OTHER BOOKS BY NANCY SHERMAN

Stoic Warriors:
The Ancient Philosophy behind the Military Mind

Making a Necessity of Virtue:
Aristotle and Kant on Virtue

The Fabric of Character:
Aristotle's Theory of Virtue

Aristotle's Ethics: Critical Essays
editor

NANCY SHERMAN

W. W. Norton & Company
New York · London

More Praise for

THE UNTOLD WAR

"[Sherman] offers penetrating portraits of the individual struggles of soldiers and profound insights on aspects of war that civilians rarely consider." —Vanessa Bush, *Booklist*

"[An] illuminating inquiry into the psyche of our fighting men and women." —*Kirkus Reviews*

"At a time when suicide rates among veterans [are] increasing sharply, this empathetic examination of 'the moral weight that soldiers carry on their shoulders' is essential reading." —*Publishers Weekly*, starred review

"[Sherman's] nuanced book blends both her practical experience and her academic background as a military ethicist conversant with Aristotle, Seneca, Freud, and others.... We can see the missing limbs, but Sherman exposes the deep trauma below the surface, the kind that keeps soldiers up at 3 a.m. with images that linger in the mind long after the bombs and guns have gone silent." —Chuck Leddy, *Boston Globe*

"*The Untold War* will have a lasting effect on readers." —James R. Conroy, *America*

"One cannot overstate the importance of this book in furthering the cause of veterans.... A brilliant exploration of a soldier's soul." —Matthew Alexander, *Huffington Post*

"[Sherman] successfully makes the case that, with an all-volunteer military, the public has averted its eyes from the psychic damage of our current wars." —Andrea Sachs, *Time*

"[Sherman's] tract will, and should, provoke vigorous debate." —Maureen T. Moore, *Journal of Military History*

THE UNTOLD WAR

Inside the
Hearts, Minds,
and Souls
of Our Soldiers

Marianne Moore, "In Distrust of Merits," from *The Collected Poems of Marianne Moore*. Copyright © 1944 by Marianne Moore; copyright renewed 1972 by Marianne Moore. Reprinted by permission of Scribner, a division of Simon & Schuster, Inc. All rights reserved. Reprinted by permission of Faber and Faber Ltd. Permission for electronic use granted by David M. Moore, Esq., Legal Representative of the Literary Estate of Marianne Moore, with all rights reserved. Siegfried Sassoon, "Banishment," from *Collected Poems of Siegfried Sassoon*. Copyright © 1918 by E. P. Dutton; copyright © 1936, 1946, 1947, 1948 by Siegfried Sassoon. Used by permission of Viking Penguin, a division of Penguin Group (USA) Inc. Copyright Siegfried Sassoon by kind permission of the Estate of George Sassoon. Homer, "The Shield of Achilles" and "Achilles and Priam," from *The Iliad*, translated by Robert Fagles. Copyright © 1990 by Robert Fagles. Used by permission of Viking Penguin, a division of Pengiun Group (USA) Inc.

For information about permission to reproduce selections from this book,
write to Permissions, W. W. Norton & Company, Inc.,
500 Fifth Avenue, New York, NY 10110

For information about special discounts for bulk purchases, please contact
W. W. Norton Special Sales at specialsales@wwnorton.com or 800-233-4830

Manufacturing by RR Donnelley, Harrisonburg, VA
Book design by Lovedog Studio
Production manager: Anna Oler

LIBRARY OF CONGRESS CATALOGING-IN-PUBLICATION DATA

Sherman, Nancy, 1951–
The untold war : inside the hearts, minds, and souls of
our soldiers / Nancy Sherman. — 1st ed.
p. cm.
Includes bibliographical references and index.
ISBN 978-0-393-06481-0 (hardcover)
1. Psychology, Military. 2. War—Psychological aspects.
3. Stress (Psychology) 4. War (Philosophy)
5. Soldiers—Mental health. 6. Veterans—Mental health.
7. War—Moral and ethical aspects. I. Title.
U22.3.S44 2010
355.001'9—dc22

2009040992

ISBN 978-0-393-34100-3 pbk.

W. W. Norton & Company, Inc.
500 Fifth Avenue, New York, N.Y. 10110
www.wwnorton.com

W. W. Norton & Company Ltd.
Castle House, 75/76 Wells Street, London W1T 3QT

1 2 3 4 5 6 7 8 9 0

CONTENTS

Prologue   1

I. BECOMING A WARRIOR

Chapter 1   FROM CIVILIAN TO SOLDIER   11

Chapter 2   FOR CAUSE OR COMRADE?   39

Chapter 3   PAYBACK   65

II. THE BATTLEFIELD OF EMOTIONS

Chapter 4   THE GUILT THEY CARRY   89

Chapter 5   INTERROGATION:
IN THE MORAL SHADOWLAND   113

Chapter 6   IN THE FACE OF TORTURE   149

III. THE WAR AFTER THE WAR

Chapter 7   LOOSENING THE STOIC ARMOR   171

Chapter 8   BODY AND BODY PARTS   195

Chapter 9   FROM SOLDIER TO CIVILIAN   215

Epilogue   IN MEMORIAM: TED WESTHUSING   237

Acknowledgments   245

Notes   249

Bibliography   285

Credits   315

Index   317

To Marshall, Kala, and Jonathan

And to my mother, Beatrice

And to my father, Seymour Sherman (1921–2009),
Army medic in World War II, or as he preferred to be
known, "Handsome Sy, the ex-GI"

There never was a war that was
not inward . . .

—Marianne Moore,
"In Distrust of Merits"

THE UNTOLD WAR

PROLOGUE

THIS BOOK is not a political tract for or against a war. It is about the inner battles soldiers wage—the moral weight of war that individual soldiers carry on their shoulders and don't usually talk about. Soldiers go to war to fight external enemies, in Afghanistan and Iraq today, or in Europe and the Pacific in my father's era. But most, at least the honest among them, fight inner wars as well. They wrestle with the guilt of luck and accident, and the uneasy burden of killing and leaving the killing behind. For some, what weighs heavy is the sense of betrayal that is part of the moral shadowland of wartime interrogation—of building intimate rapport with a detainee only to exploit it. For others, the moral burden comes with killing civilians, as part of the permissible but no less wrenching collateral damage of war. These are feelings felt by the best soldiers. But they are feelings that are often unexposed, borne privately, and sometimes with shame.

That psychological anguish in war is also moral anguish is a fact too often ignored. Studies of war trauma tend to focus on the acute psychological hardship of crossing the borders of peace and war. But what that research typically leaves to the side are the ordinary moral and emotional tensions of that passage. It misses the ubiquity of the inner war and its subtle moral contours. It overlooks the full humanity of soldiering, and the healthy struggle in the best soldier to remain alive to civilian sensibilities without losing the soldier's steel and resilience.

This book digs deep into the moral conscience of soldiers. It moves beyond the traditional study of war in philosophy, which from Augustine and Aquinas's time forward has focused narrowly on the justice of going to war and prosecuting it. But it also moves beyond clinical psychological study on trauma to probe the broader issues of moral character in putting on and taking off the uniform.

At the heart of the book are testimonials from soldiers, not only from the current wars in Iraq and Afghanistan but also from the Vietnam War, World War II, and World War I. The story soldiers tell over and over again is about the battle to reclaim personal accountability within the bureaucracies that armies are. Soldiers fight in units, wearing uniforms effacing individual difference in the name of solidarity, for missions meant to rally and unite. And yet soldiering, with its residue, is always about what each individual sees and does on his watch. It is about the individual moral record, etched in emotions, like honor and pride, revenge, guilt, and shame. It is about the things a soldier has seen and done on the battlefield, and the way these things come home with him.

As a professional philosopher whose area of focus is ancient ethics, military ethics, and the emotions, I have listened to soldiers' stories through the dual perspectives of moral philosophy and psychoanalysis. Philosophy and the history of ethics have long offered a way of analyzing the moral texture of our lives that is unparalleled by other discourses. To make sense of our experiences, it is not enough to tell the story and narrate the events. Philosophy sharpens the distinctions, maps the conceptual terrain, presses us to make more systematic or coherent what confuses or defies sense or seems like one feeling or thought but really is another. It is a way of knowing oneself, as Socrates insisted, and of understanding the world. It is a form of discernment and enlightenment. But like all exercises in reason and argument, traditional philosophy can also obfuscate, rationalize, puff up, push us away from ourselves. It can turn its back on what seems irrational or too steeped in the upheaval of feeling.

Yet the irrational can have its own logic, as Freud taught us. It can be understood and, often, force us to recognize a different and deeper kind of reasonableness and humanity. And this is where my psychoanalytic training comes in. About fifteen years ago, I realized that to probe more deeply the nature of emotions and moral development, I needed the framework of a "deep" moral psychology, and so I sought out research training in psychoanalysis at the Washington Psychoanalytic Institute. My view then, and now, is that emotions need to be understood not only in the context of a conceptual, philosophical analysis but also in the lived life and in the stories individuals tell about their families and friends, the conflicts they wrestle with, and their attempts to resolve them. The ancients, whose work I have specialized in during most of my academic life, knew nothing of a sharp boundary between philosophy and psychology. In understanding the full moral psyche, we are at peril if we try to erect one.

And so I have listened to soldiers with both a philosopher's ear and a psychoanalyst's ear. Soldiers are genuinely torn by the feelings of war—they desire raw revenge at times, though they wish they wanted a nobler justice; they feel pride and patriotism tinged with shame, complicity, betrayal, and guilt. They worry if they have sullied themselves, if they love their war buddies more than their wives or husbands, if they can be honest with the generation of soldiers that follow. They want to feel whole, but they see in the mirror that an arm is missing, or having bagged their buddies' body parts, they feel guilty for returning home intact. I suspect many have talked to me so openly because they sense they are being listened to by someone who may help them find, in the chaos of war, a small measure of moral clarity.

This book looks at soldiering through the arc of combat, as civilians become warriors, go to war, and return home from war. I was not embedded with a unit and so do not follow the story of one group of soldiers from deployment to the return home. Rather, I have interviewed some forty soldiers at different points in their careers, some as they take their oaths or give them as a commander; others days after their return from the fall of Baghdad; some in their role as therapists counseling soldiers on resilience and trauma on the frontlines; others as patients at military hospitals trying to recover from the shock of war; yet others reunited with families and in their new civilian lives, with visible and invisible wounds, struggling to make sense of what they have seen and done and left unfinished. In one case, I have turned to correspondence and to my friendship with a daughter who tries to reconstruct her father's service in World War II through a trove of his letters she stumbled upon. In a few cases, I have supplemented interviews with the traditional testimony of war literature.

What I have learned in writing this book is that though soldiers don uniforms and then take them off, the transitions are rarely seamless. For many, soldiering is not just a job or career; it is an identity, it is who they become. Leaving it behind is not easy. Finding a moral self capacious enough for both civilian and warrior sensibilities becomes the pressing challenge.

This book is not just about soldiers. It is also about those who send loved ones to war and live vicariously with them throughout a war and after. And it is about those who do not go to war and cannot see the emotional anguish beneath the stolid demeanor and impeccable uniform. In this sense it is about so many of us who see only pictures of the fallen that preserve the pristine look of a soldier with its reminder of lost potential. But the experience of war is far from pristine, however ennobling it can be for some. If the faces of war don't convey the moral anguish, then the stories and their analysis should.

I urge that soldiers should not have to bear the moral burdens of war on their own. As a public, we need to understand the moral psyche of the soldier far better than we do. We need to begin to cultivate the kind of empathy that will allow us to support our soldiers properly when they return home to our communities.

I have come to the study of military ethics somewhat serendipitously. In the mid-1990s I was called into the United States Naval Academy to design an ethics program in the wake of a massive cheating scandal. I later was appointed the inaugural Distinguished Chair in Ethics at the Academy, teaching midshipmen a version of what I have taught at Yale and Georgetown for years—what ancient, modern, and contemporary philosophers tell us about how to make good choices in tough situations and how to live well in a way that gives voice to emotions as well as reason.

This association with the military reconnected me with my own past and that of many in my generation and in subsequent generations. After the Vietnam War, for many, the military became split from civilians. The all-volunteer military has widened the gap, despite the increasing roles of the reserves and National Guard in the current wars. My experience at the Naval Academy was a revelation about how close I felt to those who had served yet whose formative years were so different from my own. Some were Marine colonels and Navy captains in Vietnam while I was in graduate school; others served in the first Gulf War as aviators and flew regularly over a place little known to me at the time, the "Basra" road; others came back to the Academy after the fall of Baghdad, having led Marine battalions. Deep friendships with many have continued over the years and have, in part, inspired this work.

The lives of many in this book intersect with my own communities. Bob Steck is a Vietnam veteran in my neighborhood who was a philosophy instructor at the time he was drafted by his Texas draft board. To this day, he struggles with a philosophical problem that is all too personal: how to make sense of a soldier fighting honorably and justly in a war that is unjust. Dereck Vines is a former reservist who served in intelligence in Iraq and Bosnia. He sought me out at the Woodrow Wilson International Center for Scholars in Washington, D.C., where I was a fellow and he is on the tech staff. He wanted to talk about the way he felt "suckered" by his service in Iraq, yet still so deeply proud to have served. At Georgetown, I interviewed several students who were going off to war or returned home and were then students. One whom you will meet is Will Quinn, a former interrogator at Abu Ghraib who tells me he crossed a moral line, not because he tortured or used "enhanced interrogation techniques," but because he exploited trust in a way he would never have done as a civilian. Another is Dawn Halfaker, a former West Point basketball star and a master's student at Georgetown who lost an arm in Iraq while supervising Iraqi police. In addition, I interviewed soldiers who have been military teachers, such as Lt. Col. Al Gill, an infantry soldier who has prepared students for the transition between civilian and soldier through lessons in Shakespeare.

Another community, just minutes from my home, remains sequestered from most visitors. And that is the Walter Reed Army Medical Center, the Army's flagship military hospital. There I came to know Tony DeStefano, an Army reservist and communication specialist, who was traumatized by a near missile attack in Kuwait and has been in and out of military hospitals since. At Walter Reed I also interviewed Rob Kislow, a twenty-one-year-old at the time, who had been a sniper in Afghanistan, and killed the guy who was trying to kill him, but who came home from war badly injured and dogged by shame that he could not continue to wear the uniform and make the Army his longed-for career.

In San Diego, while giving a lecture honoring the late Vice Adm. Jim Stockdale, I met Alysha Haran, a former ballerina and advertiser in Los Angeles who had something of a conversion experience when, after 9/11, she saw a picture of her late grandmother in a military uniform. At that moment, she knew she had to serve. Her glamorous life suddenly seemed drained of all its meaning.

For an acquaintance and colleague, Ted Westhusing, the warrior life required reflective engagement with ancient Greek notions of virtue and honor. Westhusing was a top-ranked West Point graduate and elite Army ranger who went on to earn a doctorate in philosophy at Emory University. His interests and mine overlapped; we chatted at conferences and he sent me drafts of his thesis chapters for comment. I interviewed him for my last book. I was stunned when I heard on the news in the summer of 2005 that he had taken his life in Iraq with his own service weapon. I will tell Ted's story later, but one way of summing it up is to say that his moral idealism collided with the reality of the war in Iraq and the corruption of contractors whom it was his job to oversee. He went to war seeking adventure and proof of his warrior virtue. In the end, he was sullied, morally undone, morally stripped. The tragedy is complex, as most suicides are. But I mention Ted now because his death hit hard and it forced the question, all too profoundly, that I have asked myself while writing this book, of just how moral philosophy can best prepare a soldier for war and for coming home after war. Ted was the best of the best, but somehow war was able to undo him.

There is another person whom I have learned about in the course of writing this book. My father, Seymour Sherman, is a World War II veteran, and of a famous generation of laconic men who buried war deep within. Often, in the past few years, I talked to my dad about war experiences that he could never tell me about when I was younger. His war, like that of many World War II vets, was a private matter. What he saw and did must not burden the family. My ardent hope is that soldiers in the current generation do not view their war as a private burden banned from their families and communities.

This book is a philosophical ethnography of sorts, and the insights of philosophers—Plato, Aristotle, Cicero, Seneca, Epictetus, Marcus Aurelius, Montaigne, Kant, Nietzsche, and Freud among others—permeate its pages. Not only do these thinkers help to analyze soldiers' voices, but in turn, soldiers' voices bring to life these thinkers' ideas. The illustration goes both ways. What emerges over and over again in the course of the book is a theme many of the soldiers I interviewed voiced: Though they do no wrong by war's best standards, they often feel wracked by guilt, betrayal, and a need to make reparations. The questions I wrestle with in this book are, How do we make sense of the reasonableness of those feelings? How does philosophy joined with psychoanalysis give us a framework for understanding this inner war?

The topic is sober. But many of the soldiers and families I have talked to are filled with courage and hope and resilience, though, to be sure, others struggle to find meaning and purpose after seeing war's horrors. However, all have wanted to talk and bear witness. For that, I have been deeply humbled and honored.

I must add here a few words about terms. I use the word "soldier" to include all military personnel from the different services—soldiers, sailors, marines, and airmen. I have done this for ease of reading, though I am well aware the term "soldier" neither captures the distinct nomenclature within the services nor the interservice rivalries. I have also struggled with gender use. In English, we have to select a gender for a pronoun, especially if we use the singular. Sometimes I use "he," "him," and "his," at other times, "she" and "her." The contexts often dictate the choice. But the point to keep in mind is that though the military profession has traditionally been male, women are an integral part of the current military, and women's voices are a critical part of my account.

Soldiers, both men and women, often keep their deepest struggles in waging war to themselves. But as a public we, too, need to know how war feels, for war's residue should not just be a soldier's private burden. It ought to be something that we, who do not don the uniform, recognize and understand as well.

I

BECOMING A WARRIOR

CHAPTER I

—— ★ ——

FROM CIVILIAN TO SOLDIER

LIONS AND LAMBS

"Are you a lion or a lamb?" bellowed Lt. Col. Dave Grossman to a group of officers gathered for a training session to develop bulletproof minds. "Baaaaa . . . baaaa," he bleated. "Do you want to be a lamb?" he taunted. "Hooah," he yelped, giving the Army grunt for the brave and confirming that all really want to be lions.

Dave Grossman, a retired Army ranger and military psychologist, lectures three hundred days a year to military and police officers who need to be able to kill when duty calls. His books, *On Killing* and *On Combat*, and his lectures and tapes address the taboo many soldiers harbor against killing up close, and the psychological cost of that fear in war. His task is to turn reluctant-to-kill soldiers into ready-to-kill soldiers who know deep down in their bones, in motor response, physiology, and psychology, the difference between murder and justified, lawful killing in war. In one of his books he asks, "Do you know the difference between murder and killing? If you do, maybe God does too." Provocative questions like this goad soldiers into making distinctions between wanton murder and justified killing. In his view, a sense of justification supports resilience and battle readiness, and reduces a soldier's vulnerability to the stains of violent deeds committed in war.

John Rupp, a no-nonsense, rock-solid Marine colonel, also worries about the reluctant-to-kill soldier. A helicopter pilot who taught ethics at the Naval Academy between tours in Iraq, he joined me on a panel at a military ethics conference honoring the late Vice Adm. Jim Stockdale, held at the University of San Diego in the fall of 2006. To a group of soon-to-graduate midshipmen, Rupp minced no words: "If you are asking yourself in the midst of combat, 'Should I be killing?' that thought is coming too late. You should have figured that out long before you got to this point." But learning to kill does not come quickly or easily. Years ago, in response to surveys suggesting low kill ratios in World War II (that fewer than one in four soldiers may have fired their weapons), the Army switched its pop-up targets in simulation exercises to more lifelike images to speed up the senses and psyche of the trainees. Still, even if the adjustment from never killing to being able to kill is smoother, the switch from civilian to soldier and vice versa is rarely seamless. The border passing is not easy. It is complex, morally and psychologically.

The stereotype of turning a civilian into a soldier involves a radical resocialization that begins in boot camp or basic training. The grueling experience "denudes," as one observer puts it: It strips civilian and personal identity and socializes individuals into members of a cadre. It cuts down in order to build up. At the Naval Academy, the cutting down begins at the barbershop near Bancroft Hall, the world's largest dorm, by some accounts. Masses of hair tumble onto the floor as buzz cuts emerge to go with uniforms and standard-issue underwear, eyeglasses, and shoes. Grooming, like dorm rooms, is Spartan, stripped of all personal effects. As in the Garden of Eden story, a new creature is forged, ready to go forth.

But few soldiers fully shed their old civilian selves. Nor should they. Life before the uniform lingers, and especially so in the reality of present-day war. For a start, global communication allows deployed soldiers to email, text, or phone home daily—a possibility that was unimaginable as recently as the first Gulf War (1990–1991). Indeed, when I was the Distinguished Chair of Ethics at the Naval Academy,

I was flown onto the USS *Eisenhower* in 1997, which was only then being outfitted with email capability. Easy access to family can be both stabilizing and disorienting—stabilizing in allowing a soldier to stay closely connected with home (contrast my father's World War II generation, where letters to loved ones could take months to cross the seas), but disorienting in shifting a soldier's attention to the dramas of home and away from the mission.

An irony of the high-tech age is that the same technology that brings home and battlefield closer also expands the battlefield by removing any clear frontline in battle, forcing a soldier always to be battle-ready and battle-weary. That is a part of the point of asymmetrical warfare, in which enemies with inferior tactical strength exploit cell phone technology to detonate deadly roadside bombs and use the Internet to develop those bombs and amass thousands of war fighters globally who do not wear standard uniforms. With this new kind of war, the battlefield penetrates, on all fronts, into civilian life. Indeed, in asymmetrical warfare, battles are fought largely in civilian populations, with soldiers fighting an enemy often shielded by civilians. In occupations, uniformed soldiers take up civil affairs jobs side by side with their soldiering roles—patrolling and policing, building schools and bridges, getting electricity and sanitation running, working to gain the trust of locals and community leaders. The complex mingling means a soldier is always simultaneously part civilian, fighting combatants commingled with noncombatants. The identities are blurred.

Those in the National Guard and the reserves, who have served in increased numbers in the current wars in Afghanistan and Iraq, know this in a distinctive way. They often serve side by side with hometown friends, from neighborhood high schools where they were on the same teams or in the same classes. Like British regiments from World War II, they go to war together and some, though not all, return home together. They are also like the drafted soldiers who made up the American Army in World War II, who tended to maintain clear dual identities as soldiers *and* as the doctors, lawyers, carpenters, engineers, and teachers they were at home. Some might argue that reservists and guardsmen, like draftees of former eras, bring "civilian values" to the fight in a way less common among the all-professional, full-time military that makes up most of today's forces. Perhaps so; professional, full-time militaries can be insulating and work hard to cultivate the military ethos. Still, and this is the point to emphasize, in the current battle scenarios, the boundary between home turf and battleground gets blurred, and with it the psychological and moral space. Sloughing off civilian skin is never absolute. Nor should it be. Humanity is too bound up in the capacity to move back and forth.

At an international symposium on military ethics held a few years ago in Washington, D.C., an officer approached me about my work and said, "What you really need to explain, Prof. Sherman, is the switching—the switching from civilian to soldier and soldier to civilian." His point was that being both a civilian *and* a soldier is always in the background. The border is always there to be crossed. Sometimes it seems porous, at other times not so. The moral challenge is to negotiate between "cask and cushion," to use Shakespeare's terms in *Macbeth*, and not betray one's humanity in either.

For some, turning to the cask is precisely because the cushion, or civilian life, has become too "cushy." Joining the military becomes a search for a lifestyle that is disciplined and tough. That story is familiar. What is less familiar is joining the military because the cushiness of civilian life leaves out caring. This brings us to Alysha's story.

A CONVERSION EXPERIENCE

Sitting across from me at a formal dinner during the military ethics conference in San Diego was a striking young woman in Navy dress whites, her dark hair rolled and pinned around the nape of her neck in a retro hairdo. When the conversation moved to physical fitness requirements in the Navy, she volunteered that her former husband, an enlisted Navy pallbearer, was unofficially exempt from the usual running requirements so that he would not lose the muscle mass needed to lift a coffin with a 250-pound person in it. "Never underestimate the weight of a dead body," Midshipman Haran joked, holding her own in the company of senior academics and Navy brass.

Alysha Haran is an unlikely Navy enlistee and just as unusual a naval midshipman and junior officer. In her early and mid twenties, she was a successful Los Angeles–based producer of advertisements. Her work started in the theater, first as a ballet dancer and then as a conservatory-trained actress. At home, as young children, she and her sister (who studied opera in New York City) were "always on stage," taught to stand straight and act as poised adults. "I had a propensity to be an ingénue, and my parents did not discourage it!" she says. Then 9/11 happened, and her life as a producer turned vapid. "I had been making Mercedes commercials. The most important thing in my circle of friends was washing your BMW. Making Mercedes commercials—what does it matter?" she asked with her newfound cynicism.

A career in the military came to have its own dramatic attraction. Alysha's grandmother passed away in February of 2001. At the funeral, Alysha found herself transfixed by a photograph of her grandmother in her WAVE (the Navy's Women Accepted for Volunteer Emergency Service) uniform. "I had never seen my grandmother in that uniform until then. She looked beautiful," Alysha sighed. "It was a moment filled with nostalgia." Though Alysha had never dreamt of the military, that image planted a seed. Four months later, she was filming on a ship. She re-creates the scene: "The smell, the feel was right. I said to a friend, 'I should have joined the Navy.' He said, 'Why don't you?' I said, 'Don't tempt me!' Then 9/11 happened." But "the hooking point," Alysha says, didn't come until a few weeks later, in a conversation that underscored the banality of her current job. She had been assisting a director who asked her to book a first-class flight for under six thousand dollars. After much to-and-fro with a travel agent, she finally got him a flight on British Airways that came just under his price ceiling. " 'Not Virgin?' he complained. 'Can you find out what kind of food BA is serving, because I don't usually fly them because I don't like their food.' That was the hooking point for me. At that point, I said to my friend, 'I'm thinking of joining the Navy Reserve.' 'Just reserve?' he said. That was it."

What struck me was Alysha's near conversion. She recalled, "In my opening statement for officer candidacy, I said, 'I'd be a nun if I were Catholic!' I have that level of commitment!" Even after boot camp and enlistment, and then four years of ROTC (Reserve Officer Training Corps) candidacy as a student close to ten years older than her classmates, Alysha still exuded a palpable thrill about the naval uniform and the authority it represents. Unlike most enlistees, Alysha found boot camp not particularly arduous, and even comforting at times. Years that were spent in Russian ballet school, she says, comprised "my first boot camp." She was already in "a corps": a *corps d'esprit* was part of her dance world that transferred to the military. Her training in sleep deprivation came from shooting car commercials on the West Coast using every moment of the seventeen hours of summer daylight.

Alysha's enlistment is a conversion experience but one that does not come from a prophetic encounter or a born-again moment. At work is a homier metamorphosis where the focus of life shifts and a new organizing principle takes hold. The early-twentieth-century Harvard psychologist and philosopher William James gives insight here. In *The Varieties of Religious Experience*, James devotes two chapters to conversion. He introduces the topic in the Gifford Lectures, delivered in Edinburgh, with a public figure that Scots, and not just Americans, would readily recognize and with an experience meant to demystify the phenomenon:

> The President of the United States, when, with paddle, gun, and fishing-rod, goes camping in the wilderness for a vacation, changes his system of ideas from top to bottom. The presidential anxieties have lapsed into the background entirely; the official habits are replaced by the habits of a son of nature, and those who knew the man only as the strenuous magistrate would not "know him for the same person" if they saw him as the camper.

If now he should never go back, and never again suffer political interests to gain dominion over him, he would be for practical intents and purposes a permanently transformed being.

In this picture of Teddy Roosevelt, there is no religious conversion. Nor is James arguing that the core personality or character of Roosevelt in his camper role is different from that in his "full pride of office." Rather, it is simply that his habits and focus of activities *shift*. Roosevelt leads an alternate life, with different commitments, attire, expectations, demands, and vulnerabilities than he has as "magistrate." As James puts it, an interest that was peripheral now becomes central and moves to "central parts of consciousness." James couches his theory in the quasi-mechanical terms of his new empirical psychology: There are "excitement shifts," and "shifts in the habitual centre of . . . personal energy," everything is "re-crystalizing" around ideas that have become "hot and live," and these replace "dead feelings," "dead ideas," and "cold beliefs." But what he is describing is essentially phenomenological: Conversion is a shifting of consciousness and attitude—Teddy Roosevelt switching from "the official habits" of president to the "habits of a son of nature," something Roosevelt, in fact, did in mini-version most days with an afternoon horseback ride. (Indeed, to one such request to join him again in the great outdoors and bring "his worst clothes," the French ambassador replied, "At this point, I don't have any worst clothes left.") Roosevelt would accomplish the transition most thoroughly during his African safari in 1908.

Entering the military represents, for many, just this kind of shift of center of gravity. "The military owns you" is a comment about a soldier's temporary sacrifice of civilian liberties, and also about how the military reorganizes a soldier's life and priorities. Recently, at my doctor's office in D.C., one of the nurses in the practice told me that she was married to a colonel in the Marines. She parroted her husband's standard quip when she demanded more of his time: "If the Marines wanted me to have a wife, they would have issued me one!" She knew the line. Her father, also a career marine, used to say the same thing to her mother. Of course, any profession can dominate in this way if it is sufficiently demanding or passionately embraced. The military is not alone in this regard. But it does require a degree of service, separation, and sacrifice of civilian liberties and roles that few other jobs demand. So, for example, a hardworking, sacrificing lawyer might be dominated by her profession, putting in long hours at the office and traveling many days each month. But the work is still in a realm that is similar to the realm in which the lawyer's spouse operates. There is no comparable arena divide or sacrifice of liberty and life characteristic of the military.

It is a familiar point that many sign up precisely because they want or need that external discipline and restriction of liberty. Will Quinn, a former Army interrogator and now a Georgetown undergraduate, enlisted, in part, because, as he puts it, he needed his "butt kicked." He needed the kind of discipline that he couldn't find in his midwestern Catholic school or at home. Alysha's case puts an interesting twist on this. Highly driven and very successful in the fast world of Los Angeles, she wanted a break from the heavy hand of her own internal whip. Once liberated from her project of self-management, she could care for others. "I always wanted a bedtime at school and my parents never gave me one. And so boot camp was heaven: to have an organized, scheduled day was a sheer relief. In a way, it took away stress and responsibility," she said. "I got to take care of people and they got to take care of me. Some of the girls would cry themselves to sleep. Then they would get used to it. To see them growing up under your eyes, that was wonderful," she added with a sense of maternal pride.

Few would describe their entry into the military in quite these idealized terms, though many do speak in the language of "caring for others" and "public service." For Alysha, what her civilian life left out was altruistic service and mutual care. For others, signing up is a less lofty matter—it is a way of getting an education, job training, an "out" from boredom or gang violence. For some, it is a promise of citizenship, sometimes, sadly, only posthumously. For still others, military service remains the surest way to prove manhood. The military advertises that promise: The ads show steely strength and an image of tough moral fiber. Putting on the uniform is a way to grow up and prove your mettle, for a man or a woman.

What Alysha's story illustrates so well, however, is that there can be other psychological longings at work. She needed to find what many associate with the best in civilian life: caring and being cared for. For her, the military was a way not to turn her back on her humanity, but to make her more whole. She was after a spiritual renewal, not unlike what some seek in other kinds of conversions. Here the influence of Lubavitch Hasidism on prestigious college campuses today is insightful. Hasidic rabbis draw students into the fold who are in search of close connection, spiritual uplift, and a community life filled with traditional food, prayer, and festival that marks a sharp alternative to ordinary, secular life. The military obviously does not share the same recruitment goals. But for some, like Alysha, it does promise a new, tight-knit family tied to a mission that has history and gravitas.

BENEATH THE UNIFORM

Alysha's story is a romance with the uniform. But it is, of course, more than that. Through the Jamesian lens, a deeper metamorphosis unfolds. Becoming a sailor involves a recrystallization of who Alysha is, in habit, activity, and attitude.

The idea of internal change, however, is often obscured by the focus on the public face of the soldier—the spit-polish shoes, the creased uniforms, the stolid demeanor and gaze, the stiff salute, the parades, the "yes, Ma'am-ing" and "yes, Sir-ing." Even in death, there are the official photos that become the faces of the fallen. Erving Goffman, the great sociologist of roles, teaches that social role involves the "language and mask" of highly stylized rituals and social interactions. Any civilian who walks onto a base is struck by just how rich military costumes and props are. In that world of uniforms and stripes and ribbons, it is easy to focus on the pageantry and forget the purpose of it all in marking rank and chain of command. In a peacetime setting, it is just as easy to forget that the uniform is, at bottom, a conventional marker of who puts themselves deliberately in harm's way and who does not.

That outer world of uniform might also suggest a role that someone can take on and off easily, like clothes. But soldiering, and especially wartime soldiering, does not grow skin that a soldier sheds lightly. Combat is nothing if not existential: It pits an individual against life and its ultimate challenges. It requires seeing the unspeakable and doing the dreaded. It is a role that is immersed and transformative and lingers long after a soldier takes off the uniform. Because of the stressors it involves—unpredictable attack, helplessness in the face of that unpredictability, pervasive and gruesome carnage—it embeds deep.

In this sense, and in an obvious way, becoming a soldier is not just a *social* or *sociological* phenomenon. It is a *psychological* phenomenon, a *deep* psychological phenomenon. And it is deep, not just because it involves attachment or investment—*kathexis*, in the Freudian lexicon—and the internalizations and conflicts of an intrapsychic world, but because war *sears* memories, it brands the soul with images that can overpower and overwhelm. It requires young men and women, often eighteen to twenty-five years old, to take on responsibilities of a magnitude and order unlike most they have available to them in civilian life. Thoughts about what they did and did not do, what they saw but could not prevent, may haunt them for the remainder of their lives. The idea of uniform, and a role, simply does not convey that weight.

Nonetheless, various philosophers have pressed hard the idea of a role or occupation as something you can step in and out of without residue. What you do in a job ought not affect who you really are, in the deepest moral and psychological sense, and who you are in that deepest sense ought not affect who you are in your different professional roles. The Renaissance essayist and philosopher Michel de Montaigne preaches the view in high style. "The Mayor and Montaigne have always been separate," he boasts. To lawyers who may have to be liars in their adversarial roles of defending clients, he advises, always serve others, as if on "loan" with the "mind remaining quiet . . . without distress, without passion." The moral and psychological point is clear: Insulate job and career from other walks of life. Compartmentalize:

We must not turn masks and semblances into essential realities, nor adopted qualities into attributes of our self.... It is
enough to plaster flour on our faces without doing it to our
minds. I know some who transubstantiate and metamorphose
themselves into as many new beings and forms as the dignities
which they assume: they are prelates down to their guts and
livers and uphold their offices on their lavatory-seat. I cannot
make them see the difference between hats doffed to them and
those doffed to their commissions, their retinue or their mule.

Aspects of Montaigne's instruction have broad intuitive appeal. Many
workplaces have their own specific ethics codes, and various professions—
lawyering, notably—tolerate and require a level of lying and concealment
that simply are not the norm in ordinary moral life. Montaigne's message
also has appeal to the military. A soldier salutes the uniform, not the person in it. The salute is a strong deferential nod to status and not esteem
for moral character or respect for personal dignity. The military model of
the uniform's honor is a vestige of a Homeric world in which a military
leader's *timē* or honor is an external matter of accumulated booty and
status. The stripes on modern uniform sleeves and the stars on collars
and epaulets are similarly conspicuous signs of differential status.

The point was driven home to me during my years as the Distinguished
Chair in Ethics at the Naval Academy. When I traveled and stayed in
military accommodations ("Bachelor Officer Quarters"— BOQs), the
staff making the arrangements typically had to book me in at a rank.
They were told by those higher up, much to my embarrassment, that a
distinguished chair was ranked at the level of a one-star admiral. On one
occasion, another time when I was visiting San Diego, the commanding
officer of the Naval ROTC, Jerry Singleton, a captain (the equivalent of
an Army or Marine colonel), drove me to my quarters, a beautiful, two-
bedroom cottage on the shorefront that Prince Charles of Great Britain
had stayed in as a guest of the Navy. I asked this senior officer if he had
ever stayed there with his family. He peremptorily said, "No," and then

pointed to the one-star flag that had been hoisted in my honor. I looked
at it and immediately blanched. That night, at a reception, a number of
folks chatted about the one-star flag they saw flying on base and wondered who the visiting admiral might be. At that moment, I slipped into a
corner, too embarrassed to reveal that the Navy bureaucracy had slapped
a military rank on my professorship in order to process its paperwork!

Montaigne, like Goffman, is insightful in calling attention to the
mask and ritual of the workplace, and the familiar idea that with different stations in life attach different duties, whether we are parents, lawyers,
teachers, therapists, or soldiers. Moral codes and practices appropriate in
one walk of life may have less relevance in another; moreover, psychological health can demand a modicum of distance between who we are
in these different walks. But Montaigne surely gets it wrong in thinking
that this entails no moral dialogue across the borders. It is precisely as a
result of internal dialogue that a soldier may discover that she can no longer fight in uniform because of an emerging belief in pacifism, or that she
can no longer fight *this* war because she does not believe in its cause, or
that obedience to authority would itself be criminal, or immoral because
an order goes too deeply against what she believes is right or required of a
good commander responsible for her men and women. These are cases in
which a soldier's duties conflict with her overall virtue, or with her view
of what, in fact, is virtuous, *as* a good soldier. Duties a soldier may be
called to perform and what that soldier sees as being virtuous in general
or as a soldier collide.

Montaigne is dismissive of these tensions. He urges us to insulate ourselves so that who we are morally and ethically in our professions and
who we are, at core, in the deepest sense of our character and virtue are
separate. The reward will be peace and detachment. Perhaps, but at far
too high a price. Most roles stand no chance of becoming enlightened
with that kind of insulation, and most individuals do not act in fully
moral ways when they insulate themselves from the reflection of robust
moral reasoning. It is to take a limited, but all too familiar view of moral
accountability.

Col. Tony Pfaff ruminated on this with regard to his own tours of duty in Iraq. He is an elite Army ranger and foreign areas officer whose work in military ethics was background for his job in Baghdad advising the Iraqi Ministry of Interior in its training of police. He has a master's degree in philosophy from Stanford University and is now working toward a doctorate in the philosophy department at Georgetown. Tony is also a father of two middle school–age children. His wife, Julie, a former Army officer herself, once joked to me that she and the kids used to "channel" Tony in at the dinner table in order to stay connected during his deployments. In fact, they "instant messaged" most days. For Tony, that empathic connection with day-to-day life at home fed into his work. "When you are receiving instant messages from home and are required to empathize, it is more difficult not to transfer that empathy to other situations and roles." Those roles involved mentoring young officers and reforming a beleaguered police corps that had grown accustomed to doing business through abuse and corruption. In Tony's case, building complex working partnerships across cultural and sectarian divides not only required being tough and having rank but also required compassion for the plight of the many Iraqis squeezed by conflicting loyalties and the need to bring home a paycheck. His humanity as a parent and spouse—and friend, I might add—permeates his humanity as an officer.

Immanuel Kant, the preeminent eighteenth-century German rational Enlightenment philosopher and champion of the notion of a cosmopolitan moral humanity, is surprisingly ambivalent on these issues. He does not go so far as advocating Montaigne's professional detachment. But as a sixty-year-old observer of the French and American revolutions, he worries about the power of unfettered freedom to throw over the convention of traditional roles whole cloth. The point is missed if we fail to go beyond the thunderous opening lines of his popular essay, "What Is Enlightenment?":

> *Enlightenment is man's emergence from his self-incurred immaturity. Immaturity* is the inability to use one's own understanding without the guidance of another. . . . Dogmas and formulas, those mechanical instruments for rational use (or rather mis-

use) of his natural endowments, are the ball and chain of his permanent immaturity.

But Kant's polemic soon turns cautious. Reforming roles, and critiquing them, enriching them by robust moral reflection "on the inadequacies of institutions," he goes on to say, is a job to take up outside office, as a public and civilian intellectual. In uniform, the job is to obey as "part of the machine." The soldier "gets on parade!"

> Thus it would be very harmful if an officer receiving an order from his superiors were to quibble openly, while on duty, about the appropriateness or usefulness of the order in question. He must simply obey. But he cannot reasonably be banned from making observations as a man of learning on the errors in the military service, and from submitting these to his public for judgement.

Kant's remarks have teeth for many in the military. Soldiering is not membership in a debating club; the command structure depends on obedience to authority and acceptance, with limited exceptions, of conventional role and substantive orders. Kant concedes that in the case of the clergyman who is unable to "carry out his official duties in good conscience," he ought to resign. Yet perhaps not surprisingly, we do not hear this Prussian openly reflecting on the comparable military case. But *we* certainly would want to add a similar caveat, even if we acknowledge that for the soldier who protests unlawful or immoral or unwise orders, court martial or expulsion—not graceful resignation, transfer, or retirement, as with a clergyman—is often the price of acting on conscience.

Kant's own position is disappointing. It is precisely *in uniform*, and in order to be true to that uniform, that military personnel may have to disobey, question authority, choose not to bow to institutional pressures, if what they are being asked to do violates conscience. To be sure, cases of unwise orders present difficult tests for moral judgment, far harder than outright illegal or immoral orders. In the case of illegal or immoral orders, a soldier has a clear duty to disobey. Unwise orders test a soldier's conscience more subtly. For though an order may be unwise, the only way to disobey it may threaten the general good order and discipline of the military (presumably Kant's predominant worry) or the notion that the military is subordinate to the civilian (often our own worry). Still, for the virtuous soldier, moral courage may at times require just such action.

Unlike Kant and Montaigne, most of us do not view our public voices as fully separate from our professional identities, nor should we. Too much compartmentalization puts at risk the very reasonableness and "enlightened" transformation of the roles to which we commit ourselves. It also puts at risk our own moral integrity. The self splinters. True, many in the military often speak publicly "off the record," "without attribution," precisely in order not to jeopardize their careers or stamp personal criticism with an institutional imprimatur. Some "leak to the press" in order to serve the public without self-destruction. Others wait to retire before they speak out, sometimes effectively, but often forfeiting the very clout they would have had in office. Some wait until they are retired and become media analysts and commentators, where they can speak not only publicly from experience, but also independently (at least when they are not also working for the military or contractors). Others know that if they are to achieve any kind of honest excellence, they have to critique what they do while in uniform. Recently I was at the Pentagon talking to a former Annapolis colleague who now is one of the top brass in the Navy. He told me that one of the most valuable lessons he learned from his earlier years as an elite aviator came from the grueling, postmortem critiques after flight operations. The critiques lasted longer than any of the flights. A productive group review often depended on a unit leader prepared to acknowledge mistakes before subordinates. Absent that kind of candor and internal analysis, the burden on outside critique, from the media and public watchdog groups, becomes all the more urgent.

For soldiers who struggle to hold on to their humanity in the face of war's evils, Kant and Montaigne's message about insularism may confirm their worst fears: that soldiering is ultimately at odds with who they are as full human and moral persons. Soldiers may conclude that barrier walls have to be erected if the job of soldiering is to be done. If the gates are opened and emotions flood in, confusion about what to do and how to feel might undo the precarious balance. But cordoning off cask from cushion is not the way for a soldier to hold on to humanity. Militaries that encourage that put themselves at risk of becoming perfunctory bureaucracies of the worst kind, prone to treat both their own and their enemies in dehumanizing ways. The limitations of Kant's teaching on professional ethics was to be played out all too dramatically a century and a half later in his own Germany, where diffuse responsibility in highly bureaucratized roles of all sorts—military, political, industrial, medical, legal, historical, clerical—enabled ordinary men and women to insulate themselves from their participation in the abhorrent evil of Nazism. The cost of making impregnable boundaries is simply too great, both to self and to the armed services and country, to which soldiers give of their lives. The types of decisions they make and the magnitude of the actions they take require the full force of their humanity, not the suppression of it. Flourishing requires breaking down barriers, not building them up.

THE OSTRICH AND THE HYDRA

The topic at hand is the humanizing of the soldier: How do civilians become soldiers who preserve their humanity in the midst of killing and witnessing killing up close? How do they become tough without loss of human vulnerability?

At Georgetown University, the commanding officer of the Army ROTC battalion in recent years was Lt. Col. Al Gill, a former artillery officer who came from West Point, where he taught English literature and his passion, Shakespeare. On Georgetown's Collegiate Gothic campus, Gill cuts a distinctive image in his pixilated fatigues, combat boots, and green beret. He has a five o'clock shadow early in the morning, and in the middle of a conversation, he sometimes jumps outside the French doors of his office to light up a cigarette in the adjoining courtyard. His deep Tennessee drawl inflects his drill commands and his Shakespeare. It is Gill who gave me an informal lecture one day at lunch about how the theme of "cask and cushion" weaves through many of Shakespeare's plays.

Gill often turns to literature to prepare cadets for the moral and emotional complexities of war. He teaches not only from Shakespeare but also from memoirs. One essay he assigns is a short piece by John Wolfe, a Vietnam vet who survived a rocket barrage in March 1969. Wolfe's left leg was shredded; his right one was badly mauled and eventually amputated at the hip. He suffered severe damage to his trachea. After three cardiac arrests, he was almost left for dead by two senior surgeons, but a junior surgeon convinced the anesthetist "to postpone his death." Wolfe's writing is brutally frank:

> Few things in this world are as unforgiving, pitiless, ungovernable, and irrecoverable as lead and steel loosed from a weapon. The transfigurations they affect on the bodies of friend and foe alike form a permanent backdrop to all of a man's future visions. While others experience intervals of silence between thoughts, a combat veteran's intervals will be filled with rubbery Halloween mask heads housing skulls shattered into tiny shards, schemeless mutilations, and shocked, pained expressions that violent and premature death casts on a dead boy's face.
>
> These images are war's graffiti. They are scrawled across the veteran's mind defacing the silence and peace that others enjoy. At times the images may seem to fade, but an unguarded glance into the gloom is sufficient to exhume them.

The essay is an exposé of vulnerability—physical, emotional, and moral. Over a burger and fries at Georgetown's popular Tombs restaurant, Gill explains why he introduces his young recruits to such graphic horrors. Gill is a storyteller, and he tells the following story to me: "One year when we were discussing the essay, one of my brighter cadets said, 'Sir, don't you hesitate to have us read things like this?' 'Why?' I asked. 'I mean there may be another war. People could conclude, you know, that we should back out of this commitment,' explained the student. I thought about what he was asking me. I had recently been watching a public television show with my son. It was on ostriches. . . . The ostrich was threatened by something and it stuck its head in the sand. My son, Josh, a ten-year-old at the time, just thought this was hilarious. 'Josh, Why is *that* so funny?' I asked. He thought really, really hard. He goes [Gill now paraphrasing]: 'It is funny because his method of dealing with this situation has nothing to do with reducing the threat, only his ability to see it.' I related this story to my student. 'Do I need to embellish the story any further?' And the student said, 'No, I believe that just about does it, sir!' "

Burying one's head in the sand is not permitted in Gill's battalion. Cadets openly debate the war and whether soldiers are responsible for fighting not only with just conduct but also with just cause; they simulate and analyze battle choices that young officers will face in scenarios involving roadside bombs, mortar attacks, ambushes, checkpoints, warlords, journalists caught in the fray, collateral damage, and community building. They engage in tactical exercises on weekends in the Virginia hills, sometimes for sixteen hours at a stretch. And they read war literature in order to test and feel, vicariously, the emotions of war.

This sort of training of the emotions through literary and dramatic immersion has a venerable history. Aristotle famously argues in *Poetics* that the performance of tragedy enables an audience to learn through *mimēsis*—through imitation and vicarious experience. To appreciate tragic drama requires an empathic identification expressed in the cathartic feelings of pity and fear. That catharsis, or moment of moral clarity, occurs when an audience grasps that a good and decent person of some stature falls not through moral depravity but through an unwitting error or choice (a *hamartia*, as Aristotle calls it) that can lead to terrible, bad luck. The catharsis crystallizes in pity and fear for their own lives: They shudder at being fallible and subject to tragic luck. They feel pity that what happens on stage could happen to them—that "there but for fortune."

It is precisely this kind of pity that overwhelms Wolfe as his unit suffers one casualty after another. He compares the unit to the Hydra, the mythical many-headed beast slain by Hercules. The unit loses troops impersonally replaced "in a process of constant generation." Fresh replacements are reminders of what is lost and what will be lost, and that one's number may be next. The feeling is of profound pity.

We moderns, influenced by the eighteenth century, tend to look at pity with condescension. It is a soft and soppy emotion. To show pity is to be "sentimental." When pointed toward self, it looks worse, like a narcissistic whimper. But that is not what Aristotle means by tragic pity, nor is it what Wolfe has in mind. Pity, says Aristotle, is what we feel "when we are reminded that similar misfortunes have happened to *us* or *ours*, or expect them to happen to *us* in the future." This is just what Wolfe's Hydra depicts: He and his buddies are merged. Chopping off one head is as good as chopping off another. Solidarity binds them, and feelings of betrayal and guilt bleed into intense pity and fear.

For cadets who are just being initiated, reading Wolfe's essay is to dive in headfirst. It is a raw immersion in the tragedies that could be their own. "I am not going to *not* expose them just because they might not like the answer," insists Gill. Gill, himself, may not explicitly emphasize emotions. But what he is demanding, in essence, is that his cadets be exposed to the unsavory early on and pay heed to the testimony of their full reactions. Preparing for the threats of battle demands skill, weaponry, strength, and moral leadership. It also demands emotions that put soldiers in touch with their humanity and the sacred bond that connects them with other soldiers. Exposure is to stress and carnage, real and literary. It is also exposure to the anguish of love and loss.

But this is not the prevailing conception of training a soldier. Soldiers need to be hardened. They need to suck it up, not show pity or fear. The warrior ethos, today and throughout much of history, is a Stoic ethos. And on a traditional reading of ancient Stoic texts, often taught by military educators, training is a rehearsal in detaching from emotions that can make a soldier vulnerable. We should prepare for tragedy and evils that can befall us by saying of them, as Epictetus, a popular Stoic of the late first century in the Common Era (read by many in the military community), put it, "They are nothing" to me. In this view, to indulge in fear, grief, or pity is to exacerbate the effect of what is beyond our power; it is to give in to ordinary desires and aversions and to "corrupt" self-sufficiency. If instead, the Stoics argue, we minimize the emotions of want and distress, then we can learn to protect ourselves from the impact of tragedy. This is how to build strong, psychic armor.

The distance between an Aristotelian and Stoic-inspired training for war is considerable. For the Stoics, exposure to tragedy is an occasion for inoculation by essentially rehearsing the thought that what happens to me, as opposed to what I do willfully, does not affect me at the core. For Aristotle, in contrast, toughening is precisely through emotional suffering and an honest acknowledgment of friendship, love, and loss. Presumably there is some truth in each of these ancient views. And contemporary clinical psychology draws on the wisdom of each. Exposure to stress, we now know, can desensitize, but it also can teach us how to connect more deeply to our emotions and to the judgments they record. The military cannot afford to neglect the fact that emotions, just like skill and physical endurance, need cultivation and expression. Full detachment from emotions is not a viable way of building courage or resilience.

For some in the military to feel emotions and show them is not stoic, and not macho. Here I am reminded of a conversation I had in late 2006 with an Ohio Army reservist, Tim Boggs, who had just returned from his second tour in Iraq to finish his degree at Ohio University in Athens. He said he "had never thought of life in Iraq as scary." Soldiers just do a job, "like a mechanic fixing a car, a garbage man picking up the trash, or a teacher delivering a lesson each day." Like many in the military, he was raised on the view that psychological war trauma was a problem for the weak-minded; "strong-minded people just won't get it," he said. But his second tour shook things up. He saw good friends, "really strong-minded people," break down. It was eye-opening for him. He came home from his second deployment feeling angry and lonely, wondering, "Where's my life now?" He was pretty certain he didn't suffer from war trauma or post-traumatic stress disorder (PTSD; the diagnostic markers include symptoms such as recurrent nightmares, flashbacks, emotional numbing, and feelings of hyperarousal and hypervigilance). Still, coming home from war was a "tough adjustment." For Tim Boggs, at age twenty-five and after five years in the Army, the myth of invincible stoic armor was no longer sustainable. Perhaps Tim is a soldier who might have profited early on from an exposure to the emotions of tragedy and to the mix of pity and terror that can blend with pride and glory.

Aristotle reminds us of the general point: We must hit the mean in actions *and* emotions. Roughly put, emotions must be appropriate to situation and role. Of course, emotions that are apt on the battlefield as commander or subordinate may not hit the mean at home as teacher, parent, or spouse. But this is no argument for hardened detachment or dulled empathy in soldiering. Rather, it is an argument for a broad swath of emotions, sensitive to time and place and need. Emotions of all sorts are required on the battlefield, both in caring for life and in taking it. Alysha Haran is a reminder of that need for caring and being cared for in the fleet. Gill's teaching is a reminder that exposing young soldiers to the tragic emotions of battle is yet another, often ignored, part of making a soldier battle-ready.

Uttering the Oath

Gill's final act to his cadets is to commission them at graduation. Several times in recent years, I have looked on as midshipmen and cadets take their oaths of office. May of 2006 at Georgetown stands out because the graduates were high school seniors in the fall of 2001, then applying for military service in a country that had just been attacked and was now at war. Four and a half years later, in the early hours of graduation day, twenty-one of Gill's ROTC candidates from the Hoya Battalion (drawn from a consortium of five universities in Washington, D.C.) filed into Georgetown's historic Gaston Hall for their induction as commissioned officers in the Army. On a campus where few wear military uniforms, and often self-consciously in the classroom on designated ROTC days, this occasion was when students openly showed the colors. I learned that day (belatedly, after twenty years of teaching at Georgetown) that Georgetown's own colors are military in origin: the Union Army camped in Georgetown's dorms during the Civil War, and Hoya blue and gray came to symbolize the reconciliation after that war. But few on campus know its military history or associate the blue and gray of their college paraphernalia with war, or the peace after.

Most of those commissioned on this graduation day, whether into Army branches in engineering, military intelligence, nursing, armor, or transportation corps, would soon be headed to Iraq or Afghanistan. The chaplain offering the invocation did not shy away from advertising the dangers, speaking openly about what parents dared not utter.

One cadet read from an informal exit survey about motivations his peers had for signing up. For some it was clearly financial—a way to pay for an education otherwise unavailable; for others it was a way of honoring parents and ancestors who served; for yet others it was a direct response to 9/11. One said he signed up because he didn't "want to be fat any more." Another, a nurse, knew all along that she wanted to "comfort the wounded." Whatever their reasons for entering, these twenty-two-year olds, unlike most of their classmates at Georgetown, knew from their first day on campus what they would be doing the day after graduation, and in some cases, for the next eight years.

Becoming formally commissioned (or enlisted) begins with an oath. Roman soldiers took such an oath. Soldiers today do the same. Lieutenant Colonel Gill, in his measured Tennessee inflection, swore in the cadets as second lieutenants. They repeated the oath after him, inserting their names in the blank. To take an oath, the British linguistic philosopher J. L. Austin teaches, is not to state or report something but *to do* something. It is an action performed through words. By repeating the oath, these soldiers "committed" themselves to their future duties of office, and accepted, as their burden, armed defense of the Constitution. They committed themselves to a sacrifice few at their age make.

MORAL ANTICIPATIONS

One of Gill's poster boys from that class of 2006 is Ripley Quinby IV from Ridgefield, Connecticut. Quinby, a tall, square-jawed, strikingly handsome blond, majored in political economy. After graduation, he recruited for the Hoya Battalion. We spoke several times during that summer as he prepared to head out for infantry training and then ranger school.

Quinby, who at the time had "killed" only members of his own cadre in mock battles, imagines how he will conceive the real enemy. As he speaks, I can feel the live tension between civilian and military sensibilities. In his mind, he owes the enemy discrimination in terms of motives, beliefs, and character—the ordinary tools we use to evaluate others with whom we interact. And he imagines he owes them, too, the usual range of excuses, on the grounds of coercion or ignorance. But on the battlefield, he knows there is no room for these niceties. The enemy is just your opposite number, vulnerable to your fire because they have made you vulnerable to theirs. Character is opaque. Extenuating circumstances don't matter: "I recognize probably the majority of terrorists, or at least insurgents, in Iraq's case—the people actually going out and doing the roadside bombs—aren't people who are ideologically committed to the cause; they're just people who are trying to get by in an uncertain security environment and they're being offered money or incentives by the true evil masterminds and the plotters."

Quinby then muses, "So how would I feel about killing someone who wouldn't do evil things, wouldn't kill others, wouldn't try to destroy the security of his own country except for the fact that he has to feed his family? That's where it starts to get a little more difficult," he answers. "As an officer, there may be the necessary evil in killing someone who could have been redeemable but . . . if allowed to continue to do whatever they're doing" poses a threat.

What bothers Quinby now, before his baptism in battle, is that the practice of war does not allow him to "redeem" the hapless enemy foot soldier, to excuse or exempt him in light of his socially or economically coerced position, to segregate the believers from the doubters, the masterminds and plotters from the children and men who take up arms for money or uncertain security. He does not think of his own position as in any way comparably coerced by duress or ignorance, though some enlisted American soldiers surely fight under far more duress than he does and with less opportunity and ability to constructively reflect about the cause for which they fight. Quinby frames the problem of self-defense in military terms and, in particular, in terms of counterinsurgency. But the problem he alludes to has a civilian analogue. Imagine that your life is endangered by an "innocent threat," a threat coerced into attacking you by a remote manipulator, an evil third party. To give a philosopher's stock example, "imagine you are in an elevator with a mild-mannered colleague when she suddenly goes berserk and tries to stab you, having earlier drunk coffee that some villain had laced with a mind-altering psychopathological-behavior-inducing drug. More prosaically, perhaps your life is endangered by the movements of someone in the throes of an epileptic fit." The innocent threat may be "hapless," not just redeemable, but truly innocent, free of evil or criminal intention. But it is your life or hers, and in the circumstances, there is no time for redemption or more honest respect for character or goodness of will.

What Quinby here anticipates is an aspect of the tragedy of all war that many soldiers think about only when they are in battle—namely, that protection from vulnerability in war has little to do with goodness or character. The fact that soldiers agree to put themselves in danger's way does not mitigate the pity a soldier feels in seeing decent men and women fall, or the fear, I suspect for some, that they are similarly exposed. It is no surprise that many have resorted to dehumanizing the enemy, whether in World War II, my father's war, by turning the enemy into "krauts"; in Vietnam, by turning them into "gooks"; and in our current wars in Afghanistan and Iraq, by calling them "rag-heads" and "A-rabs." George W. Bush, as commander-in-chief, did something similar by calling suspected terrorists "the worst of the worst." It is itself a way to dehumanize and keep the empathic judgment of the troops at bay.

Again, Wolfe, the Vietnam vet, offers sharp lessons for Quinby's generation:

> Some individuals seemed to acquire additional stamina by nurturing a hatred for the "gooks," by creating a dehumanized image of the enemy at which to direct rage. I could never see the NVA [North Vietnamese Army] as other than our dusky companions in misfortune.... The scanty bric-a-brac found in the pockets and packs of the dead dramatized not their differences to us, but their essential sameness. We found family pictures, a few small bills, a comb, and maybe even a bag of marijuana. Assuming the role of nemesis to poor, rice-eating sub-proletariats yanked from their lives of subsistence farming, seemed ridiculous.

Quinby's worry that he fights the coerced, hapless soldier is not much different from Wolfe's, except that Wolfe served in a draft army where many Americans themselves felt coerced. Young Quinby's quandary also brings to mind Robert Graves's reflections in his well-known memoir of World War I, *Good-Bye to All That*. Graves reports that he "refrained from shooting a German" only once, and not because the German was wounded or a prisoner of war, but because "he was taking a bath in the German third line. I disliked the idea of shooting a naked man, so I handed the rifle to the sergeant with me. 'Here, take this. You're a better shot than I am.' He got him; but I had not stayed to watch." During the Spanish Civil War, George Orwell, who served as a sniper, reports a similar reluctance. He held back his fire once when he saw one of the enemy running with his trousers half down. "I didn't shoot partly because of that detail about the trousers. I had come here to shoot at 'Fascists'; but a man who is holding up his trousers isn't a 'Fascist,' he is visibly a fellow creature, similar to yourself, and you don't feel like shooting." John Rawls, the eminent twentieth-century Harvard political philosopher, whom I was privileged to have as a teacher, echoed similar sentiments. At his funeral, which I attended, his son said that his father never spoke much of his experience in World War II, but he did share one story with the family. During his years in the Pacific, he could not bring himself to be angry against the ordinary Japanese foot soldier, though he did harbor anger for the Japanese authorities responsible for the war. On one occasion, face-to-face with his counterpart, he and his opposite looked at each other and chose to retreat rather than fire. It was again a case of pity for the hapless soldier.

I ask Quinby what would be one of the hardest situations he might face as a junior officer. Without hesitation he sketches a scene in which soldiers case a house harboring suspected terrorists. A soldier ends up killing innocent civilians, maybe because he was "scared," "stressed out," or caught up "in a chaotic gun fire." Or maybe, it was "due to sloppiness," "ignorance," or "poor discipline." "That's the sort of thing which I think would probably weigh most heavily on my mind and give me a lot of trouble—being responsible for the accidental killing of someone who's completely innocent" when "it could have been avoided."

In the scenario Quinby limns, he doesn't do the shooting or authorize another to do it. The fog of war—chaos and ignorance—may be factors; his men's psychology—their fear, stress, or desire for revenge—may enter; their failures in skill—sloppiness or lack of discipline in executing a maneuver—may also figure. No matter. It is his command responsibility, his watch, and if innocents die, he is accountable. "As an officer it will be my responsibility to keep my troops in rein, so anything that does happen on the part of my soldiers . . . anything that they do that is against rules of engagement or just against good morality, it's going to be my responsibility." Some might say this is cheap talk, pie in the sky, an easy time to take responsibility. (Maybe the young Janet Karpinski would have said the same, well before the Abu Ghraib scandal unfolded under her command; or similarly, the scores of top brass and civilian leaders who after the fact said Abu Ghraib had nothing to do with command climate or official torture policy but was the work of "rogue" elements among the lower enlisted.)

Fair enough. Still, Quinby's view of commander accountability is in earnest. And we should not be too cynical. We can imagine him taking

Aristotle on moral education to heart: that "we become by doing." Trying on responsibility, in advance, is a way to recognize in the real test how it is all too easy for those in power to pin blame on subordinates, and for those at the bottom to find commanders, orders, and rules of engagement to help dilute personal accountability.

In taking his oath of office, just a month earlier, Quinby surrendered the pared-down moral accountability that most Georgetown graduates still enjoy. The cost of command is the responsibility that runs up the chain. A year and a half after graduating from Georgetown, Quinby will rise to a first lieutenant in charge of a platoon of forty soldiers, some older, some younger, some in their second or third deployments, engaged in massively complex conflicts with shifting enemies and scores of independent sectarian gangs and militias willing to use all and any means of terror. The responsibilities are more than most twenty-three-year-olds carry on their shoulders.

Civilians become soldiers, but the civilian who becomes the soldier is always just one—a soldier *and* civilian, or to paraphrase Montaigne, a soldier *and moi*. A soldier may kill with legitimacy under the conventions of war. But the moral conventions of war do not always or enduringly penetrate the moral soul. Killing the enemy often does not sit easy—even less so, killing an innocent child as the real "collateral" damage of a military targeting. What presses is the weight of a soldier's full humanity, and not just a soldier's duty. Perhaps we could not ask more of a soldier who accepts the awful duty of killing fellow humans.

How war morally feels becomes further complicated when honorable soldiers fight for causes they cannot fully embrace, though their governments view the aggression as legitimate.

CHAPTER 2

——— ⋆ ———

FOR CAUSE
OR COMRADE?

FIDELITY

The well-known motto of the U.S. Marine Corps—*Semper Fidelis* ("Always Faithful") does not make explicit just what the object of a marine's fidelity is. For most marines, it is unquestionably a commitment to each other, and by implication to the corps. For many in the Marines, and the military in general, there is also loyalty to mission and to the overall cause of war for which the mission is a part. Warriors prepare for war by rallying behind a cause. But what happens when they feel deep ambivalence about the justice of a cause?

In preparing to write "the true story of GI Joe" for a Hollywood war movie in the early 1940s, Arthur Miller warned that soldiers abhor an ideological vacuum. Unless the American people can "explain and justify this war," they are "going to injure and sometimes destroy the minds of a host of their returning veterans." At issue for Miller was not just how to rally the troops but also how to return them home whole. The rationale to go to war can be motivating, as it was for Miller's World War II generation and for a generation of soldiers who enlisted sixty years later in immediate response to the attacks of 9/11. But the rationale to stay at war, as we know all too well from our engagement in Iraq, can shift over time, be more or less rooted in fact, be more or less responsive to the realities on the ground. Cause, unlike camaraderie, can erode a soldier's morale. What remains the central battle motivator in most wars is care for buddies and the knowledge that they care for you. "To bring each other home becomes the cause," as lawyer and former Army reservist Capt. Phil Carter told me. At the time, Phil had recently returned from Iraq, where he had served with the Army's 101st Airborne Division as an adviser to the Iraqi police. Retired Army reservist Sgt. Dereck Vines put it more bluntly: "You go because you don't want to let your fellow soldiers down."

The sentiment resonates throughout all militaries. One of the most striking examples comes from Siegfried Sassoon, the English poet and World War I soldier. Even in the face of his own political protest against the war, and a growing pacifism inspired by conversations with Bertrand Russell, Sassoon, as a young officer, felt a profound obligation to the men with whom he fought, "shoulder to aching shoulder." And so after a long psychiatric convalescence at the military hospital Craiglockhart, outside Edinburgh (a stay his good friend Robert Graves arranged to stave off possible court martial for Sassoon's dissent), Sassoon insisted on returning to the front in France to share the burden of battle with his troops. In Plato's *Symposium*, a celebration of love at a drinking party, Phaedrus sings the praises of love in battle. An army of lovers, he insists, is the most courageous kind of army, for shame engendered through love and mutual admiration will check cowardice and self-interest. Plato had in mind homoerotic relations, and Sassoon, to some degree, did too. But the point is a far more general one. Profound mutual love and care are what bind soldiers together and motivate battle. And they are also what heal soldiers after war.

But cause has its place too, in motivating battle and, just as critically, in a soldier's personal sense of accountability for participating in war. Many soldiers whom I have interviewed—draftees, reservists, National Guardsmen, and career military alike—insist they are not responsible for the decision to go to war; that is for those at a higher pay grade, they often tell me. And yet those same individuals feel morally accountable not just for how they fight but for what they fight for. They feel accountable for their participation in the collective end that defines a particular war. To the person, they are patriotic and often speak movingly about their responsibilities to do public service and their willingness to sacrifice. Some remind me of the vast public investment in them as soldiers, trained to fight when the call comes. But none want their willingness to serve exploited for a cause that is unworthy or for a war grounded in unjustified fear or waged for a pretext.

When they believe that has happened, the betrayal felt is profound. Some view it as a kind of breach in the family, a rupture of the deepest kind of trust and care. They are hurt and angry, and frustrated about being caught internally between the role of servant and that of conscientious free moral thinker. For those who are professional soldiers, the tension can be much greater. They have chosen the military as their careers, and they know well, from years of service and command, the military benefits of discipline and order. But they also know that a good officer does not obey unlawful or unjust or morally unwise orders.

How does war feel to individual soldiers who are caught between conscience and obedience to legitimate political authority? How do honorable soldiers prepare themselves for battle when they don't fully embrace the cause of war? How does the duty to take care of each other factor in? The questions are merged in the minds of soldiers: They fight for each other, but always within specific wars fought for specific causes. The war they are part of is not something they can wall off in their minds, however they may try.

HENRY V AND CAUSE

Over lunch at the Tombs restaurant, I ask Lt. Col. Al Gill, then professor of military science at the ROTC program at Georgetown, in what sense cadets are accountable for the wars they will fight. Gill, sitting tall in his fatigues with lynx eyes that peer behind Army-issued black wraparound glasses, answers by way of Shakespeare's *Henry V*. He takes me to act IV, scene V, where the king, cloaked in darkness, visits the troops the night before battle. "Here are these enlisted guys," says Gill with his deep Tennessee accent. "They don't know who Henry is, and they have these very frank discussions about the rightness of the cause." In the famous scene, Henry baits the soldiers on, "Methinks I could not die any where so contented as in the king's company; his cause being just and his quarrel honourable." One soldier pleads ignorance of cause: "That's more than we know." Another counsels: "Ay, or more than we should seek after." The soldiers conclude that responsibility for just cause rests with the king and that their own ignorance is not culpable: "For we know enough, if we know we are the king's subjects: if his cause be wrong, our obedience to the king wipes the crime of it out of us." In other words, mere participation in an unjust war is not wrongful action for a soldier. What a soldier is accountable for is conduct, not cause.

Gill puts his own spin on Shakespeare's verses: "I don't know much but I know this . . . if the cause is not good, then all these guys with their arms and legs chopped off, all these wounded—the king is to blame for that shit." It is the spring of 2006 and many of Gill's young officers who entered the Hoya Battalion in the wake of 9/11 are now in Iraq and Afghanistan. "This is the sort of thing cadets need to see," he insists. "There has always been this stuff. As I tell my class, the thing that makes Henry less to blame is that in those days, the king was there with sword in hand. . . . Now we have this situation of guys making decisions for those who have arms and legs cut off, but they themselves have never done this stuff and never will. It's very difficult." The weight of his own responsibility to his cadets hangs heavy.

That ordinary soldiers are not responsible for the cause of war remains a dominant part of the philosophical tradition of just-war theory. Michael Walzer, in his landmark post-Vietnam *Just and Unjust Wars*, defends the traditional view: "By and large we don't blame a solider, even a general, who fights for his own government. He is not the member of a robber band, a willful wrongdoer, but a loyal and obedient subject and citizen, acting sometimes at great personal risk in a way he thinks is right." This implies that soldiers on both sides have "an equal right to kill" and enjoy a kind of "moral equality" on the battlefield. What they are accountable for is *how* they prosecute war—for conduct free of atrocities and crimes and excessive collateral damage—not for *what* they fight for.

Francisco de Vitoria, the sixteenth-century Catholic theologian advising the Castilian crown, puts forth a kindred view in one of his lectures. With the Spanish conquest of the New World the catalyst for his remarks, Vitoria argues, "Even though the war may be unjust on one side or the other, the soldiers on each side who come to fight in battle . . . are all equally innocent." Yet the moral equality of soldiers does not preclude, urges Vitoria in another lecture, a soldier's individual responsibility to conscientiously reflect about what he ought and ought not fight for. "If their conscience tells subjects that the war is unjust, *they must not go to war even if their conscience is wrong*," and even if "ordered to do so by the prince." To this, Vitoria adds the rider: *Merely* to have doubts is not itself to violate conscience and does not warrant disobedience. Soldiers need more than doubt alone to renege on their obligation to fight.

Vitoria also addresses the moral responsibilities of leadership, with thoughts prescient for our own recent times, during which we have witnessed unprecedented executive power. It is not enough, he says, for a leader to believe that war is a just cause and the last resort. "The king is not capable of examining the causes of war on his own, and it is likely that he may make mistakes, or rather that he *will* make mistakes. . . . So war should not be declared on the sole dictates of the prince, nor even on the opinions of the few, but on the opinion of the many, and of the wise and reliable." In the back of his mind is Aristotle's standard of the judgment of the practically wise person. However, Vitoria critically revises it: Wisdom is not the province of one; it rests on the informed deliberation and scrutiny of many, who are duty bound to counsel against war and a leader if circumstances demand it. "One must consult reliable and wise men who can speak with freedom and without anger or hate or greed," propounds Vitoria. "If such men can by examining the causes of hostility with their advice and authority avert a war which is perhaps unjust, then they are obliged to do so." Vitoria does not mince his words. He is counseling a monarchy worried about its perilous position as the universal protector of Christendom and Christian values. In a different time and place, he could be counseling a democratically elected leader about the moral hazards, for a nation and world, of shutting out opinions that do not agree with his own.

Taken as a whole, Vitoria's remarks actually push us beyond the traditional view that foot soldiers are not accountable for the causes of war for which they fight. True, he grants, foot soldiers, unlike advisers privy to a leader's ears, will be limited in their power to prevent a war. But still, given the fallibility of a leader's judgment and the magnitude of the destruction of war, soldiers ought to reflect conscientiously about what, in good faith, they are willing to fight for. The claim has continuing appeal today. It seems plausible to hold that individual citizen-soldiers, especially of liberal democracies such as our own, ought to bear *some* modicum of responsibility for the causes of war for which they fight, particularly when they are not conscripts. Given unprecedented access to information and critical debate through enhanced media modes, shouldn't soldiers be more reflective than they often are about what they are willing to fight for? Moreover, wouldn't such reflection tend to curb governments from too casually going to war?

The philosopher Jeff McMahan has voiced these concerns in an important series of public addresses and articles, arguing that soldiers act morally wrongly in fighting for unjust wars; they are "unjust combatants," he says, though they are not criminally liable for mere participation. That is, what they do is morally wrong, though excusable. Others have argued that it makes sense to have exit options that allow citizen-soldiers to refuse to fight specific wars they believe unjust, without the imposition of crippling penalties. To deny them reasonable exits, they claim, is to hold the liberal state ransom to the military.

However, it is easy to see the practical problems with selective conscientious objection. Especially in the case of a volunteer army, it would be hard to raise troops for unpopular wars. Doubt about the cause of war might mushroom into rationalizations not to fight. The defense needs of a country would be left to the discretion and motivation of each soldier.

But then how do we take into account a soldier's responsibility to reflect on the justice of cause? Despite its merits, McMahan's view seems too harsh and to miss too much about the practice of soldiering. However much we might like citizen-soldiers to be more reflective about the causes for which they are willing to fight (and indeed all citizens who send soldiers to war), it seems too much to expect soldiers on the verge of deploying, or having deployed, to track the shifts in official rationales and to puzzle whether they are now, at this point in time, fighting for a cause that justifies the use of lethal force. Army tours, as I write, are twelve months long, with another three months for preparation operations with a unit. During that time, soldiers are either immersed in training or marching to the tempo of missions. Days are long and emotionally and physically grueling. This is not the optimal time for the deepest reflection and analysis of war's causes and rationales. There are other practical matters. Militaries work by coercion and command structures. While few good leaders want or expect blind obedience from their troops (and this includes responsible commanders-in-chief from their top brass), they do depend on mobilized cadres that operate with good discipline and order. This doesn't efface individual responsibilities soldiers have to object to unlawful, immoral, and unwise orders, including the ultimate order to go to war, but it does recognize the collectivizing and coercive force of armies and raising armies.

What I found throughout my interviews is that soldiers actually do struggle hard with their individual accountability for participating in a war of others' making. But the struggle is often internal and not a matter of others judging them. True, the boundaries are not always sharp. What others think and say is sometimes reflected in self-assessments. But the debate goes on largely inside, as a soulful struggle with conscience. Few think in the abstract terms of just-war theory or its legacy in international law and the United Nations' doctrine—that justified wars are conducted only to fend off attack or in the face of "immediate and imminent" attack. Most don't worry, as theorists and political, legal, and military advisers do (and did in the run-up to the war in Iraq), about whether fending off "immediate and imminent" attack allows not only preemption but also prevention. But what they *do* worry about is whether they are going to war on a pretext for other actual causes. In a deep and personal way, they worry about whether they are being betrayed or manipulated by leadership, and how they can serve honorably in those circumstances. This is the worry of soldiers whose stories I tell. It is the worry of Dereck Vines, who served in Iraq in an intelligence unit. It is the worry of Bob Steck, who served in the Army in Vietnam, and of Hank McQueeny, who was a naval officer in that war. And it was the worry of Ted Westhusing, for whom the war in Iraq would become an unlivable internal war (as I detail later).

Put more globally, soldiers worry about the goodness of the ends of their wars and whether those ends will outweigh the destruction. I get insight here from my father. Seymour Sherman, now eighty-eight and a veteran of World War II, wrestles with that question over and over again, whether he is reading the papers now and following the current wars in Afghanistan or Iraq in Gaza, or was doing the same, some forty years ago, in the Vietnam War era. He looks on, often, through the eyes of a soldier, as the Army medic he was. Somewhere in his reveries, he is back on the *Queen Elizabeth I*, Cunard's luxury liner that was refitted as a U.S. Army transport and hospital. He is zigzagging across the Atlantic some sixteen times on a slow five-day journey to Gourock, Scotland, in the Firth of Clyde, and then on to Normandy. In his case, he does have time to reflect, and wonders if the fight is worth the horrific ruin and devastation he anticipates and then sees up close in dying men and mutilated bodies. That sense of his own responsibility for the specific war he fights is there, whether he talks about it openly or not. The worry is about proportionality, the ratio of the good anticipated to all the carnage. Is it worth it? In the war he fought, he believes it was, then and now, as most do. But the point I am making is that the moral oversight is internal. Yes, it is not just about what he did as an individual soldier, in his case, administering inoculations and relief to the war-torn and maimed. It is also about the war he was in. That frames his perspective and his responsibility. Perhaps, at some level, there is also appreciation for the role of luck in arranging for which war was his to fight, and the fact that moral luck is not itself equitable.

My father's worries are shared by many of the soldiers I have interviewed, whether they are engaged in Iraq or Afghanistan, or served in Bosnia or Vietnam. They carry on their shoulders the burden of the wars they fight, and not just their individual conduct in those wars. But the debate is often internal, and for many it has never been fully verbalized or exposed.

Philosophers often miss this inner debate. And it's not just because they don't talk to soldiers. It is, in part, because of a long philosophical tradition that casts morality in terms of our praise and blame of others: the address is "second personal," to use philosophers' jargon. A conversation between McMahan and a soldier who fights for an unjust cause might go like this: "Your participation is unjustified. But because you may have been coerced, deceived, understandably afraid of the authority of the state, or because of the unfeasibility of trials (who would conduct such a trial? certainly not the state which demands you fight, and if the trials fall under the jurisdiction of international courts, then not in their courts, given their overextended dockets and underfinanced budgets), you are not held individually responsible or culpable. Given mitigating factors and pragmatic consequences of holding you, and others like you, liable, you are excused for your participation."

But soldiers have a reply. They might respond to McMahan by saying, "Even though I *think* that this war is immoral, I don't know it. I worry about it, but I also worry about deserting my country in its time of need. I am a professional soldier. You have spent a lot of money and resources ensuring I would be ready when you called. You trust me to be there. What if I thought the call to war was just, but I still had my doubts? If I then said 'I won't go, unless I am certain the cause is just,' what, Dr. McMahan, would you say to me then? Would you honor me for my dissent? Or condemn me for being a coward? More importantly, what would history say? This is what I worry about when I worry about whether a war is just or not. I don't just worry that the war might be unjust. If that were the case, my doubts might be enough to get me to quit. I also worry that it is just. If that were the case, giving in to such doubts would be an act of cowardice."

This, in fact, is one soldier's reply. I have quoted here Army Col. Tony Pfaff, the military attaché to Kuwait at the time of this conversation, and a ranger and infantry officer who served twice in the current conflict in Iraq, advising Iraqi military police, and earlier, leading a company in the first Gulf War. Undoubtedly, he is more philosophical than many, and indeed, he writes on issues of just war and military ethics. (I disclose here that he is a Ph.D. student at Georgetown whom I supervise.) Still, his remarks voice something implicit in many soldiers' minds: that moral accountability for taking part in a particular war is part of a larger inner moral debate framed in terms of virtue and cowardice, certainty and doubt about cause, obligation to fellow soldiers and to country.

Many soldiers I have spoken to hold themselves accountable for the wars they fight in, whether expressed in the fact that they feel proud or tainted, accomplished or disillusioned, compromised or angry. The feelings are typically mixed and complicated. Some try to compartmentalize their portion of war as a way of fending off more complex feelings. It may be true, as McMahan charges, that traditional just-war theory is too limiting, because it too neatly pries apart cause from conduct. But it is also too limiting because it doesn't invite us to look at soldiers' own struggles with what they are asked to fight for. As a public that sends its citizen-soldiers to war, it is our duty to understand better, and help heal, their inner wars.

TAINTED

Bob Steck got his greetings to go to Vietnam a few days after he turned twenty-six. At that point he was too old to be drafted, but the letter from his Texas draft board had been postmarked before his birthday. Officially, he was still eligible. "There was a sense of the absurd," Bob said. "It was 1970, and I was against the war at the time." He had recently finished graduate course work in philosophy at Yale and was teaching at Washington and Lee University in Virginia. He even hired the firm of Rabinowitz, Boudin, and Standard, New York attorneys well known at the time for their opposition to the war. The strategy was to test his orders to go to war as illegal, based on the fact that the war was illegal. "It was a way of trying to bring cause to the courts." The case didn't go very far, and ultimately he faced, as many drafted did, an existential crisis. Canada was not much of an option for him. It was jail or going to the Army: "I decided to go to the Army because I didn't think it was a one-step inference from 'I don't believe in this war' to 'I won't serve in this war.' I reasoned, if I don't go, someone else will, who is maybe younger without my resources or someone who would be less likely to keep his wits and be more tempted to commit atrocities. It was very difficult, obviously. Maybe it was all rationalization. I never was entirely confident with my decision. Also my dad had died five years earlier, and my mother was on her own. My going to jail would have been terribly hard on her."

Bob Steck served in Vietnam for a little less than a year as a radio operator with the Army's 3/17th Air Cavalry ("A" Troop), keeping networks open so that helicopter teams could communicate with each other. Back then his light brown wavy hair fell onto his forehead, and he sported a thick brown mustache that matched his tortoiseshell specs. In one picture, taken in Quan Loi in 1971, he looks youthful in his fatigues, sleeves rolled up, seated on a pile of sandbags at a sentry post, with his rifle and cigarette in hand.

I first met Bob in 2005 at a reading of my book *Stoic Warriors* at Politics and Prose, an independent bookstore in northwest D.C. During the question-and-answer session, he was one of the first to speak. In his early sixties at the time, Bob briskly stepped up to the mike, but then choked with emotion as he tried to talk. When he regained his composure, what followed was a fairly dry academic question: "Can you distinguish the justness of a war from the justness of a warrior?" he asked. But it was clear that for him, the question was much more than academic.

I hadn't addressed the issue of just war in my talk, so I was a bit taken aback. As I paused, he offered his own answer: "Those of us who became anti-war veterans about Vietnam used to insist that we could—that we must—distinguish the war from the warrior." Some thirty-five years after his war over Vietnam, Bob had to believe that the cause for which he fought, and his conduct in fighting, were separate if he was to make peace with himself. Still, believing that was not easy.

As I was to learn later, through many conversations with Bob over the last several years, the wars in Iraq and Afghanistan have led him and scores of other Vietnam vets to relive some of their worst war trauma. Some have returned to therapy; others, including Bob, have regularly visited hospitals, such as Walter Reed Army Medical Center, to share their own hard-won lessons with returning, war-torn soldiers. (One such vet who has been public about his returning depression is Max Cleland, former senator from Georgia and a decorated Vietnam veteran and triple amputee.) In Bob's case, what weighs heavily is a felt impotence at not being able to save soldiers from the suffering he went through.

This was on his mind when I interviewed him in February 2007 at my office at the Woodrow Wilson Center in downtown D.C. "I think my works and days are kind of marinated in a sort of melancholy," he said sullenly. He had felt betrayed by World War II veterans who did not really tell him the truth about going to war—what it feels like, what it requires of soldiers, and what it does to them. The commitment he has carried since Vietnam, and in his activism in Vietnam Veterans Against the War, is to not betray a future generation of soldiers.

Bob reflects back to an incident early in his military career that was formative. He was standing in chow line in basic training when a drill sergeant "came down" hard on an African-American soldier for being dressed sloppily. "He kicked the hell out of his leg and then kicked him again when the guy flinched.... I was just livid," says Bob. But maybe that's how you have to make an army, he rationalized. Maybe that's how you have to prepare for "the contours of what combat was really like." But the anger really never subsided, nor did the resentment that he had been kept in the dark about the true price of combat: "Why in heaven's name didn't the combat veterans from the Second World War come back and tell us, even though theirs was a war worth doing: 'Hey folks, here are the prices of this kind of thing. We don't go into this stuff lightly. We don't go into wars of choice. We don't go in on a bet or a theory. We go in if we have to stop Nazi Germany.' Why didn't they tell us? So one of the things I sort of resolved for myself standing in that chow line out in Fort Lewis, Washington, was that I'm not going to let people forget. I am not going to let this be just passed over."

Returning to the present, he says with disbelief, "I thought we had talked enough. I thought we had talked enough. I thought we had talked so much people had gotten tired of it. I thought at least they knew."

Bob Steck is visibly anguished about his own generation's ultimate failure to inoculate future generations of soldiers. He is a man of strong moral sensibilities; he is well read, knowledgeable, and an activist. He has returned to Vietnam several times to heal himself and fellow vets, on one occasion riding on a tandem bike from Hanoi to Saigon with George Brummell, a vet who lost his eyesight from an explosion during the war, seated behind. Over the past thirty-five years, Bob has not taken his mission lightly. Part of the anguish comes from the sense of political impotence, but part also comes from the underlying fact that he can't psychologically or morally fully separate himself from the war he fought. Wars and warriors don't easily come apart, even if they do in some theoretical formulation.

Shortly after Veterans Day in 2007, Bob told me in a phone conversation that he had gone down to the Vietnam War Memorial to commemorate the day. At the time, I was trying to understand the notion of shame some soldiers feel for their engagement in war, and so we began to talk about that. In his case, he said, the predominant feeling wasn't shame, but a sense of taint. "We *all* felt a sense of taint," even those in the nursing corps who were "on the side of the angels in that they did not carry weapons." Michael Herr puts his finger on the feeling in his famous memoir of his years as a war correspondent in Vietnam: "I went to cover the war, but the war covered me."

Taint is a feeling seldom discussed in the philosophical or psychological literature. Researchers write about moral feelings such as guilt and shame, remorse and regret, indignation and moral protest. Some with a more legal bent write about complicity. But taint is rarely mentioned. So just what does it mean when Bob tells me that he feels tainted?

"Taint" implies pollution, staining, fouling. In the Vietnam era, returning soldiers sometimes met jeering crowds who yelled, "Baby killer" and "Murderer," even though the enlightened public, and probably many of the jeerers, knew well that not all returning soldiers committed atrocities and that many (such as Bob) fought hard to prevent them. Still, honorable soldiers felt vulnerable to the criticism, for they viewed the remarks as not only about *how* they fought the war, but also *that* they fought the war. Being blamed for conduct was a way to get at the fact that they fought at all. The soldiers were held, in some way, complicit, even if the preponderance of public criticism was reserved for those higher up, in particular, the civilian administration.

In the case of taint, the complicity is often of the mildest kind. In Bob's case, it is clear that as a young soldier he was far from the center of power, where decisions were made and policies formulated for why the war was fought or continued. He was a draftee who went opposed to the war. Like most foot soldiers, he participated at the extreme periphery of a collective end and was, by any measure, far less complicitous than the top civilians and brass who called the shots. Yet Bob feels tainted—not corrupted or sullied. Those words are too strong, and not his. In his mind, there is a passive yet pervasive association with a policy that is wrong or unjust. The tinge spreads, irrespective of his moral protest. What is toxic permeates. In that physical metaphor, taint fills the pores so that cleansing and purification seem impossible.

Bob tells me the taint was reinforced when people would later say to him, as a member of the Vietnam Veterans Against the War movement, "You are not in a position to criticize the war since you fought in it." Taint mingles with the shame of internalizing something you don't really believe but that "has traction"—that you are guilty of hypocrisy. Some fellow veterans worried precisely about the risks of open dissent. So, he noted, veterans who did not join the movement (perhaps some of whom would later become part of the "Swift Boat" attack against John Kerry's 2004 presidential bid) may have privately felt that they fought an ill-conceived and unjust war, "but did not want to make it public because it would cast shame on veterans" for being less than patriotic.

As Bob describes it, the taint comes from outside in. Others—and the circumstances of his war—stick it on him. Yet it sticks. This veteran was, and forever will be, part of a war he didn't believe was just. There will always be that felt lack of confidence about his moral position for agreeing to fight. "Maybe it's all rationalization?" he muses. "I will probably go to my grave not knowing if I made the right decision." But his own doubts get exacerbated when others see him as part of an undifferentiated force prosecuting a misguided war. He is implicated, not for some specific action or accident. Rather, he is implicated because of bad, circumstantial luck that has caught him in its snare. In a different war, in a different generation, he might have come home from war feeling pride and a sense of courage for putting his life on the line for the sake of what is noble. Instead, because of the war he fought, he feels contaminated. His assessment of himself, and how he views others assessing him, are wrapped up with moral luck and a coerced choice.

SUCKERED

Dereck Vines served in the Army Reserve in both Bosnia and Iraq. He is pensive and soft-spoken, and there is a sadness in his eyes and voice. Now in his early fifties, he deployed to Iraq at age forty-five, with the 404th Reserve Unit in Fort Dix, New Jersey, as a civil affairs sergeant in an intelligence unit. He retired at the rank of Army sergeant first class. I first met Dereck at the Woodrow Wilson Center, where he was on the tech staff and had come to my aid many times when my phone or computer acted up. When he learned about my project on soldiers, he asked to sit down with me to chat. We talked on Memorial Day of 2007 and again, several times, later that year and into 2008.

Each time we spoke, Dereck compared his experiences in Iraq and Bosnia. Bosnia was a war he could believe in, and he felt good about being part of it. He went feeling he had a mission, and had come home feeling proud. "In Bosnia we had a purpose. The Serbs were about to wipe out the Bosnian people altogether. If we or the UN hadn't stepped in, it would have been a catastrophe," he says. The war in Afghanistan, too, had a mission he said he could rally around and did when his unit was put on an alert roster to go there. "I felt the importance of the mission in Afghanistan, to try to find Bin Laden and to get back at them [Al Qaeda] for their attacks. Otherwise we'd be suckered. We'd let them just get us." But orders shifted and his unit was deployed to Iraq. "Iraq was the complete opposite of Bosnia," he says. It was a war he just couldn't believe in.

The word "suckered" jumped out at me. It had come up before, the first time we talked. In fact it was the theme of that interview. In going to Iraq and in serving there, *he* felt "suckered." Dereck wasn't talking about a public that had been suckered or blinded into going into war. And he wasn't analyzing a history of America or other countries "suckered" into war by blind patriotism or the beating of the war drums in effective propaganda. He was talking painfully about his own feelings, the notion that his life might have been squandered on a pretext, for a mission whose purpose he couldn't believe in and still believes was ill-formed: "The whole thing with the weapons of mass destruction. Did we ever find any? And that's what we always say—did we ever find any weapons of mass destruction? All of the chemicals and stuff that Iraq was supposed to have—and we never found any. . . . It's just like: Okay, I've been suckered."

"I try not to think about it," Dereck says with muted anger. "The more and more you hear in the commissions, that this was false information and that was false information. You're sitting there. You're just like, 'Okay, I was almost killed. I was almost not here and they haven't really given me a clear reason.' You hate to be against the president and I don't care if he's a Republican or a Democrat or whatever. But for your upper echelon to really sucker you—that's kind of a hard pill to swallow."

What Dereck Vines means by being suckered is that he feels duped, deceived, toyed with by those in charge, to whom he has sworn fidelity and for whom he has put his life on the line. To be sure, like many soldiers, Vines is adamant about his patriotism: "When you are feeling these thoughts [of being suckered], pride in America and the uniform—that's what kind of holds you together," he says. But what fractures is the sense

of betrayal, the feeling of being abandoned, misled, unsupported, manipulated by those who have put you in danger's way. Even those terms are
too abstract to capture Vines's feeling. The betrayal is raw and existential:
"I was almost killed. I was almost not here."

The words are a soldier's shorthand for traumatic moments imprinted
in his psyche—in his case, images of picking up and bagging body parts of
buddies caught in a fire bombing; of watching his convoy get severed by a
roadside bomb, which thrust him against the windshield of his armored
vehicle; of being medevaced, half-conscious, to a hospital. The memories
are seared in his mind and return intrusively. But the trauma is exacerbated by moral anguish and resentment that his trust was misplaced and
abused. The shock and the disappointment are tangible as he speaks. To
be suckered by "your upper echelon" (by top military and civilian leaders, he means) is almost unfathomable to him. "You serve your country,"
he says passionately. "You don't want to let your fellow soldiers down." In
his case, there was never the thought that he wouldn't go. But still he felt
duped. He felt betrayed. He wanted, and morally felt he was owed, wiser
leadership and better analysis of the intelligence from the military and
government agencies. The teachings of Vitoria press here: A leader cannot examine the causes of war on his own, nor can an insulated coterie
of advisers. The likelihood for mistake is too great. The wisest and most
reliable must deliberate and provide counsel. Again, in Vitoria's words,
"If such men can by examining the causes of hostility with their advice
and authority avert a war which is perhaps unjust, then they are obliged
to do so."

"Betrayal" is a word not to be taken lightly in military contexts. If we
turn to the *Oxford English Dictionary* for instruction, the first definition
is "a treacherous giving up to an enemy." Next is "a violation of trust or
confidence, an abandonment of something committed to one's charge."
The primary definition of the verb "to betray" again makes the military
context central: "to give up or place in the power of an enemy by treachery or disloyalty."

The military connotation is suggestive, but it doesn't tell the full story.
It is not, at least in Dereck's case, that he is given up to the enemy. Rather,

what counts as the betrayal for him is that a sacred bond of trust is broken, a "sacred band," like those Plato and Plutarch write about, founded on military honor, loyalty, and a sense of shame. For some, the betrayal is experienced as a rupture of the most basic caring bond: the family that a soldier becomes part of when he or she joins the military. The reciprocal caring from those cared for and served breaks down. The betrayal is experienced profoundly, as perfidy. Here it is critical to remember that bonding in the military is not just horizontal, toward comrades, brothers and sisters in arms, though that undoubtedly is the most intense attachment. Bonding also runs vertically, up chains of command: Soldiers give allegiance and respect to superiors with the trust that that service and sacrifice won't be squandered. Their trust is betrayed when a country and its soldiers are duped into going to war.

The attachment element in military life cannot be underestimated. Many young recruits, just out of high school, join the military in search of a new family. What they have at home may no longer, or, never did, satisfy. They want new role models that give them something to believe in and idealize. They want to be part of something bigger than themselves, where there is community and caring if they are willing to work for it. Others don't so much seek a new family as find it through the radical socialization process of initial training. Markers of old attachments (first name, easy contact with home and family, civilian clothes and hair, comfort objects and personal styles) get effaced and replaced with new attachments; look-alike images stamp the recruit with a new family identity. Boot camp and basic training are about molding a new self, but also about becoming a part of a new family, with all its aspirations and promise of care.

The Marines' *Semper Fidelis,* again, speaks volumes. To be betrayed by this new family is devastating, especially for those who sought it out because of earlier betrayals or traumas within their families of origin. Nancy Meyer, a psychotherapist who has treated scores of patients at Walter Reed hospital for some five and a half years, twenty-five to thirty hours a week, once commented anecdotally, that there is often an element of betrayal experienced by those who are wounded psychologically by war. The attachment bond has been snapped, and with it the belief that fidelity ought to be reciprocated by support and care and empathic leadership. It is a betrayal often not easily resolved, given the distance between ranks, and the implausibility of "working it out" in the way individuals do in healthy families in or marriages, face-to-face. The betrayal may have to be accepted as a fact, a bitter fact.

The soldier's implicit wish, voiced by Dereck Vines, is that commanders not betray subordinates' willingness to serve and make sacrifices. When commanders do, they act with treachery and perfidy. Dereck went to war as a graying noncomissioned officer (NCO). He was "Pops" to his troops, not a naive, wide-eyed boy. Yet he feels suckered, taken for a fool. He is angry at others but also angry at himself for being gullible. If called again, knowing what he now knows, he tells me he'd still go. That is what he signed up for. Like many enlisted and reserved, he is willing to fight because he accepted that responsibility as part of his job. But still he feels betrayal—a sense that his willingness to make the ultimate sacrifice for his country and comrades ought to be mirrored by the gravest of responsibilities from higher-ups. If betrayal is about the rupture of trust, perfidy and treachery are about the risk and danger to which abuse of trust exposes one.

Shakespeare's Henry V again makes the point, but this time from the perspective of the compassionate commander. If *I* live to see the king ransomed, says Henry under wraps to his troops, "then I will never trust his word again." Henry projects his wishes onto the soldiers: He desperately wants them to have faith in him, to believe that he won't be ransomed or lose the war. He wants them to feel that it will not have been wrongheaded or in vain, and that they will not feel exploited or expendable. But the soldiers can't and won't share the luxury of his lofty fantasy. They are, after all, just subjects. Ransomed or unransomed won't make a hoot of difference once they are dead, they say. They are (or in death will have been) just the king's instruments. But Henry wishes they were more and he were less. In the shadow of soliloquy, he deflates his own "farced" (stuffed) pomp and title that inspires "awe and fear in other men." Still, deflation in status is just for the sake of a "proud dream," a wishful fantasy that he might share the weight of his responsibility for war. But the moral reality is that he remains the king and calls the shots. At the end of the day, the soldiers still take his orders and die for his causes. They can only hope that their faithful service is not abused.

Dereck Vines carries that feeling of being someone else's instrument. What smarts is that he is no king's subject. He votes. He is informed. He now works in a Washington policy institute, whose director he much admires and feels special affection toward—Lee Hamilton, the former Indiana congressman who with James Baker headed up the Iraq Study Group in 2006 to advise on American policy in Iraq. Vines never uses the word "tainted," as Bob Steck does. For Vines, Iraq is not toxic in the way Vietnam felt and feels to many veterans of that war. Vines was not a draftee. He did not feel coerced to serve in the way many draftees did going to Vietnam. He went willingly, as part of his duty. But he still felt "suckered." That feeling of being lied to and of letting himself be lied to is what tears him up.

DISILLUSIONED

Hank McQueeny is a retired naval officer who served in Vietnam and always wanted to be in the Navy. Of all the military uniforms, Navy summer whites, officer summer whites, "dress whites with the stiff neck and the bridge cap," were those he loved best. He also loved battleship gray "and the smell of the ship oils and resins and paint and the sea all mixed together." As a young boy, he could remember himself saying, "By God, if I'm in the service when I grow up, I want to be in the Navy." Growing up in Boston, he had a local naval hero—John F. Kennedy, the young lieutenant and captain of the PT-109 that was ripped apart by a Japanese destroyer in August 1943 in the Solomon Islands. For Hank, the Navy called. And so in 1960, after graduating from Boston College, Hank McQueeny was commissioned, went to intelligence school, survived simulated POW training, and was assigned as a junior officer to a squadron in fleet. By 1964, he was aboard the USS *Ticonderoga* off the shores of Southeast Asia.

It wasn't long before disillusionment set in. His centered on the ruse that led to the Gulf of Tonkin Resolution (August 5, 1964), in which Congress, in a near-unanimous vote, authorized President Lyndon Johnson to use "all necessary measures" to repel armed attacks against U.S. forces in Vietnam.

The surrounding incidents are well known (and were narrated to me earlier by another officer on board the *Ticonderoga*, Vice Adm. Jim Stockdale, who one year after the Tonkin incident was shot down in Vietnam and held as a POW for seven and a half years in the Hanoi Hilton). The circumstances are these, as Hank retells the events: Two U.S. destroyers were ordered to enter the claimed sovereign waters of North Vietnam. "The idea was to prompt the North Vietnamese to send small vessels . . . —the little fast PT boats—against the destroyers to have them back away from their port. . . . That would be an excuse, a reason to accelerate the war."

From the *Ticonderoga*, two A-1's (single-seat aircrafts) were sent overhead to inspect the damage. "But they saw no PT boats. They saw nothing" and reported as much through their command structure up to the Pentagon. All they saw was "the flash of the weapons aboard the destroyers shooting aimlessly against the presumed target." As one of the skippers of the aircraft told Hank at the time, "Hank, there's nothing up there, no shit, nothing up there." In Hank's sober words, "They said that the ships were attacked, falsely said that, and they used that as a ruse, manufactured a ruse, to thereby enlarge the war. That was a big disillusionment. . . . Everybody on the ship knew the truth, or practically everybody," even if many accepted it as the cost of moving the war forward. But for Hank, the reality of what happened loomed large in his consciousness.

His disillusionment is a brooding anger in being deceived, toyed with, made party to a deception. The treachery is a kind of triple abuse of respect and dignity: You are lied to (or at least what you know to be true is denied) in order to play a role in a public deception (the ruse), which then puts you at great risk (the war's acceleration through the Gulf of Tonkin Resolution). "I was disillusioned. I thought, I still think, that this country ought not to be above ordinary standards." From then on, as he puts it, "there was just a sense of going down a slippery slope real quickly." His way of coping, like that of many soldiers in all wars, was self-medication and avoidance: "We did a lot of drinking, carousing, a lot of running around. We played bridge." Drugs would come later in the war, after Hank's time.

The general tenor of this narrative is familiar to those for whom the Vietnam era was formative. But the point that emerges over and over again in my interviews is that combatants internalize their conflicts about the justification of war, suck it up, truck on, keep fighting, and perhaps only later, if they are reflective and empathically supported, expose their anger and ambivalence. Like Dereck Vines, Hank McQueeny clings to the uniform as something that idealizes his service and helps him tolerate his disillusionment. "I used to enjoy my uniform," he says tenderly. "I used to greatly enjoy my uniform. I still have dreams about my uniform." He confides on a lighter note that he once failed to show up in his dress uniform because he refused to spend a hundred dollars on a ceremonial sword that was a mandatory part of the dress code. He chuckled as he relived the moment of youthful defiance: "I stood up the guy who wanted me to wear a sword to the party!" Musing about this and his mention of dreams, I asked if he ever dreamt about his sword. "No, that's too phallic," he shot back. "I never dreamed about that!"

Of course, in Hank's case, if there weren't the uniform, there wouldn't be the disillusionment. For what he is saying is that there is still an important place in him for the military at its best—for the ideal of the military and the protection and support it represents, captured for him in the gleam of bright summer whites. Holding on to that idealized object removes some of the taint, alienation, and loss, in service for a cause he fears may not have been worth it, and in service to leaders who may not have deserved his trust.

To my ears, Hank McQueeny's disillusionment is morally and psychologically distinct from Dereck Vines's feeling of being suckered. True, Hank feels betrayed, but what hurts most is the *deflation* of himself and his ideals. What he imagined he stood for in his whites got drained of meaning and with it his image of self, defined by commitment to worthy public service and sacrifice. The disillusionment is the deflation that follows the betrayal. It is that deflated self that is so hard to reconcile with who he envisions he was in uniform, and who he was supposed to be.

THE CESSPOOL OF NAPLES

As a public, we tend to idealize World War II and have a tendency to think that American soldiers and Allies who fought in that war, by and large, did not have to struggle with the anguished feelings I have just been documenting. They went to war rallying not just for each other, but for a cause that was popular. The evil of Nazism and Hitler's tyranny was real. Defending homeland and allies against attack was justified. The internal doubts and conflicts were, on the whole, fewer. Perhaps that is so for most. But consider one soldier's voice from that war. The voice is from John Horne Burns's underread World War II novel, *The Gallery*. Written in 1947, it is more memoir than novel. The setting is northern Africa and Naples, and the "gallery" in the title is the Galleria Umberto Primo, a bombed-out glass arcade that was "the unofficial heart of Naples," where Americans, British, and Neapolitans commingled in sin.

Through Burns we see again the internal tensions soldiers experience in fighting wars that they have come to lose faith in. Though World War II is portrayed by most as a war to save the world from evil, Burns, writing with fresh eyes, just three years after the war, paints a picture that is not so noble. Whatever sense of righteousness he felt going to war soon evaporated in war. Naples was a cesspool of soldiers selling their rations for an hour at a brothel, of child-pimps with their prostitutes, of Neapolitan ladies showing up en masse at a public concert in winter coats sewn from purloined Army-issue blankets, of Army freighters, tanks, and wheels of military vehicles stolen by a population that was bombed out and starving. This we might say is an indictment not of the cause of war, but of how it is prosecuted and the reality of post-bellum occupation. But it is also about cause. For Burns, a writer schooled at Andover and Harvard, the lofty rationale for World War II never fully stuck. What he saw daily was war's corruption, "its annihilation of everything" that "the sensitive, shy, and gentle" stand for, and the fury of those who die, who leave "this life angry, but not hurt," some wrestling "with the larger issues" when it is not even clear if they can read or write.

Many of the soldiers he writes about see themselves as participants in the grotesquerie and hold themselves liable. They are their own persons, not just marionette-servants of someone else's decision to go to war. It is *their* war. It frames what they do and their engagement. To disconnect from their feelings about the war comes at too great a psychological price, though some will pay the price for the protection.

Hal is a character in one of Burns's "gallery portraits." He has crossed the Atlantic to arrive in the "gummy city" of Oran, Algeria. He visits the bars, as he used to in New York, from Central Park to Greenwich Village. There, he had been a looking glass in which others could feel understood and enlightened. But here, after ten minutes, conversation with the "Joe" next to him freezes in a subconscious sense of shared complicity that indicts them all:

> Hal found it difficult, after a few drinks, to look them straight in the eye. There was some vast and deadly scheme in which they were all working; only they didn't know it.
>
> Hal himself had an inkling of what was upsetting him. Casting about for a rational explanation of why he felt so *odd*, he decided it was because the war was beginning to seep into his bones. This war was the fault of everyone, himself included.

To read Burns's words is to feel the nausea, booziness, loneliness, and terror young boy-men evince as they leave home for the first time and steam across the world. But it is also to feel the ache of searching to justify the violence of war with a worthy cause, a fine and noble end that will ensure that courage is genuine, as Aristotle might put it. And when such an end isn't easily found (and when war sucked of its glory is seen at best as the least immoral option), characters like Hal turn war inward and line up enemy positions inside. The corruption of soul becomes war's collateral damage: "Something in him seemed to be chasing another part.

Often this hunt between sections of himself became so vicious that he had to put his head between his hands, as a man with a hangover expects his heart to stop in the very next moment, and prays for even the distraction of a bowel movement." Ghoulish incubi "with no bodies or faces" inhabit his mind, scuttling around "squeaking in furry voices of doubt and doom." "Hal knew that actually they were playing with him—that each of these vague animals was himself in pieces." But to know it was not to relieve the self-persecution and fragmentation.

This is where deep conflicts about the reason for which a soldier fights can recede—to an unsavory interior, where a soldier turns the battle inward and relives unresolved battles of betrayal, complicity, and taint. From ancient Greek and Roman philosophy to contemporary philosophers such as Harry Frankfurt, the moral and psychological quest is often about becoming a unified or harmonized psyche, "wholehearted," in Frankfurt's words, the enemy "beat back" at the gates, as Seneca puts it in a Stoic plea for tight self-control and hegemony. But for most of us, and certainly for soldiers who sometimes see themselves as fighting the wars of others in large tyrannizing bureaucracies, Freud seems more convincing. Battles are turned inward. Psyches fracture, and self-empathy with the warring parts is often in short supply. There is not only a sense of accountability for one's part in collective ends, but also a sense of being manipulated, beyond easy control, to carry out others' mistakes or deceptions.

Soldiers are good at compartmentalizing, I've been told over and over. But as the above stories attest, conflicts about complicity and personal responsibility for participation in collective ends don't just disappear. More often, they are displaced, deferred, put on hold until soldiers find the safety and trust needed to express personal doubts and torments.

What soldiers have said over and over in the above narratives is that they don't just fight war—they fight specific wars, the wars that it is their luck to be in. And they fight against specific enemies. For some, revenge is part of an unspoken pact a soldier makes with himself in preparing to face the enemy.

Chapter 3

PAYBACK

Wild Sweet Revenge

Soldiers go to war for each other and, often, to punish an enemy. When Dereck Vines, the senior NCO from Washington, D.C., was put on alert to go to Afghanistan "to look for Bin Laden," he felt psyched for the job. "We've got to get back at them," he said, "otherwise we'd be suckered and just let them get us." When he talked about his preparation to go to Bosnia, he had spoken of feeling a sense of moral outrage at an impending genocide. So I asked him if what he was talking about now was payback. "Yes, it's payback," he replied.

Anger often fuels a soldier's fight, and revenge is one of the common forms it takes. As Aristotle tells us, anger and the impulse toward revenge have to do with a perceived unwarranted injury to oneself or to the group to which one belongs. From ancient times forward, it is one way soldiers rev up for war. The desire for revenge "whets the mind for the deeds of war," says Seneca, reporting the conventional view that he will vehemently oppose.

However, for many of us, and not just a Stoic critic like Seneca, the thirst for revenge seems one of the more primitive and noxious sentiments in war. It brings to mind personal vendettas and lawless punishment, feuds where blood becomes the coinage for exchange. It conjures up the grievances that militias, gangs, and armed kin stand ready to carry out and pass on from generation to generation. It calls to mind the massacres of My Lai or Haditha. It speaks to the sectarian violence and reprisal killings that, as I write, compete with the insurgency and counterinsurgency for number of lives taken each day in the wars in Afghanistan and Iraq.

Yet feelings of vengeance are a close cousin to other sentiments of anger we are less quick to find fault with, such as a retributive sense of justice, righteous indignation, moral outrage, and a fiery courage to stand up to threat. As negative as many of our associations of revenge are, the desire for revenge is something most of us know intimately and sometimes even savor. It can mingle deeply with patriotism, as it did in the wake of 9/11. Soldiers who mobilized shortly after 9/11 did not always use the word "revenge," but many spoke unflinchingly of their anger. Consider Walter Clark, a National Guard NCO from the Midwest and father of two teen-aged daughters, whom I interviewed during his convalescence at Walter Reed in the spring of 2006. Clark went to Iraq with vengeful feelings, though he worked hard to rein them in. "Have you ever seen those pictures of Hamas prisoners?" he asked. "I admire some of those guys. . . . They are doing push-ups, sit-ups, they are reading Koran. That's what I am doing. I am channeling my anger into fighting a constructive war."

One prominent philosopher put the general point provocatively years ago: Revenge may be part of a "package deal," "conceptually inseparable" from love of country and solidarity with countrymen, and "psychologically inseparable for people anything like ourselves."

This is a strong claim that I am not prepared to endorse. But I do believe that we need to consider revenge with greater equanimity. Given our natural propensities as well as the close conceptual links between revenge feelings and other less overtly offensive emotions, it is too heavy-handed to proceed, as Seneca does in *On Anger*, and ban wrath outright from the moral psyche of the decent person. It is critical to understand wrath on its own terms, as part of the general task of understanding ourselves. And then, and only then, will we be in some position to assess its reasonableness. Military leaders especially need to understand the emotion, for their soldiers are likely to feel it when their closest buddies are blown up before their eyes. They may feel rage, however harnessed, when losses mount and their grief and pity mingle with frustration and exhaustion. In the face of an enemy that flouts the laws of war and uses terrorism and insurgency to exploit the morality of its opponents, feelings of revenge may seem all too inevitable.

In short, vengeful feelings in war merit a fresh look. Soldiers' inner debate is part of an ancient debate about the proper place of wrath in a warrior's life.

REVVING UP AND REINING IN

In December 2002 I interviewed Ted Westhusing, then an Army lieutenant colonel finishing up a Ph.D. at Emory University on military honor and ancient virtue. We knew each other from the conference circuit and had reconnected the spring before at a lecture I gave at Emory on virtue and decorum. More recently, I had been thinking about warrior emotions, in particular, warrior anger, or what Plato in the *Republic* depicts as the noble fire in a warrior's belly. Was it so noble? In Plato's view, warrior spirit, the *thumos*, is sandwiched between reason and appetite. It does the bidding of appetite yet is responsive to reason and its chastening. With the right training, that anger is the source of warrior courage, and a central part of a harmonized virtuous soul. I wondered if for the modern soldier, stoking anger was a morally defensible way to rev up the war machine. Was anger an appropriate combat motivator?

Ted was an Army ranger who had spent most of his career in infantry as a paratrooper in the 82nd Airborne. He had taught at West Point and commanded troops in Korea and Kosovo. At Emory, he stood out as an older philosophy student (he was married with a family) who in civilian clothes was still a warrior at core. He had a combative argument style and a "can-do" efficiency about his work; he kept in shape by running to campus in combat boots with an Army rucksack weighted down with heavy texts. I asked Ted, "Was warrior anger not only sweet but noble?" He answered methodically: "Without exception, all the leaders I've admired employed anger at some form at garrison, in the field, in serious training exercises, and in life and death situations, to get soldiers to do what they knew they were supposed to do, but yet would not do if anger had not been present. . . . It's not only that it's critical, . . . but that really excellent leaders are artists in the use of anger."

His last point piqued my curiosity. Even Seneca, outspoken critic of anger that he was, had recommended mock anger as a part of motivational technique in oratory. So had Cicero in his elaboration of Stoic texts. Faking anger was something a great orator could do without losing control or risking self-contamination from anger's venom. So I pressed: "In the leaders that you've admired, was it real or fake anger?"

It was both, Ted replied. On one occasion, he remembered watching a drill commander chew out a subordinate and then turn to Ted, in a private aside, with smug pride, chuckling, "Yeah, I really turned that on well, didn't I?" But on other occasions, he said, it was not mock anger at work, but anger that really seemed to come from the depths of a leader's soul. Yet even here, in cases of what he called "soulful anger," the person was always still in control, "had not gone beyond the pale, so to speak, and did not do or had not done things that he would later regret. He was still within some acceptable moral limits, yet it was soulful."

Had he ever experienced that "soulful anger" in his own command experience? I asked. Ted thought for a moment and then recounted a grueling nine-week ordeal in Ranger school, in particular, the desert phase of the course at Dugway Proving Ground in Utah, where candidates go through a live-fire exercise. It was make-it or break-it for him. At that point in the Ranger course, he said, "I had failed one patrol already, and you're only allowed to fail two patrols. And you get recycled or either kicked out. So I was on the edge, I was blade running as a Ranger candidate. I was tasked to be the leader of a patrol that would execute a live-fire exercise where you're firing live weapons and you're assaulting an objective in the desert. My fellow rangers were tired, and we'd been up for several days, with long movements, and clearly the morale was very low. We began this live fire, and my fellow rangers were obviously not moving and assaulting in a manner that was going to get us to go on this patrol. So at some point I found myself literally jumping out in front of them and shouting at them every name in the book, getting almost in the way of some live fire. At that point it was almost magical in the effect, because it—for whatever reason, the anger I was showing—motivated this small patrol to do what they should have been doing."

Ted said that the group ended up doing quite well and that the Ranger instructor told him afterward that it had been the best-led live-fire exercise he had seen at Dugway. "He attributed it to the point where he saw me become angry." Ted ruminated on the moment: "I realized that I had, . . . that I was at the point where it was 'do or die' for me at this course. . . . That emotion, I think, was the piece that got me over the top. It really put me on the edge, both danger-wise and edge-wise in terms of getting the entire unit over the top. So I always look back on that and say: 'That was a case where anger was effective.'"

For Ted, relying on anger had come "almost by accident," as he put it. Getting the Ranger tab had always been paramount. He was disappointed at his troops for not performing at the "level he knew they were capable of." That was clear. And he was disappointed at himself as a leader for not being able to get his troops "to do what was needed to be done." Still the outburst of fury totally surprised him. It was not how *he* led troops.

In Seneca's view, it is just such moments, when anger threatens to take over, that we need to keep vigil against it. For even if anger can be effective on occasion, in general it is a dangerous tool that tends to excess. It puts at peril rational control and nimble mastery. It is a runaway emotion, hard to stop once started. It revs up easily but subsides only slowly. When turned toward the enemy in war, it is often indiscriminate. "You will see . . . militaries sent in to butcher the populace *en masse*, . . . whole peoples condemned to death in an indiscriminate devastation. . . . No plague has cost the human race more," Seneca warns. Directed at self, anger can be equally merciless: "the hideous horrifying face of swollen self-degradation." It can take us to a place where, far from adrenalizing us to perform at peak, we self-implode.

Seneca's polemic against anger is potent. It is easy to see how in the context of war, anger can mix with hatred and a demonization of the enemy to serve up a toxic brew. Still, anger takes many forms. Aristotle, whose traditional view Seneca broadly attacks, insists that anger is neither one thing nor, necessarily, unregulated. As he famously puts it, anger can hit the mean: It can be felt and expressed at the right time, in the right way, to the right degree, toward the right objects. In short, there is praiseworthy and fine anger. To never be angry, he maintains, is to be insensate or servile. It is to be indifferent to what matters and indifferent to unwarranted attacks and injuries to yourself or those you care about. To register a sense of injury or unfairness through anger, outrage, indignation, resentment, and yes, even desires for revenge, can be a reasonable response.

Aristotle's focus is often on the warrior tradition of the *Iliad*, in which wrath is "sweeter . . . than the honeycomb dripping with sweetness." Of course, anger is not all sweetness. It is precisely the pain of injury that makes the anticipation of revenge so sweet. "The images called up [in thinking about vengeance] cause pleasure, like the images called up in dreams." To be sure, Aristotle is not singing praise to the *hot-headed* warrior. Nor is Homer, for that matter. Homer passes decisive judgment on Achilles' frenzy at the moment of his desecration of Hector's body: "that man without a shred of decency in his heart." He outrages "even the senseless clay in all his fury." For both Aristotle and Homer, there is the clear recognition that certain desires for revenge and their satisfactions can well exceed limits for how a soldier fights with honor. Still, Aristotle insists that feelings of revenge need not be an embarrassment to virtue. Moreover, acting on revenge has its place in a comprehensive, noble warrior ethic.

The Aristotelian legacy poses a challenge for the contemporary military commander. In my experience of working with military leaders, anger and the spirit of revenge are not something the morally conscientious military commander typically encourages in his troops. Rules of engagement, laws of armed conflict, notions of just conduct—in short, the norms of professional soldiering—are designed, in no small part, to curb the measurelessness of revenge. For many commanders the task is precisely to rein in anger in their troops. Here the words of a Naval Academy colleague, a retired

Marine colonel, are telling. When I started teaching at the Naval Academy in the late 1990s, he told me our job is to curb the Rambo in the young fighter. In the fall of 2007, a retired Navy Seal expressed a similar view. He pulled me aside and said quietly that he worried about the effect on young troops of a commander-in-chief's message that the wars we were fighting were wars against evil. He had in mind a recent story from the war theater: A buddy commanding a unit in Iraq was giving a pep talk to his troops about respecting the enemy forces and the Iraqis. In his unit there was to be respect for their religion, respect for their culture, respect for civilians. He wouldn't tolerate any derogatory names used for the enemy. One of the soldiers reacted by pounding his right middle finger in the palm of his left hand. The commander discreetly took note and had the soldier shadowed by a senior enlisted soldier. I doubt very much that either Aristotle or the Stoics were on this commander's mind. But it is the Stoic position on anger that is implicit in his command: Once you open the gates to revenge feelings, you risk a stampede.

Of course, reining in revenge feelings doesn't mean eliminating them. It is hard to eliminate them. They brew in war and in the very making of a warrior. The denuding of the civilian the moment the recruit steps off a bus and enters boot camp or basic training—the shorn head and issued uniforms, being forced to call yourself by your last name instead of "I," the loss of all privacy and sense of home and family, all that goes into being cut down and built up into a new self—breeds loyalty to the new family, as well as a sense of shame and honor that tends to heighten revenge feelings. Paradoxically, that first training toughens, but it also softens by creating new bonds and vulnerabilities to their rupture. For some, repair in the wake of fresh loss takes the form of revenge. The retribution may mean killing not just the enemy, but civilians who are held in contempt and fused in a soldier's mind with the cause of the enemy.

Anthropologists have long studied revenge cultures. Yet it has not always been fashionable to turn to their work in thinking about the psychology of revenge feelings. Vigilantism and vendettas are hardened *practices* of revenge; they are part of honor and shame *societies*. Revenge *feelings*, in contrast, are a part of everyday moral psychology; you don't have to be a member of a traditional honor culture to have them. And yet, like it or not, the revenge described in traditional honor/shame societies often reemerges in the battleground. And it does so not just within an enemy organized by clan, tribe, and ethnic sects. It makes its appearance in our own troops who fight as modern citizen-soldiers. The moral psychology of soldiering requires a look not just at revenge but at revenge cultures.

CYCLES OF REVENGE

According to anthropologist Napoleon Chagnon, war among tribal communities is often sparked not by a land grab or conquest of mines and minerals, but by the death of a kinsman. One death can unleash generational cycles of blood revenge. Chagnon studies the Yanomamö, an Indian tribe in the Amazon. In this tribe, as in many, kinship is more or less defining of individual identity. Reprisal for the murder of a kinsman often begins with a search for the actual killer, but then devolves into killing the first man spotted in the rival group. Group identity is fungible in exacting kinship obligations. Before long, kinship debts slip into cycles of violence, and ultimately war. So Chagnon writes, "If, as Clausewitz suggested, (modern) warfare is the conduct of politics by other means, in the tribal world warfare is ipso facto the extension of kinship obligations by violence."

In this culture of kinship and honor, even natural deaths often lead to violent reprisals against a sworn enemy. Deaths become construed as enemy sponsored malevolences, persecutions that demand retribution. In the Yanomamö mind, grieving melds seamlessly into the urge for revenge. "Their very notion of bereavement implies violence: they describe the feelings of the bereaved as *hushuwo*, a word that can be translated as 'anger verging on violence.' " "If my sick mother dies, I will kill some people," is said in complete earnest. The alloy of grief and aggression can linger for years, stoked by womenfolk consuming portions of a dead man's ashes in order to rev up warrior rage for a new reprisal. Vendettas become gift exchanges between creditor and debtor, passed on to children obligated to take up the vengeance. Future generations inherit the legacy of transgenerational "killing in the name of identity," as one psychoanalytic author aptly described this transmission of trauma and violence.

It is easy to see how unresolved grieving fuels these kinship wars. But so too does traditional machismo. Quick reprisals in the Yanomamö community are public marks of manhood. They advertise courage, male strength, and mate worthiness. Men who don't respond quickly are branded as cowards, unfit for the role of group protector. They are ridiculed and shamed, and their wives become easy prey to other men's sexual attention.

The shame in shirking manly duties of revenge is a recurrent theme in honor cultures. Black-Michaud's anthropological studies of twentieth-century Mediterranean communities are instructive. In traditional Corsican society, men pressure friends to avenge the death of a kinsman by singing a folk poem. The man who sings it "levels a reproach" at the potential avenger, or in the Corsican language *"datto il rimbecco."* Traditionally, a jury would acquit a man charged with murder if it could be proved he was the object of a *rimbecco*—in essence, the victim of a public shaming. In this traditional society, the recuperation of male honor substitutes for public justice.

Revenge cultures such as these may seem remote from our own concerns, and frankly, primitive. For lessons in revenge, we tend to prefer the catharsis of tragic drama, reliving our private fantasies in the safe and sophisticated haven of the theater. We may fasten on Hamlet's wordplay in the slow and agonized vengeance of a father's death or Lear's mad revenge against a daughter who won't flatter him, as he craves, with grand professions of love. These are publicly staged revenges, though as Freud knew well, we harbor inner analogues. In the theater of stage and mind, we learn to work out our thirst for revenge without bloodshed.

WARRIOR HONOR

But those who fight in war do not have the luxury of the stage or the protected sphere of fantasy. Vengeful thoughts are often acted out, sometimes indiscriminately. Notions of tribal honor are not all that remote.

True, not all forms of warrior honor are tightly connected with revenge, and many soldiers and military leaders resist the kind of honor that demands the recuperative powers of revenge. But it is worth remembering that the honor of traditional honor codes has a storied history in Western thought. Recall Agamemnon's revenge in the opening scenes of the *Iliad*. His war bride, Chriseis, his prize and honor (*timē*), has been snatched, and he is publicly humiliated. He takes revenge by robbing Achilles of *his* bride, recuperating lost honor and reinstating his place as *agathos*, chief warlord. Revenge here is part of a zero-sum game. Agamemnon's loss is Achilles' gain. Vindication requires recovering loss, in the currency of booty, but just as often in blood.

Our own military—or at least its ethics education programs of which I have been a part—struggles mightily to dismantle this Homeric notion of warrior honor and inculcate, instead, a conception of honor rooted in inner virtue—in conscience, integrity, and doing what is right. Great efforts are made at the Naval Academy, for example, to gloss the Navy creed, "Honor, courage, commitment," in terms of the highest standards of individual, moral conscience in the line of duty. But loyalty tends to breed archaic notions of honor, as does the military hunger for an honor that is conspicuous, marked in status easily read off of stripes and medals. Indeed, it is easy to misplace loyalty and skew honor in a system that puts a premium on careerism and advancement up a chain of command. My own involvement at the Naval Academy came in the wake of a massive cheating scandal in which a number of midshipmen viewed self-perjury during the criminal investigations as tantamount to a requirement of midshipman loyalty and honor. The clan, the group, identity with those willing to protect your life, can all too quickly trump other values when survival, academic or otherwise, is at stake.

The emphasis on honor borne from group identity can also morph into revenge when one part of the group is attacked. On one occasion while I was at the Academy, Katie Koestner, who was raped when she was a student at the College of William and Mary, gave a brigade-wide talk. After the lecture, the superintendent organized a breakaway session for the female midshipmen. Many of the men were furious and reacted to the closed-door meeting as an attack on their honor. Several made life so difficult for their fellow female midshipmen in the ensuing weeks that many women later vehemently objected to official meetings that excluded men.

For our soldiers at war, affronts to sexual honor are not primarily what incite revenge. Rather, the affronts are death and grave injury, the known costs of war, but for all that, they are no less easy to accept and tolerate. The common deferral of grief in war, whether because of manly decorum or lack of leisure for private or collective mourning, can fuel revenge, not unlike the *hushuwo*, the volatile blend of grief and persecutory anger that the Yanomamö experience. Demonization of the enemy by individual soldiers or a command climate that preaches enemy evil further feeds the revenge.

HADITHA

In this regard, consider the Marine killings of twenty-four civilians in Haditha, Iraq, on November 19, 2005. The rampage by the Kilo Company, of the Third Battalion, First Marines (known as the "3/1" or "Thundering Third"), followed a roadside bomb attack of a company Humvee that killed Cpl. Miguel ("T. J.") Terrazas. The deaths were first reported as collateral damage involved in return fire, but they were later determined to result from direct assaults on civilians, ten of whom were women and young children. Four marines were eventually charged with murder and another four with dereliction of duty in covering up the facts as they sent them up the chain of command.

We can speculate, in broad terms, about what went wrong at Haditha. The list is long, and what follows are just some factors. Young marines typically sign up to fight war battles and not counterinsurgency police operations. Historically, the Marines is an expeditionary, not an occupying force. Marines are not adequately trained in counterinsurgency techniques, nor do they have a clear enough sense of how to use minimal force in the protection of civilian lives, as police models require. Some marines may feel they are in a double bind: They are taught to cover their buddies, yet fighting in civilian areas requires restraint of firearms. Sacrificing each other becomes all the harder when troops don't trust the locals they are asked to protect.

Add to this the fact that rules of engagement can often seem ad hoc. Here, it is crucial to note that at the time of Haditha, the updated field manual for counterinsurgency had not yet been written. The manual that would become the playbook for operations in both Afghanistan and Iraq was issued only in December 2006, some five years after the first troops deployed to Afghanistan. In the foreword of that manual (which was eventually unclassified and published by University of Chicago in 2007), Gen. David Petraeus, then commander of the U.S. Army Combined Arms Center at Fort Leavenworth, Kansas, and Gen. James Amos, Deputy Commandant of the Marines at the time, scarcely hide the fact that troops, currently deployed, were sent to fight with last-generation models of war: "The manual is designed to fill a doctrinal gap. It has been 20 years since the Army published a field manual devoted exclusively to counterinsurgency operations. For the Marine Corps it has been 25 years."

It is also worth noting that the Third Battalion, of which the Kilo Company was a part, had been involved in fierce fighting earlier in the year in Fallujah, where there were liberal rules of engagement. In one account about how to prevent detonation of improvised explosive devices (IEDs) by remote mechanisms, one of the commanders was reported to have said half-jokingly, "If you see someone with a cell phone, put a bullet in their f—ing head." In addition, there are the familiar psychological factors raised often in the press—the sheer fatigue and frustration of a thinned-out military, repeat deployments, fighting a war that has become unpopular at home. These kinds of conditions erode not just mental health, but moral character.

All this is pertinent. But we also need to be willing to see the events of Haditha through the lens of traditional revenge and honor. The Haditha rampage took the form of a reprisal raid, inspired by the killing of one of its own, in this case, Lance Corporal Terrazas. As in tribal raids, those responsible for the killing may have been the initial target, but the objects of payback become fungible. The point is retribution, not discrimination. Retribution often falls on those who are easier targets. And so in the Marine raid in Haditha, loose group identity becomes the salient marker, not whether individuals could or do pose a real threat (since clearly, in Haditha, infants did not). The focus on group identity becomes exacerbated, in a case like Haditha, by the fact that the enemies that set off roadside bombs are invisible; they do not wear uniforms, and once they discharge their duties, they disappear into the civilian population. Of course, the same was true in Vietnam, in a different kind of battleground, fought in the jungles not streets, thick with mines not IEDs. Maybe in having no visible enemy there is no physical contact to impose a sense of the enemy's humanity, however much that humanity may long haunt survivors of *mano a mano* combat. (Here I think of my uncle Marvin Brenner, now in his early eighties and still haunted by the faces of the Japanese he fought, discriminately, at bayonet point on Okinawa during World War II. Clearly each kind of war takes its own toll.)

Another aspect of a traditional honor culture is crucially relevant in the Haditha case and important to expose: the role of machismo. Unedited public comments from the commander of the First Division, Lt. Gen. James Mattis, some months before the Haditha incident, are telling. Of fighting in Iraq, he said publicly, "It's a hell of a hoot. . . . I like brawling." About Afghan culture, he added, men who slap women around for years because they do not wear a veil have "no manhood left anyway. So it's a hell of a lot of fun to shoot them." It is hard to shove aside the anthropological lessons here: Killing in war, in honor cultures, is a way to prove manhood before other men and a way to shame those who fall short. True, Mattis sees himself as defending an *enlightened* kind of manhood, one that protects women without abusing them. But still, he is defending the protector status of manhood *before* other men, and humiliating, just as publicly, those who lack it. It is a familiar pattern of machismo—familiar, but no less noxious. His remarks are patently offensive, all the more so because they are made from a person in a highly prominent and visible leadership role, the kind of person we expect and entrust to prosecute war using his better humanity.

REVENGE FEELINGS IN THE RAW

Machismo like Mattis's points to the glory of killing—the hepped-up, swelled-up crowing that some experience in killing. It can feel like raw carnal pleasure and potency. The sexual motif is not uncommon in war and killing. Here I recall a story that Bob Steck, the Vietnam veteran, once told. Bob's job during the war was to enable helicopter communication. One of the helicopters—nicknamed a white "loach"—looked like "an Easter egg with a hard-on," he said. Another, the "Cobra," was "thin and phallic looking," shooting red tracer rounds out of its front. One night a Cobra pilot reported back on the radio, " 'Coming hot. Coming hot.' He was almost panting as he said it. I thought, whoa, I think I just looked under the curtain."

It is the raw, carnal side of the warrior spirit that is so distasteful to Bob. But if Aristotle is right—that some warrior anger is fine and virtuous—will it preserve, in any form, this carnal sense of potency and satisfaction? To put it bluntly, what is noble about the craving for relief of pent-up feelings, the sense of urgency, and then the satisfaction of discharge? Perhaps the satisfaction is less about sex than power. It is a matter of successfully putting fear in the air: of terrorizing and paralyzing. In the case of violent payback in killing, there is a sense that revenge in blood will be an ultimate kind of potency over another person that can settle, for once and for all, the debt.

But of course that promise is typically unfulfilled. The Yanomamö keep killing new victims precisely because one corpse won't pay for the loss of one dead. If the dead cannot be resurrected, then new bodies must do. Similarly, Achilles drags Hector's corpse around Troy not once but seven times. If one corpse is all there is, then it must submit to multiple desecrations. Haditha and My Lai are not just reprisals, but rampages or massacres; the killing is unbounded. It is fed by rage and fury, by "a sheer brute force that rushes," as Seneca would put it.

At a seminar I gave at Saint-Cyr, France's national military academy, the subject of the carnal feel of warrior revenge came up. A French col-

league and military ethicist, Henri Hude, put the question provocatively
to the class of male and female noncommissioned officers, most in their
mid-twenties and thirties and soon to be commissioned officers. "Let's
be outspoken," he said shifting between French and English. "Don't you
think that when we kill somebody, we are inclined to feel powerful—to
feel a sort of absolute power over somebody—perhaps insofar as we are
overcoming some taboo? Don't you think the violence is akin to a kind
of sexual pleasure, in its relation to life, bodily life?"

Gen. Pierre-Richard Kohn, Saint Cyr's deputy commandant and official host during my visit, seized the moment as an occasion for an object
lesson to his young officers. "Thank goodness, *Monsieur* Hude is a *profes-
seur* and not a soldier!" he exclaimed with theatrics. Killing, for the professional soldier, must always be a matter of necessity, not pleasure. "The
difference between the soldier and the nonsoldier is that as soldier you
are often close to death, or close to your friend's death in accident or in
action. At that point, if you still think killing someone is a question of
revenge, then you have a problem!"

Killing, he continued, especially killing up close, is a moment of ultimate humbling; it is a confrontation with the awful power of being able
to take human life. "You never know what it is like to kill in war until
you kill someone, and then you never forget his eyes."

Maybe, he conceded after the students pressed him hard about a specific case, there are brief "wild seconds" of satisfaction, fleeting feelings
that can erupt without causing moral damage or unjust conduct. The case
was one they had all heard firsthand during a recent visit to the base by
a French colonel who had stormed a bridge in Sarajevo. His lieutenant,
sent before him, had been badly injured in a first attempt to secure the
site, and the colonel was nearly killed in the intervention. Yes, conceded
the commandant, this fine colonel had "a few wild seconds." Yes, passions raged. But they were contained. To indulge those passions would
risk turning war-fighting into the pursuit of "wild animals looking to
kill just anybody, anywhere."

The challenge, he went on, "is making sure that *you* men and women
never fight with hate. Because if you fight with hate, you will try to find

... pleasure in revenge." In words with an uncanny echo of Aristotle, Kohn pleaded, "The point is to be angry for the right reasons with the right people with the right means." He then raised his voice, making clear that he knew just how hard it is to hit the mean in war. "We are professionals. And this is the job. *This is the bloody job. Okay? This is it.*"

The commandant's lesson is Aristotelian in formula but Stoic in spirit. Revenge feelings may descend involuntarily, like a flush or a blush or a sexual twitter. The true Stoic sage doesn't assent to those impulses. He nips them in the bud and lets calmer reason prevail.

But what then do we say about Cpl. Robert Kislow, a twenty-one-year-old and veteran of the Afghanistan war whom I interviewed at Walter Reed, where he had been in residence for nineteen months, convalescing and trying to retire from the military. From the age of five, he wanted to be in the Army and carry a gun. His dream finally came true when he enlisted at the age of eighteen and became a sniper in Afghanistan fighting alongside the 82nd Airborne. His last mission, a seek-and-destroy mission, led to a fierce firefight on June 10, 2005, that lasted about fifteen hours in the Paktika Province, along the Afghanistan-Pakistan border. His unit of eight was overrun by a military group of at least one hundred that seemed "like a beehive" swarming out of the mountains. Several friends were killed. He tells me, "After a sniper killed one of my friends, I put a couple of bullets in his head." It was "the best feeling in the fucking world because of knowing that he killed a friend of mine and almost killed me." Rob suffered injuries in the head, back, side, arm, and leg. He later lost his right leg below the knee, now replaced with a prosthetic, and has one arm that is half filled with titanium.

Rob narrates his story of the battle several times in different sequences, backing up and going forward as he tries to reconstruct how he was injured. His voice and body language take him back to Afghanistan. The actual events are unclear. But what seems to have happened is that as he was raising his arm to kill a target ahead, he was hit from behind, in the arm, head, and back, by a sniper. He then tried to stand up and his ankle was taken out. After he was shot and saw that he was the last man in the formation, he put his weapon "on burst" and started spraying a thirty-round magazine of bullets. It was only at Walter Reed, after a debriefing by a senior military medic who had been in the battle, that he received confirmation that he, in fact, "got the guy" who had killed his buddy, Sgt. Victor Cervantes, who just seconds earlier had run to Rob's aid. The senior man says, "That's more satisfaction than I could have." I wanted you to know, he said, "so you could sleep better at night."

Rob Kislow's story is psychologically complex. But what is salient is that at the moment of a life-and-death battle, and in the reliving of it, this soldier is exuberant about the payback. He got the guy who took his buddy's life and who almost killed him. That part of the story feels good—indeed, it is "the best fucking feeling." His survival and performance as a sniper in battle depend on the very desire to get back, though not necessarily on feelings of satisfaction in executing that desire. Yet it seems unreasonable to deny him the pleasure of that desire, the pleasure not just of anticipatory revenge and actual revenge, but of reliving, revisiting, and reimagining his revenge. This is so even if his revenge is a mixed pleasure that involves taking life at the instant of seeing life taken. Still, Rob does not revel in killing. "It's a job, that's what it comes down to." "It's a life style," he says, but one, he acknowledges, that needs tall barriers, which he does not yet know how to build.

Rob thinks of revenge in terms of pleasure and satisfaction. He doesn't crave the satisfaction, though the act of payback yields it. And he is buoyed by it. He was a sniper, a good sniper. He practiced tirelessly for the job. At the moment of the big game, he played and played well. He can take pleasure in a job well done, even if the job requires killing.

There are other accounts, though, where revenge produces no pleasure. Consider a vignette from *Naples '44*—an eye-opening memoir of Naples in the last year of World War II. The author, Norman Lewis, a British Field Security officer, reports the comments of a prison lifer from the rural countryside outside Naples who was engaged in gang violence during the war years. The prisoner tells Lewis that he wiped out a "whole family with a hatchet. It took five minutes. It was a quick, clean job. Nobody suffered. I did it for honour. . . . Don't imagine anybody enjoys having to do a thing like this. The fact is it was a mistake to get ourselves born."

The sober assessment is about honor cultures. Revenge, for some, may be less a matter of pleasure than duty—an obligation passed on transgenerationally and never completely fulfilled by each generation. If the injury is not adequately grieved, or if grief is prolonged and stoked with a renewed sense of persecution, it may stay fresh, "unmetabolized," part of the next generation's inheritance. The "mistake," as this man says profoundly, "is to get ourselves born." Revenge, for this man, is not about pleasure in anticipation or in deed. It is simply about honor-bound duty, and a matter of moral luck.

GRIEF THAT TEMPERS REVENGE

Perhaps the point is that while we can sever the conventional notion of honor from the *pleasure* of revenge, we are unlikely to sever such honor from revenge itself. And this may be because traditional honor does not easily accommodate grief or leave room to "work through" loss. Like the *hushuwo* of the Yanomamö, grief feelings in honor cultures are channeled through anger. Loss is experienced as persecution that needs to be righted. Revenge keeps grief at bay, and with it, mechanisms for absorbing and acknowledging loss.

But significantly, one of the most honor-bound revenge cultures in history leaves room for grief—and not just private grief, but public ritual grief. Consider again the Homeric warrior, and once again, Achilles. Achilles is committed to avenge Patroclus's death and to savor the sweetness of his vengeance. But he is also expected to mourn openly. It is what the archaic Greek warrior does. And so Achilles grieves with the women keeners and with his warriors, in public and collective mourning during the lull of battle:

> *A black cloud of grief came shrouding over Achilles.*
> *Both hands clawing the ground for soot and filth,*
> *he poured it over his head, fouled his handsome face*
> *and black ashes settled onto his fresh clean war-shirt.*

Overpowered in all his power, sprawled in the dust,
Achilles lay there fallen . . .
tearing his hair, defiling it with his own hands.
And the women he and Patroclus carried off as captives
caught the grief in their hearts and keened and wailed,
out of the tents they ran to ring the great Achilles,
all of them beat their breasts with clenched fists,
sank to the ground, each woman's knees gave way.
Antilochus kneeling near, weeping uncontrollably,
clutched Achilles' hands as he wept his proud heart out—
for fear he would slash his throat with an iron blade.
Achilles suddenly loosed a terrible, wrenching cry
and his noble mother heard him . . .
and she cried out in turn.

At the end of the *Iliad*, Priam and Achilles, Trojan and Greek together, reunite and weep—Priam for his beloved son, Achilles for his beloved friend, slain by Priam's son:

> *. . . Priam wept freely*
> *for man-killing Hector, throbbing, crouching*
> *before Achilles' feet as Achilles wept himself,*
> *now for his father, now for Patroclus once again,*
> *and their sobbing rose and fell throughout the house*

In this way, archaic warriors are permitted to grieve openly and even in the bosom of their enemy. They maintain honor by revenge, but assuage some of the anguish of loss through collective mourning. Achilles' grief is complicated. It is, in part, anger turned inward: He "tears his hair, defiling it with his own hands." It is a punishing guilt. He has to live with the luck of surviving Patroclus, but worse, the stain of having sent him out to do his bidding in war. It is almost as if he killed his own.

This is a survivor's nightmare. For some, it is an untrue narrative that has to be undone. But some troops do, in fact, suffer real and intentional fratricides. One of their own fires at their own. The requirements for grieving take on a new dimension.

Such is a case that Army Maj. Thomas Jarrett, a lead mental health counselor deployed in Iraq, shared with me. His team was called in for "post-traumatic growth" work for a unit that had recently suffered a double fratricide. A member of their unit, in a moment of unleashed rage, intentionally opened up fire on other members. The fratricide hit hard the platoon of forty, which had already, prior to the incident, lost nine soldiers. "The entire platoon," he wrote in an email, "was pulled off-line and sent to an R & R [rest and relaxation] center." In a follow-up phone call from Baghdad, Jarrett discussed the case further: "There's an ancient code that you don't kill your parents, your children, or your fellow warriors. That's a deep code. When it happens, it shatters your assumptions. The bad guys are supposed to get you; not your fellow warriors." The last thing a unit wants in war, Jarrett added, is "an internal insurgence. You don't want to have to expect a sapper [an infiltrator] to be amongst your midst." Jarrett and his colleagues counseled the unit so that the troops could both grieve and "voice a group sense of betrayal."

At bottom, as Jarrett put it, one of their own had "brought shame to their house. What they felt was shared dishonor." The dishonor Jarrett had in mind was not that of an "honor culture" fixed on revenge. It was what decent people feel when their characters are threatened. The betrayal was an injury to their integrity, as individuals and as members of the platoon. What happened, he insisted, was an affront to virtue. His counseling focused on a shift in perspective, including a way to recover the unit's decency and integrity. "People felt that they couldn't stand this unit. I tried to help restructure a narrative. . . . I also preached patience and compassion and focused on post traumatic growth."

Public grieving does not come easy to the tough, stoic warrior. To be buttoned up and tight is the trained posture. To cry and mourn can appear weak, effeminate, a breakdown in macho decorum, even for women eager to be accepted as equals in the masculine military. But grieving, mirrored in the grieving of others whom one loves, is a way to detoxify rage, and a way to mutually acknowledge that what is at risk in war is not just life, but goodness. Grieving must be a part of war, so long as there is loss.

SALVAGING ANGER

It is easy to plead for warrior grief, but what of anger, and in particular, vengeful anger? It is important to clarify just what is problematic about revenge, and what is worth salvaging. The Stoics, and Seneca, in particular, are right to insist that anger's curse is its lawlessness, its disregard for proportion and regulation. It can metastasize, like a cancer. It can destroy self and others in its reckless fury. But this overlooks the very empowerment that can be essential to anger, and even revenge. Rob Kislow, the young sniper, is mobilized by his anger. An enemy sniper kills his friends and badly injures him. At that moment, to strip him of his anger is as good as surrender. As Aristotle puts it bluntly, it is to become "insensate" or "servile." It is to become impotent as a warrior.

However, the dialectic does not stop here. The Stoics have one more round, implicit in many a commander's rant against rage. And this is the Stoic insistence (later taken up by Kant in the Enlightenment) that at the heart of *moral* conduct, whether in peace or war, is a sense that our actions are constrained by respect and reverence for others. Following Diogenes the Cynic's lead, Stoics such as Seneca, Epictetus, and Marcus Aurelius argue that we are all cosmopolitans, literally world-citizens, worthy of respect and dignity. In war, it is precisely cosmopolitan values that become the constraints that make war a regulated activity, with enemies worthy of respect ("our dusky companions in misfortune," to use John Wolfe's words) and not just objects of blind revenge. Respect is rendered in prosecuting war justly, with proportionality and discrimination.

The point is that once constraints are introduced on warfare, revenge may become tamed but not neutered. The sense of biting back, of defending oneself against attack still has a place. In war, forgiveness must occur late in the game, not at the moment of armed aggression, when a battle still rages. The fiery warrior spirit, the *thumos*, must be available to serve courage and the rationale of the mission. It needs to be given room to do its job. But at the same time, that fighting spirit must respect that spirit in others. That is a Stoic lesson to preserve.

The lesson is echoed by Ernst Jünger, a German lieutenant in World War I, who writes movingly in the preface to the English edition of his memoirs, *The Storm of Steel*:

> It is not impossible that among the readers of this book there may be one who in 1915 and 1916 was in one of those trenches that were woven like a web among the ruins of Monchy-au-Bois. In that case, he had opposite him at that time the 73rd Hanoverian Fusiliers, who wear as their distinctive badge a brassard with "Gibraltar" inscribed on it in gold. . . . At the time . . . I was a nineteen-year-old in command of a platoon. . . . Of all the troops who were opposed to the Germans on the great battlefields the English were not only the most formidable but the manliest and the most chivalrous. I rejoice, therefore, to have an opportunity of expressing in time of peace the sincere admiration which I never failed to make clear during the war whenever I came across a wounded man or a prisoner belonging to the British forces

The remarks may seem quaint to soldiers fighting insurgents who have abandoned modern forms of chivalry for leverage against an enemy that outpowers them in traditional force. Still, the burden for our soldiers today is to fight justly against an enemy who fights by different rules on the battlefield—and to cope with the guilt they feel when they kill innocents, not because of rage or fury but because of accident, human error, and the moral fog of this kind of war.

II

THE
BATTLEFIELD
OF
EMOTIONS

CHAPTER 4

———— ✶ ————

THE GUILT
THEY CARRY

LIVING WITH GUILT

Lt. Cdr. Tom Webber is a Navy chaplain who has talked to thousands of marines as they prepare for war, deploy, and return home. In 2002 he was with the 1st Marine Division at Camp Pendleton, California, as it mobilized for the war in Iraq. In 2003 he deployed for eight months, advising many soldiers who had never really experienced war: "Probably the thing that was the most difficult to get the men ready . . . was to get them to understand life and death. . . . The junior troops, the lance corporals, corporals, and even sergeants had never really seen battle. Many of them up until that point had never even fired a weapon at another human being. So, just about to a man—and I was with an all-male unit—they all wanted to find out 'Will God still appreciate me if I have to pull the trigger on another human being?'"

These marines did not use the word "guilt," but that is what they worry about: How will they judge themselves or be judged by a higher being for what they do in war? Their worries are not about war crimes or indiscriminate killing—that is, killing in malice. They trust that they will not commit such acts and instinctively understand the moral issues at play there. They worry about what they regard, by and large, as *just* killing in war: despite their training, the prospect of *that kind of* killing does not always sit easy. Other military personnel, whether sailors, soldiers, marines, or airmen, struggle with guilty feelings about past acts for which they are not legally or even morally culpable. Army Maj. John Prior, who was in charge of an infantry company in Iraq, told me in an interview some three years after his return from Iraq that he struggles with his "own personal guilt" about an accident in which one of his privates was killed by a gun that misfired from a Bradley Fighting Vehicle. Still others struggle with guilt for what would be transgressions in peacetime circumstances but are less clearly so in wartime. An eighty-year-old World War II veteran who was part of the Normandy invasion in 1945 tells a younger neighbor sixty years later that the beachhead was far from glorious. It was awful, he says, remembering vividly what happened. As soon as they landed, they looted the bodies of their own dead. Stripping the dead, even of arms, offended his civilian mentality. Ralph (Rogow) Roger, a friend's father who served with the Canadian army in World War II, wrote home in February 1945 about the plentiful German chickens they had been feasting on: "Naturally we don't steal the chickens. We just happen to be passing by when they fly into our vehicles." As his daughter Robin Roger later commented in poring through his letters, "Even in the relatively minor matter of helping themselves to food, my father needed some rationales." But as the war drew to a close, "empathy provoked by direct contact with Germans" made the "guilt of triumph so significant that it can't be spoken of." A psychiatrist who has supervised cases at a Department of Veterans Affairs (VA) hospital tells me that one veteran reported feeling that his act of killing the enemy was fine until he approached the body and took out the wallet, which contained family portraits. The pictures were like those he carries in his wallet. That empathic moment unleashed a torrent of guilt.

The emotion of guilt, as these examples suggest, is Janus-faced. We think of it, in part, as focused on the past, on the thought of having wronged another, or on the future, in contemplating wrongdoing, where the bite of conscience, the "pang" of guilt, acts as a check against it.

But in addition, as we know well, individuals can feel guilt about actions for which they are not at fault, yet they nonetheless hold themselves responsible. In some cases they may be *causally* but not *morally* responsible. That is, the injury or death is something they "brought about," but as the result of nonculpable ignorance, as in the case of the Bradley misfiring. In other hard cases, it may be a soldier's finger that pulls the trigger and kills an innocent; though he foresees the risk, he does not intend it. In yet other cases, an individual knowingly and intentionally kills justly in the role of soldier, though if he steps out of role, it feels like a gross transgression of his humanity.

Guilt for these various actions can seem both rational and irrational. Personal agency is implicated, but there may be legitimate excuses or, indeed, justification. What is typically overlooked in discussions is that even when guilt is irrational, it can be an important sign of a soldier's humanity, and something admirable. Though we might not blame those who lack a feeling of guilt in comparable cases, we still tend to feel moved, morally moved, by those who show it. In the case of a soldier, guilt is often a testament to a sense of moral accountability in the use of lethal force. It is an expression of personal responsibility often squeezed out by fighting in large, bureaucratic armies.

Of course, guilt that can be admirable can easily turn excessive and pathological. So Friedrich Nietzsche warns, standing morality on its head: "Bad conscience" can become "torture without end," undoing any prospects for happiness. Sigmund Freud famously elaborates upon the theme: Enduring the recriminations of a harsh superego (his term, more or less, for "conscience") is the cost of civilization. The anger of the superego, like Seneca's notion of the thirst for revenge, can leave its possessor more tormented than satisfied. Soldiers feel this double bind all the more intensely, for if recognizing the incredible responsibility they bear is necessary to wage war justly, the weight of this terrible recognition deepens the guilt they may feel when they exercise their wartime duties, justly or not. And whereas wrath is punishment outward, guilt is punishment inward, a self-indictment of having harmed or violated or betrayed another. It is an accusation and conviction against self for actions done.

We tend to worry about war desensitizing warriors, about soldiers getting used to killing and accepting how cheap life can be. This may happen to some. But this was *not* the prevalent theme I heard in my interviews. The soldiers with whom I have talked feel the tremendous weight of their actions and consequences. Sometimes they extend their responsibility and guilt beyond what is reasonably within their dominion: they are far more likely to say, "If only I hadn't" or "If only I could have," than "It's not my fault" or simply leave things at "I did my best."

Yet for all this, the subject of guilt does not come up easily in conversations with soldiers. It is often the elephant in the room. And this is so, in part, because guilt feelings are often borne with shame. Shame, like guilt, is also directed inward. Its focus, unlike guilt, is not so much on an action that harms *others* as on *personal* defects of character or status, often felt to be exposed before others and a matter of social discredit. But on the battlefield, where the destruction of others is the *modus vivendi*, it is the guilt for causing that suffering that is the potent emotion.

KANT AND FREUD ON GUILT

Immanuel Kant, the eighteenth-century German Enlightenment philosopher, sets the scene in the modern world for the vigil of conscience. Under Kant, Socrates' dictum to "know thyself" becomes "the first command of all duties to oneself"—a highest-order duty to "scrutinize, fathom" your heart for rightness of conduct and purity of motive. The self becomes both the judge and the judged: The spotlight is on *me*, on what *I* have done or failed to do, and not on others, neither on their actions nor on their characters. But despite the focus on self-judgment, Kant is not particularly interested in what from ancient times forward has been described as the "bite" of bad feelings for doing wrongs or in the fear of punishment that can prod us to do what is right. The absence is deliberate. Kant is concerned with the mature conscience. The attitude of that conscience is not punitive pain or fear, but respect or reverence in the sense of attention and submission (*Achtung*) to our own authority as moral legislators. Kant imagines us in awe of the capacity to issue laws to ourselves. This legal capacity is neither that of a despot nor that of a capricious lawmaker, but the capacity of a just and fair lawmaker making law for self that can apply to others similarly situated. We are not free riders. Before our internal moral legislator, we stand ready, at attention, capable of following duty's call, even and especially when it conflicts with our strongest self-interests.

This is one reason why we find little talk in Kant's works of moral distress of the sort that bites and gnaws, or of fear that goads and bullies. The idealized emotion we feel before genuine moral authority is far more dignified. Indeed when the subject of repentance comes up, Kant warns against a morality that is "cheerless, morose, and surly"—a self-punishment that becomes "self-torture." Beware of "hypocritical self-loathing " and the moral melancholy that detracts from the real work of morality, he warns. True virtue ought to be cheerful and soar with the sublimity of respect for its law. But in all this, Kant doesn't appreciate that harsh self-judgment is not necessarily self-righteousness. It can be inseparable from empathy with those we harm and a sense of responsibility and duty of reparation even when the harm is not intentional, or intentional and warranted but no less loathed, as in just killing in war. Soldiers as inflictors of the horror of war often bear this kind self-judgment, complete with its bite and gnaw. It is not self-righteousness or pious melancholy they are feeling. It is more a "moral remainder," as philosophers have called it, a reasonable reaction to being a human and of having humanity. The good soldier does not lose that humanity simply by donning his uniform.

We might think Freud can do better than Kant in recognizing the rationality of guilt felt for actions for which we are not, strictly speaking (in a juridical sense), culpable. And he does in some ways, but not entirely. Freud famously tells a developmental story, a "just so story" of sorts, of how morality comes to be internalized as part of our personalities: Our conscience is the product of a childhood battle. As children we both want parental love and fear its loss and repudiation in punishment when we do wrong and "are found out." With moral growth and independence, we move that tension inside ourselves, into an internal representation of authority and regulation that stands over and above our ego or self; thus, the superego is born. Through that superego we become our own judges, vigilant and fearful of self-indictment. So, Freud declares, "the superego" is the Kantian "moral law within us." Guilt, in Freud's view, is a kind of leftover tension from childhood; its predominant feeling is fear of punishment and retaliation.

But despite the Kantian legacy, Freud does not really offer an account that internalizes the *moral* law. Indeed, he does not offer an account of *morality*. Moving parental or conventional authority from outside to in is not enough to ensure that that internal authority and judgment is legitimate or really moral. We can bully ourselves and be harsh tormentors without justification, just as parents can be cruel or military leaders overbearingly harsh. What the move from outside to in *does* do, as Freud rightly insists, is set up "a garrison" whose watch is inescapable. That is, if childhood morality is about "being found out," then once an internal garrison is set up, "nothing can be hidden" from self, "not even thoughts." Of course, Freud famously leaves room for the work of repression and self-deception. We need to veil ourselves from ourselves precisely because we have become our own watchdogs. Still, without some clever philosophical patching up of his theory, Freud cannot explain why some self-indictments from that watchdog have at their base guilt that is more rooted in morality than in just the bullying of a harsh superego. Nor does he really seem to appreciate how very thin the wedge can be between the two. This is at the heart of understanding "the personal guilt" that Maj. John Prior carries with him.

ACCIDENT GUILT

The guilt, as Prior explains, is the result of an accidental fratricide in 2003 in which twenty-year-old Private First Class Joseph Mayek was killed. Prior, who was then commander of the Charlie Company, 6th Infantry, First Armored Division, was tasked to provide security around the U.S. Army headquarters just after the fall of Baghdad. Private Mayek was taking up his post when a Bradley blast ripped through his face. He had been standing no more than a foot in front of the muzzle. Prior reconstructs the scene. He is calm, but he is eager to lead off the interview with the accident: "I lost a soldier, which was extremely traumatic," he says without hesitation. He narrates every detail precisely, the way a person who has relived the scene over and over does: "One of the Bradleys misfired. It was on the front gate, and had a malfunction and it took off a third of his face. It was as if an ice cream scoop just scooped out his face. . . . He survived the initial blast, if you can believe it. We were in the medic tent with him. It was one of the most traumatic things I have ever seen in my entire life. To literally see someone's face completely scooped out, to see just the very bottom part of his jaw working. . . . He couldn't see, couldn't hear, couldn't scream. . . . I mean he had no eyes, obviously. No face. I can only imagine the terror, the fear, the pain he was in. He obviously couldn't breathe because he had no nose or mouth to take in air. . . . It was one of the few times in my life I've really cried—tears just streaming down my face because I'm watching ten people work over this kid. . . . It was an unbelievable thing to see. . . . It is one of those images that will be in your head until you die."

If Prior's immediate response to the incident was visceral, what followed was profound guilt and an ongoing tug-of-war with his rationality. He continues: "The aftermath of that was the guilt of the situation because I'm the one who placed the vehicles; I'm the one who set the security. Like most accidents, I'm not in jail right now. Clearly I wasn't egregiously responsible. But it is a comedy of errors. Any one of a dozen decisions made over the course of a two-month period and none of them really occurs to you at the time. Any one of those made differently may have saved his life. So I dealt with and still deal with the guilt of having cost him his life essentially. . . . There's probably not a day that doesn't go by that I don't think about it, at least fleetingly."

The malfunction, as Prior explains in lay terms, had to do with a faulty replacement battery. When the Bradley's ignition was turned on, the replacement battery in the turret failed to shut off current to the gun.

Prior had authorized the replacement after consulting with his maintenance team and after a thorough reading of the manuals. The replacement was a Marine battery, the only one available at the time for a Bradley. It had the same voltage as the original one, but different amperage. The amperage, they learned too late, was all-critical. Army manuals now prohibit the use of that Marine battery.

Prior was formally investigated by the military and ultimately exonerated. By the standards of the legal and moral community, he is not guilty in the sense of culpable or at fault. Yet he carries guilt and holds himself responsible. "On a personal note, I definitely felt tremendous personal guilt over it because of the placement of the vehicles and ... the decisions made. I felt very personally responsible." He speaks of a "comedy of errors," but a tragedy of errors is closer to his experience. "I knew that clearly it was an accident," but "I kept wishing I had made other decisions." When he says he doesn't hold himself as "egregiously responsible," he means that it wasn't a careless blunder. But he still doesn't think of himself as fully, morally cleared.

In a very important way, Prior's guilt is not irrational. We understand it and admire him for it. We would think less of him as a commander, ready to lead his troops and have them follow, if he viewed what happened as just an accident, only remotely connected with his own choices. The guilt is reparation for harm done. It records something morally significant, something that marks his deep connection to his troops and his moral accountability to them, and to himself. It is not just a response to the fact that he was *causally* implicated. He feels *morally* implicated. Still, for all its reasonableness, the guilt oversteps moral accountability, even for a commander responsible for his troops and tied to them by the "sacred bands" that form in war. Prior's anguish needs to be alleviated in some way. What happened *was* an accident, a *flukishly unlucky* accident. This is a situation where, surprisingly, we don't get much guidance from Freud. It is a case where we hold ourselves morally responsible for bringing about bad consequences we couldn't reasonably expect or prevent.

Nietzsche has just this kind of case in mind when he says, "Bad conscience" (his hyperbole for *subjective* guilt) doesn't grow in the soil where you would most expect it—such as in prisons where there are actually "guilty" parties who should feel remorse for wrongdoing. Rather it is often a "question of someone who . . . caused harm," someone who causes a misfortune for which she is not really responsible. He appeals here to the earlier philosopher Spinoza for support: The "bite of conscience" has to do with an "offense" where "something has gone unexpectedly wrong here"; it is not really a case of "I ought not to have done that." Personal agency is implicated in the accident, though involuntarily through ignorance. Guilt is felt, but there is no wrongdoing for which we can be held morally or legally guilty.

Melanie Klein, a student of Freud and pioneering child psychoanalyst (and founder of the object relations school of psychoanalysis), elaborates the point in terms of the dynamic and lasting influences of childhood morality. To the notion of offense or harm, she adds the element of empathy. Our principles of guilt are rooted in notions of harm and injury and not principally, *contra* Freud, fear of retaliative punishment. More critically, the guilt is inseparable from empathic love for those we hurt, however hard the mind tries to keep separate and pristine ("split," in her terms) what we love from what we have damaged. The "bite" of guilt comes from our recognizing that what we love we may destroy, often unwittingly. In the case of the young child, Klein envisages a primal drama between love and hate of the parent, and empathy and reparation for fantasies of destruction. Of course, guilt of the kind Nietzsche and Klein point to— focused on harm, often unintended, and a harmed victim, with whom we empathize—is certainly not the only kind of subjective or personal guilt. But the conception helps make sense of the kind of guilt Prior carries, and that which many other military men and women bear as the emotional fallout from decisions made in the fog of war, under stress and urgency, and often with nonoptimal information. An illustration from Greek tragedy helps to sharpen the contours of this kind of guilt.

DOING "UNWITTINGLY
THE WILL OF THE BEAST"

Tragic errors (what Aristotle calls *hamartiai* in *Poetics*) teach us that we are vulnerable to misfortune incurred through our own fallible agency. If "I had made other decisions," Prior says, it wouldn't have happened. Yet he knows he took due care in making that choice. Aristotle's own favorite example is from Sophocles' *The Women of Trachis*. The botched choice is this: Deianeira is unaware that the "charm" she uses to woo back her husband, Heracles, is in fact a lethal substance that, when applied, literally eats away at its victim. In her case, perhaps she should have known better: The potion was a gift to her from the centaur Nessus. As he ferries her across the River Evenus to meet her new husband, Heracles, the centaur puts lustful hands on her. Deianeira cries out for help and Heracles heeds the call, killing Nessus with his bow and poisoned arrow. In his dying moments, Nessus concocts a potion from the poisoned blood of his clotted wound for Deianeira. It is a love charm, he tells her, to be used should Heracles' love ever wane. Wane it does while Heracles is away at war, and he sends back home a new war bride as proof. It is just this "erotic diversion" that Deianeira aims to cancel with the potion.

Deianeira, it seems safe to say, was duped; Prior was not. Deianeira did "unwittingly the will of the beast." But it was, after all, a beast seeking revenge for being rejected. She should have suspected his motives. Even after the disaster, she focused not on the likelihood of that revenge, but on her own defense, on how she followed the beast's instructions to a tee; there were no "egregious" missteps here: "I neglected none of the instructions that beast the centaur explained to me. . . . I kept them like an inscription on bronze that cannot be washed away. And I only did what I was told to do." Even so, in her case and certainly in Prior's, there is ample space between full moral responsibility and the kind of luck where a person is more victim than agent. Neither Deianeira nor Prior was picked up and blown along by the wind, as Aristotle might put it, forcibly moved by external forces. Rather, the impetus comes from within, from choices and actions performed voluntarily. Still, these choices have unexpected, heinous results that those who made the choices could not readily foresee. Each does awful things unknowingly, fallibly but not necessarily culpably. They feel tremendous guilt and regret. In Deianeira's case, she takes her own life when she discovers what she has wrought with her hands.

"Regret" for these kinds of tragedies is, in fact, too light a word, not close enough to remorse and too close to the kind of regret we feel about inclement weather. Philosophers of late have worked hard to beef up the notion. But even the philosopher's term of art, "agent-regret," doesn't capture the kind of feeling Prior experiences. The sheer weight of guilt—its heaviness, its identification with the victim, and the assertion of the need for repair—is what Prior feels. It is not just that things turned out badly and he happens to be involved instrumentally. It is that he stands indicted before himself and must make reparation. There is a perceived moral element to what he has done. To call it "regret" is to miss that.

After the fratricide, Prior and his first sergeant wrote a letter to Mayek's mother. For some time after, he tells me, she continued to send care packages to the company with letters. "Oh, it was terrible," said Prior. "It was horrible." The letters weren't "just very matter of fact—here's what we did today; it was more like a mother writing to a son." For this mother, Prior and his company became the son who was no longer. "It was her way of dealing with the grief. . . . I had a responsibility to try to give back." Allowing himself to feel that mother's grief, so intimately, was part of his reparation.

He gave back, but he held back, presumably, the graphic image of Mayek's suffering. The agony was simply too hideous, undeserved, and unrelieved to share with a mother. Prior told me that in watching Mayek's last moments, he wished he would die quickly so his torture could end. In *The Women of Trachis*, Sophocles does not spare us the details of Heracles' final torment. This man of mythic labors, whose body once subdued so many, is now eaten away by a "ruthless, devouring malady" that never leaves him "without torment." The pain sears like "sharp points brought to burning heat." His only relief is a quickened but horrific demise: to be burned alive on a funeral pyre, a gruesome task he delegates his son to oversee, instructing him, as he is laid on the pyre, to set a "steel bit in my mouth" to "hold back the shriek." In point of fact, there is no holding back, Sophocles teaches (and Prior knows well), on the uncompensated physical agony humans can undergo as the result of mistake.

LUCK GUILT AND BETRAYAL

Guilt like that which Prior experiences is the moral cost of making choices. Other kinds of battlefield guilt may also seem, at first blush, irrational, but less so on further inspection. In the fall of 2005 I met with two small groups of Marine and Navy officers who had recently returned to the United States Naval Academy from Iraq. I never specifically asked about guilt, nor did the soldiers touch the feeling by name. Yet it was there at every turn.

One kind of guilt that surfaced in the interviews is a variant of survivor guilt that I will call "luck guilt." Several marines felt that by being in Annapolis, and no longer in combat zones, they had been the recipients of "undeserved" luck. They spoke of needing to return to their brothers and sisters in arms. The guilt is a kind of empathic distress for those still at war, mixed with a sense of solidarity and anxiety about betraying that solidarity. For some, abrupt ruptures from units exacerbated the guilt.

Maj. Michael Mooney, an intelligence officer, was part of a lead battalion that on March 23, 2003, took catastrophic losses during an attack in Nazaria, Iraq. Eighty were killed and nearly another eighty were wounded in one day. The attack came just after a rescue operation in which the same battalion pulled out the dead and wounded from the freshly ambushed convoy of the 507 Maintenance Company (made famous by Jessica Lynch's story). Two months later, in mid-May, the battalion was ordered back to Nazaria for peace and stability operations. The troops were jittery about returning to the site of so much carnage. "I remember driving into this city from the north this time, almost flinching, bracing as we were going down Ambush Alley, because I remember the last time I was in it. . . . [We were] still seeing the charred marks on the road where we lost amtraks [amphibious tractors]—catastrophic kills where every marine in that amtrak was killed in action." Soon after a battalion-wide memorial service was held on the very fields where marines had fallen, Mooney got orders to report immediately to the Naval Academy. He left behind his regiment, which would take a ship back to the States. He was put on a commercial, not military, flight, sitting next to civilians who simply occupied a different world from his.

The rupture with his unit is palpable, but so too the expectation that, as a marine, he should be able to carry on: "I didn't have the same experience or opportunity as the other marines leaving the combat zone. I had orders to report to the Naval Academy. I had to get here very quickly or I wasn't going to be able to execute those orders. It was around May 15.... So as my unit was backloading, moving down to Kuwait, I had caught a plane, got shuttled down to Kuwait City, and was thrown on a British Airways flight. Seven hours after being in Iraq, I was in Frankfurt, Germany, sitting in a first-class lounge. It was very surreal. Trying to actually look at the porcelain toilets—'cause the last time I had taken a shower was, I think, March 7—and then ten hours after that I was meeting my family and my wife-to-be . . . in Reagan National, which was also very surreal. There wasn't a decompression time.... Basically, I just had to start at the Academy.... It was a very interesting dynamic being transitioned so quickly . . . boom, boom, boom."

When I ask him if he was able to manage with the transition, he answers, without pause, "Yes, ma'am."

But seconds later he reveals the true weight he bears: "Just for me, personally, I don't think there's a day goes by that I don't think about those times, just because of the accomplishments we achieved and the incredible loss of potential for the marines, even though I didn't know them personally. Just seeing and being present when the marines were being pulled out of the amtraks . . . " He says he "reflects back" often on the "lost potential," his restrained words for the grief he feels for those he saw die far too young in Nazaria.

Mooney talks about the horrific with steel-like comportment. He carries his feelings tightly inside. But there is unspoken guilt that he is in tranquil Annapolis while others continue to fight. He is ready to go back and he is preparing his new wife for that reality: "'I say, You've got to prepare yourself for this because after sitting here in Annapolis for three years, after wonderful air conditioning in Annapolis, while my brothers and sisters have been out on their second and third tours . . . you need to come to grips with that I'm going to be away for a while.'"

Mooney's guilt while at home, separated from comrades in battle, recalls that of another young officer, Siegfried Sassoon, the British World War I officer and poet whom we met briefly in chapter 2. Against the wishes of his doctor, the eminent Freudian-inspired physiologist and anthropologist Capt. W. H. R. Rivers, Sassoon returned to the trenches out of a profound mix of love and guilt and a sense of futility at his war protest. He experienced his separation from his troops as at once abandonment and banishment. To return to the front line might well be a kind of "death," he writes in his memoirs, but it is also "my only chance of peace."

> I am banished from the patient men who fight.
> They smote my heart to pity, built my pride.
> Shoulder to aching shoulder, side by side,
> They trudged away from life's broad wealds of light.
> Their wrongs were mine; and ever in my sight
> They went arrayed in honour. But they died—
> Not one by one: and mutinous I cried
> To those who sent them out into the night.
> The darkness tells how vainly I have striven
> To free them from the pit where they must dwell
> In outcast gloom convulsed and jagged and riven
> By grappling guns. Love drove me to rebel.
> Love drives me back to grope with them through hell;
> And in their tortured eyes I stand forgiven.

Another poem, "Sick Leave," concludes with the battalion whispering softly to Sassoon, "When are you going out to them again? Are they not still your brothers through our blood?"

"Brotherhood" is often an unanalyzed term in war. It speaks to attachment, a new family, and the trust in being able to count on another to cover your back. It is, to say the obvious, a gendered term: The masculine profession of war is precisely what the more inclusive "brothers *and* sisters in arms" is meant to counter; the brotherhood of arms is what some desperately wish to keep pure. They want the profession of arms to remain free from the taint of women. Yet Sassoon, writing almost a century ago, implies that the brotherhood he has in mind involves "mothering" activity at its core—including caregiving, profound emotional love, and a willingness to die as if for your own child. Those traditional "mothering" roles have always been part of a cohesive, effective army. They are inseparable from solidarity.

Sassoon's guilt is complex, but it is, in part, the luck guilt of a survivor. "Survivor guilt" (a specific kind of luck guilt) is itself a relatively new term, but the phenomenon is not. The term, when introduced into the psychiatric literature in 1961, referenced the severe guilt felt by survivors of Hitler's genocide of European Jewry. Those who survived the genocide felt they were the "living dead"; they carried the unconscious belief that "merely remaining alive was a betrayal of the dead." Strictly speaking, survivor guilt is not rational guilt, for surviving the Holocaust—or surviving battle, our theme—did not typically happen because a person deliberately let another take his place in harm's way. To be sure, it may be like that. Achilles' guilt over the death of his beloved war comrade, Patroclus, is, perhaps, one of the earliest records we have of a soldier's survivor guilt. And in this case, Patroclus was killed, to reconstruct the moment, because Achilles refused to fight and Patroclus took up Achilles' shield and armor and did battle for him. What Achilles wants more than anything is to undo the original switch, to trade places, to suffer the harm and endure the death himself: "My spirit rebels—I've lost the will to live." "The man I loved beyond all other comrades, loved as my own life —I've lost him." He can't undo the switch and he feels unbearable guilt.

But the guilt of surviving war buddies, or of not being exposed to exactly the same lethal dangers, is not always or typically like this. It is often a matter of dumb luck that a soldier makes it out alive, and tragic luck that others do not. And yet many who have that good luck feel that it is a betrayal of those who don't—a betrayal of solidarity. It is not unlike what is sometimes felt in a family, when one sibling does well and another does not. The child who succeeds may feel guilty, experienced as if the distribution of goods is based on a zero-sum game: To do well means she has deprived, in some non-innocent way, her sibling of limited goods. Psychoanalyst Arnold Modell describes aptly this kind of guilt. There is "in mental life something that might be termed an unconscious bookkeeping system, i.e., a system that takes account of the distribution of the available 'good' within a nuclear family so that the current fate of other family members will determine how much 'good' one possesses. If fate has dealt harshly with other members of the family the survivor may experience guilt." Soldiers, as a result of tight unit cohesion and solidarity, may have similar unconscious thoughts—that the cost of their good luck is another soldier's bad luck. To be lucky is to deprive a buddy of comparable good fortune. Though they do no wrong, they blame themselves as a way of sharing the ill fate. Sharing the evil helps to negate the awful sense of betrayal.

As a form of guilt, survivor guilt (and more generally, luck guilt) points the blame inward and pins moral responsibility on self, though there is not even the causal involvement that characterizes accident guilt. Still, feeling guilty, in general, puts oneself at the center of the story. It is a way of repossessing moral agency and control, however much we overextend the orbit of our actual dominion. We do so unconsciously to make intelligible a terrible thing that has happened and claim agency in a chaotic world. Not surprisingly, that overextension may lead to good effect: In the case of the military, strong feelings of solidarity and fidelity mobilize fighters. Sassoon's luck guilt, like Mooney's implicit guilt, is part of the cohesion of the fighting cadre. But still, the guilt itself is an awful burden to the individuals who privately bear it. And it is a burden that persists long after wartime, as soldiers know and civilians don't often fully appreciate.

Maj. Daniel Healey, another marine I interviewed that morning in Annapolis, was the commander of a rifle company in Iraq during the early years of the war. Healey was in charge of over two hundred marines, most of them having joined his unit shortly before what he refers to as "the race to Baghdad." Only two in the entire unit were combat veterans, both in the Gulf War, where they had served as junior marines twelve years earlier. His job, he tells me, is to build trust and faith in those whom he does not know personally or have time to train. He has to cultivate "empathy," he says, know his troops implicitly, no matter how different their levels of training and experience are from his own.

It is hard to overestimate the gravity of the command responsibility he feels, and that informs many commanders' sense of responsibility, and guilt: He must prove himself and convince his troops to trust him as a competent authority. He has to rely on those who know him to convey the decency and wisdom of his command to those who don't. "I felt like my entire life had prepared me for that moment," he says conveying the weight of leadership. "For me, I took it as a particular challenge because I had the potential of having to write to their parents, saying that they had died under my command." Stalin's famous remark presses here: "One death is a tragedy, a million deaths is a statistic." To Healey, individual or aggregated death on the battlefield is never just a statistic: "I was thirty-seven years old, I was a father of three, and I had been in the Marine Corps for seventeen and a half years," says Healey. "I was leading people who had been in the Marine Corps for five months and were eighteen years old. So in many ways, although it was my first time going into combat, I truly felt that everything I'd done up until this point had prepared me for this. And I had to make sure—I had to make a constant effort, to look for and try to understand how those young marines' experience was not necessarily mine. How *I* was responding to something—how well prepared *I* was—was not necessarily how well prepared *they* were. It's called "empathy." . . . And as a commander, as a leader, you really have to put a lot of energy into that. Because you're busy, because you're genuinely busy, and it's very easy to just overlook."

Healey does not speak of losses, but like Mooney, he alludes to the unfair burden other marines are shouldering while he has been in Annapolis. "You got twenty-year-old marines over there for the third time while we've been here trying to be in touch, but not much being asked of us personally." Like Mooney, Healey is trying to get back to a unit that will go overseas. "There are so many people out there who have had to reach so much deeper than we have and for so much longer and so many more times."

The unspoken guilt that Healey or Mooney feels is different from Prior's: Neither is triggered by events that led to a tragic death. Rather, theirs is a more generalized kind of guilt rooted in omission rather than commission. In leaving the war zone, they have let others take their place. Their guilt or moral anxiety is experienced as if a betrayal. Admittedly, this is an interpretation made outside a clinical setting. I am in no position to plumb the depths of their souls, nor pretend to do so. But the point I am trying to make is as much conceptual as psychoanalytic: Guilt is a part of the battlefield that often goes unrecognized. And while its general form may be single—about apparent transgressions against others for which an individual indicts himself and seeks reparation—its shapes are myriad.

Are these feelings misplaced or marginal cases of guilt in so far as they do not track objective culpability? Should we minimize them, as some philosophers urge, and spotlight instead clearer cases of what we might think of as rational guilt or rational remorse? This would be a grave mistake. The conception of guilt and its phenomenology, like that of all emotions, includes the rational and the irrational and the many imperceptible degrees in between. Proper emotions are not just the sanitized ones, responsive to our best reasoning, as the Stoics famously insist. Rather, they include the full array of what we feel. They are real by virtue of the fact that they are felt. This is important not just in treating pathology, but in understanding the nature of emotions and the psychic and moral reality they can express. For soldiers, who often feel alienated from those who do not fight or bear directly the costs of war, it is essential that their subjective experience of war be understood and their feelings accepted and given due consideration.

THE GUILT OF COLLATERAL DAMAGE

But what of cases where wrongdoing is not so easily ruled out? In particular, what of guilt feelings that arise from killing civilians, where civilian deaths are part of the "collateral damage" of attempts to discriminate legitimate from illegitimate targets? This kind of guilt is different from accident guilt or luck guilt. Yet it shares with them a similar theme. Even if limited collateral damage is widely regarded as permissible within just-war theory, those who incur it do not always live with it easily.

Marine Col. Bob Durkin commanded a battalion in the Sunni Triangle, just south of Baghdad, during Operation Iraqi Freedom II. He recalled how "emotionally upset" his marines became when Iraqi children were injured or killed when cars ran the "trigger lines" at vehicle checkpoints. In some cases, elaborated Lt. Cdr. Irv Elsten (a Navy rabbi), families would be put on the hood of a car that was followed by a pickup truck with armed fedayeen (Ba'athist loyalists) intent on running the checkpoint. If the injuries or deaths were of an adult man whom they suspected was a suicide bomber or a woman who might be concealing explosives under a large burka, his marines, Durkin said, would "generally fluff it off and justify it to themselves, rightly or wrongly." They would reason counterfactually: "Even if I couldn't find out, it *coulda been* this or *coulda been* that." But when children were involved, "there was a dramatic psychological difference." The soldiers would immediately become "visibly upset when they killed children." In the case of a badly hurt child, "they would go out of their way to try calling in medevac aircraft to get the kid out to the hospital." It was just different, he said, when kids were involved. The marines were more vulnerable. They couldn't shake what they had done.

One way to think about this is psychoanalytically, with a twist. The sight of the helpless, injured child may throw the marine back to an image of himself, as once, not so long ago, a child dependent on adults for protection and survival. In that child's world, adults are supposed to construct sound moral order. They are the moral legislators. This is true for the marine in a special way. The combatant in an urban counterinsurgency war is never just a war-fighter; he is also a policeman and peacekeeper. He is tasked to fight as well as to help create a sustainable civic order. The dual role is never easy: When to be a policeman and when to be a fighter is often a tough decision; the rules of engagement don't always settle the matter. Yet the wish to be the good cop, who can restrain his fire when innocent children's lives are at stake, is part of what Durkin's marines feel profoundly.

Checkpoints make vivid the moral ambiguity and the anguish of killing civilians caught in the cross-hairs of war. The purpose of security checkpoints is to help sort out combatant from noncombatant, threat from nonthreat. But as these marines attest, the opportunity for mistake is great. After the heat of battle, with time to reflect, they struggle to make sense of what they have done.

This is the force of a remark Lieutenant Commander Webber makes: "It is a hard thing to gun down innocent people." He is not talking about marines who kill out of malice. Nor is he talking about causing collateral damage impersonally, in the way that air strikes do. What he has in mind is a specific case he knows well: that of Sgt. Rob Sarra of Illinois, who, speaking about his experience in Iraq on a PBS television special, claimed he shot an innocent woman on March 26, 2003. Webber worked with Sarra while in Iraq and then again for a few months after they returned home, until Webber was transferred to another unit.

Sarra's case is wrenching. It was reported in detail in the *Chicago Tribune*. During the early days of the war, Sarra was part of a convoy of armored vehicles in the push toward Baghdad. According to his war journal entry for that date, a woman walked toward the assault vehicles ("amtraks," as the marines call them). The marines shouted at her in Arabic to stop.

> So she's walking and walking and walking.... I'm like, OK, we've had reports of suicide bombers, she's wearing all black, she's carrying a bag under her arm.

One of two things is going to happen. . . . Either she's going to stop or we'd better drop her or [else] she's going to blow up and kill a bunch of guys. . . .

So she's walking. She's walking. She's walking. I perceived her as a threat. You know what, I've got a shot. Two shots. The first one, I think I missed her. Second one, I saw her buck. And then the Marines from the other amtrak opened up on her. And I was the only guy in my platoon to fire.

And she hit the ground and when she hit the ground, there was a white flag in her hand, a piece of white flag in her hand. And I was like, "Oh my God."

The general lines of Sarra's account are corroborated by Marine official reports. Given the perceived threat the woman presented, the shooting was regarded as within the rules of engagement. Furthermore, the official report concluded that even though the woman was killed by Marine fire, it was most likely the fire from the platoon in the second amtrak that caused her death. Yet this far from settled the question in Sarra's own eyes of his moral responsibility and guilt. Sarra was irreversibly shaken by his experience, and despite counseling and rest, he was unable to resume his position as platoon guide. He returned to the States and eventually was given an honorable discharge from the Marines.

THERE IS A FINAL perspective to bring into the conversation. Col. John Rupp is a Marine Corps aviator who sees war from the relatively safe distance of an F-18 cockpit. Part of the interview group in Annapolis, he has been quiet until the very end: "All the baggage that comes with combat—stress, anxiety, fear—is directly related to the proximity of the action. And all the baggage that comes after the war is, I think, directly related to the proximity. Aviators, because they are in a jet that's above the fight, that's sometimes thousands of feet above the fight, don't nec-essarily get the full impact of what they're doing like a ground officer or infantryman would."

Rupp is insulated by distance, and he feels almost the guilt of it in front of these ground troops. He doesn't see the faces, the child's or the adult's or the woman wearing the big burka. He is focused on targets and nontargets. He is not being callous. The gut, moral experience of war is just different for him than for his colleagues on the ground.

For these marines, the intimacy of indirect killing may simply can-cel out other judgments about its permissibility. Indeed, empirical moral philosophers have argued that even if we generally think it is morally all right to cause harm as a side or collateral effect when the overall benefits are great enough, in cases where that harming is "up close and personal," we are less likely to think it morally permissible. We might speculate, given the testimony we have heard, that when a child is harmed or killed, the act seems to cancel out permission in an even more visceral way.

There is a more general lesson as well: In experiencing certain kinds of guilt, soldiers try to reclaim a sense of personal agency and moral auton-omy minimized by putting on a uniform and marching in step as part of a cadre. They take personal responsibility for what they have done, even if that responsibility exceeds what they can in fact do. In so doing, they reaffirm their own humanity in fighting war.

There are myriad other ways in which soldiers, each in their differ-ent roles, struggle to validate their humanity in the face of harming the enemy. Interrogation, in particular, presents a complex challenge to the morally conscientious soldier.

CHAPTER 5

———— ✭ ————

INTERROGATION: IN THE MORAL SHADOWLAND

A YOUNG INTERROGATOR

In early December 2006, William Quinn sat down in my office, looking tired and stressed out, like most undergraduates in the weeks before exams. Yet Quinn was no ordinary undergrad. Before enrolling at Georgetown that fall, he was an interrogator at the Abu Ghraib prison in Iraq. He had enlisted in the Army in the spring of 2001, after having a blowup with his father and getting sinking grades at school. "I needed to get a kick in the butt," he said. He was hoping to become an infantryman, but after scoring well on a test for language aptitude, he was assigned to interrogation duties, with a five-year commitment to the Army. On September 11, 2001, he was two weeks away from graduating from interrogation school at Fort Huachuca, Arizona, where he was trained in how to interrogate Korean prisoners of war. He arrived at Abu Ghraib in February 2005, almost a year after the first photographs of the torture scandal had surfaced.

As we spoke, I had the unsettling thought that Quinn was prob-

ably sizing me up faster than I him. Still, I had my first impressions—
that Quinn, dark-haired with piercing eyes, was remarkably mature and
poised for a twenty-two-year-old; he had an understated charm and sensitivity that would serve him well as interrogator. At one point in our
conversation, I asked him if he felt he had ever "crossed the line" in his
interrogations. Without flinching, he cited three examples that he felt
really badly about. In one case, a detainee who was in isolation and
wasn't talking had requested recreation time. Quinn arranged for it, but
made sure that he, a Sunni with Al Qaeda connections, was paired with
a Shia detainee: "I knew that they were just going to sit there and hate
one another and be miserable for two hours, so that they may as well have
been in solitary confinement for the whole time." In another instance, he
and a fellow interrogator were aware that a detainee had had extramari-
tal affairs, "and so we just harped on it constantly. Every time we thought
he was being difficult, we brought up the fact that he had been immoral
in the past." In a third, a female detainee showed signs of falling in love
with him, and he felt badly about having manipulated her feelings.

Frankly, I was taken aback by his examples. I had expected to hear of
the harsh "fear-up" tactics associated with Abu Ghraib, Guantánamo,
and the CIA—waterboarding, religious or sexual humiliation, sensory
deprivation, stress positions. But what he was telling me had more to do
with betrayals of trust, the infliction of what to me seemed mild emotional bruisings yet in his eyes were acts that caused the detainees "a lot
of mental hardship," and himself, remorse and moral quandary. I was
genuinely puzzled, and my puzzlement, in part, informs this chapter.
Was Quinn just being morally queasy, too "touchy feely" or unhardened
for the job? Or was he, in fact, being a good interrogator, insofar as interrogation requires building trust with a detainee in an overall environment that fosters distrust and hatred; and did he feel that he squandered
that trust for uncertain gain? Or was it simply that now that Quinn had
returned home and had time to reflect on what he did as an interrogator, he had become cynical about what he once did so easily? Was it a role
that no longer fit? Was it a little bit of each?

Some of these questions touch on more general issues of negotiating military/civilian relations within a given psyche. "Border passing"—that is, moving between civilian roles and the roles required in uniform and in war—is neither morally nor psychologically simple. The passage can subject both psychologically strong and morally good persons to feelings of shame and remorse, as well as to traumatic syndromes. In Quinn's case, deception and betrayal, manipulation and exploitation, tools morally questionable in ordinary transactions, had become standard tools of his specialized trade. And this did not sit perfectly well.

Deception and concealment are, of course, routine in war. Surprise campaigns depend on deception, as well as concealment and confusion, whether the ruse is the Trojan horse or high-end art and optics in digitized camouflage designs or in the "Dazzle" paintwork of World War I ships used to evade submarines. Aquinas, in laying the foundations of just-war theory in the thirteenth century, argued the general point against those in the church who worried that a soldier's "ambushes and deceptions" are sins "opposed to faithfulness." He appeals to the Bible, Matthew 7:6, for his defense: "Give not that which is holy, to dogs." He explains: Just as elements of the Sacred Doctrine ought to be concealed from unbelievers, "lest they deride it," "much more ought the plan of campaign to be hidden from the enemy." The soldier, Aquinas concludes, must learn well "the art of concealing his purpose." In intelligence gathering (in peace and war), the point holds in spades: Deception comes with the territory. If killing under the right circumstances is morally permissible in war, then certainly deception must be. On a scale of harms, it is surely a lesser harm.

But as Quinn's story reveals, even if deception is just in war, moral and psychological challenges remain. Interrogation involves close relationships and the building of rapport. It involves what psychoanalysts call "transference," the projection of real feelings and attachments onto substitute objects that are close to hand. The transferences can go both ways, with attachments building mutual rapport. Individual interrogations can go on for months at a time, day in and day out for many hours at a stretch. These are intimate encounters, where empathic identification, however unconscious, is critical if the interrogator is to enter into another's mind.

Even in wiretapping, where there is no face-to-face encounter with the source, there can be strong identification, as the remarkable depiction of the Stasi police agent in the movie *The Lives of Others* makes vivid.

Yet the current public debate has barely touched on the psychological and moral complexity of the interrogator's role. Perhaps this is so for good reason. As a public, what we have debated and continue to debate is torture, and what is now accepted by most as a policy under the Bush administration of state-sponsored torture. At first, the word "torture" was only whispered behind closed doors in places of power and secrecy in Washington. Soon the word was uttered publicly with moral outrage. We now use it easily and with confidence that many of the stories of torture were not made up. The graphic images of Abu Ghraib flooded the media in the spring of 2004, including the chilling image of a detainee, hooded and robed in black, with fingers wired to electric current. Others depicted human pyramids with detainees in sexually compromised positions. Still others involved military dogs terrorizing crouching naked prisoners. Sexual humiliation using menstrual blood, stress positions, extreme sleep and sensory deprivation, sustained social isolation, nudity, exposure to extreme cold, disorientation by prolonged blaring of loud rock music, simulated drowning or "waterboarding"—all became part of a lexicon of "enhanced interrogation techniques." We learned that many of the torture techniques used at Abu Ghraib had migrated there from Guantánamo under a command structure. Indeed, Susan Crawford, the retired judge in charge of the tribunals at Guantánamo, reported in a public interview given to the *Washington Post* in early January 2009 that the life of Mohammed al-Qahtani, a Saudi national accused of being part of the 9/11 plot, had been seriously endangered by his detention in Guantánamo: "We tortured Qahtani," she said openly.

Guantánamo Detention Center (and its predecessor, Camp X-Ray) became shorthand for an outlaw prison set up off American shores in order to evade legal and public scrutiny. As I will explain later, I was brought to Guantánamo as an observer in the wake of a series of hunger strikes, force-feeding, and charges that confidential psychiatric reports on detainees had been breached in order to design individual interrogation plans. Military health leaders asked for advice about how to discharge their official duty to give medical care to detainees, but their real worry was about how they could continue to use mental health workers in a system that had, in essence, condoned torture.

The defining issues of the torture debate have been sharpened in the halls of academe and in scores of books and conferences devoted to the topic: Is there really a moral difference between physical and psychological torture? Are ticking-time-bomb scenarios a cogent way to frame limited exceptions to torture bans or are they themselves blanket invitations to torture based on ill-conceived hypotheticals? What are the legitimate applications of the Geneva Accords in a counterterrorist war against an army that fights without uniformed combatants? Among senior officers with whom I have spoken, and young sailors and soldiers in ROTC programs whom I teach, many express profound shame that we have become a country that has morally and legally justified the use of torture. For them, the fact of torture has opened disturbing questions of identity— just what does the uniform stand for and what are the ideals that they have signed up to defend?

The nearly exclusive focus on torture has silenced a more general debate about the moral shadowland in which the interrogator dwells, even when he does not practice torture. To interrogate is to occupy a complex moral space. True, all soldiers occupy a moral space that at times is hard to reconcile with civilian life; this is a recurrent theme in the stories soldiers tell. But the space the interrogator inhabits has its own special moral demands. And with it comes a distinct set of moral and psychological vulnerabilities.

The sense of moral trespass that Quinn describes comes from the fact that interrogation typically involves not just deception or ruse, but exploitation, and, crucially, exploitation in the context of an intimate relationship. But what exactly is exploitation in this context? Again, there has been deafening silence on this topic both in academic writing on exploitation and in the more mainstream current discussion of wartime detention. In academic accounts of exploitation, the context is often economic and focused on sweatshops or the selling of sex; or legal and connected with fair bargaining and unconscionable contracts; or medical, directed at the ethics of experimentation and obligations of care toward subjects. A few have taken up exploitation within the family. But exploitation in the context of wartime interrogation is still, by and large, a moral black hole. Yet it is a hole which many interrogators struggle to climb out of. Most interrogators never cross the line to torture, though they do routinely exploit. And at some point, in reflecting on their role as exploiter, they may feel they have crossed, or come close to crossing, a significant moral line. This is Quinn's worry.

It is our worry as citizens as well. We can't ignore Quinn's moral worries any more than we can dismiss the guilt a soldier feels when he kills nonculpably. In the case of interrogation, we can't let ourselves be voyeurs of torture, with our views more influenced by TV programs such as *24* than by actual conversations with professionally trained military interrogators. Those, like Quinn, know that torture is by and large ineffective and don't use it but nonetheless struggle to make moral sense of what they do that falls short of torture.

EXPLOITATION

The operative concept in the Army intelligence manual that Quinn used in his training, FM 34-52 (a revised version of which is still current), is exploitation. Consider a sample of guidelines from the manual:

> Interrogators are trained to exploit sources.

> An individual's value system is easier to bypass immediately after undergoing a significant traumatic experience. The circumstances of capture are traumatic for most sources.

> [The following] factors must be considered when selecting tentative approaches:

The source's mental and physical state. Is the source injured, angry, crying, arrogant, cocky, or frightened? If so, how can this state be best exploited during interrogation?

Regardless of the type of EPW [enemy prisoner of war] or detainee and his outward personality, he does possess weaknesses which, if recognized by the interrogator, can be exploited. These weaknesses are manifested in personality traits such as speech, mannerisms, facial expressions, physical movements, excessive perspiration, and other overt indications that vary from EPW or detainee.

Each interrogation is different, but all interrogation approaches have the following in common. They—

+ Establish and maintain control over the source and interrogation.
+ Establish and maintain rapport between the interrogator and source.
+ Manipulate the source's emotions and weakness to gain his willing cooperation.

These are general principles. The manual proffers more specific techniques for exploiting the source's emotions and attachments, such as love for fellow soldiers and family, or a depressive sense of futility, or a sense of pride, shame, and overwhelming fear. The "fear-up harsh" and "pride and ego-down" approaches, widely discussed in the press, are directed precisely at these vulnerabilities. Key to successful exploitation, according to the manual, is building rapport through feigned postures of empathy and sympathy and through the semblance of shared preferences, interests, and knowledge. Interrogators are to avoid overt promises or guarantees and to dispense incentives strategically, whether through flattery, "comfort items," or psychological help in "exonerating guilt." In unambiguous words written well over a decade before pictures from the Abu Ghraib scandal flooded the Internet, the manual flags harsh fear-up tactics as having "the greatest potential to violate the law of war," citing specifically the Geneva Convention Relative to the Treatment of Prisoners of War (prohibiting "mutilation, cruel treatment and torture" and "outrages upon personal dignity, in particular humiliating and degrading treatment"). The point of inducing fear in the detainee, the manual insists, is to cast the interrogator not as its object, but as "a possible way out of the trap" for the detainee.

The clear take-home lesson for practitioners, such as Quinn, is that exploitation is the principal tool of the trade, and a morally legitimate one. It becomes morally and legally problematic only when it is used in excessively harsh ways, however hard it is to define that limit. Like lethal force, exploitation used proportionately and discriminately is a permissible part of the prosecution of war.

Yet to ordinary ears, "exploitation" is a morally freighted term. It feels pejorative even to Quinn. He doesn't take morally for granted what he does in interrogation. But, of course, exploitation, in everyday life, isn't always bad. We exploit things all the time, such as mines and quarries, and exploit each other, or at least our vulnerable spots, in games like chess and tennis, and in professions, such as the legal profession, where it is strategic to get the upper hand. To exploit is to take advantage, to take advantage of a weakness. It becomes morally suspect when taking advantage is *unfair*, when it is somehow foul play, disrespectful of the rules or disrespectful of another as a person and not just as an opponent in a court of tennis or law. To exploit the enemy seems like what we do when we exploit opponents. It is strategic. It is what you do *in role*. A detainee, POW, or enemy combatant seems fair game for exploiting in permissible ways in order to extract information.

But what, then, are we to say about the moral queasiness Quinn sometimes feels? Even if nonharsh exploitation is regarded as conventionally permissible in war, in what sense do those who exploit to extract intelligence sometimes *reasonably* view it as a moral violation or trespass? Again, the question is a variant of one woven throughout this book: Soldiers may do no wrong by war's best standards and yet feel wracked by guilt, betrayal, and a need to make reparations. How do we make sense of the reasonableness of those feelings?

The interrogation manual carefully circumscribes exploitation as taking advantage of the subject's "state" and "personality traits" rather than the subject herself. But in practice, the boundary between an individual and her outward manifestation is harder to define. Key here is that an interrogator, like Quinn, exacts a benefit by taking advantage of a detainee's *acute* weakness or vulnerability. It is the exploitation of abject human helplessness that feels so cruel. At bottom, he is exploiting the detainee's basic need for human connection and sociality, her fundamental longings and fears, her psychological disorientation and trauma from captivity and detention. The detainee may begin weakened by the circumstances of captivity, but she is also made weaker by detention conditions, in which the interrogator becomes a looming, central figure poised to help her in her psychological death from isolation. There is a "total imbalance of power," as Quinn put it to me: "I interrogate for eight hours a day and can then leave the cell and talk to my friends or call my family. These detainees can't. They are totally under my control. They are at my mercy."

Philosophers often try to locate the moral wrong of exploitation with the absence of consent. Some have said it is a necessary condition of exploitation. There seems to be some application here: Detention is a kind of enslavement. Detainees don't consent to being detained, exploited, subject to extreme deprivation. If anything, detention is aimed at weakening the will and squeezing out autonomy. This may be, but face-to-face with an interrogator, detainees may nevertheless tacitly consent to cooperate in order to avoid further harm. In this regard, they are a bit like the sweatshop worker who may choose exploitative work simply because it is better than starving to death. In both cases, there is a kind of consent, however coerced by the dread of something worse.

More helpful than the philosophical debate about consent, I believe, is the psychoanalytic insight that detention, and the exploitation that is part of it, induces a regressive transference in the detainee. Exploitation in the context of that regression can feel morally problematic to an interrogator.

Consider the power dynamic here. In one common scenario, the detainee becomes the small child, and the interrogator, the omnipotent parent onto whom the detainee transfers longing, love, fear, dependence, and hope. At some level, an interrogator may not just fake rapport, but come to feel actual attachment. There is "countertransference," a feeling or enactment, however unconscious or slight or fleeting, that he *is* in the parental and confidant's role, meant to responsibly take care and be in charge. At a psychoanalytic conference in which I presented some of this material, one of my co-panelists was Stuart Twemlow, a psychoanalyst and professor of psychiatry at the Menninger Clinic who does extensive work on bullying and violence in tough schools. He pressed the point about transference. Psychoanalysts know that you can get people to talk without exploitation, he suggested. To resort to exploitation is to put "unconscious sadism at work." It is "indulging" the bully in us. "What makes people talk" to psychoanalysts, Twemlow counters more generally, "is that you are open to them and want to understand." The transference—not the exploitation— gets people to talk. Perhaps so, and this is no doubt part of the psychology of the rapport dynamic, even in interrogation. But so too is the exploitation built into the system, in the total imbalance of power, in the hopelessness of the conditions, in the deprivation of a detainee's life, in being isolated for years from family and friends, religious community, and country. The transference takes place within an extremely exploitative intimate relationship that fosters a dependence on the interrogator's picture of reality, including, at times, his ability to correct a detainee's own sense of what is real or fictional.

In some cases, the exploitation is designed to induce a dependence in which the victim sees herself not as helpless but as actually having both the power to care for interrogators and the ability to protect them from superiors (the so-called Stockholm or Patty Hearst syndrome). Like children who want to protect their parents from harm, the detainee may assume the role of protective teacher, instructing a star pupil about her world and culture. This sort of thing happened with Quinn and the female detainee who fell for him. He had reached a stalemate in the interrogation. The detainee wasn't talking, so he turned to a behavioral consultant on the interrogation team who advised him to induce a Stockholm syndrome. He more or less succeeded: During interrogation sessions, the detainee would put her hand on his knee. She expressed interest in understanding his religious and cultural values and explained her own Muslim beliefs to him. The situation heated up quickly, and Quinn tried to temper it by bringing a female colleague into the cell during interrogation sessions. The detainee viewed her as a romantic rival. She mocked her Arabic and said that it wasn't as polished as Quinn's. She did her best to make the colleague know that she was unwelcome during future interrogations.

What Quinn struggled with was that he had "messed with her feelings," that he had consciously "manipulated her." He had built up what psychoanalysts dub a "working alliance" in order to get her to talk. He had gone further and induced an "erotic transference." Unlike a psycho-therapeutic relationship, this was no voluntary arrangement, where a patient comes in for help and understands at some level that there may be regression, feelings projected and relived, exposure and psychological vulnerability that come with the therapeutic process. Here, the rapport was a setup for exploitation, betrayal, and rejection, without a therapeutic piece. The point was extraction of critical intelligence. The end justified the means, Quinn believed and continues to believe. But he still didn't feel good about what he did.

In the scale of enduring war's harms, it is easy to think what Quinn feels are minor moral and psychological bruisings. In ordinary life, we sometimes mislead others by our overtures; we reject those who love us, purposely inflict harm on them out of anger; we do things that make us seem, or even become, betrayers. But Quinn did this to someone debilitated by days, weeks, months, and years of social isolation and psychological disorientation, trauma, and physical weakness. He was the betrayer, but he was able to betray because he was also the lifeline. He made someone feel more alive, more human, but then ultimately extinguished all that hope. He abandoned and degraded, up close and intimately.

Some who theorize about exploitation point to its specific wrongness as having to do less with taking advantage in a way that exacts unfair ben-

efit than with taking advantage in a way that fails to respect the dignity
or worth of a human being. Put this way, to exploit is to take advantage
in a way that *degrades* another's humanity. This may help us understand
Quinn's moral struggle. To say he took unfair advantage doesn't begin to
get it. Warfare and the power structure of captor and captive make that
point moot, or at least it redefines what counts as fair. What survives the
role shift, for Quinn, is degradation within a relationship. He engineered
the setup. He helped strip her down. He then offered himself as ally and
love object within this carefully choreographed relationship in which he
had all the power. The earlier lessons of revenge should not be forgotten
either, echoed here in Twemlow's worries that interrogation can indulge
sadistic urges. (This, no doubt, is at the heart of the famous experiments
psychology professor Philip Zimbardo performed in 1971, when he re-
created a mock jail of prisoners and guards in a Stanford University
basement. The experiment had to be stopped because of the sadism it
unleashed.) But more perspicuous, as I listen to Quinn, is simply the recognition of the very awful raw power he has as interrogator, of being able
to undo a person and unravel her humanity, face-to-face.

Quinn tries to monitor that power by "microswitching" in and out
of roles, reining in "pride and ego-down" approaches by recognizing that
a detainee's worth is not exhausted by her "intelligence value." She has
dignity and not just "a price," as Kant would put it. Perching, at times,
on the rim of his interrogator *persona*, Quinn leans to the side of sav-
ing his own humanity and that of his subject. A story Quinn told me
speaks to the point. On his first day of interrogation school, Quinn was
asked to sign an informal contract stipulating, as he put it, that "I do not
have or will not allow any religious views or moral or ethical views of
mine to interfere with my completion of the mission." "That was odd," he
thought. "I eventually came to the conclusion that it didn't matter what I
signed on a piece of paper. They could never make me do something that
was illegal or immoral."

I was struck by his remarks. To one who has taught military ethics to
midshipmen and officers, including case studies on the crimes of obedi-

ence, his words spoke volumes. It is all too easy for those in positions of command to exploit those ready to make sacrifices and serve. And it is all too easy for those commanded to insulate moral conscience for the sake of the mission. But to do so is to subscribe to a kind of moral relativism, generally reviled in the military, though here it is disguised as duty. Quinn is essentially rejecting this. To be sure, professional duties can stand in extremely complicated relationships to what we would do in private, outside of institutional obligations and roles. But Quinn's initial response is skepticism to the kind of blanket statement Montaigne makes in his famous boast that "the Mayor and Montaigne have always been separate."

Still, there are consequences of rejecting moral insulation. Indeed, some would argue a person cannot be a good warrior, whether his job in war is to kill or interrogate, if the cushion between civilian and soldier is not amply thick. Some compartmentalization, some cordoning off of role, decorum, and demeanor, is psychologically necessary and morally requisite to do the job. But how much? And when do the borders become too impervious?

Quinn and I talked again at least a half-dozen times in the spring of 2009. He was twenty-seven then and a junior at Georgetown. He had signed up with ROTC and was planning for a career in the Special Forces, as a "quiet professional," the Army's lingo for the Green Berets. Once again, I was struck by his maturity and wisdom. When we first reconnected, I told him I had ruminated often on his cases of rapport building, and in particular, the female detainee case. Did he still think about those cases? I asked. "Often," he replied. And then he offered an analogy for what it felt like to be the interrogator he once was: "I am fairly religious. I don't very often go to Latin Mass. But when I do, there's a sense of mystery, a kind of solemnity. It is more than that. It's the Gregorian chants. You walk into that world, and then out. It's like being in a different universe." Going in and out of a war zone was like that: "War takes place in a different time and space." To behave toward his friends at Georgetown the way he behaved toward detainees in interrogation "would be reprehensible," he said. "And so it becomes very difficult to deal with psychologically. For I know I am the same person who was doing those things. It tears at your soul."

Some might dismiss this as convenient dissociation. To enter the church with its rituals and mysterious language is to go to a sealed-off place, severed from everyday life. The war zone, too, is a sealed-off place; to be in it is not to have to reconcile what one does in it with what one does outside it. The betrayer is outside the detention cell; inside is the soldier working to get intelligence to save lives, to prevent a suicide bombing, to avert a disaster. There are *actual, imminent* ticking-time-bomb scenarios, not just hypotheticals, Quinn insists, citing cases where he has had to get someone to talk truthfully *now*, not in two days, or three days, or a week or a month, but *now*, though that is never, in his view, a moral or legal justification for torture.

Yet Quinn never compartmentalizes in a way that fully seals off, morally or psychologically. He "stands in the spaces" between personas, to adapt the suggestive phrase of psychoanalyst Philip Bromberg. He travels between selves, knowing that what he does in one place he dare not do in another, and yet that "dare not" reminds him, "tears at him," about just how awful what he did do was, even though morally and legally it was justified and permissible in role. Recently, I bumped into Quinn while he was picking up his lunch at a deli across from where I teach. I told him that I keep thinking about our conversations. He said, returning to the moral remainder, "You know, what's legal isn't the same as what's moral." His point, I take it, is that what he did is legal. However, to his noninterrogator self, it feels immoral.

In his ability to go in and out of role, Quinn is different from the Israeli soldier in the movie *Waltz with Bashir* who has suppressed much of his memory of what he did twenty years earlier in the 1982 Lebanon war and in the massacres at the Palestinian refugee camps of Sabra and Shatillah, at which he was present and feels complicit. The lead character in that animated documentary, the film's director, Ari Folman, pieces together his memory by talking to others who fought with him and who tell him their stories of which he was a part. Perhaps Quinn can talk and remember and hold on to his different selves because he did not do something egregious as a soldier. And perhaps he did not do something as egregious because somehow the passage between roles, between civilian and soldier, was porous, even in the war zone.

For another interrogator whom I have come to know indirectly, the challenge is not the residue that exploitation leaves, but moral insulation from feeling any residue in the first place.

"LETTING OTHERS DO IT"

If Quinn's implicit approach to his work as an interrogator is to maintain enough psychological distance to be able to step back and reflect on his moral conduct, Capt. Ray Longworth's approach is to stay immersed and treat his moral stress merely as psychological symptoms that need relief. Longworth is a retired Air Force and U.S. counterintelligence liaison officer whose twenty or so years of work throughout the world involved him in routine interrogation and counterterrorism activity. The account that follows is based on an extended correspondence (from September 2002 to January 2006) between Longworth and Jean Maria Arrigo, a researcher studying the psychology and ethics of intelligence work.

In his correspondence, Longworth spoke candidly about the stresses and strains of the job, though rarely in ethical terms. Indeed, what is striking is the absence of morality in his reflections on day-to-day work. What matters for him is psychological, not moral, forbearance. As a case study, his offers a telling counterpoint to Quinn's.

Here is a thumbnail profile he paints of the interrogator: "Interrogation is a combo of fishing, chess, observation, being a stand up comic, sniper, IED [improvised explosive device] expert. [You have] to live on Coke and beef jerky, love movies and trivia, have a huge sense of humor. You learn to bribe the correct way so no offense is taken." He continues with the sketch: "We all had a degree in liberal arts ... with classes or degrees in Anthro or History. We all did crossword puzzles, collected antiques, spoke several languages, were always known as quiet and were calm. . . . We were multi-level lateral thinkers, able to switch between interrogation strategies."

The portrait of the interrogator is one of cultural sophistication, resourcefulness, flexibility, and extreme intelligence. Adaptive switching occurs, but typically "between interrogation strategies," and not between the self in and out of role. Indeed, "the quiet" and "calm" that a professional like Longworth aims to embody is, in part, the achievement of insulation from what lies beyond role. To feel too much in this career is to give in to its unbearable pressures: "The actual stress this job had on interrogators was immense," he writes. "Some drank, some could not sleep." Some "kept dwelling on what they had seen or done" and "became depressed." "Some lost weight," some "had migraines or wanted to be alone." Some reported that their wives were "shocked" at their "lack of emotion" or "affection." Some of the stress symptoms, as he suggests at one point, are reactions to "what one has seen or done," whether as witness, agent, or complicitous partner.

Still, the remarks are veiled and reflect the general tenor of the seven-volume correspondence in which, despite much open psychological talk, there is little open *moral* talk, whether in terms of felt conflicts or compromises, or moral residue, registered as slight as twinges of regret or remorse. Perhaps an important background factor here is age and professional investment: Longworth writes as a career defense intelligence operative who for more than twenty years has seen terrorists and counterterrorist operations up close. He views his work in terms of expedience, subject to legal restraint and protected by the secrecy accorded those working in human intelligence. The stress of the job is *professional* stress that he, as a senior team leader, must help to alleviate if he is to develop an effective working team.

In this regard, it is not surprising that Longworth sees himself a benevolent doctor of sorts. He knows how to take care of his troops (and himself), and how to relieve stress by distraction, cultural immersion, and gallows humor. "Recall," he says casually to his correspondent at one point, even "the German SS had to have relief now and then from camp duties." He boasts about the respites: "I took out tours on our days off

to local archaeological ruins, markets, museums.... I had the base theater guys open the theater so we had movies not only each night but during the day.... I guess I am to blame, but all of my guys are now movie
and TV trivia experts and we hold competitions.... We would often go
out for dinner together. I had high ranking local military or police set
up hunting days for us where we could go out and walk the hills, chase
game, and be outside. Some had trouble sleeping so we kept them going
until they were almost passed out. I had the best-fed and exercised unit."

In order to encourage trust and closeness, he instructs his men to call
him by first name. They know that they "can come to me any time to talk
about what is troubling them." "They know I will not file a report stripping them of their security clearance unless they are around the bend,
unsteady, forgetting the cultural boundaries or too aggressive for no reason." He addresses his correspondent, an academic Ph.D., as "doc," with
a deferential nod to the authority of medical and mental professionals.
Like many trained in intelligence, he is no stranger to clinical psychology
and the physical manifestations of stress: "We had so much psychological
warfare training from all the various services and agencies, we could spot
... when any of our own began to have a problem."

At first glance, Longworth's doctoring stance is mildly reminiscent of
that of another group of practitioners famously committed to building
a resilient psyche. The ancient Stoics view their Stoicism as a "therapy"
for the soul that can arm against vulnerability. "I am both doctor and
patient," confides Seneca, writing to friends in need of Stoic doctoring,
but also always to himself as a fellow sufferer. But while Stoic therapy
shares Longworth's goal of quiet and calm, the ultimate Stoic aim is to
insulate not against sensitivity to moral compromise, but quite the opposite, against the pulls and tugs that threaten to make individuals suscep-
tible to moral compromise in the first place. That is, moral compromise
is the evil, and Stoic therapy teaches to be ever vigilant against it. In
this regard, the Stoics profess to instill calm and quietude by teaching
patients about the self-sufficiency of good character. Any suffering individuals endure from the harsh vicissitudes of life can never compare, the
Stoics say, to the genuine loss of happiness that comes from wrongdoing,

moral self-compromise, or denial of others' moral status as fellow "citizens of the universe."

Indeed, though Longworth's gloss on his own work may sound Stoic, in fact it isn't, for it lacks the keystone of Stoic doctrine—namely, that psychological resilience is, at bottom, moral constancy. That is, Stoic therapy aims at mental toughening, but it professes to do so by keeping vigil against the corruption of virtue. This requires keeping a wary eye on conflicts of conscience, including being wary of the very defenses one raises against those conflicts. It may turn out that the Stoic view of moral integrity is itself ultimately too narrow, too cordoned off from what happens to us through forces outside our own personal agency, such as luck and tragedy. So the portraits in the previous chapter of soldiers who feel profound guilt for faultless accidents or for the luck of surviving or even for doing justly in war what civilians don't do, may simply not be a part of a proper Stoic narrative. Still, the Stoic narrative is one of *moral* girding, absent in Longworth's approach.

Longworth speaks explicitly about his efforts to alleviate stress in himself and his teammates. We can also assume that he avails himself of less conscious mechanisms that help morally insulate what he sees and does. One such mechanism is all too familiar in the history of war—namely, the use of pejorative epithets to dehumanize the enemy. The names help morph others into subhumans, whom it then becomes easier to demonize. Longworth tries to keep himself at an arm's length from such practices: that's how foreign agents speak, he says; that's what *they* say and do. But "mention" can quickly slide into "use," as when he remarks, "The Turks say that 'a terrorist is like a rabid dog and has to be put down.' That was still and is our/my way of thinking, but we can drain his mind of information before he goes to 'donkey heaven.' "

At other times, Longworth enlists euphemism to help neutralize the moral valence of what interrogators do. So he urges his correspondent not to use the word "torture" if she is really going to understand the mindset of an interrogator: "I never met anyone who actually used the word 'torture' in the field or at HQ [headquarter] level. It was always 'softening up' or 'intensive interrogation techniques.' " But euphemism is at times only a thin veil: An agency, Longworth says, "once told me that captured terrorists are like tissue paper; you use it up in interrogation and then throw it away."

Black sites for coercive interrogation also help to make involvement disappear. So Longworth comments at one point that while his liaison work with specific foreign nations is part of his record (i.e., his OERs—office efficiency reports), "there will be nothing about interrogation as we were not there 'officially.'" "It's so nice to be secret. No trouble over human rights."

Perhaps most troubling in this self-portrait of moral vanishing is the insistence that to "let others do it their way" does not make him, in any substantive way, complicit. One year before the news of U.S. military involvement in torture at Abu Ghraib, Longworth writes, "I do not know of a single instance, outside of Vietnam, where a US intelligence member actually went to Level 1 [i.e., "harsh coercive interrogation"] on a subject all by themselves. I guess I came about as close as anyone in even gaining access to the facilities where the interrogation took place. The US military has various levels in an interview and interrogation. The idea of torture is viewed as uncomfortable by Americans, so we let our allies carry it out. I would not say it was done on our behalf but as it was being done in the course of their investigation, I saw nothing to be lost by submitting questions and then talking to the subject before and after the sessions." He elaborates further: "There are free lance interrogators available used by some nations to keep their own hands clean. . . . By using third party Level 1 agents, the nation can freely claim under oath that they are not involved in intensive interrogation techniques."

In fairness to Longworth, he makes clear that as a liaison officer, his dealings with Level 1 intensive interrogators were not a common occurrence. And he holds, like many experts in the field, that for the most part, torture does not produce good intelligence: "It is always a last resort, with vague results and to be used only after all interview techniques have failed."

When his work *does* involve the infliction of torture or use of harsh, coercive methods, he sees himself on the sidelines, a passive spectator, willing to exploit the already softened-up subject, but not an actual collaborator or co-participant in the harming. It may be that he does not feel implicated in torture because he takes himself as not actually making a difference to its infliction. And yet, presumably, some of the "Level 1" harming with which he comes in contact are cases where he *does* control the harming, if not in the sense of directly producing the harm, then in the sense of both being able to prevent it and not commissioning others to do it in his place. Still, he does not hold himself or his American colleagues as accountable in such cases: "My team could at least come home and be assured we did not go out of our way to hurt anyone. We may have tricked them, confused them or out thought them, but we never did harm them." In other parts of the correspondence, he restricts real "harm" to a narrow class of physical interventions that exclude the use of electric shock, prolonged forced kneeling, light deprivation, deprivation of sleep, hooding, and systematic confusion as to day and night.

Techniques like these have been subject to intense public scrutiny of late. Surely, it is self-deceiving to think that only the worst of physical abuses can harm, and that physical abuse through prolonged forced stress positions, or psychological manipulations through sensory manipulation or sleep deprivation, are benign forms of trickery. Psychological suffering can leave marks that endure just as physical abuse does. Albie Sachs, justice in the Constitutional Court of South Africa and himself the victim of state-sponsored torture in that country, speaks passionately to the point. At a public lecture at the University of Chicago Law School in the spring of 2008, he insisted that "torture lite" is every bit as much torture that scars: "You don't get stronger by torture by sleep deprivation, by people shouting at me, by banging things at me, by being given food that may be drugged ... It is not about information. It is about breaking me. It is about who is the stronger. It is about destroying you, your will, your self-esteem." The abuse is designed to leave no telltale signs; it must be hidden from the public: "Judges could not see broken bones or blood. And so the judges would say, where is the proof of torture?" It is only from the point of view of those who wish to hide tangible evidence that practices like hooding, sleep deprivation, forced stress positions, and sleep deprivation do not count as harms.

Longworth maintains that the peripheral nature of his involvement, in these practices and others, does not make him morally accountable. When it comes to the actual torture, he remains on the sidelines. He is not a participant. But interrogational torture is typically an institutional practice, carried out by some, sanctioned and supported by others who know the clandestine sites, keep them clandestine, and create liaisons precisely to benefit from the cooperative arrangement. In the case of the work Longworth describes, there are clear systemic lines of collaboration, alliance, and intelligence sharing. There is an elaborate, collective enterprise, and there is a denial of complicity. At work, presumably, are familiar mechanisms of moral self-deception. These habits of mind are not striking in and of themselves. What *is* striking in this case is the degree of opacity they offer—that the burdens of doing the nasty business of counterintelligence are rarely raised as *moral* burdens of any sort, whether in terms of complicity, dirtying one's own hands in doing what is required for security, feeling the subsequent moral weight of actions stigmatized outside of the context of mission, or experiencing moral betrayal by agencies that later disavow actions they earlier authorized.

At stake here is Longworth's missing moral assessment of himself as interrogator. Why it is absent in his case, and present in Quinn's, is not clear. Perhaps religion plays a role in what Quinn brings to his job as interrogator, or again, perhaps youth, that he is not the hardened professional that Longworth has become. Or again, there is the moral luck that Quinn arrived at Abu Ghraib a year after the scandal, having benefited from a national debate on torture and in being in a prison in the spotlight. Or, again, it may be as basic as differences in conscience and character.

What is easier to probe is Longworth's moral perspective on the detainees he interrogates. Does Longworth ever express empathy for the detainee? Or respect? Or admiration? Significant here are his comments on interrogating skilled suicide bombers. On occasion he will muse, "It may seem odd, but ..." The caveat that often follows is a confession of praise or esteem for the terrorist, because of his smarts or because he is well educated or because he is an amazing bombmaker who has engineered an impressive device that is discriminating and precise: "You appreciated a good bomb, which sounds funny to most people ... You appreciated the work it took to make this bomb design." "You give him the respect for his accomplishments. . . . [I]n other circumstances he might be in intelligence agencies or Special Forces units." Viewed in this light, the detainees' status as enemy combatants rather than intelligence officers or elite soldiers becomes the result of their own moral luck, or rather, lack thereof. And if we were to assume that Longworth might feel differently about the use of harsh interrogation techniques if these skilled and accomplished detainees' circumstances were different, we would be left with the unsatisfying conclusion that the morality of torture hinges less on intrinsic human rights than on the relative arbitrariness of circumstance.

In this regard, it is critical to remember that respecting skill is distinct from respecting the dignity and humanity of the person who has that skill, whether a suspected terrorist or not. Quinn fingers the point in an editorial in the Georgetown University newspaper on the sixth anniversary of 9/11:

> In my meetings with detainees, from members of the Ba'ath Party to Islamic terrorists, it was often hard for me to understand how the calm and pleasant person with whom I was speaking could have committed the brutal acts to which he confessed. I couldn't help but wince every time I heard an American refer to the people we were fighting as "barbaric" or "inhuman." I had learned never to dehumanize my enemy, but to maintain a concrete understanding of him as a human being. That realization helped me understand that I was every bit as capable as they were of committing their crimes.
>
> A person's involvement in an organization that practices terrorism does not put him or her beyond our comprehension. They are still people with similar wants and fears. . . . I suspect that, when we are successful [in counterterrorism], it will be because we recognize our enemies as human and develop plans that recognize their humanity.

It is instructive to frame the remarks as part of an imaginary dialogue with Longworth, one professional interrogator to another. Quinn's point is that however horrific and perhaps unforgivable the deeds of a terrorist, he or she is still worthy of respect, sharing common humanity and due the protections of international law and human rights. Moreover, he insists, the very skill of interrogation depends on a capacity for empathy that is both bolstered and constrained by concrete respect. As he says, we "develop plans that recognize their humanity." Empathy is not just an epistemic tool, in his mind; it is the source of a moral restraint.

The portrait of Longworth raises troubling issues about professional moral accountability. Even if as a liaison officer, Longworth's relationship to direct harming is attenuated ("he lets others do it"), still, he knowingly and willingly plays a systematic and functional role in an organized practice of torture. He intentionally participates in a collective end designed to inflict torture. True, his role is at the periphery rather than at the core of that process; he nonetheless shares *some* degree of accountability, for he actively cultivates an ongoing relationship with those at the core and relies on that relationship and their methods to do his own work. Indeed, as a "liaison" officer, his role is specifically to form dynamic and ongoing relationships with foreign operatives who can help achieve ends of mutual interest. In bringing about those shared ends, he is part of an ongoing "we," not an isolated "I." He acts as part of a partnership that allows him to get done what he needs to get done, even if he doesn't do it himself. However attenuated his role in torture, there is still broad complicity.

To this, of course, he might reply that in assessing his accountability, it makes sense for him to focus primarily on what he is exclusively the author of. What did *my* hands touch, what harm did *I* directly do, what did *I* directly bring about through my own agency? This is how we often think when we assess our moral responsibility for wrongdoing—exclusively rather than inclusively. It is a pervasive part of commonsense morality. But in Longworth's case, and in cases that involve collective harming (whether in government, business, or militaries, national and transnational), the focus on the "I" fails to capture the "we" that makes collective work possible. Longworth may not directly intend torture, but what he does intend is to use the product of torture—a softened, ready-to-cooperate detainee. And he lets others know that he is counting on them to deliver that product. He thus gives a nod to the system and encourages the cooperative scheme. This is the point of liaison work, to fit into and sustain a larger, choreographed plan. To associate and closely collaborate with others precisely because of their moral flexibility is to be morally pliable oneself.

Indeed, what is most disturbing in this portrait of Longworth is the absence of what is so striking in so many of the military men and women I have interviewed: an expanded sense of personal agency, often borne at heavy moral and psychological cost. The moral dimensions of the space Longworth inhabits as interrogator, whether he acknowledges them or not, provide a good introduction to another morally freighted area—namely, the role of health professionals in interrogation.

CLEAN OR DIRTY HANDS?

In October 2005 I was invited to visit Guantánamo Detention Center along with a small group of civilian psychiatrists, psychologists, top military physicians, and Department of Defense (DOD) civilian health affairs officials to observe the medical and mental health care of detainees and the role of physicians and mental health workers in their care and interrogation. Among the unspoken reasons for DOD concern was a steep rise in the number of detainees on hunger strike in mid-June 2005, as well as the bruising criticism the administration had received, over that summer and fall, for its use of psychiatrists and psychologists in interrogation procedures. More specifically, there were well-publicized allegations, now well documented, that "resilience training" for our own soldiers at Fort Bragg was "reverse engineered" at Guantánamo for the infliction of torture. There were reports of the breach of confidential psychiatric records in order to tailor interrogation tactics. And there was concern about large-scale force-feeding of hunger strikers through stomach tubes.

As an observer, I expected to see, even if at a safe distance, some of the secret world of Guantánamo. But despite the costly and elaborate trip, that world remained hidden. The trip ended up being a fairly cocooned visit with officials at the base. It began with a two-hour PowerPoint briefing by the commander of the base at the time, Army Maj. Gen. Jay W. Hood, around a conference table at the Navy hospital on base, and ended with a visit to the detainee hospital, where we met staff physicians and psychiatrists in the hospital corridors. My only sighting of the detainees was a stolen glimpse into the distance: Behind a barbed wire fence and translucent screen were two white tunic–clad bearded men in a guarded area outside their cells.

I later pieced together my impressions with those of others who have been to Guantánamo—journalists, defense attorneys, DOD health officials, human rights workers, and released detainees. One I have spoken to a number of times over the years is Josh Colangelo-Bryan, a thirty-eight-year-old attorney at Dorsey & Whitney in New York who has made dozens of trips to Guantánamo representing five Bahraini detainees there, all of whom have now been released.

Colangelo-Bryan, who is of medium height and build, says he learned early on, during grade school in the New York City public school system, how to size up kids physically in his class. It came back to him when he first peeked into one of the maximum security cell's meeting rooms, where he was about to meet one of his clients. "After all, I was about to meet the worst of the worst," Colangelo-Bryan recalls. The guards picked up on his apprehensiveness. As he reports it, the guards told him: " 'Don't worry. We'll be watching for your protection ...' So it was with some trepidation that I stepped into that room for my first interaction with a detainee."

Across the very small room, Colangelo-Bryan saw Jumah Al-Dossari, his first client. He estimated Al-Dossari to be about five feet six inches tall and weighing 130 pounds—someone he thought he could hold off for a minute or two if necessary before the guards came to his aid. Al-Dossari was sitting at a table, his feet shackled to the floor. He extended his hand and, with a broad smile, mumbled, "Thank you, welcome," in his limited English. "This is a good sign," thought Josh.

But other signs gave him pause. "Joshua," Al-Dossari repeated at one point in the conversation. "That is a Jewish name, right?" he said, through the interpreter in the room.

"Oh," thought Colangelo-Bryan, "we are about to have the anti-Semitic moment!" He explained that his name was Jewish, but that he was not; it was just a popular name in his neighborhood when he was growing up. As he tells it, "Jumah looked a bit disappointed. 'Oh, I had heard that the best lawyers were Jewish.' I must have looked a little upset, for Jumah then said, 'But I am sure you are very good.' At that point I figured I probably wasn't really in danger that he was going to reach across the table and strangle me."

So began their first three hours together. They talked not just about the court case, and who Colangelo-Bryan was, but about Al-Dossari's family, his young daughter, Middle Eastern cuisine, and films. It turned out that Al-Dossari's favorite movie was *Jumanji*, the Robin Williams movie based on the children's book by Chris Van Allsburg about a magical board-game. "Not usual terrorist's fare," he thought. Colangelo-Bryan, in fact, worried about the hunger for emotional connection: "It was just so evident that he was soaking up all of the interaction that he could get and had just been starved for this kind of personal connection. He seemed to be trusting, very quickly, which was something I worried about, and open and just ready for this conversation."

By his own account, Colangelo-Bryan is "cynical by nature" and takes all his clients' reports with a "grain of salt." When he took on representation of detainees at Guantánamo, he read clients' reports with an even "bigger grain of salt" than he would for a typical case of commercial litigation. And so he listened with suspended judgment, over the next few days, as Al-Dossari told him of interrogation sessions in which his hands and feet were short-shackled to the floor while interrogators wrapped him in an Israeli or U.S. flag; of being chained to a floor while a female interrogator smeared what he believed to be menstrual blood on his face; of having his face banged into the floor and being beaten unconscious by the immediate-response, anti-riot forces. Al-Dossari spoke of being so desperate at one point that he got hold of a razor, cut his arms, and wrote on the walls of his cell, "I killed myself because of the brutality of my oppressors." Some of the claims didn't seem credible. Would someone really use menstrual blood in this way? Could you write that many words on a wall, with your own blood, after the trauma of slitting your arms? Would you have enough blood? Would you be stable enough to do it? Colangelo-Bryan remained cautiously skeptical until a month or so later, when he read a series of emails and FBI memos released through the Freedom of Information Act for a court case. In those memos, with names redacted, was a report of a guard having seen a detainee in a cell wrapped in an Israeli flag. Also mentioned was a description of a menstrual-blood tactic, where a woman would smear red dye on a detainee just before prayer time to make him unclean for worship and so sap him of religious strength. Finally, in a book written by a former Guantánamo guard and interpreter, the author described being called in an emergency to translate a message written in blood on a shower wall. He translated the words as: "I killed myself because of the brutality of my oppressors." Colangelo-Bryan's skepticism lifted.

During the course of their legal consultations, Colangelo-Bryan watched Al-Dossari's growing psychological desperation. He was kept in isolation for several months at a time, with the only access to the outside world being a food-tray slot on a door that opens to a hall where large industrial fans drown out any attempt at conversation. He was denied books and calls to his family. He was kept in stress positions. Colangelo-Bryan reached out to him as best he could. He told Al-Dossari to write to him at those desperate moments, and to know that he would always read what he wrote.

Al-Dossari's treatment raises pointed questions about the role of health professionals at Guantánamo. What was the role of the psychiatrists caring for his mental health? Did they intervene? What was the role of the psychologists in an interrogation plan like the one Al-Dossari was subjected to? In short, what is the complicity of health professionals in detainee abuse at a detention center like Guantánamo?

Guantánamo, like many military detention centers in operation during the wars in Afghanistan and Iraq, represents a crosscurrent of different professional and culture streams in interrogation and health care. The personnel environment is complex, and so too are the systemic and structural factors that can erode independent moral judgment. On the interrogation side, there is the influence of interrogation communities from different subcultures—from the DOD, the National Security Agency, the CIA, the FBI (which was outspoken in its repudiation of the DOD civilian leadership's advocacy of harsh techniques). In some cases, there is the additional influence of interrogation methods imported from domestic police work and law enforcement. Both civilians and military personnel work in interrogation, and those in the military do not always advertise their uniforms to detainees. Inserted into this community are the health professionals. At Guantánamo clinicians of various stripes have been in charge of the medical and mental care of detainees. Here, too, some are in uniform and some are military contractors. In addition, behavioral scientists are attached to interrogation teams. Beyond these health professionals are the various professional organizations that represent them, and the "ethics" debates and positions they have taken over the years.

COMPLICITY, WHETHER of a health professional involved in coercive interrogation, or of a foot soldier fighting an unjust war, must be understood in terms of various economic and social constraints that come with participation in an institution. There are moral and economic costs of speaking out, and institutional pressures and social rewards for toeing the line. On the side of moral costs, ethicist and lawyer Jonathan Marks describes well the limited and exhaustible "intervention capital" that military health professionals often have, such that they frequently save "objections for the most egregious cases" in order to avoid being "dismissed as unpatriotic" or accused of "crying wolf." Specific cases are not hard to imagine: Some in uniform have had expensive military medical educations that they must "pay back" through service. They may not have asked to be assigned to Guantánamo; they simply ended up there and reassignment may not be in the cards. Others may become attached to interrogation units with young, untrained interrogators. Though the consultants may begin as fairly independent-minded outsiders, they may slowly drift toward the internal norms of the group, morally seduced by leadership in a fight against terror that requires "taking the gloves off." Furthermore, by international law, those attached to intelligence units surrender noncombatant status. The legal shift may encourage a subtle identity shift away from the image of support staff role (like the roles occupied by chaplains and doctors) to the idea of being a kind of fighter, with all the machismo and gumption that it takes. None of this is to excuse complicity, though it may help to explain it.

But there are other more specific psychological mechanisms that lead to moral numbing in an institutional setting such as Guantánamo. Here, a lesson from history is critical.

FROM NUREMBERG TO GUANTÁNAMO: MORAL INSULATION

The involvement of health professionals in detention is not new. On October 25, 1946, three weeks after the handing down of the verdicts of the International Military Tribunal at Nuremberg, the United States established Military Tribunal I for the trial of twenty-three Nazi physicians. The charges, delivered by Brig. Gen. Telford Taylor on December 9, 1946, form a seminal chapter in the history of medical ethics in war. The list of noxious experiments condemned as war crimes and crimes against humanity on civilians and prisoners of war is by now more or less familiar—high-altitude experiments, freezing experiments, malaria experiments, sterilization experiments, experiments with poison and with incendiary bombs, among others.

What remains less familiar, and critical for our concerns, is the moral mindset of the health professionals involved. In his 1986 work, *The Nazi Doctors*, Robert Jay Lifton interviewed doctors, many of whom for forty years continued to distance themselves psychologically from their deeds and from moral accountability. Though by all accounts the Nazi doctors' participation in World War II is vastly different from the engagement of health professionals in our own ongoing wars, we still can learn from history about how those professionals, not unlike some interrogators, insulate themselves morally and psychologically from the deliberate, and in some cases, blatantly evil, infliction of harm. Lifton's own research, it is worth noting, is a follow-up study. It is about the conflict and moral residue that linger, close to a half a century later.

The follow-up story of the health professionals who are part of the war on terror has not yet been told. There have been no trials of doctors or health professionals and no charges brought. Nor is it clear that there should be. But the absence of the *legal* spotlight makes it all the more imperative to shed *moral* and *psychological* light on their involvement in centers where harsh exploitation, psychological abuse, and torture have taken place.

During the Nazi period, euphemistic and scientific language sanitized medicalized killing. Killing "life unworthy of life" (whether the term came to denote Jews, homosexuals, Roma, Catholic critics, the mentally ill, the physically feeble, or other "impure" strains) was a matter of "euthanasia." The Greek word, to the ears of some Nazi doctors, retained the positive overtones of its etymological root, as Adolf Wahlmann, medical director at the killing institution Hadamar, was eager to insist in legal testimony: "The term euthanasia comes from the Greek *eu*, which means beautiful." Imageries of "therapeutic killing," "killing as healing and cure," and "killing for the sake of the strong and the healthy" helped to further promote the myth of "special treatment" as therapeutic. Medical questionnaires, evaluations, and statistical analyses under professorial leadership and management—in short, the stuff of institutionalized science and academe—all added to the legitimization of the process.

Institutions such as Guantánamo are not killing centers like Hadamar was—that's not the comparison to make. But they have been torture centers, and euphemistic and scientific terms, beyond the euphemism for torture—"enhanced interrogation techniques"—have helped insulate practitioners from moral conflict. At the entrance to the Guantánamo center, visitors pass under a gateway that reads, "Honor Bound." The sign has been kept in place for years, despite the desperation of inmates about their treatment. Behavioral Science Consultation Teams (BSCTs, pronounced "biscuits") are typically military or contract psychologists who help tailor individual interrogation plans. The acronyms insert psychological distance between mental health and interrogation, as does the fact that a "biscuit" is never physically present in an interrogation room with a detainee, but on the other side of a two-way mirror. Yet the authority of BSCTs is present and felt. They can exert considerable influence on the interrogator, both as professional authorities who have expertise in matters of human behavior and as moral authorities who sanction programs of action. The point was demonstrated well by Yale psychologist Stanley Milgram in his famous experiments on authoritarianism conducted in the mid-1960s. In analyzing the experiment (in which subjects were instructed to administer increasing levels of electric shocks to students— actually confederates in the experiment—who gave wrong answers on a test), Milgram concluded that subjects were willing to inflict harm, in part, because orders were given by Milgram himself, an authority figure in a prestigious academic setting. In psychoanalytic terms, the transference he induced as a powerful authority figure must be factored in.

Studies from the Nazi period also make clear how a highly bureaucratic division of labor and roles works to diffuse a sense of individual accountability. Psychological and moral numbing results in part from individuals seeing themselves as not really "in charge" of decisions. Actions are perceived as being beyond their own doing, making, or stopping. As the Longworth case reveals, participation in collective ends can diminish the sense of ownership for those accustomed to think in terms of direct causal pathways and of the exclusive "I" rather than the inclusive "we."

At Guantánamo, too, the military has divided labor in a way that aims at professional insulation. During my visit, one of the pressing questions posed to the visiting team was not *if* psychologists or psychiatrists should consult on interrogation plans, but *which* professional should. The clear preference among some Pentagon advisers was to use psychologists rather than psychiatrists for intelligence gathering. One reason seemed to be that psychologists, as nonphysicians, are not regarded as strictly bound by the Hippocratic maxim, first do no harm. Also, psychologists, as professionals, have a strong tradition of working in forensics, where the client is not the patient.

However, the very discussion about which kind of health care provider ought to support harsh interrogation practices should raise moral suspicions to anyone sincerely worried about torture. If the "ought" is a moral one, then it is questionable whether health professionals of any stripe ought to be involved in interrogation where there is strong institutional pressure to use coercive techniques and torture. No one should torture, physician or not. It is a violation of humanity, not just of the doctoring role. But there are role-specific arguments as well. Complicity with torture runs counter to the doctor's humanitarian stance of healing and of providing comfort and pain alleviation when healing is not an option. Doctors, of course, sometimes do hurt intentionally, but typically as a means to healing; at other times, they may hurt knowingly, as the side effects of procedures with anticipated benefits for the patient that outweigh the harm. But torture answers to neither of these descriptions of how a doctor might harm, nor to more basic conceptions of what morally decent persons do. Plato warned us long ago of the specific risk of conceiving of doctoring as just a technique (a *technē*). A doctor's skill, abstracted from good character and wisdom, is a neutral ability: It can be used to heal or harm. The good doctor is always wary of that moral hazard.

But what then of the role of the nonclinicians—behavioral psychologists or other criminology or forensic experts—who are part of interrogation teams in an institution that may pressure to torture? Here, it may be important for psychologists to be involved precisely to craft more humane approaches. They may even be regarded as those in whom resides the chief institutional responsibility, on the ground—away from the fighting—of responding to a moral imperative in war to collect information about the enemy in a timely but humane way. Still, that responsibility can become degraded, and a once-strong moral voice can become corrupted by institutional pressures. What remains may be a co-opted authority who gives green lights to clear moral breaches. Without clear moral leadership from the top, the moral compass on the ground can thus get easily lost, or the consequences for following it too onerous.

At Guantánamo, institutional segregation of psychiatrists from interrogation served as an attempt to insulate clinicians from knowledge of specific interrogation plans. But consider, again, the case of Al-Dossari. At various times, as his psychological conditions worsened, he requested help from mental health clinicians both with his release from the extreme isolation of Camp 5 (the maximum-security center) and with access to meaningful social contact. According to his attorney, their reply was that they could do nothing and that he had to speak to his interrogator. The point relevant for us is that there is often seepage of information across institutional lines. Even if clinicians do not breach confidential records to interrogation teams, there may be a flow in the other direction, with information about the ordeals a patient has endured coming to clinicians. In this case a clinician was aware of a detainee's reports of suicidal depression, presumably induced to some degree by detention conditions, and yet made clinical treatment secondary to the interrogation plan. The clinician's duty was subordinated to the interrogator's role. The more general point is that clinicians, though not in interrogational roles, are not necessarily ignorant of what goes on in interrogation and confinement. In ignoring that information, they cede their professional obligation to give adequate and appropriate mental care.

One final vignette from my trip to Guantánamo is relevant to our concerns. At the time of the visit, seven detainees were on hunger strike, a steep drop from the higher numbers the previous summer. We were assured that the hunger strikers were being treated humanely. The commanding physician at the time, Capt. John Edmonson, showed our group a tube used for feeding—a thin nasogastric tube, a 10-French Dobhoff—and explained that lubrication and anesthesia were routinely used before insertion. The senior military and civilian physicians listened attentively as they were told of overall "compliance" in that most strikers did not forcibly resist insertion of the tubes or remove them once they were in place. Not one physician asked about the consequences of not acquiescing to the insertion of the tube; none openly worried that acquiescence might not be the same thing as consent; none voiced the concern that pulling out a nose tube funneled down the back of one's throat to the top of one's stomach might, in some circumstances, be painful, and that failure to do that might at best be a weak form of consent. Here, medical and technical talk about equipment displaced responsible moral discourse about care. It shielded an elite group of DOD civilian and military medical leaders from asking themselves the hard questions about whether what they were doing was right.

The scene is disturbing in light of confirmed reports, just four months after my visit, that striking detainees had been strapped into restraint chairs during and immediately after force-feeding in order to prevent, according to officials, purging and asphyxiation that might result from being fed in a prostrate position. Some detainees alleged that while in the chair they were force-fed not only nutrients but also diuretics and laxatives. The result was that they urinated and defecated on themselves. The allegations raise serious questions about the role of physicians in authorizing the procedure. If diuretics and laxatives were used, who approved their use? I later raised this question with a senior medical official in the Pentagon but never received an answer on the specific issue. The question remains: Was this practice approved by those at the head of the chain of command—namely, the army surgeon general and assistant secretary of defense for health affairs, who are ultimately "charged with assuring quality medical care for all beneficiaries of the DOD, including detainees and prisoners of war"? Did physicians at lower levels or mental health workers raise questions about the degrading and dehumanizing methods used for force-feeding? Were they bothered?

This is not to assess the morality of force-feeding itself. It may well be that many hunger strikers are not in the position to think carefully and reflectively through the consequences of their actions. They are without family contact and consultation from spiritual counselors. Some have spent months in isolation. Others have endured repeated physical and psychological abuse. They are not in conditions that promote autonomy. In such circumstances, force-feeding may be a humane option, although a far more humane approach would be to ameliorate the background conditions that deprive them of more meaningful autonomy.

What becomes salient not only in this discussion of health professionals, but also in the discussion of Longworth's case, is that torture is rarely solo work. It is a systematic practice, institutionalized by nations and states, supported hierarchically, and requiring the participation of professionals of many stripes. The collective nature of the enterprise works to diffuse ownership of actions. Still, collective ends involve individual, intentional participation, however peripheral or central that participation might be. Achieving these ends entails complicitous action, in varying degrees. Insulation through bureaucratic divisions of role, use of euphemism, and absorption in scientific detail and technique may explain moral numbing, but it doesn't doesn't excuse it. Furthermore, even nonclinical health professionals have strong moral professional duties and moral influence. Detainees are not the only ones who may undergo transference in the presence of a powerful interrogator. Interrogators can also undergo that same kind of unconscious influence in the presence of an adviser who has pedigree and polish.

At issue, ultimately, are demands on moral character: how to be effective without being ruthless; how to build trust without betraying it; how to foster meaningful relationships without taking unfair advantage of their intimacy. The business of gathering "human" intelligence is not without moral risk. Interrogators face these moral risks, as do the professionals who support their work. Moral insulation is one response. Honest struggle with the moral burdens of profession and conscience is another.

CHAPTER 6

IN THE FACE
OF TORTURE

THE TORTURE VICTIM AS
"PROFESSIONAL STOIC"

Some soldiers, like Will Quinn, are interrogators. Others are interrogated, and the unlucky among them are tortured. One account of torture I know fairly well is that of Vice Adm. James Stockdale, the naval aviator and senior POW who spent more than seven years in the Hanoi Hilton during the Vietnam War. At the Naval Academy, I read his accounts, taught from them, and watched many midshipmen and officers become inspired by them. I met Stockdale several times, once on the occasion of inaugurating a symposium series in his honor at the University of San Diego. My book *Stoic Warriors* was motivated, in no small way, by his embrace of Stoicism and its influence on the military. In writing that book, I wanted to know what kind of resilience ancient and popularized Stoicism offered that the military found so attractive.

In June 1997, well before I had even conceived the idea for that book, Stockdale sent me a signed copy of his *Thoughts of a Philosophical Fighter Pilot*. I pulled the book off the shelf recently, and a handwritten note tumbled out. Stockdale wrote that he had read about my work as the first

Distinguished Chair of Ethics at the Naval Academy in the alumni magazine and was "delighted" that my students were "becoming acquainted with writings on Stoicism, and Epictetus, in particular." He praised my work, gave me a "roadmap" of the territory covered in his book, and volunteered a "classroom appearance" if it would be of help. Maybe unconsciously the letter was in my mind as I went on to write *Stoic Warriors*. But quite frankly, I am not sure I had even seen the letter until just now.

Jim Stockdale died in the summer of 2005, a month after *Stoic Warriors* was published. The last time we met was in October 2001, the day after the United States invaded Afghanistan in response to the September 11 attacks. There was no Guantánamo Detention Center yet, nor had the public heard of prisons at Bagram or Abu Ghraib. The accounts most familiar in public discourse were of our own soldiers who had been tortured, including Stockdale and John McCain, during the Vietnam War. Little did they know that the stain of torture, this time enacted by Americans, would be part of the legacy of Operation Enduring Freedom, and later, Operation Iraqi Freedom.

While writing *Stoic Warriors*, I flew out to California to meet Stockdale in person. I went to the Stockdales' home on a tree-lined street in Coronado, just outside San Diego. His wife and co-author of *In Love and War*, Sybil, was at the time healthy and robust (she is now confined to a wheelchair), and she popped in and out of the conversation as she served us coffee and home-baked cookies. Sybil was a force of nature in her own right. She had advocated tirelessly for the protections of the Geneva Accords on behalf of the men in the Hanoi Hilton. By 1968, thoroughly disenchanted with the "keep quiet" policy of the United States toward its POWs, she organized a national committee of wives of downed pilots. One year later, she was face-to-face in a private meeting with President Nixon's secretary of defense, Melvin Laird, whom she convinced that the official silence about American POWs needed to end.

As we sat at the dining room table, Stockdale's left leg jut out from the hip socket at a 60-degree angle as it had for some thirty-five years. It had been badly broken when he was shot down on September 9, 1965, by the North Vietnamese and pummeled on the ground by a street gang. On the day he was shot down, Stockdale uttered prescient words to himself: "Five years down there at least, I'm leaving behind the world of technology and entering the world of Epictetus." As a young officer, Stockdale had enrolled in graduate studies in international relations at Stanford, but, as he said, his "heart wasn't in it." How governments worked was tedious stuff for him. "I had been beating back systems for years." And so he found himself migrating over to the philosophy department for an elective course. Philosophy caught his imagination, and before deploying to Vietnam, his professor, Philip Rhinelander, handed him as a parting gift Epictetus's *Enchiridion* (the Greek means "ready at hand," hence, the *Handbook*). The text looked esoteric. "What would a martini-drinking aviator want with a book like this?" he mused at the time, and chuckled as he thought back to the moment. But despite the initial chilly response, he made the *Handbook* his bedtime reading while aboard the USS *Ticonderoga*. Before long, he had committed it to memory and absorbed its lessons.

Epictetus was a slave, probably by birth rather than by seizure, in the outer reaches of the Roman Empire in Phrygia, or modern-day south-western Turkey. Born in the middle of the first century of the Common Era, he was acquired by a prominent secretary in the court of Nero, who permitted him as a slave to attend lectures in Rome by a preeminent Stoic, Musonius Rufus. With Musonius's blessings, Epictetus, ultimately emancipated, began a teaching career of his own, and after the expulsion of philosophers from Rome by the emperor Domitian, he continued teaching philosophy in Nicopolis in western Greece. Like Socrates, Epictetus was an oral philosopher who left nothing in his own hand. What is extant are four of the eight volumes of the lecture notes of his devoted student Arrian, compiled as the *Discourses*. The slender *Handbook* is a collection of the pithiest of Epictetus's teachings.

As a slave, Epictetus may well have been subject to the common treatment of slaves in ancient Rome: punitive torture by masters for small infractions and state-sanctioned judicial torture to extract confessions about masters suspected of political plots. (Who better than a slave would know what the master was up to?) Epictetus's repeated message is that there is freedom even in bondage. With proper practice and therapy, we can expand our orbit of control, understanding what is and what is not "up to us," and how what is up to us is the sole source of our well-being. "Our opinions are up to us, and our impulses, desires, aversions—in short, whatever is our own doing. Our bodies are not up to us, nor are our possessions, our reputations, or our public offices."

Stockdale relied on these teachings during his seven and a half years of imprisonment in North Vietnam, two and a half of which were spent in solitary confinement. As head of the chain of command of POWs in the Hanoi Hilton, he made Stoicism the backbone of his leadership style. Though he never preached or tried to convert others to Stoicism (including Sybil), it was his own personal mode of survival. At the time of his imprisonment, Stockdale knew there was an irony in his lame left leg. Epictetus had one as well, perhaps as the result of torture. That day in Coronado, with his leg jutting out, Stockdale quoted from memory Epictetus's teaching on lameness: "Lameness is an impediment to the leg, not to the will; and say this to yourself with regard to everything that happens. For you will find such things to be an impediment to something else, but not truly to yourself." Stockdale embraced and continued to embrace the Stoic lesson that self-sufficiency was sustainable, however infirm a body and however cruel the torturer's tools.

Others in prison have turned in less explicit ways to Stoic armor. Consider Jacobo Timerman, an Argentine Jew who was editor and publisher of the newspaper *La Opinion* from 1971 until the time of his arrest, in April 1977, by an extremist faction of the Argentine army. He was held captive for thirty months and tortured and interrogated inside the army's clandestine prisons. He offers advice for those who may face torture: "Memory is the chief enemy of the solitary tortured man—nothing is more dangerous at such moments. But I managed to develop certain passivity-inducing devices for withstanding torture and anti-memory devices for those long hours in the solitary cell. I refused to remember anything that bore on life experience—I was a *professional stoic* dedicated to this task."

As Timerman fashions it, "professional stoicism" is a "mechanism of withdrawal" that helped him avoid lapsing into "that other mechanism of tortured solitary prisoners"—namely, rapport building with a jailor or torturer. It allowed him to cast aside "all logical emotions and sensations—fear, hatred, vengeance—for any emotion or sensation meant wasting useless energy." Memories of his wife and children, and emotional longings for them, could be viewed only as "penetration from the outside world" that a victim of torture cannot afford to indulge. "The image of my wife's face is unbearable in this place." To survive, he had to imagine himself a "blind architect," reconstructing a world from the stimuli of his new, perverted environment—the moans and hysterical screams, the odor of the latrine that matches his own skin's stench, the violent sound of metal and barking dogs, the constant shouting of guards meant to "intimidate and confuse prisoners."

More recently, a colleague of mine at the Woodrow Wilson International Center for Scholars, and director of its Middle East Program, Haleh Esfandiari, described a similar approach she took to enduring three months of solitary imprisonment at the notorious Evin prison in Iran in 2007. While visiting her ninety-three-year-old mother in Tehran, Haleh, a sixty-seven-year-old who holds dual American and Iranian citizenship, was detained on political charges of fomenting a velvet revolution in Iran through her work at the Wilson Center. During her months of captivity, she said she kept her sanity, in part, by trying not to think of "my husband, my daughter, and my grandchildren. That would lead me to despair." Once a week she was served an Iranian dish of lentils and rice that is her young granddaughters' favorite. She refused dinner on those nights because the association with the children was too painful. The memories she *did* allow were of her long-deceased grandmother, about whom she wrote a nearly complete biography in her head. To dwell on these memories, of someone whose loss had been resolved long ago for her, would neither raise hopes nor create despair. Haleh was stoic in her own fashion, "disciplined," she tells me, from her years as a journalist, when she had learned to write in large noisy rooms, shutting out other people and their din. Given her age, she also took comfort in the thought that her loss would not disrupt the fabric of her family. There were no small children at home who depended on her. Still, there were places she could not go in her mind if she was to endure. Her job was to control where and what her mind visited.

Stockdale's, Timerman's, and Esfandiari's stories return me again to ancient Stoicism, in particular, the ancient ideal of Stoic detachment. How plausible is Stoic armor as a protection against the deprivation of military (or, as in Esfandiari's and Timerman's case, political) imprisonment? Of course, not everyone turns to it, explicitly or implicitly. As Stockdale put it to me, other Vietnam POWs "had their ducks lined up in other ways." For some, it was their faith or religion that kept them going. In a parallel way, in Guantánamo and Abu Ghraib, the Muslim call to prayer is a time and place for strengthening spirit and resolve. Still, among the American soldiers I have spoken to, stoic resilience, in some form or other, retains its allure. And often it is modeled on ancient teachings. The leadership often read Epictetus. And they read Stockdale on Epictetus. Some read the emperor-philosopher Marcus Aurelius. (One West Point colonel said apologetically to a Georgetown colleague that he didn't read much philosophy himself, but does read Marcus Aurelius's *Meditations* several times a year.) Sucking it up, or being stoic, is as much part of the military ethos as ever, and the writings of the Roman Stoics provide some of the details. Torture is an extreme case for testing Stoic ideals.

But can Stoicism protect against a fundamental vulnerability that torture aims to lay bare—that the victim will break at some point and use her will against herself in acts of collusion and self-betrayal? An interrogator's job is to build trust in order to exploit it. Can Stoicism protect against the sense of complicity and shame of yielding to an interrogator's will?

STOIC LESSONS ON THE EMOTIONS

For Stockdale, Stoic consolations were a way of strengthening will and regulating unwanted emotions. To survive and lead, he needed to be free of debilitating despair and the press of appetite and attachment. To long for a cigarette or a tasty meal and to be grateful when he got it, Stockdale reminded me, was to make himself vulnerable to exploitation by his infamous interrogation team of men, who came to be known as "Pigeye," "Rabbit," and "Cat." Better to not want those things, better to detach and fortify your will against the clamoring of want and longing.

It is important to understand the ancient Stoic doctrine here. Stockdale himself, in his later years, became more and more immersed in the philosophical underpinnings of his survival tool. He joined the British philosopher of ancient philosophy Richard Sorabji in London in a seminar that focused on his "lived" life of Stoicism. He was delighted to receive a copy I sent him of A. A. Long's book on Epictetus when it first came out. He was reworking Stoicism until the end.

At the core of Stoic teaching is the doctrine that ordinary desires and satisfactions, and ordinary emotional attachments to conventional goods and family, honor, health, fortune, and the like, are disturbances from which the healthy psyche should detach. To want and need and long for, whether in detention or not, is a vulnerability that destabilizes virtue and ultimately happiness. The Stoics go further. Virtue, and virtue alone, constitutes happiness. And virtue is an expression of cultivated reason and rational self-control.

In Stockdale's own case, "taking the ropes"—that is, submitting to torture—became an act of will and self-mastery. There were things he would and would not take torture for. Stoic teachings also guided his command order that the POWs should resist the captors' use of them as propaganda before American viewers. "My mind-set was, 'We here under the gun are the experts, we are the masters of our fate. Ignore guilt-inducing echoes of hollow edicts, throw out the book, and write your own book.'" His orders came down in easy-to-remember acronyms: BACK US, short for "Don't *Bow* in public; stay off the *Air*; admit no *Crimes*; never *Kiss* them good-bye." "US" was for the "United States," but also for "us," a "unity over self."

Stoicism is about empowerment, but it can be a harsh philosophy to those who seek its consolations. One famous ancient critic of the Stoics is Cicero, writing in the century before the Common Era and a principal transmitter of the early Greek Stoics to the Latin-speaking world. He turns to Stoic self-help to cope with his profound grief at the death in childbirth of his much beloved daughter Tullia. But he's never a believer, nor is he convinced that he's really been helped. "People come eagerly expecting to hear why pain is not an evil. The Stoics tell them that pain is a tough, unpleasant burden, contrary to nature and hard to bear—but not an evil, because it involves no wrongdoing, dishonesty or vice, no blameworthiness or cause for shame. Will anyone who hears this know whether to laugh or cry? They will certainly not leave any more resolute in enduring pain than when they arrived."

The Stoics will insist that you *can* learn to detach from ordinary pleasures and pains. You can learn to regard the despair of psychological or physical pain as not a *real* evil, and as such, something that need not undermine your happiness. True, in most circumstances a Stoic sage would prefer a life off the rack rather than on it, a life liberated rather than imprisoned (and Stoics even have a technical word to signal preferences that are prudential and "in accord with nature"). But even if the rack and prison are the sage's bad fortunes, they need not derail his virtue and well-being. For they are external conditions, not things he *does* but things that are *done to him*. As such, they don't impugn his virtue. You don't *do* wrong when you suffer evil at others' hands, as Socrates had propounded earlier. Moreover, with the right philosophical and emotional training, a sage can understand what is really important and get beyond emotions, which are reactions to things outside one's control.

But what requires probing is that thesis: Is it reasonable to assume that in conditions of detention, the POW or detainee, even the strongest, remains morally invulnerable to another's cruelty? Won't he feel some dread at being exposed to yet more torture, some sense of betrayal or shame at saying more than he wished he had when subjected to the torturer's tools?

Seneca along with other Stoics, such as Philo Judaeus and Aulus Gellius, concede that even the most resolute and trained Stoics will still experience involuntary jolts and startle to things outside their control. They are residual tendencies—"preemotions," as they call them—to become aroused by intense external stimuli that we cannot fully eliminate, however hard we row the Stoic "oars of dialectic." There is that "first mental jolt which affects us when we think ourselves wronged," Seneca explains, indicating a preemotion of anger. It "steals upon us." The phenomena are familiar. Consider the shiver that runs through your body when you are startled by a loud noise, or the involuntary racing of your heart when you narrowly avoid a collision while driving.

But first feelings, like starts and startles, are not full emotions, according to the Stoics. They lack "the mind's assent" necessary for a full-throated emotion. The sage who experiences them knows how to nip them in the bud by withholding assent from the provocative impressions or appearances that are at their base. Similarly, we know, when we are startled or avoid a crash, that there is no real reason for continued fear, no *real* evil or *real* threat, even if our body is reacting as if there were.

Yet it is unlikely that even the most resolute subjects can regain full mental control after experiencing prolonged or violent versions of these jolts. Torture is a lab for just that kind of experiment. And while training in extreme stress conditions may minimize fear, it is unlikely to completely eliminate it. Indeed, there is a substantive difference between prolonged or harsh exposure to what psychologists call "traumatic stressors" and more titrated exposures in relatively controlled or simulated conditions, such as at training schools for surviving torture, like the U.S. SERE (Survival, Evasion, Resistance, Escape) program at Fort Bragg. It is not hard to imagine that even the most resilient Stoic would suffer degraded capacities for resistance after chronic exposure to the tools of terror in non-pretend situations, where the victim knows he is in true enemy hands and there is no knowledge that the torture will end soon.

Seneca himself suggests the limits of Stoicism in the face of the cruelest torture. Although ever eager to dismiss most types of fear as idle, and insistent that "rehearsal" of dreaded situations can remove much of their shock and awe, he singles out torture, particularly its "visuals"— the "spectacle" and "paraphernalia" of "the violence of the stronger"—as dreaded by the toughest of us. "It is not surprising, then, if our greatest terror is of such a fate."

Seneca is prescient on *why* the spectacle of torture can psychologically traumatize its victims. "Displays" of imminent and intimate brutality "coerce and master the mind," leaving us powerless, he says. They over-whelm the human capacity for coping. The brute and violent images—"the disemboweled entrails of men," "human limbs torn apart by chariots," "the cross," "the rack," "the hook," "the stake"—all are meant to convey that human sensory and reactive capacities can absorb only so much before shutting down in terror. Seneca anticipates the point that psychiatrist Judith Herman makes forcefully in her landmark 1992 book, *Trauma and Recovery*. Certain threats and encounters with vio-lence are traumatic "because they overwhelm the ordinary human adap-tations to life."

Seneca has in mind not only interrogational torture but also torture that serves as punishment, spectacle, or simply, a brute sadistic need. It is likely that non-interrogational torture is harder to endure than torture aimed at extracting intelligence, for in the latter case, the victim may believe, correctly or not, that he has some control in stopping the tor-ture. But the principal point to stress is Seneca's acknowledgment that some impressions of dread lead not only to jolts and shocks, but to full-blooded terror in most of us. Even if the responses are involuntary, even if we call them preludes to real emotions, they nonetheless grip, last, and are not easily thrown overboard.

"There are no virgins here," Stockdale famously told a POW who felt tremendous shame for having broken when he "took the ropes." The spe-cifics of this modern ordeal are not likely to be in the public imagina-tion. Stockdale rehearses just what he went through. What strikes me, as I listen, is the utter banality of the torturer's techniques: "They would start by clanging a big heavy iron bar [about eighty or ninety pounds in weight] down, and then tie your feet to it so that you couldn't lift it. Then they'd sit you up and jackknife you over and tighten the ropes around your arms. Next, they'd put you through extortions to the point that they would be pulling the rope so hard that the blood circulation in your upper chest would shut off." At this point, the guard would then dig his heels into the back of your head and push your nose into the cement. With panic and claustrophobia setting in, the prisoners could be made to blurt out information, some of which would be false, but other bits of which would be true. The confession was followed by a "cold soak"—six or eight weeks of total isolation "to contemplate one's crimes."

In the context of this ordeal, Stockdale's comment that "there are no virgins here" is more than just a palliative. It is an insistence that the shame this POW feels is morally apt and reasonable. It is a decent person's response to being coerced to do what is ignominious. Moreover, the fact that a victim feels shame for breaking does not mean that *others* should see him as morally culpable, even if he appears so in his own eyes.

Not surprisingly, the Stoics offer little guidance on this kind of feeling, proffering more concrete lessons in how to *avoid* entrapment with evil and even allowing that there are recalibrated, enlightened emotions that go with the avoidance. One "good" emotion they endorse is "rational wariness," an empowering alternative to crippling fear. Stockdale created his own version of it, modeling himself like Solzhenitsyn's Ivan Denisovich—a "slow moving cagey prisoner" who could outthink the torturer and anticipate evil before it befell him. Another POW kept a long list of dead baseball players in his head (apparently, an old American POW technique) so he could quickly spout out names when his captors demanded intelligence. All this is a kind of Stoic moxie survivors learn for keeping torturers' corrupting forces at bay. Holocaust survivors, such as Jean Améry and Primo Levi, tell of how clever use of their skills kept them alive, though those skills did not always spare them moral corrosion and the awful sense that they were living on the edge of an amoral state of nature. Similarly, it is unreasonable to think that even in the case of the Stockdales of this world, wily caution can *fully* eliminate breaks, missteps, and the desperate vulnerability that detention and torture seek to instill. The toughest warriors need to anticipate the limits of the will as well as what the will can steel itself against.

And so there will have to be a place for the shame and guilt of revealing information, and also the shame of coming to see oneself with contempt through the eyes of the torturer. When I taught at the Naval Academy, my midshipmen, "youngsters" or sophomores, repeatedly said that what they feared the most, were they to become POWs, was the shame of breaking and the sense of betrayal that would come with it. To compromise the mission or their mates because they capitulated under torture was absolutely mortifying to them. They had trouble talking about it in class; it was almost as if it were a place they couldn't force their minds to go to. In a strict Stoic world, this is a place you don't have to go to. If, in fact, coercion and the duress of circumstances do force your hand, then you have not really been compromised. It is, as Epictetus says, "nothing to me," nothing for which to feel shame.

But this was small comfort for my students, and I suspect for most who are up against a torturer. Even if it is duress, soldiers need instruction about the anguish of being caught in its grip—in the helplessness of torture or cruel, inhumane, and degrading treatment, of being forced to do or endure things that are profoundly demeaning (recall here the cases reported to have occurred at Guantánamo, such as that of a Muslim male detainee who was chained to the floor while a woman interrogator smeared what appeared to be menstrual blood on his face). Simply put, and morally speaking, soldiers need to be able to feel and acknowledge not only emotions of empowerment, but also their opposite, and at times, the self-torture that comes with torture.

THE BODY IN PAIN

There is another way to cast the protection of Stoicism in torture. And this is through the Stoic's radical view of the body. Epictetus insists that physical torture cannot really harm you because your body is not really you. On or off the rack, the body is an "indifferent," something apart from both self and ultimate happiness. For the Stoic, there is no notion of what Sigmund Freud will later call "the bodily ego," the idea of a person embodied, with the body as the frontier of self. Rather the body, for Epictetus, is more of a disembodied medium in which things just happen passively. Pain may be in your body, but *you* are "out of body," to give it the modern gloss. "Our body, then, is not our own, but subject to everything stronger than itself," teaches Epictetus. "Do you not know that it is a slave to fever, gout, eye-disease, dysentery; to a tyrant[?]" It is just a "poor," "overburdened ass" weighted down by its physical needs and baggage, so many "bridles, pack-saddles, shoes, barley, fodder for the ass. Let these go." The humor and hyperbole are Epictetus as Socratic gadfly for his young listeners. But the general view is in earnest.

Cicero registers a blunt complaint about the call for bodily detachment. The Stoics "show concern for nothing but the mind, as if human beings had no body." "When it comes to a happy life," he complains, the Stoics argue that "the amount of bodily advantage has no relevance at all." Stockdale, in his own writings, registered a similar complaint about the Stoics' unreasonable marginalization of the body and its pain.

Still, there is something appealing in the idea of experiencing pain passively, whether through Stoic detachment or other forms of dissociation. Here the experiences of victims of rape and child abuse shed some light on enduring torture. Wynona Ward, a lawyer and advocate for abused women and herself a victim of repeated sexual child abuse, told me once that after a car accident in which she badly injured her leg, she reported to the doctor that she was experiencing no pain at all. Her leg did not even seem to be a part of her. She explained this to me as an attitude of disembodiment that she had internalized after years of abuse by her father. Another victim described "depersonalization" aptly to her therapist. She saw her childhood abuse from the vantage point of someone "floating on the ceiling," detached and dissociated from the site of unbearable pain. Out of body, she could watch passively, as a spectator, safe and distant.

However for other victims of rape and abuse, shame and complicity are the predominant feelings, even if there is also detachment or dissociation. They experience the conflict of being forcibly and brutally acted upon, without consent or the possibility of retaliation, *yet* feeling like a player in the drama, acquiescent, giving parts of their body to another for abuse. The passivity/complicity poles produce a sense of disgust and shame—disgust at the alienated and polluted body that can long bear the marks of someone else's brutal will, and shame that through comportment, appearance, or gesture, they have been agents in the act, however compromised that personal agency is. In other cases, the shame is not so much about complicity as about a failure to block an *impression* of complicity.

Torture often reveals a similar inner conflict. In addition to the physical and psychological pain of torture, there is the moral anguish of experiencing oneself as complicit in the torture. Torture subjects view themselves as accepting the terms of their existence and as at once resisters and partners in their own cruel torture. Consider the remarks of a freed Guantánamo detainee from Britain, who described the kind of actions that landed him in solitary isolation for a month. He said he had been punished for "hogging" an apple at mealtime. He "hogged" it, he explained, because he thought he might become "peckish" later on. His words are telling. What he describes here is a kind of complicity, the complicity of accepting the complete patheticness of being reduced to justifying his ravenousness in terms of his future desires. He forced himself to be accountable for a reasonable response to the press of his bodily needs. But he knows in the perverted world of his detention, no rational account will excuse. He did what he wasn't supposed to do. He lives in two worlds: one in which he rebels against the perverted sense of justice in order to keep sane, another in which he is forced to accept its rules and regulate his most basic wants and needs according to its logic. In the end, he makes himself accountable.

The conflict suggests that resisting torture is not primarily or simply a matter of dissociating from bodily or psychological pain. Torture invokes a sense of personal and moral agency in the very experience of helplessness. The victim is not *just* a victim. There is engagement, a feeling of accountability for what is happening. In this sense it is an environment, *par excellence*, in which to be Stoic and show effort and mastery, an environment in which to be cautious and wary, and deny that *real* moral evil is happening. It is also an environment of severely *compromised* personal agency, where the victim experiences himself as both internalizing the perverted governance and attitudes of torturers and being frustrated in his ability to resist them. It is an environment of shame.

The body and what is done to it are not so easily split off from the will, even when that will is coerced in the worst way. We are bodily beings, subject to the reactions, desires, and injuries inherent in our bodies, however much we protect ourselves by techniques of disembodiment.

Torture and Self-Betrayal

Stoic detachment from the body and ordinary emotions is an attempt to bolster self-mastery and minimize the use of self against self. In Jim Stockdale's own Stoic lab in the prison in Hanoi, he seized moments for mastery and resistance. He did sit-ups in leg irons, commanded an active chain-of-command within the cell block from solitary confinement, devised ways to bloody himself so he would not be paraded on TV as a propaganda item, instructed others on how to resist in similar ways—much of this conveyed through code tapped on walls, swished in the sound of brushes against the inside of a crap bucket, and so on.

These are all acts of defiance, attempts to resist the collusion and rapport that the torturer or interrogator wants so desperately as the preferred method of conducting business. Haleh Esfandiari similarly speaks of doing rigorous step exercises for hours on end each day. She washed her clothes each day and hung them out to dry; she dressed in a clean T-shirt and pants for dinner daily, like a British schoolgirl, though this was for a meal in solitary confinement. Being in charge of ritual and decorum was her way to restore her dignity. Jacobo Timerman, too, describes trying to resist the wished-for image of the torturer as omnipotent, as the author of ever-new ignominious forms of torture and degradation that could fully subordinate him. But he concedes, in some cases, in "unimportant matters," "it's best to acknowledge and accept the torturer's omnipotence."

His point is that some acquiescence to the torturer's omnipotence will not be self-annihilating; other moments of compliance may. It is a matter of selective acceptance (and at times, strategic acceptance—a matter of giving the torturer a little leverage).

But of course the choices aren't always a person's own, and some moments pick themselves and force collusion without particular caution or wariness. Consider being prevented from exercising control of bodily functions that are typically loci of self-control. From detainees just released from Guantánamo, I have heard some speak of their ordeals of being "processed" for eight to ten hours by U.S. troops at Bagram airfield base, where they were skimpily dressed in freezing cold weather, made to walk in circles with bare feet on sand mixed with shards of glass, denied use of toilets, urinating and defecating on themselves, and then shackled in stress positions for a ten-hour flight to Guantánamo Bay, hooded, eyes taped, and again, denied permission to relieve themselves, except on themselves.

Peeing or shitting on yourself, because you are denied more decent forms of relief, is a salient form of experiencing yourself as an agent, a doer, without agency—you *let yourself* do it. The case is neither like that of a toddler who has not yet mastered bladder control nor like that of an infirm person who has lost it. This is actively *doing it* (and of willfully controlling it up to a certain point), and yet it is *being made to do it*. It is experiencing oneself as helpless in one's adult agency. It is humiliating and it is regressive.

Here, what is vulnerable is the will and the psychological distress of using that will against yourself. Even if you are somehow dissociated from your body and its pain, as a trained Stoic may be, and identified, rather, with your capacity to make choices guided by virtue and reason, this is still an affront. It is a misuse of your will and power to choose. You are consigned to use your agency in a betrayal of what you know, in principle, is still a matter of your control.

"The chair," a device used in force-feeding hunger strikers in Guantánamo, presents a slightly different case of force and collusion. A decision to go on hunger strike is itself a complicated matter, and depending on varying circumstances, it may or may not be an autonomous or reflective choice. But assume a hunger striker makes the choice to strike in a modestly reflective way and *accepts* or, better, *acquiesces to* the consequence, in the sense of not forcibly protesting the anesthetized insertion of a feeding tube in the nose. In such cases, the victim is unlikely to have accepted as part of the anticipated bargain that he would be strapped to a chair, prevented from movement or purging, force-fed diuretics and laxatives, and then forced to urinate and defecate on himself. Here the issue, again, is less about physical pain than about a particular form of psychological and moral anguish—namely, anguish directed at the perversion of your will, experienced as if it had been brought about (at least partially) by your own hands. A cruel mockery is made of the victim's attempt to take charge of his body by a hunger strike. Inserting a feeding tube is itself a way to undermine that agency. Making the victim then defecate on himself is a way of getting him to experience himself as colluding in the mockery.

Here, a scene from J. M. Coetzee's *Waiting for the Barbarians* illuminates. The reflections are those of the old South African magistrate, who as punishment for consorting with a tribal woman, becomes the victim of state torture, like the tribal barbarians over whom he once ruled:

> In my suffering there is nothing ennobling. . . . What I am made
> to undergo is subjection to the most rudimentary needs of my
> body: to drink, to relieve itself, to find the posture in which it
> is least sore. . . . My torturers were not interested in degrees of
> pain. They were interested only in demonstrating to me what
> it meant to live in a body, as a body, a body which can enter-
> tain notions of justice only as long as it is whole and well, which
> very soon forgets them when its head is gripped and a pipe is
> pushed down its gullet and pints of salt water are poured into it
> till it coughs and retches and flails and voids itself.

Coetzee describes a version of "the water cure," or what the drowning torture was euphemistically called by American troops who practiced it in the Philippines at the turn of the nineteenth century. "Waterboarding" is its newer name, but the practice is at least as old as the Spanish Inquisition. The point, Coetzee writes, is to reduce the victim to a body that gasps for air and craves only to breathe and to stop the suffocation. The torturer takes away the most basic areas of human functioning and control—breathing, drinking, urinating, and defecating. And in being robbed by another of what a person could otherwise and "should" otherwise be able to control, the victim is mocked and humiliated in his helplessness.

To this sort of scenario, Epictetus instructs that we ought to practice greater detachment. We should say of our body, and of the persons who torture, "they are nothing to me." In short, we should practice the indifference (or the dissociation) that trauma itself might induce. That indifference may at times be adaptive in enduring torture and ordeals, though current evidence suggests the contrary, that extreme dissociation may exacerbate traumatic symptoms afterwards. Perhaps this is so because it perverts a healthy sense of how we live in bodies that *we*, and not evil outsiders such as omnipotent tormentors, use to express our intentions, emotions, and will. Even when a tormentor has control, individuals may still feel they betray themselves by the very fact that another *can* control them.

In this way, a broadly Stoic view may still leave the torture victim vulnerable to being forced *to use herself against herself* in the most degrading ways. To claim that this is viable mastery just because it is a use of one's own will is a perversion of what mastery is about. Stoic armor is not fully impervious. Full Stoic control, in some circumstances, is neither humanly possible nor advisable.

STOIC LESSONS FOR THE TORTURER

Perhaps not surprisingly, Stoicism's more durable lesson is in staving off the temptation to inflict torture rather than in learning to endure it in a bulletproof way. The point seems an obvious one. After all, that is what virtue is about—avoiding evil. But there are still questions to be settled.

In symposia on my work, some have argued that military immersion in Stoic culture trains for torture. In a more popular version of the argument, training in torture-resistance schools (such as SERE) offers as much a lesson in becoming a torturer as it does in surviving torture. It is easy to see a flaw in this argument, but it is worth pointing it out in Stoic terms.

Stoicism teaches toughening and detachment from the body *not* so that a person can become indifferent to intentionally inflicting harm on others, but so that she can better endure personal frailty. Of course any skill may be used for good or ill. This is a cornerstone of Socratic teaching. The Stoics are committed to the related thesis that "indifferents"—external phenomena that we should relinquish our desire to control—are so precisely because they are not unconditionally good or evil in their own right. Their goodness depends on regulation by virtue or wisdom. The skills of resistance in the hands of the wrong person can lead to torture. Similarly, as we saw earlier, the medical science of trauma in the hands of a psychologist advising on torture becomes a tool not of healing but of harming. The Stoics are far from simpleminded about the challenge of subordinating such goods to the work of virtue. Indeed, here is where Stoic notions of "good" emotions may play their strongest role: A good person feels and registers the pull of institutional pressures and the forces of others' evil. But for her, it is a moment to beware and take stock rather than to be afraid and capitulate to pressures. It is a moment to hold tight to personal virtue. Still, the cost of standing one's ground may be high. And the Stoics may indeed underestimate just what enduring others' evil may involve.

III

THE WAR AFTER THE WAR

CHAPTER 7

———— ✦ ————

LOOSENING THE STOIC ARMOR

THE AFTERLIFE OF WAR

When Maj. Tony DeStefano returned home from Operation Iraqi Freedom, he thought he had "survived the war scot-free." As a forty-eight-year-old Army reservist and electronic signals expert, he deployed to Egypt and then Kuwait in the wake of 9/11, to lay the communication infrastructure for troops bound for Afghanistan and Iraq. In the winter of 2002, he was in charge of coordinating communications at the critical military port at Al Shuayba, Kuwait. About the same time, he also helped to set up the telemedicine circuits for transmitting medical data and expertise from Landstuhl Regional Medical Center in Germany and Walter Reed Army Medical Center in Washington, D.C., to local medical facilities in the theater. A year or so later, he coordinated the signal tracking for hundreds of coalition ships and aircraft for integration into the Operation Iraqi Freedom battle plan. For his work on this, he received the Joint Service Commendation Medal. He was at the top of his game.

In August 2003, just shy of two years after first deploying to the Middle East, Tony returned home to New Jersey with a respiratory condition, probably from inhaling fine sand in the scorching desert winds, and a back injury from an accident that happened while he was on duty. Otherwise, things seemed more or less all right. Then one night, about eight months later, he and his wife, Noi, went out to celebrate her birthday. The two of them went to a romantic Italian restaurant. But the background chatter of diners slowly started to bother him, he remembers. All of a sudden, a loud noise sent him into a panic attack. "Two seconds, two seconds, the missile is two seconds from killing us," he began screaming in the restaurant.

Noi's birthday falls close to the anniversary of a failed Iraqi missile attack at Camp Doha (where Tony was stationed) on March 27, 2003. When Tony first told me about the incident, he pulled a Palm Pilot from his pocket. The screen brought up a digital photo of an Al-Samoud missile, which was like the one with a massive payload that had narrowly missed his headquarters, thanks to a Patriot missile interception. "If it had hit I would have been annihilated," Tony said, staring at the screen. "There would not be enough of me to find to bury."

For Tony, the close call was as good as a hit. The trauma left him deeply scarred. Complex factors about susceptibility and resilience, as well as an individual's history of trauma and stress exposure, combine to determine a person's reaction to traumatic events. Moreover, most psychologists since the time of Pierre Janet and Sigmund Freud have agreed that traumatic responses are imprinted and stored in memory differently from more ordinary emotions. They are typically laid down nonverbally and dissociated from other experiences, making conceptual and linguistic integration difficult. As noted trauma researcher Bessel A. van der Kolk states, "Every contemporary study of traumatic memories has essentially corroborated Janet's and Freud's initial observations that traumatic memories persist primarily as implicit, behavioral and somatic memories. . . . For over a century it has been understood that traumatic experiences can leave indelible emotional memories." The consequence is that traumatized individuals repeat and relive their traumatic memories, reexposing themselves to their original traumas. Hyperarousal and other responses, which humans have adapted to deal with violent and unexpected situations (including "fight or flight" instincts, in layman's terms), are triggered by the traumatic memory, but are maladaptive now that the original dangerous stimulus is no longer present

Before their night out, neither Tony nor Noi knew much about flashbacks, anniversary or otherwise. Then the flashbacks started coming more regularly, often set off by car alarms or sirens. Tony began to have trouble concentrating at work, burned his hand in a flash electric accident, and felt like "just another employee," no longer the "major in the Army" engaged in "life and death" missions. At home, he snapped at Noi and his young teenage daughters; in the car, he drove so fast that the girls cried in fear, though they knew that this is how he had to drive in a war zone.

Tony struggled on his own for a year and a half, and then finally sought help from Veterans Affairs (VA) counselors, who sent him to Walter Reed Medical Center for war-related injuries. After more than a year there and treatment primarily for physical symptoms, Tony returned home and to his job and thought things were going to get better. But then he spiraled downward. One day, he simply couldn't rise from the breakfast table to pick up his keys to go to work. "It was like waves, then the tsunami hit," he said. He had had a massive panic attack, though he was sure it was physical—a diabetic attack, he thought. When his internist suggested he become an inpatient at the VA hospital, Tony balked at the suggestion of "going into live-in" treatment. "It would be a disgrace to the officer class," he thought. As he put it to me a year later and after a suicide attempt and multiple protracted stays at VA facilities, "We're taught to suck it up and truck on."

THE STOIC CULTURE OF THE MILITARY

For Tony, to not be stoic in the face of his agony was to fail as a warrior. The myth of the soldier is that he will be invulnerable both on the battlefield and off. Yet according to an influential study by Charles Hoge and others at Walter Reed Army Institute of Research, 30 percent of soldiers will return home from Iraq with emotional problems. Another recent report by the Army surgeon general's Mental Health Advisory Team indicates that there are steep increases in the incidence of anxiety, depression, and acute stress among combat troops sent to Iraq for third and fourth deployments. According to the study, 27 percent of noncommissioned officers (a critically important group in combat tours) suffer post-traumatic stress symptoms after three or four deployments, compared to roughly 12 percent who exhibit those symptoms after one deployment and 19 percent after a second deployment. With American military casualties from the Iraq conflict at over thirty-three thousand, and a survival-death ratio of 8.3 to 1 (compared to 3 to 1 in Vietnam), the number of those who will need physical and mental treatment is high and growing. From all reports, the military health and care system is strained, with clear impact on combat readiness. The signature injury of the current wars is traumatic brain injury (TBI), a concussive disorder caused by roadside bombs and explosions with symptoms that overlap with the psychological injuries of combat trauma.

In early 2008, the military set up the Defense Centers of Excellence for Psychological Health and Traumatic Brain Injury to better treat these wounded warriors. But some senior medical military staff I have spoken to worry about segregating centers, even under the same program, for the treatment of psychological health and traumatic brain injury. It may preserve the stigma of mental injuries, they fear. One top military medical officer told me quietly, "We're still Cartesians here. It's as if the mind and brain were totally separate." The point was delivered home at a meeting of veterans who volunteered their time and expertise to assist wounded warriors at Walter Reed. One veteran spoke as the "point man" for traumatic brain injury. He had a brain injury from combat in Vietnam. The worst thing for mentors, he suggested, would be to confuse the kind of injury he suffered with post-traumatic stress disorder (PTSD). Traumatic brain injury was a real injury, he implied; PTSD was not.

Indeed, for many in the military, psychological injury is more of a scarlet letter than a badge of honor. The issue received public attention in January 2009 when the Pentagon rejected the idea that troops suffering from PTSD might be eligible for the Purple Heart. "PTSD is an anxi-

ety disorder caused by witnessing or experiencing a traumatic event; it
is not a wound intentionally caused by the enemy from an 'outside force
or agent,' but is a secondary effect caused by witnessing or experiencing a
traumatic event," said a Defense Department spokesman. As one senior
military medical officer at the meetings told me afterward with disbelief,
"So an enemy bullet could graze the cornea of your eye and that would
be an injury by an 'outside force or agent' that could earn you a Purple
Heart!" The hardliners betrayed their real reason for the rejection at the
end of the meeting. "Who would wear it anyway?" one quipped.

Jonathan Shay, a psychiatrist who has worked with Vietnam veterans,
has long maintained that labeling psychological war trauma with the term
"disorder" is itself stigmatizing. In a joint session we presented at an international military ethics symposium, he made the point passionately. Limb
injuries incurred in war aren't called disorders, he argued. "Psychological
injuries *are* war injuries no less than the amputees' [injuries]." To think
otherwise, he insisted, does a grave disservice to the soldiers. I have argued
that Stoic and Stoic-inspired models of perfection in the military can also
reinforce the stigmatization of mental illness. Those models project super-
hero images of resilience and psychological and moral purity. Ancient
Stoicism famously divides the world into sages and fools, a binary, all-or-
nothing division. The goal is to be a Stoic sage, a wise man. Anyone who
fails this lofty goal is left a fool. Who would want to be a fool?

But there are ways to read Stoicism in the great tradition of ancient
ethics as focused less on absolute perfection and more on moral education and development. As Cicero puts it, reporting the view of the early
Greek Stoics, the learner must "row for a bit with the oars of dialectic."
Epictetus and Seneca often put the emphasis on the striving or moral
"progressing," as they call it, of the individual who may never make it to
sagehood but is willing to work hard and take philosophical therapy seriously. So Seneca, as philosophical therapist, acknowledges that he may
never reach the high bar set by his teachings: "No doctor lives here, only
a sick man."

In a parallel way, Epictetus fashions himself as a Socrates-like figure
teaching young men bent on moral improvement and sincere reflection

about character. He expects moral progress, not absolute perfection or freedom from all mistakes or defects. "Is it possible to be altogether faultless? No, that is impracticable; but it is possible to strive continuously not to commit faults. . . . We shall have cause to be satisfied if . . . we shall escape at least a few faults." In short, there are ways to soften the Stoic message. And the Stoics themselves work on it.

All this is an important reminder for the military. Striving, even extreme striving, is fine and admirable so long as it is part of an institutional culture that is not overly shaming about failures to meet high goals. And yet the military can be harsh in just that way. To be less than the best, less than what one once was, can meet with severe personal and social rebuke in a culture known to promulgate a "zero-defect" mentality. While for some, physical injuries such as limb amputations are badges of honor—visible testimony to having faced battle and sacrificed for the cause—in that same culture of conspicuous honor, suffering psychologically without visible battle wounds can feel like moral weakness. It can cause profound shame.

Consider again Tony DeStefano. When I first visited him in February 2006 at Malone House, a guesthouse converted to an inpatient unit at Walter Reed Army Medical Center, Tony did not dwell on his physical injuries. What worried him was his mental state—that he slept most of the day, was listless yet agitated, and feared he was losing his memory. He slumped in his easy chair as we talked, often rubbed his head, stared out the hospital window, and several times complained that he didn't feel "sharp." He worried that he might not be on the ball enough to return to his private-sector job in telecommunications. He often curled up into the fetal position at night, cried at the drop of a hat, and let "his appearances go." He was pretty sure he suffered from some form of post-traumatic stress, and had received helpful treatment from the Deployment Health Clinical Center at the hospital. But he had limited access to that unit. His primary physician, an officer higher in rank than he, had evaluated him and said he did not suffer from PTSD. When Tony asked for a second opinion, the doctor "chewed" him out and threatened, "If I order tests and they come back negative, I will charge you with malingering."

Tony complained, and the doctor offered his own diagnosis of narcissism and rated him zero percent for disability.

The threat was delivered around the time Tony learned that although he was selected for promotion to the rank of lieutenant colonel, he would have to retire before he could be pinned. "I was a medical file," he said, "that had to be pushed out of Walter Reed and active duty care, into the VA hopper." This, on top of the doctor's denial of his psychological condition, was humiliating. He loved the Army and served it with honor. Now he felt like he was being punished. "I understand we still have to be soldiers, but we fought for this country," Tony said tearfully.

Tony's story makes palpable the anguish of shame and shaming soldiers endure for psychological injury. Of course, the Stoic culture of the military and the internalization of harsh Stoic ideals aren't the only sources of the stigma. We live in a larger culture in which mental illness is not medically insured at parity with physical illness, despite the indisputable and acute mental suffering of many. Popular views of psychological injury as not real or as mere problems of the will abound inside and outside the military. Private and public resistance to recognizing mental illness may be on the wane, but it is far from gone.

In the case of the military, what needs destigmatizing is not just mental injury, but mental anguish. Even if soldiers don't suffer acute psychological injuries, they reasonably suffer mental and moral anguish from what they have seen and experienced. Some suffer profound grief and guilt. Yet anguish of this sort is often not respected. Within the military and civilian communities, many believe that the soldier worth his mettle can tough it out, and that toughing it out is part and parcel of moral courage.

This raises a more basic issue. Failures to meet personal ideals can bring on harsh self-rebuke in the most psychologically enlightened of us. Freud put it in terms of "ego ideals" that we internalize and try to live up to: when we fail, self-punishment is meted out by internalized authority figures—"the super-ego." But what the culture of harsh Stoicism adds is the myth of an indomitable will: We should be able to stand our ground against all foes, especially internal ones, by the right kind of mental attitude. Our opinions and desires are "up to us," Epictetus would say, whatever the externals are. But again, there are limits to what the will can endure, however much that may vary from person to person. From the view that the will is indomitable, shame for weakness and cowardice is inevitable.

Consider Tony once again. It is possible to consider Tony's failure to keep "sucking it up" in a way that does not unleash quite the same shame. If he were a thoroughgoing Stoic, maybe he'd believe that his response to the missile strike was, in fact, beyond his control. "It is nothing to me," he'd say, echoing Epictetus. "It's out of my hands." But, in fact, Tony doesn't really think matters are beyond his control. He feels that he has failed to live up to standards expected of an officer. In addition to the sense of personal deficit, Tony experiences profound social discredit. He failed to do what role and office require. The shame for having failed mixes with other symptoms of PTSD that Tony has, such as intrusive memories, hyperarousal and sleep disturbances, numbing and retreat from the world. The brew is toxic and makes for a moral and psychological wound that does not heal easily, especially in the absence of a supportive community.

Tony's story about the stigma of not being stoic enough is not isolated. I hear it often from active military personnel and veterans. And I suspect part of the appeal of my work within the military—and the reason many in the military have opened up to me—is that I am deeply attracted to Stoicism's pull, both as an intellectual tradition and as a practical philosophy, but am willing to say publicly that Stoicism can be too severe. The point has come home to me at book signings of *Stoic Warriors*, when military personnel ask me to inscribe their copies for friends or, in a case or two, for commanders who apparently take Stoicism too far. In one memorable case, a Navy captain said he had a close buddy who just could not let go of his hard, military bearing at home. He was a kind of Great Santini figure who barked out orders to his family as if he were still in command. The captain wanted his friend's children to be able to remember their father, once he was gone, as a compassionate man who could show some feeling. And so I inscribed the book, with his coaching, "To ———, who is a Stoic *and* compassionate warrior." In the back of my mind were prescient words from Shakespeare, uttered by Coriolanus, the archetypal Stoic warrior: "It is no little thing to make mine eyes to sweat compassion."

On another occasion, Walter Clark, the National Guardsman from Wisconsin convalescing at Walter Reed, wanted to talk to me about his own self-described "Stoicism." He wasn't sure it was an altogether good thing. He described to me what was essentially a Stoic way of preparing to go to war: He channeled and controlled his anger as a way of toughening himself. He tried to inoculate himself against crippling fear by rehearsing potential threats. "When you are trained to face the impossible, like getting blown up or the things that most of us would never think about . . . you become inoculated, you become numb," he explained. "I'm not afraid of anything or anybody. My normal fears have dissipated."

Now out of a war zone for the better part of a year, he was trying to let go of some of the Stoic armor, but was finding that he couldn't shed it as easily as he'd expected. "Time will tell. Time will tell. But I thought some of these things would go away, like I would regain normal fear of things, but I haven't," he said. What bothered him especially was his reaction to being mugged outside the Walter Reed complex during a morning walk. He didn't feel any fear; he just went into automatic self-defense mode and then worried that he had "kicked the guy's ass" too hard. "Every day I feel there is another layer of the onion being peeled away, another layer of the stress of having been there," and of the numbing that is the antidote to the stress. But the process is gradual and the protective layers thick.

Walter Clark tries to let go of his Stoicism, as does Tony DeStefano. For the one it is overprotective and numbing; for the other, it is too unforgiving. Of course, sometimes soldiers should be tough on themselves and ask, Am I measuring up? And if there are psychological breakdowns, they might plausibly wonder, Could I have taken my training more seriously? Did I learn what I needed to learn from conditioning and prior exposure to stress? These are the questions an Army ranger who has trained troops tells me he would begin to ask.

Still, there is always the question of the reasonableness of the standard. Not all soldiers go to war with the training of elite forces. Not all go with a lot of battle experience. Tony was in communications, in the National Guard and in the reserves. It's not clear how much training he had before facing the stress and chaos of a war zone. He mobilized quickly in the wake of 9/11. He barely had time to make sure everything was in order at home. What is clear, though, is that he felt he failed as an officer. He felt shame and shamed by those in authority. And he felt shamed at a time when he was most vulnerable and most in need of real help.

SHAME AND SHAMING

What exactly is shame? One conventional place to begin is by distinguishing it from guilt. Guilt is the bite of self-punishment we feel when we wrong another; it often comes with a desire to make reparations. It is what Maj. John Prior, whom we met in chapter 4, feels when he thinks about the Bradley misfiring and obliterating Private Mayek's face. Prior may have done no wrong, but he feels as if he did. He feels morally responsible for the accident.

Shame, like guilt, involves self-condemnation, but it has to do more with "what I am" than "what I have done." It is about falling short of ideals. Still, the deflation from failing to meet goals is often just disappointment, even when it cuts deep into a sense of self-worth. Real shame, like that which Tony DeStefano experiences, requires, in addition, social discrediting—an affront to a person's status or dignity. Others judge you negatively, and their opinions and judgments matter. As one philosopher has put it, shame has to do with a compromise in being able to control your public persona. At stake, in a painful way, is the presentation of self and its limits.

Aristotle, philosopher of the fourth century before the Common Era, puts the point well, and as often, his teachings bear returning to. To feel shame, he says, is to suffer a feeling of disgrace by those "like ourselves," or those whose opinions matter to us—even though we may not always share the same opinions. The critical element of shame is the feeling that "eyes are upon us," real or imagined. The Greek language makes the point vivid. The word for shame (*aidōs*) comes from the word for genitalia (*aidoia*). When we feel shame, it is as if we are exposed, found naked, without our fig leaf. It is a Garden scene of sorts—to draw from a different ancient tradition—of exposure and judgment. Jacobo Timerman narrates such a scene in the clandestine prison where he was held in Argentina in the mid-1970s. He tells of a guard passing in front of an elderly naked Jewish male prisoner, standing with his circumcised penis, "his clipped prick," exposed to the guard's gaze. "The Jew smiles . . . and blushes. As if apologizing" to the guard. The old man then looks at Timerman and "again blushes." "I imagine," says Timerman, "that I'm being implored to understand. The guard forgives him. I understand him." The scene is of exposure and power and humiliation.

As Aristotle implies, shame is often felt because of *shaming*: perceived or actual judgment from others whose opinions carry weight. For people in positions of authority, shaming can be an explicit way of maintaining superiority by degrading others or humiliating and exposing them. It is the essence of bullying. And it is the essence of demeaning forms of punishment. Being shamed is a public shunning meant to control others' appearances and to present their characters publicly in degraded or devalued ways.

At Walter Reed, Tony DeStefano, like many senior soldiers, took on the role of mentoring younger soldiers who struggled with the trip wires of the behemoth military medical bureaucracy, including some of its bullying managers. One such soldier was Cpl. Robert Kislow, the twenty-one-year-old sniper who was injured badly in Afghanistan and lost his right leg.

When I interviewed Rob at Walter Reed on Valentine's Day in 2007, what struck me was a quiet sense of shame that dampened his pride and spirit. He had been home from Afghanistan for almost two years, at Walter Reed the whole time, but he had still not talked to a beloved uncle, a marine who was the inspiration for his own choice to go into the military. Rob's accomplishments as a sniper are impressive, by any account. He ultimately "got the guy" who had killed a friend who seconds earlier had saved his life.

Still, despite that satisfaction, he came home ashamed of his injuries.

He felt that he had let his uncle down, and let himself down by having to leave the Army and a career in the military that had dreamt about his entire life. "To this day I still can't talk to my uncle. I feel like I've failed something in some way," he said. Rob knows that his uncle has always been there for him. "I've had hard times going through training and stuff. I've called him . . . crying on the phone because I missed home or just wanted to ask him for guidance on decisions. But to this day, I still haven't had the courage, the guts to call him and talk to him about what happened."

Rob's grandmother tells him that his uncle is ready for Rob's phone call. But Rob can't bring himself to pick up the phone. "It is no use pushing the envelope," he says. His uncle will wait. "He knows. He's been there."

Rob's shame has to do with self-condemnation and an exaggerated view of what his uncle would expect of him. It also has to do with crushed dreams. His grandfather and uncles were in the military. It was "almost like a kind of legacy." He smiles, reminiscing about a photo his grandmother found of him as a little boy of five, carrying a toy machine gun she gave him for Christmas. "I had this awesome pose . . . a perfect pose of me running towards the camera with this M-16 in my hand." A career in the military as a sniper or member of the Special Forces was Rob's goal, the dream that shaped his identity growing up.

In addition, there is a pervasive institutional factor to the shame Rob feels, one that Tony knew well and, as a senior officer, was trying to protect Rob from. It had to do with how business was conducted at Walter Reed while the two of them were there. The hospital could be a punishing place that treated severely wounded soldiers as if they were still on the battlefield.

Rob told me how he was repeatedly threatened with Article 15 disciplinary punishments for minor infractions that occured while he was at Walter Reed. (Article 15 of the Uniform Code of Military Justice allows for nonjudicial limited punishments for discipline offenses at the discretion of a commanding officer, parallel to the Navy's "captain's mast.") Shortly before we spoke, he had official weekend leave to return home to Pennsylvania. He wanted to explore job opportunities for life beyond

Walter Reed. After a few beers one night, he found himself frozen at the bar, staring at his feet, with tears streaming down his cheeks. The next thing he knew, he was in combat mode, on the ground with his hands gripped around someone's neck. The incident terrified him. On Monday morning, his grandmother called Walter Reed to explain what had happened and to let them know that Rob needed an extra day or two at home to recuperate before reporting back. But Rob feared what would, and did, happen: that when he got back "they were still going to yell at me like I was just some Joe who partied for the weekend, got drunk, and didn't wake up for two days and came back to base, ready to get his ass kicked," he recounted. "The E-6 sergeant had no sympathy, nothing whatsoever.... All he cared about was the paperwork.... They wanted to bust my pay. They wanted to drop my rank.... They didn't care what I was really going through."

The punitive and shaming environment deepened Rob's own personal shame. "All the training you go through, nothing whatsoever can prepare you for the afterlife of war," he says. He failed in his own eyes, but the military rubbed it in. The irony in all this was the relative ease with which he made peace with his *physical* injuries. "I was so happy" to get the leg off, he says of the below-the-knee amputation. And the prosthetic "was like a gift from god. It's like a second life." But Rob still felt dogged by the shame of failing to have a career in the military and being treated with disrespect by those who couldn't see what he was going through.

Tony suffered similarly. After a year at Walter Reed, he returned to his wife and two daughters in New Jersey, and to his job in telecommunications. From his emails to me, it seemed that things were going to be okay. But then the *Washington Post* broke an in-depth series exposing punitive conditions at Walter Reed. Tony had been interviewed for the story. Everything came rushing back. Tony plummeted into a deep depression with panic attacks. That's when he checked himself into a VA facility for a forty-five-day PTSD treatment. As he put it to me in an email, "The whole *wally world* mess put me over the edge." ("Wally World" is a fictional family theme park and Tony's sarcastic nickname for Walter Reed.) Tony relived what he calls his "war after the war." In clinical terms, he was retraumatized by reexposure to the conditions at the hospital that had exacerbated his original postcombat stress.

The *Post* investigation made public what he and Rob Kislow had gone through and what was customary at the time for soldiers returning from the theater, not yet formally discharged and technically still eligible for mobilization from Medical Holding Companies. There was mandatory attendance at crack-of-dawn formations (often irrespective of injuries and sleep patterns, where soldiers only drift off to sleep at 4:30 in the morning); there were threats of punishment for nonattendance at formation; there was bullying by doctors and administrators. Tony posted the following letter on February 9, 2007, about ten days before the story broke in the newspaper:

> Harsh discipline is the last thing most of these people need. They need dignity and compassion. They need to be treated with the dignity of their status as wounded warriors.... While I fully understand the need to remain soldierly when the prognosis is to Return to Duty (RTD), I cannot understand the value of said discipline for those who we already know will be culled into retirement.... Shouldn't these soldiers be preparing for a return to civilian life rather than maintaining the military routine? This is very frustrating to a person who wanted to remain in the Army and cannot through no fault of his own.

Tony's and Rob's stories are just two, though they are emblematic of what many have gone through. The administration's formal response to the *Washington Post* exposé was fairly swift, with a public apology to soldiers from Secretary of Defense Robert Gates. "They battled an enemy. They should not have to battle an American bureaucracy." Shortly after that, there was a purging of the top command who had overseen the Walter Reed debacle. Army Secretary Francis Harvey resigned, Maj. Gen. George Weightman was relieved of office as Walter Reed's commanding general, and three-star Army Surgeon General Lt. Gen. Kevin C. Kiley, the Army's highest-ranking medical officer, submitted his resignation. What followed was a sweeping internal reorganization, with Army teams of combat-seasoned officers and sergeants assigned to help wounded soldiers navigate the medical bureaucracy and "buddy" each other as they would on the battlefield. It was clear that wounded warriors had been inappropriately punished and shamed. The mission now was to change the culture at Walter Reed and ensure soldiers and their families an honorable process of recovery, through a program dubbed "The Warrior Transition Brigade." What Tony did—buddy and protect younger, hurt soldiers, out of conscience and sense of duty as a senior officer—was now to be protocol.

THE BADGE OF THE STOIC WARRIOR

This is the harsh side of Stoicism in the military. But there are those in theater and at home who insist that ancient Stoic ideals can be part of healthy resilience training and therapy. They embrace the more compassionate side of Stoicism.

One such person is Maj. Thomas Jarrett. Jarrett is the former Green Beret and now Army social worker who trains soldiers in battlefield resilience. A former corporate coach, he served as head of mental health operations at the medical center at Camp Liberty in West Baghdad, where his job, as he describes it, was "to sell mental health care to therapy-resistant soldiers." In 2006 he was providing resiliency training classes, and by 2008 he was taking his message on tour throughout Iraq as part of a four-person team training combat soldiers in resilience, stress inoculation, and warrior ethos. Initially, Jarrett called his program "Stoic Resilience Training," and with others he trained, he proudly wore an unofficial "stoic" patch on his uniform sleeve. He later branded the program "Warrior Resilience Training," stressing the possibilities for thriving and growth after traumatic experiences.

Like Jim Stockdale, Jarrett embraces ancient Stoicism as the philosophical core of the warrior ethos. He has studied Epictetus and Marcus Aurelius and liberally cites those authors as well Seneca and Cicero in his workshops. I was flattered to learn that he has even taken my books on Stoicism and ancient virtue with him for tours in Iraq. His formal training in social work from New York University is in cognitive behavior therapy, which he sees dovetailing nicely with Stoic principles.

Jarrett's approach is eclectic, blending cognitive theory with Stoic-style exhortation and military "can-do." He takes advantage of the overlaps: Ancient Stoicism's account of emotions as cognitive (with emotional change as cognitive change) anticipates modern cognitive therapy's view of appraisal of circumstances as being at the core of emotions and emotional growth. Stoicism's perfectionism resonates with the military aspiration to "be all that you can be." In Jarrett's own case, his elite Green Beret training and military family background—his father was a captain and later a major during the Vietnam War—infuse his counseling style. "I don't believe in restoring people to average functioning. I believe in exceeding. My goal is to exceed the factory specification. I want them to come thinking they're gonna be helped and leave thinking that they've been strengthened beyond what they came for," he says. The "can-do" is meant to have force in the toughest cases.

Over the years, Jarrett and I have talked often by phone and email. We finally met in person at Fort Bragg, North Carolina, during Jarrett's leave home from Iraq in June 2006. I flew into Fayetteville and spotted a tall man waving at me; he was wearing cuffed woolen trousers, brown wing tips, and a white dress shirt. For a subliminal moment I was sure I had botched my schedule and had put myself on a flight to go to a college campus to give a lecture rather than to Fort Bragg to meet Jarrett. But once we were in the car, I knew I was sitting next to a soldier who had just come home from a war zone. Jarrett slowed down several times when he spotted debris on the road, apologetic and self-conscious that he had brought home a triggered response to the threat of hidden IEDs (improved explosive devices).

He was eager to show me Fort Bragg and I was just as eager to see it. It was hallowed ground for him, home of the Army Special Operations and headquarters of the SERE course for resistance training. It was a "hooah" place, where you dare not make a fuss while in line at a K-mart or Golden Corral, unless you are prepared to take on a phalanx of Special Ops soldiers likely to be standing next to you. He knew Bragg from his Green Beret days in the 1980s, when insiders knew it as home of the "STRAC" soldier, "skilled, tough, ready around the clock." For Jarrett, it is that bearing of the "trained, quiet professional"—of knowing your limits and extreme strengths—that meshes so well with Stoicism.

While Stoic models of resilience training are not particularly common in mental health circles, cognitive therapies are, and they remain a mainstay in the treatment of psychological trauma in and outside the military. Roughly put, cognitive therapy aims to challenge and loosen the beliefs and distorting self-judgments that underpin feelings of low self-esteem. John Rodolico, a fifty-year-old Army Reserve clinical psychologist on tour with Jarrett—and now back at Harvard's McLean Hospital—offers a capsule version of how he uses the technique with his patients: In a safe and trusting environment, "you try to challenge their guilt in some way. You want to ask, 'What makes you think about the guilt? Tell me more. Plead the case that you're guilty to me.' . . . The idea is to subtly put holes in their case. You don't want to dismiss the irrational belief too much. And in some cases you may not be able to put holes in it." The hope is that through the construction of new and more accurate narratives, patients will dislodge maladaptive emotions and come to feel greater self-empathy.

Jarrett's resilience training uses this kind of cognitive therapy, with narrative and renarration as key to the process. Jarrett is dynamic and theatrical, and at near-performance pitch, he rehearses a generic session in the field. Gathering young soldiers in a small circle, he empathizes about how aspects of their lives seem well beyond their control. He jokes with them about their leaders at the time: "Some of you have not been able to influence Bush or Rumsfeld lately. Nor have you had much luck influencing the insurgents." He continues: "Some of you can't influence your commanding officers." That quip elicits a complaint by one of the young enlisted men. His first sergeant is out to get him and he's now on his blacklist. Jarrett seizes the moment. "We can debate the truth of that statement. But what if he *is* out to get you? What are *you* going to make of it? What are *you* going to do about it?"

In training sessions with medics and commanders who are potential sources of referrals, he is likely to supplement PowerPoint presentations with detailed handouts from Epictetus's *Handbook* or the *Meditations* of Marcus Aurelius, the Roman emperor and military leader who in one of the great ironies of history found inspiration in the teachings of the slave Epictetus. Jarrett's message is that mental health resources are not just for postcombat therapy, but for resilience training before and during combat. Counseling is a matter of "keeping a warrior resilient," he insists. "We're not here to help you get it off your chest; we're here to help you not create it in your chest to begin with. This is not just a palliative thing. It's designed to strengthen you." It is for growth and thriving, before and after. In a Memorial Day letter, written May 31, 2006, from Iraq, Jarrett casts his work historically: "My work here is to polish many ideals these soldiers already know, and remind them of their Grecqo-Roman [*sic*] tradition of excellence and emotional control. . . . We have the same blood and ideals as those who defended (to the death) Thermopylae."

Jarrett is zealous about his mission and committed to improving battlefield mental health. He left the private sector and went back into the Army after 9/11 so he could dedicate himself to the task. His Stoic approach underscores self-mastery and the empowerment that comes from curbing excessive or maladaptive emotions and of distinguishing between what we can and cannot control. He works with soldiers, many of them in their late teens and early twenties, some newly engaged or just married and worried about whether their sweethearts will be waiting for them when they return home from long and repeat deployments. Some worry about who their sweethearts are seeing at night, back home, when they go out for a drink at a bar; some call home or email daily and bring the stress of combat home and the stress of home to combat. Some call each other too often, and become codependent and too enmeshed. On the war front, many have seen too much blood and carnage, too many buddies blown up, too many body parts strewn, too many innocent children killed—in short, the detritus of war. Jarrett's task is not easy.

Part of the resilience training he offers includes lessons—stressed by cognitive psychologists, such as his teacher, the late and noted cognitive therapist Albert Ellis—in how we tend to magnify or overgeneralize or overpersonalize or think in too black-and-white terms about events. So Jarrett might help a soldier who bears terrible feelings of guilt about an accident in which a buddy was killed, by trying to explore if the soldier really could have done things differently, given what he reasonably knew then and the constraints of the circumstances. Renarrating events in a way that distinguishes real personal agency from grandiose views of it—while not minimizing soldiers' felt need to take responsibility—can help loosen guilt in those in need of relief and healing.

All this has Stoic resonances that are therapeutic. Emotions, most research psychologists and philosophers now agree, are cognitively mediated. Here, they implicitly follow the Stoic lead, and Aristotle's earlier insistence on the cognitive basis of emotions. Clinically, getting clearer about the beliefs that ground our emotional reactions can help us correct mistaken beliefs, and so slowly transform emotions. Healthy Stoic counseling, such as Jarrett's, works toward a realistic assessment of our strengths and power to change externals. This is a common thread in other techniques too, whether the therapy is cognitive or more psychoanalytic and psychodynamic.

COMPASSIONATE STOICISM AND ARISTOTLE REDUX

Jarrett is convinced that Stoicism within the military needn't be overly severe or shaming. It can be a can-do philosophy that has a heart. He is right; moreover, a more compassionate Stoicism is absolutely critical for the moral and psychological health of the military. But what would it look like and can it still draw inspiration from the Greek and Roman Stoics whom military leaders themselves so often turn to for lessons?

I believe it can draw sustenance from the ancients, but it needs to loosen itself from the notion that we aspire to be sages, or perfect, "zero-defect" warriors. Key is how we read a core teaching, such as Epictetus's, to distinguish what is and is not in our power, or what we do and what is done to us. I take it as an exhortation to strive and exceed, but always mindful of real limits. Here an example outside of the military helps. Anyone in the role of caring for aging parents knows that movable boundary between what is acting and being acted upon, how age and the slowing of the body and mind shift the border gradually from independence to a new kind of dependency. The elderly are constantly being tested by what is beyond their control, and asked to draw the lines anew, in ways that reclaim dignity for what they can do. This is what my parents experience in adjusting to new, more fragile lives; this is what Jim Stockdale did in devising his own kind of mastery while a victim of torture; this is what a soldier like Tony DeStefano struggles with in recognizing that he isn't as sharp as he once was, that he may continue to be haunted by images of a missile just missing his warehouse, that he came home from war a different man, as he says, a man far more fragile and shaken than the one who went.

The task is to find a kind of agency in passivity, in captivity, in fragility, in situations that overwhelm and frighten. In some cases, agency will seem disappointing, a mockery of what we once were and could be. In other cases the push "to do it on my own," as my 103-year-old Aunt Ann tells me, can be ennobling and a daily test of autonomy and self-sufficiency. Her mantra is "No aches, no pains, no companions!"

So how do the ancient Stoics offer enlightenment here? Clearly, many teachings appeal to the can-do of the military but fall short on the side of compassion. Marcus Aurelius, for example, can be unduly severe in his self-therapy. His *Meditations*, private reflections penned in the quiet evening moments of commanding the Germanic campaigns, offer tough discipline to a near god whose giant gold statue is wheeled out by day to inspire the troops. "Get rid of judgment; you are rid of the 'I am hurt'; get rid of the 'I am hurt,' you are rid of the hurt itself." The commander's bark in a more familiar vernacular, "snap out of it," is almost audible.

But Marcus's Stoic lesson is, of course, subtler: Rethink what is of value to you and what is in your orbit of control. It is virtue. Remember that virtue alone is sufficient for happiness. "Not in being acted upon but in action is the good and ill of the reasonable social creature." So just as virtue rests on what you do (and not what happens to you), so too does happiness. Still, these are tough lessons for soldiers trying to relieve them-selves of the burdens of exaggerated moral agency and self-blame. There is little that is soothing here, when losses that happen are felt as real hurts and real ills, and reasonably so. Marcus is blind to the fact that virtue is neither fully of our own making nor rock solid. It is nurtured by others and can get eaten away by what happens to us and by what others do to us or fail to do.

Seneca is the Stoic we should be reading for the more compassionate voice. He is well aware that his commitment to Stoicism neither always motivates nor absolutely binds. "He who writes these words to you is no other than I, who wept so excessively for my dear friend Annaeus Sere-nus," he admits in a letter, that "I must be included among the examples of men who have been overcome by grief." He is a "progressor," a learner who is striving but keeps hitting hard limits. He is a mentor to others but also always to himself. He's the coach and the coached. "Tears fall, no matter how we try to check them. . . . What, then shall we do? Let us allow them to fall, but let us not command them do so; let us weep according as emotion floods our eyes, but not as much as mere imitation shall demand." These are soldierly lessons about decorum with a heart: If we cry, it should be because it is our natural inclination, not merely because theatrics or protocol calls for it. Try to find "a comeliness even in grief," by focusing on the sweet memory of the lost one. Seneca entreats with pep talk and exhortation. He demands striving and a refocus of energy. But he also urges compassionate acceptance of limits. The task is to make the limits, the fear, the grief, the disappointment feel like "stings," not paralyzing, permanent impediments.

For some, Stoicism will always put the accent note in the wrong place. "We teach Aristotle more than the Stoics," urged Navy Capt. Roger Her-bert, who has served as head of the "schoolhouse" for the SEALs in Cor-onado, California. True, the Stoics offer a great deal to candidates, he conceded, in how "to intellectually isolate circumstances beyond their control" from those they "can (and must) do something about." Still, he said—wary of oversimplifying—many Stoics "overemphasize the value of immunizing oneself against the 'passions.' " Yet it is precisely

emotions like fear, love, and pride that are potential lifesavers in combat. "Fear heightens our sense of danger and our physical capacities to
respond. Love infuses warriors with a willingness to sacrifice for his
brother. Pride might be the only reason a SEAL takes one more step even
though he's utterly exhausted."

In the background here is the Aristotelian view in which virtue
requires right action as well as right feeling. In that view, there is simply
no viable notion of good character or happiness divorced from emotional
investment in external goods and actions, complete with their successes or
failures. Herbert brings Aristotle back to his SEALs in the modeling of
resilience. "Even though we celebrate the image of the quiet, unaffected,
laconic warrior, most of us acknowledge the fundamental value of emotions. . . . We don't want SEALs thinking you should get rid of emotions."

The lesson is more general for the military. Proper emotions that register vulnerability and the cost of attachment and investment have a crucial
place in all soldiers' lives, on the battlefield and off. They have a place in
facing death and loss, including the loss of a career in uniform. They have
a place in recording the real hurt in adjusting to a new life with impairment and injury. They are the medium through which soldiers acknowledge the hard battle of reintegration after war.

Still some of the emotional battles of the war after the war are unduly
hard and involve wrestling with a Stoic ideal too severely imposed by
military culture. The battle to regain dignity in the face of psychological trauma is arduous enough without, in addition, having to battle the
image, internal and external, that a real warrior is self-reliant and can
"suck it up" no matter how tough the going is. As Tony DeStefano and
Rob Kislow have taught, that shame of being less than fully Stoic can be
unbearable.

The military can recognize, at times, its own need to change. So the
U.S. Army in 2006 jettisoned its 2001 recruiting motto, "An Army of
One," replacing it with "Army Strong." The 2006 message gets it right—
that the soldier who fights always fights with and for others. The cadre
is the unit, not the solo soldier. The perimeter goes beyond self and self-
reliance. So, too, how things turn out goes well beyond the perimeter of

control. No matter how thoroughgoing the training or preparation, personal wars often end in ways that no soldier would expect or want. All this sits in uneasy tension with Stoic ideals that extol self-sufficiency and the notion that true goodness is an excellence that cannot be weakened or corrupted by forces from within or without. All but the most callous soldiers are affected by what they have seen and done and let others do in war. The lesson is, again, Aristotelian: Our happiness, and even the full realization of our virtue, are fragile and depend on more than what is "up to us."

Still, I suspect Stoicism will retain its appeal to many in the military. And it will retain its allure to many outside as well, myself included. And Greek and Roman Stoic texts will continue to inspire, as well they should. But they need to be read always as showing our limits as well as our striving. Here Seneca could not be clearer about mortal limits and mortal striving: "While we still remain among human beings, let us cultivate our humanity."

CHAPTER 8

——— ★ ———

BODY AND
BODY PARTS

DAWN'S STORY

In the late spring of 2004, Dawn Halfaker was in Iraq for her fifth month. Just three years out of West Point, where she was a star basketball player, she was now in Baquba, the capital of the Diyala Province, on the edge of the Sunni Triangle, and in charge of training newly minted Iraqi police officers. She liked her command and bonded well with the local officers, many of whom were her age or younger. But despite good relationships within and outside the police office, her troops became a target of hostile fire. It wasn't long before she learned "to question everybody and everything." "You never know who is really your friend. Even the Iraqis you work with, you feel like you can trust them, and you feel like they want the same things you do, but you even end up questioning them. Sometimes you question your interpreter. There is just a lack of deep trust."

Late on the night of June 19, the police divided up the city in preparation for a flushing out of insurgents the next day. As a senior U.S. trainer, Dawn went out with one of the Iraqi squad patrols. One of the units took light fire, but by local standards it was a quiet night. Then as her own unit veered around a corner, they were ambushed. A rocket-propelled grenade blasted through the front of her armored Humvee and tore off its side. The explosion hit the Iraqi squad leader in the arm and chest, and he slumped over in his seat. Dawn was seated behind him in the rear. The blast collapsed her right lung and tore up her right arm, leaving it to dangle by a thin ribbon of skin. But she didn't see any blood. "Blinded by the flash, deafened by the sound," her "senses completely in chaos," she could barely make sense of what was going on. Still, she mustered enough consciousness to instantly resume command and order the unit back to the station. She surprised herself by her own resilience. "I was able to sort of stay in touch with things and give orders, even though my body was shutting down."

Dawn describes the accident to me some three and half years later in my office at Georgetown University, where she is studying for her master's degree in security studies. She is professional and poised, and on this cold December afternoon, she is wearing a gray flannel pantsuit, with the right sleeve dangling empty by her side.

"You don't get trained thinking you're going to get hurt," she laughed, remembering some mandatory medical training at West Point that she didn't think was especially helpful. "What they do is *really* train you to fall back on your instincts and trust them." It was that confidence and resourcefulness that kept her going.

Her next clear memory was of lying on the ground at the station, in excruciating pain, realizing that pain so severe on her right side could only mean something serious happened to her. "Your mind catches up." The sight of people working on her side sent her into a tailspin. She remembered thinking, "I can't feel my arm. Oh, they better not be putting on a tourniquet, because, oh my god, a tourniquet means I'm going to lose my arm!" But still she had no awareness of her blood-soaked clothes or shattered shoulder blade and broken ribs.

Within fifteen minutes of the accident, a helicopter medevaced her out, just in time for her to receive emergency care during the remainder of the critical "golden hour," the sixty minutes after a severe battle injury occurs when speed of treatment can mean the difference between life and death. Two weeks later, she awoke from a coma to find her parents at her side at Walter Reed Army Medical Center in Washington, D.C. But in her mind, she was where she had been before she went unconscious: on the ground in Iraq, yelling to the medics, "Don't cut my arm off! Don't cut off my arm!" But her arm was already gone. The doctors at Walter Reed had had little choice. The humerus bone near the scapula was completely destroyed, the blood supply in the arm was choked, a lethal infection was poisoning her body. By day three at Walter Reed, the doctors had amputated at the shoulder. "I remember looking over and seeing a big white bandage over here [pointing to her right shoulder], and I remember thinking . . . wow, but it didn't really sink in at all at first. . . . When you are lying in a hospital bed and you're not moving or doing anything, it's easy to pretend it didn't happen." And so, while she could pretend that nothing had happened, she did. "Well, let's deal with that later," she told herself.

Unlike Maj. Tony DeStefano, Dawn came home from war with acutely visible injuries. No one would dare call her war injury "amputee disorder," or try to trivialize it in the way some have regarded posttraumatic stress disorder. Moreover, diagnostic abuses, like those Tony DeStefano and others have suffered in which military doctors have withheld proper psychological diagnoses in order, according to some reports, to save the military money, are hardly temptations in the case of a gangrenous limb. Limb injury is a visible wound and one that has long been publicly recognized as a cost of battle. Images of legless World War I veterans in wheelchairs, like August Sander's 1928 austere photograph of a disabled ex-serviceman who is sitting at the bottom of a staircase he can never ascend on his own, are part of photojournalism's early war record. In the more recent public view are heroes such as decorated Vietnam War veteran and former Georgia senator Max Cleland, a three-limb amputee who has long advocated on behalf of wounded warriors.

Though there is no attempt to discredit the reality of war's limb injuries as there is in the case of psychological injury, amputees often feel stigmatized by their injuries, self-conscious that others view them as freakish or disfigured or just different. Some wear military paraphernalia to mark themselves as not just "disabled," but as warriors wounded in action. Among some there is a sense of not being properly honored, of not being "shown deference" for their sacrifice or heroism. This is how Will Quinn, the former Army interrogator and ROTC candidate, describes it to me, referring to acquaintances who have lost their limbs. "If you see a guy in his early twenties who is an amputee, there is a good chance he's been injured in Afghanistan or Iraq." "He's not just someone who lost his leg in a car accident."

Indeed, the yawning military-civilian gap, a legacy of the end of the Vietnam-era draft, has meant that many in the public are simply unaware of the extent of the limb injuries produced by the wars in Iraq and Afghanistan. Given the nature of explosions and the coverage of body armor, injuries are often to the exposed body parts—head, face, and limbs. In some cases, enemy snipers deliberately target unprotected body regions, including the side of the chest, a young soldier at Walter Reed who lost his closest buddy to such a shot tells me. It is not uncommon to return from current wars with multiple limb injuries as well as some degree of traumatic brain injury. Traumatic brain injury is a literal kind of shell shock, with symptoms that can include memory, motor, linguistic, and cognitive impairment, as well as mood disorders.

At Georgetown one evening, Army Sgt. Juan Luis Alcivar, a Walter Reed patient and Purple Heart recipient, talked to a small group of students who wanted to learn more about the recovery of wounded warriors and opportunities for volunteering to help. Alcivar (known as "AC") is twenty-five, and has been at Walter Reed for over two years, in the new Warrior Transition units, recovering from a sniper shot that tore up his femur, now replaced with a metal rod. He also suffers from mild traumatic brain injury. He has a decided limp and uses a cane with a handcarved handle in the shape of an American bald eagle head (though he is originally from the Dominican Republic and only just received U.S. citizenship, four years after joining the U.S. Army). As he talks to the group, he toys with an empty twelve-ounce plastic water bottle, and tells us how in Iraq, in enemy hands, these banal objects can become deadly and absolutely feared improvised explosive devices (IEDs). Over a period of a week, he says, the trap is set: One day someone digs a hole; the next day, the bottle, filled with high explosives, is thrown in with a simple electrical fuse; the next day the hole is filled; the next day, an unsuspecting U.S. armored vehicle goes over the patch in the road and the explosive goes off. A leg or an arm is blown off, a femur or shoulder blade is shattered. For those who survive their injuries, *visible* wounds of war remain. Yet most of us in the public don't see these wounds up close. Access to military hospitals is restricted. We don't see the wheelchairs, the canes, the stumps, the prosthetics, the burns, the empty eye sockets. We are shielded, but we also shield our eyes.

Historically, the image of the returning warrior has been idealized. We owe something of this to the Greeks. The perfect Greek body goes to war and returns home nearly as perfect. The wounded Homeric warrior, depicted on Attic amphorae and vases, leaves the battlefield with only a few pencil-thin streams of blood on his chest. Other than that, there is no disfigurement of body. Consider, too, the remarkable imperial Roman marble statue—a copy of an earlier Greek one—that commands a prominent space in the great hall of the classical wing of the Metropolitan Museum of Art in New York City. A stunningly beautiful Amazon returns from war, perhaps having battled Heracles, or Achilles, or Theseus. Her right arm is raised, and barely visible by her right breast are two or three irregular skin marks, the site, presumably, of slight bleeding from wounds. Her weapon is lost, but she departs from the battlefield essentially unmarred. She is serene and tranquil, heroic still in strength and uncompromised in physical integrity.

To be fair, the human cost of war followed a different calculus back then. The technology used to create the explosives that can cause instant, catastrophic injuries obviously had not yet been invented. And the state of medical technology was such that those who did suffer grave wounds—a gaping slash from a sword, the crushing blow of a mace— did not survive to return home. Nonetheless, the depictions of classical war heroes are deliberate idealizations. But that is the point. That is how war is often depicted: It does not shatter the body or psyche of the warrior. Even today, newspaper reports of soldiers injured or killed in combat are accompanied by pictures of the warriors before the injury, often as smiling, idealistic young men, unblemished. Until recently, flag-draped caskets, arriving from the war theaters in Iraq and Afghanistan, were censored from public view. Though we may feast our eyes on Hollywood's depictions of violence, we have a far lower tolerance for real war's detritus.

War is fought on "credit," Will Quinn tells a class of my undergraduates, twenty-seven in total, with one in the Army Reserve, another in the Navy Reserve. For most in the public, it is like running up a credit card bill. "There are thousands and thousands of dollars of debt, but it doesn't feel like a personal debt. It is only money anyway. That is the American relation to war," Quinn says. "All the debt will be borne by the Army and Marines, and to a lesser extent, the Air Force and Navy." This is by design, he says, to make the costs of war easy to bear.

Quinn returned from Iraq physically uninjured. He also believed that he returned without psychological injury, or at least if he had PTSD, it was "very mild." Still, there was a profound "disconnect" and tremendous "emotional anguish" that he knows only "time can cure."

Dawn Halfaker, in contrast, returned from Iraq without her right arm. Its absence set the parameters of a personal mission in which she put to work West Point's teachings: "They teach you that you can be thrown into anything and figure out how you make the best of it and accomplish your mission, regardless of the resources you have, the time you have, the problems you have, the challenges you will encounter. You're going to get it done, one way or another." Walter Reed became another "can-do" place where she was pushed, but she then pushed herself even harder. It helped that Halfaker is a self-starter: "I'll make my own plan and probably be more aggressive than the average person" in following it. Originally right-handed, through physical therapy she has become self-sufficient in the use of her left arm and hand—tying her shoes, putting on her clothing, writing, and typing. She opens jars and wine bottles with the help of her knees. She has been fitted with several prosthetics, both high-tech, functional models and others that are purely aesthetic. But of late, she prefers to wear none. The prosthetics are too uncomfortable, she says —the high-tech model weighs fifteen pounds, and while the aesthetic one is lighter, it offers little more than a dummy arm.

In addition to her studies, Dawn is the CEO and founder of a hundred-person defense contracting firm, which she started after leaving Walter Reed. She drives, uses a BlackBerry, plays tennis left-handed, and does yoga. It is easy to think that the mission is accomplished.

But Dawn sometimes lets down her guard a bit and shares a glimpse of her loss. On the tennis court, she says she remains a competitive athlete but is self-conscious about her inability to serve. During her first year at Georgetown, she would sneak into the back of the classroom before others arrived and then leave early to avoid the gaze of her classmates. She gets frustrated trying to keep up with email and the expectation that she can respond to all of her messages at the same pace as others. Though a native of San Diego, she says she is unlikely to ever wear a tank top or sleeveless bathing suit again. She has gone swimming once since the accident, with a group of amputees. (She wore a suit with a slightly capped sleeve, and the cool ocean water felt wonderful on her skin.) Her back often hurts from overuse of her left side, and she worries about falling on her left arm and injuring it. She suffers daily from phantom limb pain, where her right arm feels as though it is pinned behind her back in a contortion; sometimes there is a sensation that her skin is being twisted, "like an Indian burn; other times, it feels like a knife stabbing through you." There is daily physical and mental stress and frustration and grief. But there is also stunning courage in the face of a new kind of battlefield.

Part of the adjustment Dawn has to make involves skills that are the familiar stuff of occupational therapy—how to open cans and jars one-handed, or in her specific case, how to hold a computer bag and pocket-book with only one shoulder, or how to type on a BlackBerry with only one thumb. But what is not a skill of the same sort, yet requires no less time and emotional adjustment, is the feel from within of occupying a new body, and the feel from without of the real and imagined gaze of those who see that struggle. In the case of a wounded warrior, all this can mix with the resentment of shouldering a terrible loss that is not adequately recognized or honored as the public sacrifice that it is.

LIVING IN NEW BODIES

The general idea of how we occupy our bodies is a fairly trendy subject these days. Some talk about not feeling "at home" in their bodies; others, of "feeling trapped" in the wrong body. "Body image" and "body identity" are fashionable terms associated with cosmetic enhancements and reductions, surgical augmentations and replacements, scarrings and piercings, procedures to suck fat from one place and use it to plump up another. A familiar condition often associated with body image is anorexia, typically manifest in women and in many cases focused on the ideal of the thin body (though also often it is about eating itself, or about orality, digestion, elimination, and sometimes a flight from sexuality). Less recognized by label but familiar enough in gyms is what Harvard psychiatrist Harrison Pope and collaborators dub "bigorexia," the desire among adolescent boys and young men to build massive muscles through obsessive workout regimens and steroids in order to escape a body they find humiliatingly puny. In a more bizarre turn, there is a small group of self-identified wannabe amputees, individuals who feel their limbs do not belong and who beg for elective amputation, sometimes doing the surgery themselves (in one macabre case, by using a log splitter) when denied it by professionals.

Within the mental health community, excessive preoccupation with body image often falls under the diagnosis of body dysmorphic disorders, though there is no shortage of controversy as to what counts as normalcy or pathology, including whether elective amputation of healthy limbs is self-mutilation or a therapeutic intervention. Complex cultural, social, and technological trends affect how notions like health and disease and, more generally, well-being are understood.

But what does it feel like to be in a body, encased within surfaces and skin that touch the world and with shapes that move through space? For many of us, our awareness of ourselves living in bodies is, as one philosopher has put it, "attentively recessive in a high degree, it takes a back seat in consciousness almost all of the time."

Yet that bodily awareness does not recede in amputees. For new amputees, limb absence and the new posture it dictates, with dramatic changes in mobility and skill and shape, can be acutely intrusive, especially for those with multiple limb injuries. For Dawn, the harsh fact of losing her right arm did not really sink in while she was lying in a hospital bed, immobile, with a sheet draped over her shoulder. She could conveniently ignore the loss when it remained hidden from sight and when there was no question of trying to use her right side. It was only when she left that hospital bed, and tried to function as she used to, that the reality of her new body set in. Her new shape, her injury, was devastatingly present. Postponing acknowledgment of the loss was no longer a viable option.

Still, Dawn reports that most of the time she does not typically think of herself as having a new body image. "I haven't changed. I don't walk around all day looking at a mirror. I'm myself." And yet, she acknowledges, there are moments that catch her by surprise, when it suddenly hits her, "Oh my gosh, I only have one arm. And then I find myself getting a little anxious." Recently, while shopping in Target, she found herself on edge. It was an unfamiliar environment, and she felt all eyes were on her. She told herself, "I'm never going to be normal. It's never going to be easy. . . . When I lost an arm, that went out the window." There is a tension in her images of herself, then and now, of who she would like to be and who she is, filtered through the eyes of others and her perception of their gaze, and through her own grief.

During a visit to Walter Reed in 2006 shortly after Memorial Day, Walter Clark, a National Guardsman, walked me past a grassy knoll under a flagpole where a soldier at the hospital base had recently had a ceremony for his lost leg. As Walter spoke, he choked up. "What civilians don't get is that war is traumatic. It is not about politics. You are there to survive. And you're there to ennoble each other, to support each other." While at the hospital, Walter has helped roommates who smelled of burning flesh—one had his armpit blown off, another his right leg. "I cleaned them up. I bandaged them. Walter Reed is like being on the *Battlestar Galactica*." He meant that it was removed from life as many of us know it. Like so many soldiers with whom I speak, he regards his own injuries, three ruptured disks and visual impairment, as minor compared to the injuries sustained by those with leg stumps or arms missing. Some soldiers feel profound "luck guilt" that their losses are not greater. And the grief they feel for others' losses does not easily cancel out that guilt. And as Walter spoke, it was difficult not to feel as if I had a share in that guilt as well.

Perhaps what the experience of grief at limb loss touches is that who we are, as "carved at the joints," as hinged, shaped, and with a specific perimeter and gait and way of moving in the world, is something we carry deep within us all the time, albeit tacitly, as part of a "long term body image." It lingers in the back of our minds, part of our basic identity, though much of the time it yields to more conscious awareness of specific movements that we do *with* our bodies as parts of skills, whether it be lifting weights with proper form, becoming a good shot with a rifle, or parachuting from a plane. In the case of an amputee, that long-term body image, taken for granted by most of us, has to be reconfigured, replaced with a new representation, at the very same time effortful attention must be paid to a host of new instrumental and technical skills required to make prosthetics and remaining limbs perform basic functions. Older body images and routine behaviors and movements get tested and challenged and supplanted. All this is hard work, filled with frustration and filtered through loss.

Dawn tries to move her right arm, but she has no arm to move. Another wounded warrior falls out of bed because he forgets that he is missing a leg. Another is hounded by phantoms that telescope a missing foot out of a leg stump and radiate a "trapped pain memory." Others have dreams of being in their old bodies, doing what they could do with those bodies. Still others, like Sergeant Alcivar, have wakeful dreams—hopes and wishes and the aspiration that comes with hard work—that with sufficient rehabilitation, they can return to the war theater and once again be active fighters. For some, this will happen; for others, the uniform may stay on, but returning to combat is not in the cards.

Many are pragmatic and stoic about making the adjustments that come with severe bodily injury. Dawn is a take-charge manager. She does what she must to learn a new drill and perfect it. Rob Kislow, the young sniper who endured multiple limb injuries in Afghanistan, is equally pragmatic about his lost leg and titanium-reconstructed arm. "This is the way it is," he reflected, a year or so after he left Walter Reed, though he reported suffering daily phantom pains. "What are you going to do? You go on." Like Dawn, he remains active and athletic. He loves hunting and fixing cars, and his new leg and arm make that possible. When I first met him at Walter Reed, he sported his below-the-knee, springy high-tech prosthetic with Army shorts; whatever disappointment and shame he felt for coming home injured in war and bereft of a future in the military, the prosthetic was an overt reminder to himself and others of his honorable service.

For both Dawn and Rob, consciousness of their bodies—its new shape and appearance, how it has been torn up, unhinged and rehinged, and what it can and cannot do—is something they carry in the foreground of their thoughts. Making their bodies work is work. And knowing themselves, in their new bodies, is also work. It requires self-acceptance and healing, all this on top of building a new, internal body image or schema (in this regard, perhaps not unlike what young children implicitly do in seeing and moving their bodies, and then forming a coordinated mental image of what their bodies are like from various inputs across sensory modes). In this sense, there is a developmental process that comes with occupying a new body.

THE HAND AND THE FOOT

At one point in my conversation with Dawn, she tells me that the doctors initially tried to save her arm because her hand still *looked like* a hand. But it wasn't really a hand any longer, she said soberly to me. It didn't have any functioning left. Infection had cut it off from the health of the rest of the body.

Her insight is fundamentally Aristotelian. "Things are defined by their working and power, and we ought not say they are the same when they no longer have their proper quality," says Aristotle. A foot or hand sculpted from stone is only a hand in name, he says, and so too a hand that is attached to a dead body. Analogously, a dead hand that hangs by strings of flesh from a live body is no longer a part of that live whole that is the body.

And yet dead hands and feet can be more like live hands and feet than prosthetics are. None feel this more powerfully than the soldiers who must collect war's scattered detritus and return it home to families for proper memorial. Indeed, for some, the war that lasts and gets relived in anguished nightmares is less about losing body parts than about finding them. A scene from Sean Huze's play *The Sand Storm* is illustrative. Huze, an aspiring actor and playwright, enlisted in the Marines immediately following 9/11. He returned home physically injured and wrote *The Sand Storm* as a way of therapeutically processing his war. Ten characters are on stage, all marines. Private First Class Weems is obsessed with a foot he finds while wading through wreckage in search for survivors:

> My ankle rolled and I almost fell into a pile of dead hajjis. I caught my balance and looked down to see what had tripped me. It was a foot. A fucking foot. I picked it up and stared at it. I couldn't get past it. I was stuck on this foot. There I was, bodies were scattered throughout the streets and it didn't phase me, but this foot for some reason really fucked me up.
>
> I looked around for the leg it came from. It was important to me that whomever it belonged to got it back. I know it sounds crazy, but it just seemed like the right thing to do. I kicked bodies over and around, frantically looking for the foot's owner. Fuck, couldn't I at least make this right? No luck. My sergeant yelled for me to catch up with the rest of the guys, but I couldn't leave yet. I had to figure this out. He yelled again and I held up the foot thinking he'd see it and understand. He came over and slipped the piss out of me. I dropped the foot and when I did my trance was broken. I realized how ridiculous I must have looked; standing in the middle of a street, littered with debris

and death, holding a goddam foot. I don't know why it was
so important to me. I left the foot behind and continued our
search for survivors. I caught a lot of hell from everyone about
that for the rest of the war. Me and the foot.

The foot severed from the body is not a real foot, Aristotle insists.
It is no more a foot than a stone foot. Yet this marine looks for the leg
that might make the foot whole, or at least more whole than it is now.
Certainly some feet can be reattached to legs and living bodies. But this
is probably not one. The marine seems to assume its owner is dead. Yet
the foot is so much like what the living have. It is a recognizable part of
a whole that, in a sense, still belongs to that whole. And that it is frag-
mented from that whole, irretrievably so, is deeply fragmenting to this
young private. The others laugh at his obsession with the foot. But what
may be closer to his psychic reality is that intimate exposure to strewn
body parts, this foot and all the other detached parts he has seen on his
detail, presents an image of his own struggle to hold himself together in
war. He wants to make the foot whole, make it reconnect to its rightful
leg, and in so doing, somehow make *himself* whole again.

Finding body parts reveals other issues about loss. We tend to think
of grieving for the dead in terms of visual memories, remembering how
someone was in our mind's eye, or through auditory memories, how he
or she spoke with intonation and phrasings. The Roman Stoic Seneca
goes so far as to say that we do not really have to grievously mourn the
dead as painful losses, for they are recoverable and can become present to
us through such memories. But the image of the foot ironically reminds
us that when we lose our beloveds, we also lose something equally not
recoverable—namely, the tactile and physical presence of their bodies.
We grieve for the space they occupied and our tactile contact with them,
in hugging and holding, sitting by their sides, reaching to slap their
backs, stretching out a hand to hold theirs. The Marine private *can* pal-
pably touch the foot, but it is not the real thing. It is a macabre reminder
of what it would be to be beside another foot, in a boot, walking in the
scorching dust and heat of Iraq.

Here, I am reminded of a story a friend shared about her mother. As a young German girl at the outbreak of World War II, her mother found the finger of her best friend, a Jew who had been killed or taken away by the Gestapo from the apartment upstairs. Finding the finger, said my friend, was profoundly traumatic to her mother. "Think of what young girls do with each other's fingers," said my friend: They hold hands, they stroke each other's hair, they wrap their arms and hands around each other's waists. The tactile memory of the finger was buried deep for decades after the war. Her mother told no one about it until the end of her life.

The American public has little appreciation of the impact on soldiers of collecting body parts. These are not images in the media. And few dare to let their private imaginations go there. Yet for those whose duty it is to pull survivors out of wreckage and to collect body parts, the images grab hold and can traumatize. For two years after returning from Iraq, Army Sergeant First Class Dereck Vines wrestled with nightmares in which he saw the body parts he had picked up and bagged after an intense fire-bombing of a house that had two American intelligence officers in it. "We had to find one of the guy's body parts. I think one of his arms was in the tree. It was just that smell that you can't forget. . . . Just seeing bodies all over the place . . . the smell of burnt flesh, that's one thing that you never forget."

Vines describes the scene as if on a tape that plays over and over again, with him reliving the imagery "at the weirdest" moments, with all its immediacy and sensory overload. The intrusive images of dismembered, charred limbs flood him with grief and guilt that he survived and they didn't.

MILITARY COURAGE MORPHED

My own image of a soldier with missing limbs is one I carry from childhood, and that comes from my father's war, World War II, in which he served as a medic. It is the image of soldiers lined up in litters on the deck of the converted hospital ship, the *Queen Elizabeth I*, awaiting amputation or already having been operated on. The soldiers are bundled in blankets, perhaps like the brownish green Army-issue ones my dad brought home from war, which we kept in the linen closet as spares. The blankets shield, as they did for Dawn, the sight of stumps and empty spaces where limbs ought to be. But my father knew the losses that soldiers would have to live with. Under each blanket, stubs looked "like fresh cut meat hanging from a butcher's hook." "It was a butcher shop," he told me, tears welling up. The loss, over sixty years later, of all those limbs is still hard for him to talk about. Dawn's story puts a different ending on my father's. Hers, like that of so many soldiers, is of loss, but also of courage and hope in the face of devastating loss. It is a story about seeking happiness in new terms, but still constituted by a kind of military character and resilience, honed and tested sharply in war.

In a striking way, Dawn's story is emblematic of the idea that military courage and warrior spirit can have a proper venue off the battlefield as well as on. The point is not trivial. Many with whom I have spoken (including war journalists) describe the banality of life after living in a war zone for years: the snail-like pace of life without life-and-death decisions; the absence of high adventure and extreme bonding; the absence of the adrenaline rush, and the ramped-up state of readiness and terror, and the guilty thrill of killing and protecting one's own. The letdown can hit the moment a returning soldier deplanes stateside in a civilian airport. The gleam of white-tiled bathrooms, easy drink and good coffee, the relaxed faces of people unfazed by war can be profoundly alienating, however joyous a reunion with family. For some, the desire to feel pumped up again with warrior spirit and the intense sense of belonging will mean future reenlistment or signing up as a private, corporate warrior. For others, the need to stay ramped up will lead to risky and aggressive behavior: motorcycle accidents on bases, bar-room brawls, and domestic violence.

As is evident, some responses to no longer being the warrior are maladaptive in the extreme. Hyperarousal and vigilance are responses necessary in war but less so in life outside a war zone. My uncle Marvin Brenner, fifty years after his World War II service as a marine in Okinawa, pivoted on his heels in a park when he saw a bunch of boys cross his path on mountain bikes. He threatened them: "Tomorrow I start target practice." Army Cpl. Rob Kislow's enemies also materialized out of nowhere. In a bar, while home on a leave from Walter Reed, he suddenly found himself in combat mode, strangling the guy standing next to him. He had had a flashback that brought him back to Afghanistan and to combat mode. For others, flashbacks and unabated combat rage lead to homicides and suicides.

But, to return to Dawn, certain aspects of warrior spirit, what Plato called the *thumos*, a kind of fire in the belly, can be essential to the reintegration process back home. Courage, in particular, can adapt to new horizons. It can morph. And resilience, or post-traumatic growth, may depend, in part, on those adaptations.

Here, again, a lesson from Aristotle is instructive. Aristotle has courage reside primarily in the realm of fear. Fear of threat or danger is the obstacle in the face of which a courageous person stands her ground well. By fear he often cites fear of what is painful, and his own examples are typically of physically induced pain that a warrior, like a boxer, endures—"blows they take" that "are distressing to flesh and blood." But, of course, even athletic or battlefield threats need not be restricted to physical blows. The threats and risks can be psychological as well, and the pain that persists can be both physical and mental anguish.

This is a scenario for courage in war, but also for what Maj. Tony DeStefano aptly calls "the war after the war." There is still a battlefield to face, however different the enemy appears to each individual. For those who return with missing limbs, the new threats and battles pit old images of body against new ones, and old abilities and skills against those that have to be relearned from scratch, reducing one to a baby learning to take first steps. There is humiliation, exhaustion, disappointment, grief, rage, and resentment, and too, punishing Stoic ideals of demanding nothing less than perfection of oneself in each trial. In Dawn's case, there is anxiety, frustration, fatigue, phantom pain, restricted mobility, self-pity, embarrassment, shame, and the wish to retreat. There is mourning for the past and what she once could do. All these are new threats, obstacles, against which to stand her ground. They are moments for courage and resilience. To be sure, they are also moments easily abused, by too harsh a self or military environment. The battles are never easily won, and sometimes they are tragically lost. But it doesn't seem at all out of the question that for some, like Dawn, there is thriving in the recovery from war, with adaptive and robust courage playing an important role in that growth. And there is happiness.

I don't venture here to compare her well-being or happiness with those of others, or consider whether those who are able-bodied overestimate the unhappiness of those who are disabled. Some psychologists have taken up just these questions. But in general, we have good reason to be wary of the research methodology of psychologists who conceive of well-being in terms of some quantifiable report of subjective states of pleasure or satisfaction in the tradition of moral philosopher Jeremy Bentham's famous hedonic utilitarianism. Pleasure and, ultimately, happiness, insist Aristotle and later, John Stuart Mill in his famous critique of Bentham's calculus, are inseparable from the activities from which they are derived. Those very activities are constitutive of happiness. Moreover, as Aristotle argues with great insight, challenging the position the Stoics will come to defend, genuine happiness cannot be sanitized from emotions that are painful. Anger, fear, and grief may each, in their own right, be unpleasant emotions. But they are critical for acknowledging human vulnerability to threat and loss. And virtue requires just those honest assessments, which are often accessible only through the raw report of the emotions.

All this brings us back to recovery from the battlefield. In his famous poem, "Character of the Happy Warrior," Wordsworth paints a portrait of a "happy warrior" through essentially Aristotelian lenses. "The happy warrior" is one "diligent to learn"; he "abides by his resolve and stops not there"; he is "more able to endure as more exposed to suffering and distress; thence also more alive to tenderness." The image is of courage standing its ground against awful blows. The distress is felt; the soldier is "alive" to it; there is no immunity from the fear or the suffering; there is no full "insensibility," as Wilfred Owen, the World War I soldier and poet, writes in a poem that is a likely response to Wordsworth. Courage, Aristotle himself demands, requires knowing and feeling the anguish of loss. Without feeling the burden of the costs, there is only bravado and sanguinity.

Recovery from war, too, is not without horrific suffering, anguish, resentment, guilt, and grief. The battlefields live on, scarred in bodies and minds. But so, too, do warriors. The challenge they face is to harness their skills and energy—whether they come by nature, training, or luck of circumstance and environment—and to continue the battle off the field, to become whole again.

CHAPTER 9

---★---

FROM SOLDIER TO CIVILIAN

A SECURE HOME BASE

When Julie Pfaff's father, then an Army captain, went to the Vietnam War, she imagined him on an open battlefield as a member of a platoon fighting in shiny uniforms under sparkling sunlight. In her mind's eye, she was there and she could bring him home by stepping out on the field between the two sides, her arms spread out like a policeman's stopping the war. Some thirty years later, and after a stint of her own as an Army officer, Julie's husband, Col. Tony Pfaff, deployed to Iraq. During Tony's deployments, she and their two boys joked at the dinner table that they could stay connected with Tony by psychically "channeling" him.

As Julie's stories of then and now attest, families find ways to go to war alongside their soldiers. When soldiers return home, war lived vicariously becomes intimate, with nightmares, flashbacks, and unhealed wounds often commandeering a house and its rhythm. Some families and marriages implode from the strain. Others fare better; some thrive, though often the soldier who left is not the person who comes home. For some families, there are no reunions. The official knock on the door is the awful beginning of harrowing loss.

A familiar account from World War I tells the story of a French soldier who returns from the front, suffering from amnesia and without any documents or belongings to identify him. He is interned in a mental asylum with other traumatized combatants and given the name Anthelme Mangin. A newspaper advertisement shows his picture and tells his story, as best it can, in the hope of finding his real home. But that home is never found because twenty French families compete to claim him as their own. He is the son, or husband, or father who never returned. In Mangin's case, the litigation was never settled and he died an unknown man. Mangin's story is not an isolated one. From 1914 to 1918 some 250,000 soldiers vanished and their families plunged into uncertainty and the grief of not being able to have closure or bring war to a proper end.

In myriad ways, the war after the war lives on in a family's life, and not just in a soldier's. The critical unit shifts from being the squad to being the family, and it is often hard for a soldier to adjust to that because a family lacks the routine and discipline of a military unit, but more crucially, the intensity of war's sacred bands and secret suffering. Drafted into the German army in World War I, the soldier and novelist Erich Maria Remarque depicts in *The Road Back* the harrowing sense of alienation young Ernst feels as he is severed from "Number 2 Platoon" and reenters his family home. His father does not understand why he now smokes and why he is always so fidgety. His mother, ignorant—willfully and not—of the real hazards of the trenches, hands him a lamp to walk in the roadside near their home so that "no harm comes" to her boy "out there." In her mind, she now knows how to protect her son; in his mind, home is unfamiliar, his room looks tiny, not big enough for the man he has become. He longs to be with his war buddies, who know the crevices of his war-torn soul. Though only home for a few hours, he yearns to escape and march again with his comrades, "side by side, cursing or resigned, but all together."

Yet however alienating the return home, family can become for some a "secure base," to adapt the language of child developmental psychoanalyst John Bowlby, himself a British army psychiatrist during World War

II, but preeminent for his research in postwar Britain on childhood emotional attachment and separation. Just as parents, in his account, provide "a secure base from which a child or an adolescent can make sorties into the outside world and to which he can return knowing for sure that he will be welcomed when he gets there," so too it is plausible to reconstruct a developmental account for the next phase of life for returning soldiers. They too require the family's safety and nurture in order to leave behind war and "press forward" into civilian life. The expeditionary force can go forward only when there is confidence that the base is secure.

Still, Remarque's portrait of the return home is an unsettling account of the search for that trust and confidence. Neither comes easily. In Remarque's story, many of Ernst's buddies come from his hometown; they were school friends. Those who survived return to the village and the platoon lives on, substantially metamorphosed yet competitive with the family.

Other portraits of the return to the hometown are rosier. Some have become iconic, cultural reference points. In *The Best Years of Our Lives*, William Wyler's classic movie about the return home from World War II, a young Air Force captain, an Army sergeant some twenty years his senior, and a boyish sailor catch the same flight home to small-town America. The decorated captain (Dana Andrews) outranks the others, though he was a soda jerk before the war and is still a working-class guy looking for a working-class job. Married just before he deployed, he returns to a wife who is a nightclub worker and loves his uniform more than him. But true love waits for him, and he falls in love with the daughter of the Army sergeant (Fredric March). In his civilian life, the sergeant is a prosperous banker who lives in a posh high-rise apartment with his beautiful and savvy wife (Myrna Loy) and two children. The sailor, who comes from a middle-class suburban neighborhood with porches and parcels of green lawn, bears the most visible wounds of war. Two hooks replace his lower arms and hands, which had to be amputated after a massive fire on board his sinking ship. (The sailor is played by Harold Russell, in fact, a double amputee from the war.) But his fiancée is the girl next door, and she is unfailingly devoted. She fights his shame and implores him that she loves him as ever and will have him as he is. In the final wedding scene, remarkable for its candor and corn, he nimbly works his hooks to put his ring on her finger and she, her ring on his hook. The minister joins hook and hand as the couple declares their vows. Glimpses of reality appear on the screen: The captain has nightmares, night sweats, and flashbacks and can't find a decent-paying job; the sergeant self-medicates with booze and makes loans to worthy soldiers who have promise but no collateral; the sailor hides from his family and spirals into a depression. Still, this is Hollywood in the mid-1940s and it all works out in the end. Everyone is married and lives happily ever after.

Some returning warriors try to relive the plotline, whether or not they have seen the movie. Perhaps it was tacit in the mind of the young couple whose wedding photo, widely reproduced in the media in 2007, became something of a legend. A young marine in dress uniform stands next to his young dark-haired bride, a teenage sweetheart, whose hair is swept up in a tiara with a veil cascading down her nape. She looks elegant, wearing a crimson trimmed white strapless gown and carrying a bouquet of matching crimson roses. But she stares out blankly, with a hypnotic, frozen fear on her child face as she clings tightly to her roses. The groom, with both burned and freshly grafted skin pulled tight like a bathing cap over his dome-shaped skull, casts his gaze at her. He can see her through one eye. Perhaps he can smell. Perhaps he can hear. Not even that much is clear from the photo. A suicide firebomb burned the flesh off his face, now reconstructed with salvaged tissue placed around the remaining orifices of his face. The couple has said their vows, but there is no happily ever after for them. They will be separated in less than a year. The return home from war is no simple return to what was before.

"I'M HARD TO GET UNATTACHED TO"

Early one Sunday morning in December 2005, Pam Estes, a payroll director, and her husband, Mike, a telecommunications engineer, received a phone call that would radically rechart the course of their lives. Pam's son,

Private Specialist Jason Erhart, just two weeks shy of turning twenty, was in a Humvee in Iraq transporting a bomb-sniffing dog when an improvised explosive device (IED) detonated under the vehicle. The explosion hurled Jason 20 feet out of the top of the Humvee, leaving him with life-threatening injuries: second- and third-degree burns covered 60 percent of his body, and the explosion shattered his ankles and feet and shook his brain violently. His left foot was eventually amputated, and the lower part of his right leg, with twelve fractures and no heel bone left, remains at risk. The force of the blast sheared the brain tissue away from the skull, causing a traumatic brain injury that has left Jason with severe cognitive and memory deficits, and limited movement in his left hand and wrist.

I visited Jason in February 2008, two years after the explosion and more than thirty-three operations later. He was propped up on an oversized leather reclining chair in the handicap-rehabbed basement in his family's large home, located in a bucolic, exurban neighborhood some thirty minutes outside Baltimore. Mounted on the opposite wall was a sixty-inch TV screen, and at Jason's side was a computer hook-up for games, movies, and cognitive therapy exercises. Though Jason's brain trauma was a closed-head injury, his buzz cut revealed a four-inch indentation in the back of his head, the remnant of bedsores from lying immobile in hospitals for ten months.

Jason has a boyish, puckish face and an extremely soft spot for his mother. He has always been "a mama's boy," Pam says. "Can't you tell?" In Iraq his buddies would kid him about it because he called home three times a week. Diagnosed with attention deficit disorder in middle school, Jason found high school challenging and then floundered for a few months in community college, before, as Pam describes, "an extremely effective recruiter" sold him on the Army. He enlisted in November 2004, went through basic training, and was sent to Iraq, where he had been for only three months before the accident.

Despite the severe trauma and slow recovery, Jason is upbeat and outgoing. That part of his personality, Pam says, has not changed. His teachers always loved him for his bright personality, even if he wasn't the best student. "He was the kind of kid you could plop down in the middle of a room of strangers, and he could work the room. I always thought he'd be good in sales!" says his mother. Jason still beams with sunshine. "Yes, I am sunshine on a cloudy day," he grins proudly with a twinkle in his eye.

At the time of my visit, Jason had been back in the family home for a little over a year. For the better part of the year before, he shuttled to and from military and VA hospitals, with his family keeping close vigil. After being stabilized in Balad, Iraq, he was quickly medevaced to the Army's regional medical center at Landstuhl, Germany, and then on to Brooke Army Medical Center in San Antonio, Texas, for three months of intensive burn treatment, where skin protected by his flak jacket and chinstrap became donor sites for grafts to the charred areas on the rest of his body. From Texas he traveled to the VA's Richmond Polytrauma Rehabilitation Center in Virginia, where he arrived still in the coma he had been in since the day of the injury. The staff was doubtful that they could do much for Jason in rehabilitation. But then a few weeks into his stay, Jason started laughing. It was "appropriate laughter," Pam beamed. "He still couldn't swallow or eat, but he was responding!" Shortly afterwards, he began to eat again. When he asked for "a double quarter cheeseburger," a glimmer of the old boy shone through, though he was a silhouette of himself at 130 pounds, down from his Army weight of 180. "I am lucky to be alive," Jason says pensively, listening to his mother retell the story of his awakening. "I was a veggie."

For Pam, the greatest worry remains Jason's traumatic brain injury. "I thought amputation would be the worst thing. But really what is worse is the head injury. They can operate on burns. For lost limbs, there are prosthetics." But treatment for traumatic brain injury remains a medical challenge. "They really don't know how different each of us is," Jason adds, filling in her account. "I compare him with kids with autism," Pam whispers softly in an aside to me. Jason overhears and protests the diagnosis. "Mom, I don't have autism." Pam whispers again that he returned home with "zero short-term memory" and is being treated with an Alzheimer drug to slow down the memory loss. She quizzes him. "Okay, Jason, what did you have for breakfast?" "What is the day of the week?"

"Mom, I don't remember those things. Mooom, I'm just like my dad! We don't remember those things!" Jason protests laughing. Pam then points to Jason's left hand, burnt and curled up and partially paralyzed from the brain injury. "Make your head tell your arm to move," she gently instructs him. But try as he might, he can't get it to move. "It's not going to happen, Mom," he says. "As much as I'd like it to happen, it won't."

Pam is undoubtedly Jason's "secure base," and Jason, in a developmental rebirth within this trusting relationship, renegotiates new stages of attachment and separation. Like a young child, he takes his baby steps under Pam's watchful eye, confident that she is there for every new foray and retreat. Jason cannot sit up, stand, or roll over. His milestones come in different units, often centered on cognitive and memory breakthroughs. But in the background, always as enabler, is this intense parent-child bond: a gifted mother's attunement to her child, and the child's desire to impress her. "I'm hard to get unattached to," he teases Pam, youthful and pretty with long, brown hair and a playful smile. "You better like it, Mom. What can I say? I'm just a loveable guy!"

Jason has been blessed with remarkable resources at home and remarkable medical treatment. "I don't think I could have got that care in a civilian hospital," Pam acknowledges with profound gratitude for Jason's military and VA care. But she and her husband have also been tireless advocates for Jason and nimble facilitators of the military's medical bureaucracy. "Veterans who come to facilities with assets, generally come off better," remarked Jonathan Shay, a VA psychiatrist and tireless advocate for veterans. Pam and her husband also have supportive colleagues and careers that accommodate flexible hours, unlike many other veterans' parents or spouses. They played tag-team shifts during Jason's hospital stays in Texas and Virginia, overseeing his medical care by day, and telecommuting at night from the hotel. A beloved uncle of Jason's has also been a part of the vigil.

Still, finding the right care and access to benefits has not always been easy. "The medical treatment has been a learning curve. We are blazing trails," confesses Pam. Jason's home physical and cognitive therapist is a private provider contracted out through the VA, which pays for half of a day's visit, with the family picking up the cost for the rest. But until Pam did thorough homework, she was unaware that Jason would be eligible for any home benefits. Indeed, initially, she thought his only alternative would be long-term care at a VA hospital. "I cried when I brought him to the Washington VA," she recounted, remembering how she dreaded what she saw. It was filled with "old people," Vietnam, Korean, and World War II vets. Jason would be one of the very youngest. "I just couldn't leave him there," she said in a tearful moment when the strain of her grief broke through.

But despite the close mother-child bond that has helped propel Jason's recovery, his return home has not been without challenges. Jason's homecoming forced a reconfiguration of home life and the family. His teenage sister, Kerry, has had a hard time adjusting to her brother's trauma and has worked with a psychiatrist. Visiting him in the burn unit, surrounded by so many other severely burned and disfigured patients, was especially traumatic. She has tried to heal and process her trauma through poetry she has written for a high school literary magazine. Pam herself is fatigued. She is up at five in the morning and at bed at midnight and sleeps with a baby monitor hooked up to Jason's room. She dresses Jason's burns twice a day, a task that initially took four hours and that she has pared down to an efficient half-hour per session. The family eats in the basement with Jason, in his refitted suite.

On occasion, and without much warning, Jason is not all sweetness and sunshine. Because of his brain injury, Pam explains, "he cusses more than he used to" and can have quick flashes of fiery anger. Other symptoms of PTSD common with traumatic brain injury are mild, though: He has no nightmares or flashbacks, but he can startle easily, especially when someone comes up from behind. He has seen a psychologist once or twice, but when he remembered going, he protested a future visit with an adolescent whine that was a glimpse of his old self: "Mom, I don't want to go." When the family goes out, Jason is in a wheelchair, always wearing a military hat, clearly marking his veteran status. "It's important he gets the positive feedback. He's not just some young kid who got drunk and hurt," says Pam, whose protective instinct includes recognizing the role that the respect and affirmation of outsiders will play in Jason's recovery.

As I say good-bye to Jason, he is eager to add one last thing. What he wants most, he says, is to go to college, to the University of Maryland. Pam mirrors his enthusiasm with a broad smile, but she knows he is like a young child who needs not only parental empathy and attunement but also regulation, and so she puts his hopes in context. "You're on the two-year plan," she says, gently trying to reorient his expectations. There is nothing to take for granted here in the pace of progress or the need for bonding. Jason ponders Pam's words and then turns his attention to the family dog, a yellow lab named Baylee, who plays at his side most of the day.

On my way out, Pam ushers me through to her home office and shows me a picture of Jason taken just two years ago, before the war. "He's coming back," she says, tearing and reconnecting with the strapping boy in the photo. "He's even chewing his nails." "He's picking up his old eating habits," protesting vegetables. "We've come a long way and we have a long way to go," she sighs. "It's a marathon, not a sprint."

In this family, attachment and trust most definitely bind the wounds. Jason is "stuck" on his mother, and she returns his affection. But the flashes of what seems like a pubescent boy with a mad crush on Pam mix with the wisdom of a man who has seen the bottom and tells it as it is from there. "I'm lucky to be alive," Jason says, in a pensive moment. "I wouldn't trade my place. Actually," he says, pausing, "some days I'm sorry I went into the Army. But some days, I say, I've got to get over it." With that same adult wisdom finely blended with a child's naiveté, Jason embraces his mother's role in the healing process. "She's the boss," he beams at her.

"WE DIDN'T SEE THE FANFARE"

Dereck and Clara Vines were married on November 16, 2001. Two months after the wedding and a few days after sorting out their wills, Sergeant First Class Dereck Vines, then a forty-five-year-old Army reservist and veteran of the war in Bosnia, deployed for Iraq as part of a civil affairs intelligence unit. Clara and her teenage son, Brandon, waited for Dereck to return in their predominantly African-American garden-apartment community in Greenbelt, Maryland, just outside D.C.

A year after Dereck left, Clara was still sleeping with the lights on and struggling to put on a strong face for Brandon. "We wives are the ones trying to keep it together. There are the bills, the children. Where does it all end?" Brandon, who had been an honor roll student, watched his grades plummet. One day his class had to put together terrorism kits for the possibility of new post-9/11 emergencies. The reality of his father being at war hit home: "When my dad left, I was thirteen. I had just got a new stepfather," he said. "We were just getting used to each other. . . . And then he left." Even Honey, the family dog, enacted the loss that Clara and Brandon felt. "My dog missed him a lot," said Brandon. "She ran away a few times. When we'd put the phone to the dog's ear to hear when he'd call, she'd go crazy. Honey seemed to pick up on our feelings."

Clara and Brandon's new family life included Dereck's parents, who live just down the block. News from Dereck, quartered in local houses in a dangerous area between Mosul and Kirkuk, shuttled up and down the block. Before long, Clara became a familiar figure at the local Greenbelt post office, sending off care packages three times a week, often filled with a new stash of DVDs. She sent postcards that Dereck eagerly read, but he methodically burned and shredded the home address to protect his family. For six months or so, Dereck contacted Clara daily in rationed seven-minute phone calls or emails. Then for two weeks there was total silence, with Clara attempting to piece together Dereck's whereabouts through news reports on CNN. Then one day at work, Clara gathered her office colleagues to confirm an email she had just received. She wanted to be sure she was reading it right. "Coming Home," Dereck wrote.

Dereck had been on a routine supplies and intelligence run from Mosul to Kirkuk—a two-hour ride—when an insurgent car rammed into his convoy, splitting it in half and enabling a surprise ambush from the rear. Dereck was in the middle of the convoy in an SUV traveling eighty-five miles per hour. The collision hurled Dereck's head onto the windshield, with the impact shattering the glass. He sustained severe back and head injuries. Medical treatments at the military hospital at

Balad didn't seem to offer much relief. The medevac trips themselves were harrowing, with the helicopters often coming under heavy fire, despite the red cross on their wings, which signaled they were medical transports. (Dereck continues to see those flares and tracer rounds in nightmares.) Eventually, he was flown to Landstuhl, in Germany, and then on to Walter Reed, where he was treated for head and back injuries and for combat trauma.

Dereck Vines envisioned a hero's return home, with fanfare and a parade. But there was neither. "A lot us often said we felt kind of like cheated because we didn't see the fanfare. There were guys with me that still had shrapnel in their face." He continued, "There were guys who had legs blown off. They didn't get the welcome home you see on TV with all the other units coming back." There wasn't any cheering, only the Red Cross workers who handed out juice boxes. "They did as much as they could probably," Dereck said philosophically but hurt, "with the money they have."

For Clara, though, Dereck's homecoming had the makings of a romantic movie. When she first spotted him on the grounds of Walter Reed, "it was as if he came up from a hill and then disappeared into the distance." She took off work for a month so that she could spend time with him at Walter Reed. Brandon began to bond with him. "That was cool. I remember when he first got back. We went every day for three weeks for fried chicken and fish."

But soon things started to get strained. Dereck would volunteer to take Brandon to school, but then couldn't wake up easily on those mornings. Once behind the wheel, he would drive so fast that it terrified Brandon. On the Baltimore-Washington Parkway near their home, Dereck would find himself back in Iraq. "It reminds me of a highway we used to travel. I'd come over a little hill. It's like watching a movie; it is just in front of you. You're right back there." As Dereck talks, Clara senses him drifting back and she snaps him out of it. "He has that look like he first had when he just came home. Honestly, I'm scared sometimes. Now he's a vet two times round."

Dereck was contrite about his difficulties adjusting. "When I got home I had to realize this is not Sergeant Vines anymore. I always had people to jump for me." At home, things were different. "My temper was very bad," he continued. "I was rough on Brandon for a while—he was growing up," he said apologetically, the stress etched in his brow. Age and combat experience in another war didn't protect him from the flashes of hot anger and the trauma of reliving war. "He's frustrated," Clara adds. "He's tired of meds, the pain is not getting better." Dereck has flashbacks and night traumas, only now beginning to subside, that take him back to the car bombings he witnessed, the charred body parts he collected from trees and still smells, the constant fear and reality of ambushes on his convoy and attacks on his helicopter as he was being medevaced out. For him, there was no safety in Iraq, and he relives—like a rewound tape, he says—the threats and the sound of AK-47s and rocket-propelled grenades. He can sleep only with the aid of sleeping pills, and his legs twitch at night, like he's having a seizure. "Dereck was essentially a healthy person," says Clara ruefully. "But now it is one thing after another. He has hypertension and smokes a lot," a habit that got exacerbated, as it does for many, in going to war.

Medically discharged from the Army, he now receives medical care through the VA, though he believes that the full retirement benefits to which he was entitled were cut substantially at his medical evaluation. He attends a bimonthly PTSD group at the VA facility and has had therapeutic consultations with a psychiatrist and social worker, but he still struggles to navigate his way through the lumbering bureaucracy: "The VA doesn't volunteer too much information." "Once I left [the Army] I was on my own," he continued. With a touch of resentment and envy, he contrasts his own experience, as a Reserve veteran who came back without his unit, with that of a Marine unit he once saw arrive en masse at the VA hospital, headed by a commander who immediately took charge. Dereck has had to manage on his own, in a system overstrained by a flood of returning wounded warriors and in a bureaucracy separate from, and at times without easy access to the data systems and medical records of, military hospitals such as Walter Reed, where soldiers have been treated earlier. (In addition to the new wave of veterans, VA hospitals continue to serve older veterans, who as they age place new demands on the system.)

But still, despite the travail of the Vines family, there are strong signs of recovery and resilience. I first met Dereck in 2006–2007 when I was on a fellowship at the Woodrow Wilson International Center for Scholars in D.C. He is a member of the tech staff there and came to my aid often when phones or computers misbehaved. The Woodrow Wilson community, headed by former Indiana congressman Lee H. Hamilton (or just "Lee," as he is known to all at the center), is a tight-knit family, and Dereck, like many who work there, has benefited from that cohesive community. Hamilton, along with James Baker, headed up the bipartisan Iraq Study Group in the fall of 2006, often holding their investigative meetings at the Wilson Center and debating in its rooms the course of the war and troop withdrawal. It is likely that in working at the center, Dereck has felt that his war contribution has been understood and respected more than it would be in many work environments. The Wilson Center stood vigil together as a family in the spring and summer of 2007 when one of its members and head of the Center's Middle East Program, Haleh Esfandiari, was held hostage for eight months in Iran, three months of which she was in the notorious Evin prison. Dereck, like all of us, felt that sense of family, and too the sense of protectorship emanating from Lee, who was visibly anguished during the long crisis and ultimately instrumental in intervening for her release.

Dereck first learned about my interest in veterans after reading a feature story on my research for this book in the Wilson newsletter. He emailed me to ask if we might talk. We first talked in my office, during a lull in his work schedule. It was clear to me that he read my research as validation that understanding war and a soldier's return home was part of the work of the center, and implicitly, part of the center's support of his own service. Paralleling Dereck's reentry into civilian life, Clara took up a new job as a medical technician working with injured soldiers at Walter Reed. "I couldn't have done it before," she tells me. She couldn't have faced the suffering, nor had the motivation to understand and hold the raw pain. Trained as a nursing assistant, she works twelve-hour shifts, five days on, five days off, helping soldiers, like Dereck, who have come straight from the war theater with head or limb injuries and psychological and moral wounds. Long days treating injuries leaves her "mentally drained." But her work brings her closer to Dereck and to the new kind of insurgents he fights.

Unlike Pam Estes and her son, Jason, Clara and Dereck are a new couple, brought together in midlife, Clara already with a teenage son. War split this newly blended family only months after it first united. The transformative and empathic work that makes for strong unions barely had time to begin.

"Empathy" is a relatively new word from early in the twentieth century and a Greco-English translation of the German *Einfühling*, literally, to feel your way into another. To be empathic is to resonate with another. A century and a half earlier, the Scottish philosophers David Hume and Adam Smith used the term "sympathy" to mean something similar. According to Hume, sympathy is a vicarious arousal. His model is crudely mechanical: We are connected as if by a chord; a tug at one end causes reverberation at the other. The analogy has some intuitive appeal. Attunement, especially emotional attunement, requires a similar kind of tension in our wiring. But Adam Smith fills out the picture with a critical cognitive piece. I feel another's pain or anguish through acts of imagination: By trading places "in fancy," I bring another's experiences "home" to myself, back to my "own bosom." Through imaginative transports, I come to understand and feel what it would be like to "beat time" with you. In the most robust case, I don't simply put myself in your shoes, but try to become *you* in *your* shoes. As Smith puts it, I have to "become in some measure the same person" as you are.

None of this is easy, as Clara no doubt knows, especially in the case of wounded warriors, who often erect barriers as part of the emotional withdrawal and distancing symptomatic of psychological trauma. But even when there is no trauma, taking up another's perspective is no simple achievement. We are in sync and out of sync often. We are not always understood in the way that we crave. Like children, we sometimes withdraw into narcissism, feeling angry, rejected, and needy. Being in sync requires an *active* transport of imagination, as Smith insists, a letting go of narcissism matched with an openness to accept another on his own terms.

Indeed, contemporary developmental psychologists, from Jean Piaget onward, theorize that the very act of taking up another's perspective is a developmental achievement. A child before age three or four does not easily see the world from a perspective outside his own eyes; for some, cognitively impaired, reading and knowing others' minds may never come. In a loosely parallel way, both soldiers and loved ones to whom they return must work through new stages of mind reading. Clara's work with soldiers is an indirect way of learning how to read Dereck's mind and a way of him knowing, in return, that she is committed to understanding the internal war he wages.

Aristotle, in his *Ethics*, writes influentially of the friendship of families as a form of *philia*, built on mutual caring and affection, with each party mutually acknowledging the other's commitment. There can be no bond of *philia*, he insists, without that mutual recognition of goodwill and love. This is something the Vines family knows tacitly and works on explicitly in bridging the gulf that war has created.

"Squaring the Name"

On a bitter cold, snowy day in February 2008, I visited retired Maj. Tony DeStefano and his family in their home in western New Jersey, near Allentown, Pennsylvania. Tony greeted me at the door enthusiastically. He had been eager for the chance to introduce me to his wife of eighteen years, Noi, and their two teenage daughters, since our first visit, two years back. Now fifty-five, Tony's hair had grayed and he was ashen faced. After his year-long stay at Walter Reed, he had spent monthlong stints in live-in units in veterans' hospitals in New Jersey and West Virginia, treated for what was now definitively diagnosed as severe postcombat trauma and what doctors believe to be mild traumatic brain injury.

Tony was wearing a royal blue Army bomber jacket, with Little Bear, the family's Pomeranian, zipped up inside like a baby in a carrying pouch. "He's my therapy," Tony smiled. They sometimes go out for a ride on Tony's BMW motorcycle, Little Bear, the co-pilot, riding high on Tony's chest.

With Little Bear still snug inside, Tony ushered me into the family room. Noi soon joined us and later the two girls, Poi and Tony-Michelle, each with dark hair and deep features like their mother's. They had just returned from a Catholic teen retreat at their local church.

Slumped on a low couch, Tony begins to speak in a barely audible voice, his eyes often closed as he talks. It is impossible not to feel the bleak helplessness that fills the house. "It's tough," says Tony. "I'm depressed and it makes me feel much worse when I feel the strain on them." He turns to Noi, perched on the opposite end of the couch. "Noi is doing well right now, but twenty-four hours earlier, or twenty-four hours later, things might not be so good. It could be almost anything at any minute," he says. "Same with me," he continues. "My girls tell me I snap at them and completely lose it. And I don't remember it at all. There's nothing there at all—like a slug at the memory bank. It doesn't get registered." Most of the time, he says, his mind races, but his body is exhausted. He can't sleep. He is often still up when the girls wake up for school.

Tony is a working-class Italian guy from Boston who wears his heart on his sleeve. He is introspective and can talk easily about his feelings. He has set out to educate his family about postcombat stress, passing along books to the girls and explaining to Noi, who is Thai and was raised as a Buddhist, a believer in the power of mind and will, how mental illness can commandeer will and control. He has rehearsed for them many times just what happened that night in Kuwait, some five years ago, when a massive warhead barely missed his warehouse: "A 300-kilogram warhead possibly full of gas or high explosives coming at you at Mach 3; you can't even get your arms wrapped around that kind of speed," he says, transfixed once again by the scene. "It was the second Patriot that made contact. It was my last chance at living. It was like shooting a rifle at a rifle bullet. But somehow someway Raytheon [the Patriot missile manufacturer] came through. I love those people." Tony opened his eyes and then shut them to hide his tears.

Tony's job was a technical one, laying the communication infrastructure for the war in Iraq. He was called up in the reserves to do what he did well in civilian life. Underwater cables and fiber-optic wires were his focus, never missiles. He was not an infantryman or a naval aviator, trained to die in a hail of bullets. He was a communications expert who could map the intricate signals network needed to integrate hundreds of aircraft and ships into a battle plan. Immediately following the rocket strike, Tony felt "delivered." He was "ecstatic, it was almost like a runner's high." It was only months later, once home, that the combat trauma set in, with anniversary flashbacks, nightmares, sleeplessness, memory loss, lack of concentration, massive panic attacks, and suicide attempts.

Tony-Michelle, almost fifteen years old, struggles to find her dad. "The second time he came home, he was a totally different person," she tells me, in front of her family. "He wasn't the dad I knew. He snapped a lot; he'd do 100 miles per hour in the car. It's so scary." At that very moment, Tony flashes red-hot rage. He is the Army major and his subordinates have failed to show due deference: "I *hate* being told by people what to do who are not above me." Just as quickly as he flares up, he backs off, contrite about the outburst: "I've become really distant." Tony-Michelle nods, trying to see in him her old dad. "He used to tolerate us. Now he gets up and leaves the room." Then she begins to sob, the strain of holding it in and acting "like nothing's wrong" becoming overbearing.

"I am not ashamed of my dad," she says to me, wiping away the tears. "He's the greatest thing to walk this planet. It's just like I don't want to disrespect him because I know a lot of people look at him and think he's strong. I don't want people to see the weak side." There is tragic irony here: As Tony struggles to let down his stoic armor—"I have been sucking it up for twenty-three years. I am tired of it," he says—his daughter needs to rearm him with it, so that he can fulfill the image of the unassailable officer and family protector. Tony-Michele needs to protect her father in the role he plays in the public, in their family, and in her own view of what a father should be.

Tony-Michelle opens up to her older sister, Poi, but otherwise the girls are emotionally isolated. They don't talk to their friends, teachers, or church community about their father. "They wouldn't understand," says Poi, who stays at school late so that there is less time at home. "I just feel like I've been through so much that I . . . can't feel anything anymore." Noi, too, says she is emotionally numb. She used to love cooking and taught her family to savor complex Thai dishes. While Tony was at war, she nursed his dying mother, carrying her up stairs and bathing her like a baby, not long after undergoing her own surgery for a hysterectomy. But now she has no interest in cooking or home care. She doesn't work; she is afraid to leave Tony alone. During a bad patch, he burned out three kettles a month. She wants to move to the South, where they used to live, to be closer to her family and start over again.

Tony is racked with shame and guilt. He can't do for his family what he believes he is supposed to do as the man of the house. The male protector image is etched deep in military culture (women make up only about 14 percent of the active Army, and the first promotion of a woman to the rank of four-star general occurred in 2008), as well as in the more general civilian culture, and certainly in the culture of this traditional home. Tony, by his own reckoning, is failing. From a successful career, he bounced from hospital to hospital, and from short-term disability to long-term disability, and then to no job. He fears he may lose the house. He knows the family needs therapy, but they don't have enough money to pay for it. "How do you think I feel as the man of the house, when my kids and my wife don't have health insurance and I do with the VA?" he asks. "It's my role to maintain the roof over this house, to make sure the girls get into college, to please my wife. I feel like I'm not meeting those goals."

He feels the shame all the more deeply as a retired Army officer, trained to be "mission oriented," to "juggle jobs," in his case, to be the "go-to guy" in complicated technical, global network projects. "Now I'm just confused, and I can't remember, and I'm frustrated. . . . And my mind makes me physically tired. I actually get out of breath from thinking."

His mind races with what he ought to be able to do for his soldiers, "my kids," as he calls them—soldiers younger than himself whom he has met while in the hospital, like Rob Kislow, the young former Army sniper who served in Afghanistan, whom Tony came to know at Walter

Reed. More recently, Tony has worked with a recreation specialist at the VA Medical Center in Lyons, New Jersey, trying to secure funding for a project in sailing and rock climbing that will reinsert "a flash of color" into the lives of the war-torn. It may give them "a reason to come out of isolation—a reason to stay alive," he says, talking about his tutees, but clearly also himself. He worries about suicide, and about an epidemic of homelessness like that which still plagues Vietnam vets. In a series of emails and slides about his project, he leads off with a poem/song he has composed, with homage to the Vietnam vets:

> Fifty-eight thousand names in marble
> Hundred thousand more (behind them)—took their own
> I'm lookin' for a homeless veteran
> I wanna say "welcome home"
> I'm lookin' for a homeless veteran
> Just to bring him in out from the cold
>
> Iron monkey's laughin'
> Iron monkey digs in his claws
> He knows if I'm not careful
> My name's goin' on the
> Wall behind the wall . . .

He interprets the song: "The Iron Monkey is the street name for Post Traumatic Stress Disorder (PTSD). It is relentless and it is for life. The monkey wants to be paid. He wants your life." The marble wall is the Vietnam Memorial, with its etched names, which try to mark out the particularity of each sacrificed life. Once, a few years back when I was working at the Wilson Center, I met Tony at that wall. He had come to the Vietnam Memorial as part of a scheduled VA inpatient trip. He was with a small group that included Vietnam vets whom he regarded as important mentors. The visit was anguishing, and in a moment when he could no longer contain his grief, an elderly man wearing a World War II veteran's baseball cap, and visiting the monument with his family, noticed and slowly approached Tony and embraced him. "I know where you've been brother," he said, tears streaming down his own cheeks.

In the walls of the war memorials on the National Mall, generations of the patriotic dead bear silent testament to the sacrifice they have made for their country. And those who survive, who through skill or sheer circumstance are able to return home and to visit these memorials, feel the guilt of believing that they have somehow betrayed those less lucky.

Tony wrestles not only with that guilt but also with deep shame. It was a sense of shame that drove him to put on a uniform in the first place. As I get ready to leave, Tony tells a story he had not shared with me before. In 1973, twenty-one years old and living in Everett, Massachusetts, a working-class Boston suburb, Tony drew a low lottery number for the draft. His parents were dead set against him going to Vietnam, and his father insisted he enroll in a class at Harvard that could teach him how to qualify as a conscientious objector. "I learned how to quote a lot of Bible passages," Tony chortled. At the time, Tony, with a mop of shoulder-length hair, was the lead guitarist in a local rock band called Sunshyne, which had a brief recording career. When he announced to his Everett band buddies that he had been deferred as a "CO," they shot back, "Yeah, C-O . . . W-A-R-D." "That was a stiletto in my chest. It struck me and stayed with me and haunted me all my life." Tony ultimately joined the Army in order "to square the name. I had to know. I had to know if I was a coward." I ask Tony if, after all he has been through, he feels like he has squared the name. "I do," he weeps. "I do."

Tony is more reflective than many soldiers I have met. His story has deep roots in a history that he is only slowly piecing together. He adds one more piece to the puzzle on my way out. Tony's father was drafted during World War II, separated from his northern unit and sent to basic training at Fort Polk, Louisiana. The Deep South was alien territory to this Yankee, a foreign country still fighting the Civil War. He had his own psychological snap and left the Army on a psychiatric discharge. Tony has a sense that his father's insistence on his CO status during Vietnam was his way of protecting his son from his own ill-fated experience in the military and his passionate hatred of any weapons other than your fists: "I think if anything, *he* was the conscientious objector."

Tony's story has elements of every soldier's story. It is about the transformation that comes with putting on a uniform. It is about the central desire of all soldiers to be strong and to prove themselves to themselves and to others. It is about their yearning to become part of something bigger than themselves and the risk of losing themselves in that effort. It is about the desire to be courageous and hardened against the threat of bodily harm, and the risk of becoming hardened to the humanity of themselves and others.

Other soldiers' stories told here are equally emblematic of their inner wars: their wish to face the enemy without flinching, knowing that anger can mobilize the warrior spirit but that rage can destroy the warrior soul; the awful struggle to fight while maintaining a sense of justice and compassion, and the guilt of betraying others by surviving; the simultaneous pride that comes from making great sacrifices and the shame of bringing home what one has done and seen and become, in body and mind, and the strain of making it all fit into ordinary moral and psychological categories. It is about the fight to live up to the uniform, and the difficulty of living on after it has been shed. This is what weighs on the psyche of a soldier; these are the frontlines of his personal battles.

IN MEMORIAM: TED WESTHUSING

Not all soldiers come home. Some fight their internal insurgents while still on the battlefield. And some lose the battle. Army Col. Ted Westhusing is one who fought that hard battle but ultimately succumbed. His story has been with me, quietly but pressing, throughout the writing of this book. For he was a fellow traveler, of sorts: a philosopher, a lover of the ancients, and a teacher of military ethics. But unlike myself, he was above all else a warrior, a warrior who mixed the ancient and the Homeric with the modern in what turned out to be a tragic combination—he cared about virtue and honor and its public face. But he cared about excellence in a war, in the war in Iraq, in which compromise and moral ambiguity all too easily sully.

Ted was, by nature, a rigorist. At Emory University he wrote his dissertation, on the ancient virtues and their relation to the warrior, in a record six months. "He had it all worked out in advance," his adviser, Nick Fotion, told me. Even on campus, as an older student, he was the competitive warrior/athlete and could be rigid philosophically. "You never wanted to argue with him because he didn't budge an inch. He had his mind made up and wasn't going to change," commented one faculty member. Ted went on to teach at West Point, holding a prestigious tenured military professorship.

Though trained as an elite ranger, Ted missed the first Gulf War because he was working on his master's degree. He had served in Kosovo and Korea, but the wars of the post-9/11 world had reawakened his warrior spirit. The notion of justly fighting wanton terrorism resonated with the values he held dear. When the wars in Afghanistan and Iraq began, he had already started his path on a teaching career at West Point. But he itched for the battlefield. So when the opportunity came to go to Iraq, he volunteered. He had written about military honor; now he wanted to test it against a new kind of enemy. He hoped to come back a better teacher. Perhaps, too, he wanted some glory. Ted deployed in January 2005, filled with excitement. "Yippie!" was what he told his old professor, Fotion.

His mission would be a critical one for the war effort—to train Iraqi officers to take over security duties from U.S. troops. His specific job was to oversee the Virginia-based private security firm USIS, which supplied many of the trainers. USIS had contracts with the Department of Defense worth $79 million to train the elite of Iraqi police (the Emergency Response Unit) in special operations. Though Ted had little experience in military policing or contractor oversight, he formed friendships with the young Iraqi cadets and contractors. He wrote to friends at home saying Iraq was "high adventure." In March, Gen. David Petraeus, then commanding officer of the training mission, praised Ted's performance in an email: "You have already exceeded the lofty expectations all had for you." Ted replied, "Thanks much sir, but we can do much better and will."

But by April, Ted's mood began to change. He clashed with contractors who seemed more interested in money than the mission; he was irritated by the Iraqis' lack of professionalism at work. He wrote home to his father that he had failed. He complained to another officer about how hard it was all becoming; the officer told him to just buck it up and, essentially, truck on.

In May Ted received an anonymous four-page letter saying that USIS contractors had been involved in corruption and human rights violations. It alleged that they had deliberately shorted the government of a number of trainers in order to push up profits. The writer went on to detail an incident in which a USIS contractor out on a raid with Iraqi police later bragged about the insurgents he had killed, although contractors are explicitly prohibited from carrying out offensive operations. In a second incident, the letter alleged, a contractor witnessed an Iraqi police trainee killing two innocent Iraqi civilians. The letter also suggested that Ted had become too cozy with the contractors who were exploiting ambiguities in contracting rules.

Ted was distraught. He reported the allegations up the chain of command, but told one superior that he believed USIS was compliant with its contractual obligations. To colleagues he complained about "his dislike of the contractors" and their high salaries. Meetings with them became contentious. He was blunt to his wife, Michelle: "The contractors were corrupt, the Iraqis were not trustworthy. . . . The Iraqi treatment of the insurgents was deplorable." He told her he was thinking of quitting.

He became increasingly depressed, fell physically ill, and began losing weight. "That illness took the fight out of him," Fotion said. He started staring off in space and "would examine his gun at lunch." He wrote to his brother, Tim, "Nothing is easy in Iraq, nothing, and everything is important. Couple that with the corruption, evil, etc. etc. and it is tough, but [I'm] persevering." His wife detected a dramatic change: "I heard something in his voice. There was fear. He did not like the nighttime and being alone."

On June 4, 2005, Ted gave a briefing to Gen. David Petraeus at the USIS headquarters, Camp Dublin, near the Baghdad airport. The briefing was received well. He had a meeting early the next morning, and so decided to spend the night in a cabin at the headquarters rather than returning to his office in the Green Zone. He returned to the cabin after the meeting. At about 1 p.m., Ted was found by a USIS manager lying on the floor in a pool of blood.

At the time, Ted was the highest-ranking officer to die in Iraq. Three months later, Army criminal investigators concluded their report: "Cause of Death was perforating gunshot wound of the head and Manner of Death was suicide." He had killed himself with his service weapon. There was a note. His isolation and suffering at the end were excruciating. His world utterly collapsed:

> I cannot support a msn [mission] that leads to corruption, human rights abuse, and liars. I am sullied.... I came to serve honorably and [I] feel dishonored.... Death before being dishonored anymore. Trust is essential. I don't know whom to trust anymore. Why serve when you cannot accomplish the msn, when you no longer believe in the cause, when your every effort and breath to succeed meets with lies, lack of support and selfishness. <u>No more</u>. Life needs trust. Trust is no more for me here in Iraq.

Ted Westhusing's suicide is a tragic story of the war within. He went to war, as many soldiers do, filled with moral idealism. In his case, he wrote about it as well as lived it. But his idealism collided with the reality of a corrosive war. Like the ancient Greeks he studied, he believed passionately in the self-sufficiency of virtue. Yet he had to partner with those for whom war was about profit, not honor. Their values were not his values, he found them repugnant, but he felt implicated, complicit, and unable to fight for what he did stand for. He felt isolated, an intellectual who was without intellectual companions. He felt sullied, and in a tradition that the Stoics made famous, he took his life to preserve his honor. Of course, we can't rule out the possibility of some organic component in this suicide. But it seems clear that the suicide was triggered by a corruption of ideals. His devotion to ancient ethics couldn't help him. They couldn't pull him out of his profound grief and the sense that his virtue had been polluted by collective evil.

It is easy to point to a tragic character flaw here. Ted's virtue undid him. That same lofty idealism that served him so well at West Point as captain of the honor board, as an inspiring officer and professor, tore him to bits in Iraq. The honor he so wanted to test in Iraq wasn't so much "bewitched" by false honor—the theme he wrote about in his dissertation—but assaulted by it, and it could not endure the attack. The Stoic picture of self-sufficiency, and an idealization of a persistent theme in the Greek view that many in the military have embraced—that one can always retreat to a pure part of self and remain untainted—was shattered.

But it would be a terrible mistake to think that this is the full story and that the simple lesson to learn is that it is impossible to be a high-minded warrior. War is rarely morally clean. There are often shady alliances, dirty hands, mixed motives, and mercenaries. Mercenary soldiering is "an extremely ancient pastime," as one classical scholar has put it, perhaps as old as organized warfare. Fourth-century Greece (the period Westhusing studied) relied on recruitment of foreigners and "men for pay" to amass the kind of army needed to fight the Peloponnesian War. Hellenistic states of the Stoic period amplified the use of mercenaries from the earlier classical period, entering an era of "gigantism," with large professional mercenary armies, "greater specialization of arms and armor, terrifying machines of war, and huge ships." As ancient historian Glenn Bugh continues, "War was still settled 'the old-fashioned way'—by men on the battlefield, but it was no longer the exclusive province of the citizen army of the Classical polis. Warfare in the Hellenistic period belonged primarily to the professionals and to the technical experts." Whatever we may think of paid professional soldiers, nationals or otherwise, warfare even in the ancient world that Westhusing so revered was not the exclusive province of citizen-soldiers.

Still, perhaps the war in Iraq, and Afghanistan too, is dirtier than most. Private contractors operate without clear chains of command, oversight, and sanctions for abuse. The military's legal jurisdiction over civilians is limited. The fact that contractor salaries are sometimes four times as high as those of uniformed soldiers doing the same job can arouse deep envy and enmity on the part of troops. That many contractors are former soldiers and marines often deepens the sense of betrayal.

Training alliances with the Iraqis are equally morally perilous. Col. Tony Pfaff is also a military philosopher who was a senior adviser to the American commander training Iraqi security forces in the Ministry of Interior in 2006. His career track and training paralleled Ted's, and at times they competed for the same academic plums. He served during the first Gulf War and has had two deployments during the war in Iraq. He is a foreign area officer with a focus on Iraq, fairly familiar with local culture. But he was still shocked during his last deployment in Iraq by the sheer level of bribery, coercive threats, abuse, and lying. Firings for incompetence could lead to death threats and murders. Hirings that crossed sectarian lines could result in the same. Iraqi police chiefs who could keep roads safe often did so by methods that involved gross humanitarian violations. "The corrupt can come from outside, sideways, laterally," he told me. "But most of it really is someone from outside, a militia commander outside the organization making contact with a midlevel [Iraqi] major, colonel, commander and co-opting them."

I ask if that is something you learn to tolerate. "You don't tolerate any of it and you force them to do something," Tony says. "But that something may not be terribly satisfactory." Firing someone is viewed as an injury not just against the individual, "but against your tribe, your family, your clan. When you are telling them that they've got to do this, you're putting them in a box, you're trapping them. . . . You've got to be culturally astute here." The pressure of group honor and shame that our own troops have expressed acutely with revenge raids, such as at Haditha, reemerges in even sharper form for allies who come to the fight as tribal militias.

Still, for all his cultural savvy and moral realism, Tony Pfaff returned from his command vexed and morally perplexed. "Iraq is the abyss, it really is," he told me, strained by the tour. Later, he put it to me in terms of these comparisons: "You feel like a doctor or engineer with extremely complex, time-sensitive problems" or "like the inner-city social worker." "You're surrounded by corruption and crime, but you keep fighting it. You don't walk away even if that means dealing with some unsavory characters."

To be sure, there are stark personality contrasts here. These are two very different individuals working in the same corrupt environment. But Tony Pfaff's account is a corroboration of how corrosive the external circumstances were. Each in their own way struggled for honor and virtue. In Ted's case, the struggle proved overwhelming.

The Army lost one of its best from Ted Westhusing's suicide. He believed in the transformative power of soldiering to give birth to a special kind of virtue that is noble but often challenges ordinary civilian morality; he fought with fire in his belly, with a recognition that a leader's "soulful anger" can motivate troops, get an "entire unit over the top," as he put it while describing the challenges of Ranger school, but that it also can turn to fury and self-destructive rage. He struggled with guilt and shame, guilt that his attempts to fight justly got foiled by the accidents and luck of the war that was his to fight, shame that his honor couldn't stand up to the test. The complexities of reclaiming personal moral accountability in messy wars fought with partners in institutions that seemed corrupt or unjust, or at very least, at odds with civilian conscience, bewitched him. Not all soldiers suffer the same tragedy. But the honest ones wage battles inside on many of these fronts.

ACKNOWLEDGMENTS

THIS BOOK is a tribute to the men and women who have served in the military and have carried the weight of war and its moral uncertainties. I am deeply indebted to all those who granted interviews and opened their hearts to me, one who has never worn the uniform. The list is long: Juan Luis Alcivar, Tim Boggs, Mary Beth Bruggeman, Jim Bullinger, Walter Clark, J. R. Clearfield, Tony DeStefano, Robert Durken, Irv Elson, Jason Erhart, Al Gill, Jeannie Groeneveld, Dave Grossman, Dawn Halfaker, Alysha Haran, Daniel Healey, Roger Herbert, Thomas Jarrett, Erez Kerner, Robert Kislow, Hank McQueeny, Michael Mooney, Dan Moore, Tony Pfaff, Julie Pfaff, Jon Powers, John Prior, Ripley Quinby, Will Quinn, Jerry Rizzo, John Rodolico, John Rupp, Mike Simpson, Elizabeth Stanley, Bob Steck, Don Vandergriff, Brady Van Engelen, Dereck Vines, Nicholas Wagner, Tom Webber, and Ted Westhusing. I am grateful, too, to the families of soldiers, to Pamela Estes; Junko Jarrett; Noi, Poi, and Tony-Michelle DeStefano; and Clara Vines and Brandon Douglas for welcoming me into their homes and speaking to me about their loved ones so candidly. Many thanks also go to Karim Sadek, whom I interviewed about his experience living in war-torn Lebanon, both as a child and as an adult. I also remain indebted to my father, Seymour Sherman, and to my uncle, Marvin Brenner, for helping me understand the burdens World War II veterans still bear, and to my mother, Beatrice Sherman, for shedding light on the war years from the perspective of the home front.

I owe much gratitude to many who treat soldiers and who have shared their insights with me, in particular, Jonathan Shay, Nancy Meyer, and Bob Ireland. I am also grateful to Sheila Crye and Robin Carnes for welcoming me to Walter Reed and introducing me to their community of health care workers who treat wounded warriors through yoga nidra and massage therapy. I owe thanks to Barbara Lau, Michelle Pryor, and Grace Park and their volunteer group for wounded warriors, CAUSE (Comfort for America's Uniformed Services). For critical insights on amputees, I have benefited greatly from conversations with Doug Price and Peter Cappadona. For the perspective from a war journalist, I thank Christina Asquith.

I have talked to many about this project in all of its stages. I am profoundly grateful to three colleagues and friends, Elisa Hurley, Tony Pfaff, and Robin Roger, who read and commented on the penultimate draft of the manuscript. Writing can be awfully lonely; these three took a journey with me. I owe gratitude beyond words to my son, Jonathan Sherman-Presser, who painstakingly read the final drafts of the book with a literary editor's eye, a voracious intellect, and an ear for language. Blunders may remain, and I take full responsibility for them. But I owe much to these four for catching many before publication.

Others have read draft chapters of this book and commented at various points; still others have steered me in the right direction at the right time. Yet others have been part of ongoing conversations for a long time. For all this, I owe thanks to Dan Akst, Jean Arrigo, Ryan Balot, David Barham, Alisa Carse, Phil Carter, Rick Chefetz, Mark Clemente, Georges Dicker, Charlie Di Sabatino, Randy Howe, John Kafka, Judith Lichtenberg, David Luban, Coleen MacNamara, Larry May, Jeff McMahan, John Mikhail, Aaron Miller, Martha Nussbaum, Nancy Olson, Patty O'Toole, Peter Railton, Lauri Robertson, Frank Sacco, Jennifer Sims, Paul Sullivan, Stuart Twemlow, Charlie Di Sabatino, David Velleman, Rick Waugaman, and Elizabeth Waugaman.

Many research assistants were involved in the project. I owe my deepest thanks to Jeff Farrington for being by my side at the Woodrow Wilson Center for a year, tracking down research materials, transcribing scores of interviews, assembling a bibliography, and gently helping an often technically challenged person. I am also grateful to Tony Manela for his research assistance at key points and transcription of the last of the interviews. Thanks also go to Emily Evans, Lauren Fleming, and Diana Puglisi for assistance during the earliest stages of the project with transcription of the first interviews. I am also most grateful to Jack Noble for help with revising the endnotes in the final stages of copyediting. I fear there are others I have failed to mention. I hope they will understand.

I have given numerous seminars and lectures based on the manuscript, and have benefited greatly from the lively discussions that followed. Among those venues have been the military academy of Saint-Cyr (France), U.S. Naval Academy, Uniformed Services University of the Health Sciences, the Department of Defence Suicide Prevention Conference and the Defense Centers of Excellence for Psychological Health and Traumatic Brain Injury, the American Society for Political and Legal Philosophy, the American Philosophical Association, Haverford College, Duke University, Washington University Law School, University of San Diego, University of California at Fullerton, Colorado College, the Society for the Preservation of the Greek Heritage, the Woodrow Wilson International Center for Scholars, the New School, Emory University, the College at Brockport—State University of New York, Baylor University, Georgetown–George Washington–National Institutes of Health Joint Seminar, the American Society for Political and Legal Philosophy, the American Psychoanalytic Association, University of Chicago Law School, Yale University, Viterbo University, the University of Notre Dame Australia, University of Gdańsk (Poland), Washington and Lee University, University of Texas, Seattle University, and University of South Carolina. I gave many other talks around the same time focused more specifically on my last book, *Stoic Warriors*.

The Untold War owes a great debt to Jim Levine, my agent, for encouraging me to write the book and for providing inspiration, wisdom, and enthusiasm along the way. I am also deeply grateful to my editors at W. W. Norton, Angela von der Lippe and Erica Stern, whose wisdom and insights permeate this book.

The writing of this book would not have been possible without the sponsorship of two wonderful institutions. In 2007–2008 I held a fellowship at the Woodrow Wilson International Center for Scholars in D.C. A scholar could not ask for a better home for a year. I was surrounded by academics and writers who all had pressing deadlines yet found time to share ideas. I owe special thanks to Janet Spikes and her marvelous library staff there; to Lindsay Collins for her brightness each morning; to Robert Litwak, director of the International Security Studies program, for taking me under his wing; to Haleh Esfandiari, director of the Middle East Program, for sharing with me the painful details of her detention in Iran; to Gordon Adams, a fellow with me at the time, for sharing his war poems; and to Lee Hamilton, the center's director, for making the Woodrow Wilson Center such a welcoming and decent home.

The other institution to which I remain deeply indebted is Georgetown University. I wrote the penultimate draft of this book during a leave supported by a Georgetown Senior Faculty Fellowship. Wayne Davis has served valiantly as our gifted chair for many years. He has made the philosophy department another true home for me. My students at Georgetown, and especially those in the spring of 2009 to whom I lectured on this material, were challenging interlocutors and a sheer delight to teach.

No words could suffice to express my gratitude to Marshall Presser, my husband. His humor, his wit, his smarts and good nature, are the light of my life. He and our wondrous children, Kala and Jonathan, are a blessing to me. To you, my dearest loved ones, I thank you. And to my parents, Beatrice and Seymour Sherman, who have always stood by me, my gratitude and love are immeasurable.

Nancy Sherman
Kensington, Maryland
May 30, 2009

NOTES

Chapter 1: FROM CIVILIAN TO SOLDIER

11 **"Do you know the difference"**: Grossman 2004, 344. See also Grossman 1995.

12 **"If you are asking yourself"**: In remarks delivered at University of San Diego, Naval ROTC, October 2006.

12 **in response to surveys**: The survey was conducted by military historian and retired brigadier general S. L. A. Marshall (1978). The methodology behind Marshall's famous "fire ratio" has since come under heavy fire itself (see Spiller 1988 and Grossman 1995). Still, Marshall's general assumptions have been upheld in training: Training needs to meet the natural and strong aversion to killing, and this requires fear and stress inoculation gained through more realistic and rigorous drills.

12 **"denudes"**: Lifton 1973, 28.

13 **the point of asymmetrical warfare**: I thank Tony Pfaff for sharpening this point. For more on this, see Pfaff 2005.

14 **"What you really need to explain"**: JCOPE (Joint Services Conference on Professional Ethics), held in Washington, D.C., in January 2006. At that session, Jonathan Shay and I participated in a dialogue: "Suck It Up: The Proper Emotions in the Education of Warriors." The remark about "switching from civilian to soldier" came from a U.S. military officer who approached me after the talk.

14 **striking young woman in Navy dress whites**: Interview with Alysha Haran in October 2006.

16 **"The President of the United States"**: James 1902, 190.

17 **"full pride of office"**: Ibid., 191.

17 **"excitement shifts"**: Ibid., 193.

17 **"At this point, I don't have any worst clothes left"**: From conversation with Patricia O'Toole, Teddy Roosevelt biographer, in October 2006. See O'Toole 2005.

19 **faces of the fallen**: For insight here, and an appreciation of different sorts of portraits, I am grateful to Mary Challinor, an artist in Washington, D.C., who helped mount "Faces of the Fallen," an exhibit of more than 1,300 portraits of servicemen and women who died in Afghanistan and Iraq. The show was on display at the Women's Memorial at Arlington National Cemetery in 2005–2006.

19 **"language and mask"**: Goffman 1959, 254. See Luban 1988, ch. 6, for a concise sketch of the history of social roles.

20 **role that someone can take on and off easily**: For the notion of role as something you might take on and off, see Kronman 1987, 841 and 845; as quoted in Oakley and Cocking 2001, 166.

20 **"The Mayor and Montaigne"**: Montaigne 1993, 1144, Screech edition (replacing "twain" with "separate").

20 **on "loan" with the "mind remaining quiet"**: Ibid., 1139.

21 **"We must not turn masks"**: Ibid., 1144.

22 **different stations in life attach different duties**: For a classic statement of station and its duties, see Bradley 1927/1876.

23 ***"Enlightenment is man's emergence"***: "An Answer to the Question: What Is Enlightenment?" in *Kant* 1970/1784, 54, Reiss edition.

24 **"Thus it would be very harmful"**: Ibid., 56.

24 **military personnel may have to disobey, question authority**: Here, consider the cases of Gen. Douglas MacArthur in April 1951, and more recently, Adm. William Fallon in March 2008.

26 **Lt. Col. Al Gill**: Interview with Al Gill on June 14, 2006.

27 **"Few things in this world"**: Wolfe 2006.

28 **Aristotle**: For further discussion of Aristotle, see Sherman 1992. I take up the discussion of accidents and guilt, later in ch. 4. For all Aristotle citations, I am using Aristotle 1984, Barnes edition.

28 **catharsis crystallizes in pity and fear**: See Aristotle's notion of fear at Aristotle 1984, *Rhetoric* II 5.

29 **"when we are reminded"**: Ibid., Rh. II.8, 1386a11–4; a18; a25–28.

29 **Stoic ethos**: For a development of Stoicism and the military, see Sherman 2005.

30 **"They are nothing" to me**: Epictetus 1995, 1.29.7, Hard translation in Gill edition.

30 **Tim Boggs**: Interview with Tim Boggs in December 2006.

31 **hardened detachment or dulled empathy in soldiering**: Note here that the ancient Stoics do not advocate detachment from *all* emotion. Stoic "good emotions" (*eupátheiai*) resemble cultivated Aristotelian emotions that are apt and hit the mean. Yet, significantly, those Stoic good emotions exclude all trace of distress and disturbance. This means there is no place for grief, pity, fear, anger, and certain forms of empathy. In short, without a fair bit of reconstruction, the palette of Stoic good emotions cannot take into account the full range of affect required for healthy, good living. See Diogenes Laertius 7.116, in Long and Sedley 1987, vol. 1, 412, and more generally, 410–423. For excellent discussions of "good" emotions, see Cooper, 2004 and Graver 2002 and 2007. Also, Sherman 2005, 81, 106, 109, 193, and 205.

32 **Roman soldiers took such an oath**: See Davies 1989 and Watson 1969.

32 **J. L. Austin teaches**: Austin 1962, 5.

34 **Quinby frames the problem of self-defense**: Tony Pfaff's comments about Quinby's remarks are helpful here: "Note that this situation exists because the counterinsurgent forces Quinby represents have not managed to give that civilian an alternative. This suggests that counterinsurgent efforts are obligated to at least pursue providing those kinds of alternatives; simply relying on 'attrition' strategies would thus not only be unwise, but also immoral." Email correspondence, April 21, 2008.

34 **"imagine you are in an elevator"**: Rodin 2002, 80.

35 **"Some individuals"**: Wolfe 2006.

35 **"refrained from shooting a German"**: As quoted in Walzer 1977, 140.

35 **"I didn't shoot partly because"**: As quoted in ibid.

36 **he did share one story with the family**: I am indebted to Mardy Rawls for confirming the story; for a fuller account, see Sherman 2005, 91.

CHAPTER 2: FOR CAUSE OR COMRADE?

39 **For Cause or Comrade?**: The title of this chapter is a deferential nod to James McPherson's *For Cause and Comrades: Why Men Fought in the Civil War*, 1997.

39 **"explain and justify this war"**: Miller 1944.

39 **"going to injure and sometimes destroy"**: Ibid.

40 **erode a soldier's morale**: The interplay between factors is complex: If soldiers believe they are not fighting for an admirable cause, cause may *decrease* the overall willingness to fight and take risks. In taking fewer risks, soldiers are likely to incur more collateral damage. I thank Tony Pfaff for insight here.

40 **"To bring each other home"**: In remarks at a symposium on this chapter conducted at a meeting of the American Society for Political and Legal Philosophy at the eastern division of the American Philosophical Association, held in Baltimore December 2007.

40 **Sgt. Dereck Vines**: Drawn from several interviews with Dereck Vines in 2007 and 2008.

40 **Sassoon insisted on returning to the front**: For a fictional casting of Sassoon's story, see Pat Barker's *Regeneration* trilogy 1992, 1993, and 1995. For Sassoon's memoirs, see Paul Fussell's edition (1983) of Sassoon's *Sherston Memoirs*.

41 **cause that is unworthy**: On just cause and the current wars in Iraq and Afghanistan, see May, Rovie, and Viner's introduction to their anthology on the morality of war 2006, xi.

41 **How does war feel**: In *Just and Unjust Wars,* Michael Walzer is concerned with "the moral reality of war—that is, all those experiences of which moral language is descriptive or within which it is necessarily employed" (1977, 15). I extend that understanding of moral reality to what psychotherapists would call "psychic reality," and more specifically, in context, "the moral psychic reality of war." But as there is no *one* "moral psychic reality of war," the more accurate term is perhaps "the moral psychic realities of war." The phrase "the untold war" is meant to capture all of that.

41 **legitimate political authority**: See Estlund's (2007) insightful piece on legitimate political authority.

42 **"Here are these enlisted guys"**: Interview with Al Gill on June 14, 2006.

42 **"By and large we don't blame a soldier"**: Walzer 1977, 38–39.

43 **"an equal right to kill"**: Ibid.

43 **What they are accountable for**: Some might reasonably argue that not all governments have legitimate political authority. Only in regimes that are considered legitimate do we tend to think a soldier who fights for an unjust cause is not a criminal. See Estlund 2007 on this important point.

43 **"Even though the war"**: Vitoria 1991, "On the Law of War," 3.5–6, Par. 48. Note, though, Vitoria seems to contradict his earlier claim (Par. 22) that if war seems patently unjust, then killing in that war would be like killing an innocent man and therefore unlawful. The combatant who fights for an unjust cause is not the moral equal of the one who fights for a just cause. The first is like a murderer, he says.

43 **"If their conscience tells subjects"**: Ibid., 2.1–2, Par. 22–26.

43 **"One must consult"**: Ibid., 2.1–2, Par. 21.

43 **"If such men can"**: Ibid., 2.2–3, Par. 24.

44 **shutting out opinions that do not agree with his own:** For a detailed account of this pattern in the later years of the George W. Bush administration, see Woodward 2008.

44 **Vitoria's remarks:** Vitoria 1991, 2.2–3, Par. 22–26.

44 **"unjust combatants"**: McMahan 2004, 2006, 2006a, 20006b, 2008.

44 **exit options that allow citizen-soldiers to refuse:** Garren 2007. Israel is sometimes mentioned in this context, and specifically, the disposition of military courts in some cases to not punish harshly conscripts who selectively refuse to serve in the occupied territories. See Chaim Gans, "The Refusal to Serve in the Occupied Territories in the Second *Intifada*," in the *Jurist*: http://www.jurist.law .pitt.edu/forum/forunnew109.php (submitted May 23, 2003). Also, see Amnesty International's positions on this: http://www.amnesty.org/library/print/ENG MDE151692002.

45 **blind obedience:** On this, again see Woodward's 2008 account of George W. Bush's reliance on a like-minded retired military general for counsel about the proposed surge of troops in 2006, and his shutting out of the loop the strong opposition of Adm. Michael Mullen, the Chairman of the Joint Chiefs of Staff, and Gen. George W. Casey, Commanding General in Iraq from 2004 to 2007.

45 **collectivizing and coercive force of armies:** For a debate on this, see Walzer's and McMahan's 2006 exchange (Walzer 2006, McMahan 2006b).

45 **"immediate and imminent"**: In the words of Hugo Grotius, founder of modern international law, in *De Jure Belli ac Pacis* [1625], trans. by Francis W. Kelsey (Oxford University Press, 1925), and as cited by May, Rovie, and Viner 2006, xi. For further discussion of preventive war, see Luban 2004.

47 **"second personal"**: For a recent account, see Darwall 2006.

48 **first Gulf War:** Email correspondence with Tony Pfaff, October 2, 2008.

49 **Bob Steck:** Drawn from numerous conversations with Bob Steck between June 2005 and January 2009.

50 **public about his returning depression is Max Cleland**: Max Cleland spoke publicly about the resurge of his symptoms of postwar trauma at a discussion after the premiere of Sean Huze's play *Sandstorm*, about marines in Iraq, fall 2005, Alexandria, Virginia.

51 **"I went to cover the war"**: Herr 1977.

52 **"Baby killer" and "Murderer"**: From testimony of a veteran speaking at the

Vietnam War Memorial, Washington, D.C., November 11, 2007, and covered by NPR's *All Things Considered*.

52 **many (such as Bob) fought hard to prevent them**: I am reminded of Hugh Thompson, the helicopter pilot who stopped the My Lai massacre and yet was viewed by many fellow soldiers, long after the war, as a traitor. For my interviews with Thompson, see Sherman 2005, 64, 93–95, 105–107.

52 **soldiers were held, in some way, complicit**: On this, see Christopher Kutz's (2000, esp. 157–165) helpful spatial metaphor for assessing an onlooker's response to others' relative complicity in a collective end. Kutz considers a vice president of sales, an engineer, and a shipping clerk who are part of an ethically irresponsible, international arms company that manufactures and sells mines. Though all participate in the end, the vice president more directly and knowingly engages with the harm, since he arranges for sales and lines up a schedule of production. In the spatial model, he is at the core of the activity and identifies with its success and uses. He must promote the product, advertise its benefits, and deflect social criticism. Even if ethically conflicted, in role, as an effective vice president of sales, he backs the product, views it as reliable, and is its spokesman. The engineer is farther from the core. He needn't really care if the mines are ultimately sold, though he does care that the individual products he makes work and are technically well designed. The shipping clerk is at the extreme periphery. He puts objects in boxes without a commitment to sales or technically sound products. Granted, says Kutz, all have "participatory intentions" in the collective end that define their engagement. But given the workers' different functional roles with respect to the product, as onlookers, we weigh their participation differently. While a shipping clerk may be criticizable for compartmentalization or indifference if he doesn't think much about the ultimate end of his labor, in terms of participation in the collective end, he is not as complicitous as those at the core.

52 **far less complicitous than the top civilians**: See McMaster 1997.

53 **moral luck**: I thank Ryan Balot for pressing me to take seriously the issue of moral luck regarding which war one fights, in his comments on this chapter.

54 **blind patriotism or the beating of war drums**: For a discussion of American propaganda and the beating of war drums, I am grateful to Richard Rubenstein of George Mason University in a lecture delivered to Kehila Chadasha on October 5, 2008.

54 **"I try not to think about it"**: Interview with Dereck Vines on May 31, 2007.

55 **"If such men can by examining the causes"**: Vitoria 1991, 2.2–3, Par. 24.

56 **"sacred band"**: Plutarch describes the "Sacred Band" founded by Gorgides at

Thebes, around 378 BC. Within this sacred band, homoerotic ties bind individual couples. (See also Phaedrus's speech in Plato's *Symposium* on an "army made up of lovers" [Plato 1989, 178d].) But the motivational point goes beyond homoerotism: honor, loyalty, and protective shame and fear of dishonor keep soldiers fighting. See Plutarch 1906, *Pelopidas*, 14ff., and Hubbard 2003 for sources; also Williams 1999 for further discussion of Roman ideas of masculinity.

56 **bonding in the military**: I am grateful to Tony Pfaff for strengthening the point.

56 **Nancy Meyer**: Conversation with Nancy Meyer in November 2007.

58 **Hank McQueeny**: From an interview with Hank McQueeny on February 16, 2006.

59 **in a near-unanimous vote**: The vote was unanimous in the House for the Gulf of Tonkin Resolution; in the Senate only two Senators—Wayne Morse of Oregon and Ernest Gruening of Alaska—voted against it.

59 **Vice Adm. Jim Stockdale**: For an interview with Jim Stockdale, see Sherman 2005, ch. 1, and also ch. 6 of this book.

59 **triple abuse of respect and dignity**: I am indebted to Alisa Carse for discussion of this point.

61 *The Gallery*: I am grateful to Janet Spikes, head librarian at the Woodrow Wilson International Center for Scholars, for bringing this work, as well as many other works, to my attention.

61 **picture that is not so noble**: See Fussell's introduction to Burns 2004. See also Lewis 1978.

61 **"its annihilation of everything"**: Burns 2004, 87–88.

62 **"Hal found it difficult"**: Ibid., 77.

62 **"Something in him"**: Ibid., 75.

63 **"with no bodies or faces"**: Ibid., 78.

63 **"wholehearted"**: Frankfurt 1988, 159–176.

63 **"beat back"**: Seneca 1995a, 1.8.

CHAPTER 3: PAYBACK

65 **"whets the mind for the deeds of war"**: Seneca 1995a, I.9, Cooper and Procopé edition.

65 **thirst for revenge**: For earlier treatments of related themes, see my "Revenge and Demonization" in May 2008, as well as Sherman 2005, ch. 4. For other discussions, see W. I. Miller 2006, Blumenfeld 2002, Frijda 1994, and Elster 1990.

66 **Walter Clark**: Interview with Walter Clark on April 28, 2006.

66 **"package deal"**: See Lewis 1984.

69 **"You will see"**: Seneca 1995a, l.2.1–3.

69 **"the hideous horrifying face"**: Ibid., 1.1.3–4.

70 **praiseworthy and fine anger**: See, for example, Aristotle 1984, *Nicomachean Ethics* (NE) 1126a4-30; 1125b32ff; 1126b1-3, Barnes edition. For Aristotle's more popular discussion of anger in the context of oratory, see Aristotle 1984, *Rhetoric* II.2, Barnes edition.

70 **"sweeter ... than the honeycomb"**: Aristotle 1984, Rh. 2.1, 1378a35–b10.

70 **"that man without a shred of decency"**: Homer 1999, 9.857–861, 865, Fagles edition.

71 **making of a warrior**: On the making of a marine, see PBS's documentary *The Marines*, aired February 21, 2007.

71 **shame *societies***: On shame and shame cultures, especially those depicted in classical ancient literature, see Williams 1993. On revenge and revenge cultures, see Elster 1990.

72 **by the death of a kinsman**: Chagnon 1988. At the time of the study, the Yanomamö numbered 15,000 and divided into about 200 politically independent subgroups.

72 **"If, as Clausewitz suggested"**: Ibid., 988.

72 **"Their very notion of bereavement"**: Ibid., 986.

72 **"If my sick mother dies"**: Ibid.

73 **"killing in the name of identity"**: Volkan 2006.

73 **Black-Michaud's anthropological studies**: Black-Michaud 1975, esp. 43, 83–84, 79.

73 **victim of a public shaming**: Ibid., 142.

73 **Revenge cultures**: For a broad study of revenge tragedy, see Kerrigan 1996.

74 **scenes of the *Iliad***: Homer 1999, 1.217–221.

74 **careerism and advancement up a chain of command**: For an insightful study of military careerism from an insider, see Vandergriff 2002.

75 **police models**: For a discussion of these different models of the use of force, see Pfaff 2005.

76 **"The manual is designed"**: U.S. Army/Marine Corps 2007.

76 **"If you see someone with a cell phone"**: See "Probing Bloodbath," *Newsweek* June 12, 2006.

76 **moral character**: See the findings of the Battlefield Ethics Survey, May

2007, "Army (and Marine) Mental Health Advisory Team IV Findings."
According to the report, more than a third of the troops approved torture in
certain situations, most would not turn in a buddy who mistreated Iraqi civilians, and only 40 percent said Iraqi noncombatants should be treated with
dignity and respect. Those numbers were highest among troops on repeat
deployments. Available at: http://www.armymedicine.army.mil/news/releases
/20070504mhat.cfm. For a discussion, see: http://www.pbs.org/wnet/religion
andethics/week1037/perspectives .html.

77 **same was true in Vietnam**: Recall the antecedent moments of the Charlie Company's experience in the My Lai massacre in Vietnam—losses mounting
from mines without visible enemies and commanders, and Lt. William Calley
and Capt. Ernest Medina ready to exploit the rage against that invisible enemy.
For an account, see Bilton and Sim 1992.

77 **"It's a hell of a hoot"**: From "Probing Bloodbath," *Newsweek*, June 12, 2006.

78 **violent payback in killing**: See W. I. Miller 2006, 26.

78 **promise is typically unfulfilled**: Again, a point W. I. Miller (2006, 156)
makes.

78 **"a sheer brute force that rushes"**: Seneca 1995a, 3.3.

78 **seminar I gave**: The seminar was in March 2005. I owe deep thanks to Henri
Hude for organizing my visit and to Gen. Pierre-Richard Kohn for hosting this
seminar.

79 **"never fight with hate"**: Contrast what Kohn says with comments Ted Westhusing made to me during our interview in December 2002. He speculated
about a "noble kind of hatred" that might serve a warrior well: "Aristotle makes
a distinction between anger being particular and hatred being general. And I'm
almost leaning to hatred being a possible good motivating force in some circumstances. I think that in the case of what we're doing in Afghanistan right now, I
would be willing to bet that the leaders, if not most of the soldiers, are driven by
a form of hatred which has led to an increased performance over there as opposed
to perhaps what you might have seen in initial interventions in Kosovo. You recall
all the friction that we went through in getting the Apaches into Kosovo. I was
involved in that, in getting the first battalions in. I thought about it more and I'm
beginning to think that in cases where American soldiers are motivated by almost
a noble sense of hatred—that that tends to eliminate the frictions." In Afghanistan, but not Kosovo, he said, there is the sense, "Okay, we're doing this because
we've been threatened." But he conceded, "It's a thin line. You just have to go as
far as . . . My Lai to see what hatred can do in the extreme."

80 **impulses**: The Stoics call these first feelings *propatheiai*—involuntary pre-emotions, or as Seneca more elegantly dubs them, "emotional preludes." For Seneca's account, see Seneca 1995a, 2. 1–3. I take up these phenomena briefly, again, in ch. 6. For further discussion, see Sherman 2005, 82, 108–109, 134, 147, 167.

80 **Cpl. Robert Kislow**: Interview with Robert Kislow on February 14, 2007.

81 **"whole family with a hatchet"**: Lewis 1978, 87–89.

82 **"unmetabolized"**: Ibid. Pertinent here is the Israeli film *Walk on Water*, about the revenge of a child of survivors on a Nazi who persecuted his parents.

82 **public ritual grief**: See Jonathan Shay's (1994) impassioned plea for the role of collective grief on the battlefield.

82 **"A black cloud of grief"**: Homer, 1999 18.23–42.

83 **"Priam wept freely"**: Ibid., 24.595–600.

83 **archaic warriors are permitted to grieve openly**: For more on Homeric permission to grieve and comparisons with ancient Stoicism, see Sherman 2005, 134ff.

84 **Army Maj. Thomas Jarrett**: Email and conversation with Thomas Jarrett, October 2008. The case Jarrett discusses may be that involving Sgt. Joseph Bozicevich, 39, charged with the September 14, 2008, slayings of Army Staff Sgt. Darris Dawson, 24, and Sgt. Wesley Durbin, 26, at their Army patrol base in central Iraq. See Russ Bynum, AP Military Writer, "Ga.-Based Soldier Charged with Murder of 2 in Iraq," *USA Today*, posted at: 10/3/2008www.usatoday.com/news/nation/2008-10-10-2336923477.

85 **"insensate" or "servile"**: Aristotle 1984, NE 1125b3–8.

85 **we are all cosmopolitans**: On cosmopolitanism, see Laertius 1972, 6.63; see also Epictetus 1995, 2.10.3, 1.9.2–6. For further discussion, see Sherman 2005, 168–172.

85 **"our dusky companions"**: Wolfe 2006.

86 **"It is not impossible"**: Jünger 1996, ix–xiii.

CHAPTER 4: THE GUILT THEY CARRY

89 **"Probably the thing that was the most difficult"**: Interview with Tom Webber on October 21, 2005.

90 **"own personal guilt"**: Interview with John Prior on September 27, 2006.

90 **eighty-year-old World War II veteran**: Conversation, with Steven Lagerfeld of the Woodrow Wilson International Center for Scholars in Spring 2007.

90 **his daughter Robin Roger later commented**: I am indebted to Robin

Roger, a psychoanalytic psychotherapist, for sharing with me portions of her father's correspondence, and her astute analysis of it.

90 **psychiatrist who has supervised cases**: Conversation with Dr. Richard Waugaman on September 27, 2006.

91 **rational**: By "rational," I mean something like "strictly speaking, appropriate."

91 **expression of personal responsibility**: I thank Peter Railton for help in seeing this point.

91 **"Bad conscience"**: Nietzsche 1994, 61.

91 **Sigmund Freud famously elaborates**: *Civilization and Its Discontents*, in Freud 1955, 21:123–124.

92 **shame**: In the last century philosophers have talked considerably about shame in an attempt to reinstate it as an important moral feeling in the way it once was in ancient moral philosophy. For influential discussions of shame, see Williams 1993; Nussbaum 2004, ch. 4; and Velleman 2001.

The subtleties of guilt as a moral emotion may have been taken for granted or left primarily to psychoanalysts. A notable exception is in the writing of Herbert Morris (1976, 1987, 1988, 1999) and those influenced by his work; see esp. Deigh 1999 and Murphy 1999 in a symposium on Morris's work on guilt with Morris's reply (1999). Other important discussions of guilt are in Deigh 1996, especially, "Love, Guilt and the Sense of Justice," "Remarks on Some Difficulties in Freud's Theory of Moral Development," and "Freud, Naturalism, and Modern Moral Philosophy"; Velleman 2006, esp. "Don't Worry, Feel Guilty"; Scheffler 1992, ch. 5; Taylor, 1985; Wollheim 1984; and Lamb 1983.

92 **"the first command of all duties to oneself"**: Kant 1964/1797, 440, Gregor edition. For more on Kantian virtue, see Sherman 1997.

92 **"bite" of bad feelings**: See Graver 2007 on the history of the feelings that "bite."

93 **"cheerless, morose, and surly"**: Kant 1964/1797, 485.

93 **"just so story"**: *New Introductory Lectures*, in Freud 1955, 22:61, 163.

94 **Guilt, in Freud's view**: For example, *Civilization and Its Discontents*, in Ibid., 21:123.

94 **"a garrison"**: Ibid., 21:125.

94 **patching up of his theory**: Velleman (1999) tries to patch up Freud's theory by melding the discussion of the superego with Freud's notion of an ego ideal that represents enlightened moral ideals, and the inculcation of those ego ideals through parental love of children that fosters independent moral judgment.

94 **"the personal guilt"**: Interview with John Prior on September 27, 2006.

94 **accidental fratricide**: It is worth noting that the word "fratricide" in the context of war, unlike "suicide" or "homicide," does not implicitly include intent in its meaning. It typically implies accidental, "blue on blue," friendly fire. For a gripping exception, see the movie *In the Valley of Elah*.

96 **anguish needs to be alleviated in some way**: Robert Roberts commented insightfully on this chapter at a memorial conference in honor of Bob Solomon at the University of Texas, Austin, in January 2009: "The *moral* therapist has to walk a fine line between respecting a patient's character and alleviating anguish." Guilt is rational, he noted, in that it depends on construals (though not standard judgments subject to strict standards of what is veridical).

96 **bad consequences we couldn't reasonably expect or prevent**: See Thomas Nagel's (1979, 24–38) seminal discussion of moral luck. For the notion that moral luck highlights the idea of our personal agency as "impure," in the sense of requiring resources of character to meet the combination of choice *and* fortune in life, see Walker 1991.

97 **"question of someone who ... caused harm"**: Nietzche 1994, 59–66, Diethe edition.

97 **involuntarily through ignorance**: The philosopher Bernard Williams (1981, 20–39) has coined the term "agent-regret" to refer to the feeling often felt when a person is "causally" (though not morally) responsible "in virtue of something one intentionally did." But to my mind, a notion of regret, even *agent*-regret, doesn't adequately capture what is actually felt. It does not capture the despair or depth of the feeling of guilt, nor, as I indicate later in this chapter, the empathic identification with victim, so common in war. Nor does it capture the first-person aspect of the moral feeling: I see myself as morally implicated and need to make repair. It is not just that I should take responsibility because I am part of the causal chain. Guilt, it seems, is rational to feel on such occasions precisely because it is a response to this more robust moral involvement. I thank Elisa Hurley for discussion here.

97 **dynamic and lasting influences of childhood morality**: See Klein 1977, esp. "Love, Guilt, and Reparation." Also "Our Adult World and Its Roots in Infancy" and "Some Reflections on the *Oresteia*," in Klein 1975

98 **own fallible agency**: See Halliwell 1986 for a discussion of *hamartia*; also Sherman 1992.

98 **Sophocles' *The Women of Trachis***: I thank Paul Woodruff for helpful comments on the play.

98 **"erotic diversion"**: See Williams's "The Women of Trachis," in Williams 2006.

98 **"unwittingly the will of the beast"**: Sophocles 1967, Green and Lattimore edition.

98 **"I neglected none of the instructions"**: Ibid., 680ff. As the quotations suggest, there may be some culpable ignorance here, though Sophocles does not press the point too hard: Deianeira, after all, must remain a tragic character for whom we have sympathy.

99 **what she has wrought with her hands**: She acts with her own hand, but was fooled. Perhaps Prior too feels a bit betrayed by the manuals.

99 **"agent-regret"**: Marcia Baron (1988) may be pointing to limitations in the term of art when she speaks of remorse (as distinct from agent-regret).

99 **"ruthless, devouring malady"**: Sophocles 1967, 840.

100 **"steel bit in my mouth"**: Ibid., 1260.

100 **two small groups of Marine and Navy officers**: The first was a group of Marine majors who had become company officers at the Academy: J. R. Clearfield (infantry), Michael Mooney (reconnaissance), Daniel Healey (infantry), Jerry Rizzo (aviation), and Mary Beth Bruggeman (combat engineering). Some had fought in the siege of Baghdad; others served in intelligence; still others oversaw security at medical units, working to ensure safe landings for helicopters carrying the wounded. In the second group were more senior Marine and Navy officers: Lt. Cdr. Tom Webber and Lt. Cdr. Irv Elson (both chaplains), Col. Robert Durkin (infantry) and Col. John Rupp (aviation). At the time of the interview, several in this group were resident at the Naval Academy's Ethics Center, now known as the Stockdale Center for Ethical Leadership.

102 **Siegfried Sassoon**: See Paul Fussell's 1983 edition of Sassoon's *Sherston Memoirs*. For a trilogy of novels based on Sassoon's life, see Barker 1992, 1993, and 1995. For further discussion of this, see Sherman 2005, 157–162.

102 **"death"**: Fussell 1983, 138.

102 **"I am banished"**: Ibid., 140. The poem is "Banishment."

102 **"When are you going out to them again"**: Ibid., 141.

103 **some desperately wish to keep pure**: See, for example, James Webb's controversial article "Women Can't Fight," *Washingtonian* (November 1979), on women in the military. Webb was teaching at the Naval Academy at the time of the article. His article was a response to Congress's 1975 authorization for women to attend service academies; 81 women graduated from the Naval Academy in 1980, many of whom were incensed by Webb's article. When I taught at the Naval Academy in the late 1990s, the article was still widely discussed, and criticized, notably by Paul Roush, a retired Marine colonel and then professor in the leadership, ethics, and law division.

103 **willingness to die as if for your own child**: See Held 1987, 111–128. I thank Patty O'Toole for pointing out this connection to me.

103 **"living dead"**: See Lawrence Friedman's (1985) discussion of psychoanalytic writers William Niederland and Arnold Modell and their work on survivor guilt.

103 **"My spirit rebels"**: Homer 1999, 18.105, 94–96, Fagles edition.

104 **"in mental life"**: Modell 1971 as quoted in Friedman 1985.

107 **sound moral order**: Here I am indebted to comments by Paul Schwaber at a seminar I gave at Yale University, March 2008.

108 **caught in the cross-hairs of war**: As Tony Pfaff noted just after returning from Iraq in the summer of 2006, not all checkpoints are well advertised. And even when they are, some local drivers may not be used to them. Others may run them out of fear of Americans, or in defiance of "occupiers," or simply because they are teenage boys out for a joyride. Given all the ambiguity, a commander may want to have in place fairly explicit rules of engagement precisely "to limit moral culpability their guys have to buy."

108 **reported in detail**: Louise Kierman, "A Son Confronts the Aftermath of War," July 2, 2004, *Chicago Tribune*, July 2, 2004, available at: http://www.chicago tribune.com/features/health/chi-0407020125jul02,0,5055328.story?page=1.

110 **morally permissible**: There is a body of empirical studies suggesting that we may mentally represent in an unconscious and hard-wired way—as a part of some deep "moral grammar"—a significant moral difference between directly harming innocents in a way that uses them as a mere means, and causing them harm as a foreseen side effect; for discussion, see John Mikhail's (2007) philosophical computational model of double-effect dilemmas. However, other empirical moral philosophers have argued that we register the incurring of indirect harm differently when it is up close and personal. Joshua Greene's work (2008) may be particularly relevant to the checkpoint cases discussed in the text. Studies using functional magnetic resonance imaging suggest that our limbic systems step in in up-close contexts in a way in which they do not for action at a distance. I thank Rick Waugaman and John Mikhail for discussion here.

CHAPTER 5: INTERROGATION:
IN THE MORAL SHADOWLAND

115 **whether the ruse is**: I have benefited here from the Imperial War Museum exhibit on camouflage, July 2007, and the companion catalogue (Newark 2007).

Also Phil Patton, "The Art of Camo," June 2, 2005, at: http://www.aiga.org/content.cfm/the-art-of-camo?pff=1.

115 **"ambushes and deceptions"**: *Summa Theologica*, "Question XL. Of War. (In Four Articles), Third Article. Whether It Is Lawful to Lay Ambushes in War?" quoting from text reprinted in May, Rovie, and Viner 2006, 29.

115 **Deception comes with the territory**: For a discussion on deception being part of intelligence gathering, see Goldman's anthology (2006), esp. articles by J. E. Drexel Godfrey, Tony Pfaff, John Langan, Michael Skerker, and David L. Perry. Also, see Pfaff and Tiel 2004.

116 **stories of torture were not made up**: Indeed, as this book goes to press, the Obama administration has released legal memos, from 2002 to 2005, at the heart of the torture program. See Obama statement on release of torture memos in the *Washington Post*, April 17, 2009, at: http://www.washingtonpost.com/wp-dyn/content/article/2009/04/17/AR2009041700770.html. The release followed shortly after the leak, in the *New York Review of Books*, of the International Committee of the Red Cross's report on the treatment of fourteen "high value detainees" in CIA custody. See Mark Danner, "US Torture: Voices from the Black Sites," *New York Review of Books*, vol. 56, no. 6, April 9, 2009, available at: http://www.nybooks.com/articles/22530.

116 **"We tortured Qahtani"**: Bob Woodward, "Detainee Tortured, Says U.S. Official: Trial Overseer Cites 'Abusive' Methods against 9/11 Suspect," *Washington Post*, January 14, 2009, A01, available at: http://www.washingtonpost.com/wp-dyn/content/article/2009/01/13/AR2009011303372.html.

117 **defining issues of the torture debate**: For important recent collections on torture, see Levinson 2004 and Greenberg 2006. For a penetrating discussion of the misleading "exceptionalism" of ticking-time-bomb scenarios, see Luban 2005. On the notion of "torture lite," see Bowden 2003. For earlier discussions, see Henry Shue's classic 1978 article; for a discussion of Jeremy Bentham on torture, see Twining and Twining 1973.

117 **accounts of exploitation**: For a sample of philosophical views, see Wertheimer 1996, Wood 1995, Sample 2003, and Carse and Little 2009.

118 *24*: Civilians are not the only ones influenced by the TV program *24*. American troops in the field have watched the program and fallen under its allure, as have West Point cadets. The dean at West Point, U.S. Army Brig. Gen. Patrick Finnegan, has argued that the show has, in fact, undermined military discipline at West Point and the core teaching at West Point that torture is illegal. The issue has been widely reported in the press. According to one account, in the fall of 2006 Finnegan made a trip to California to impress upon the producer of

the show, Joel Surnow, the deleterious effect the program was having on cadets and throughout the rest of the military. Surnow didn't show up for the meeting, claiming a scheduling conflict. Other producers insisted that the program was just fiction, based on fictional premises. But with the times changing, the program has changed. In the 2009 season of *24*, the content has shifted away from torture, reflecting the public and now presidential insistence that torture is illegal and ineffective. For more, see Henry Berry, "Torture and Television: Effects of the TV Program *24*," February 28, 2007, at: http://americanaffairs.suite101 .com/article.cfm/torture_and_television.

118 **FM 34-52**: Released in September 1992 and approved for public release. In 2006, FM 34-52 was replaced with FM 2-22-3, though much remains the same in the new "approach techniques" section (ch. 8), with a few tweaks. So, for example, in the new manual, techniques such as "pride and ego-down" and "fear-up" remain the same with the same names, though the words "interrogator" and "interrogation" have been replaced with "HUMINT collector" and "collection effort," probably in response to the fact that the former terms, once themselves sanitary, have now been saturated with negative valence. Noteworthy also is that the term "weakness," as in "manipulate the source's emotions and weakness," has been replaced with the more neutral term "characteristic." This may be a response by the military to block the sentiment that the exploitation of human helplessness within interrogation seems cruel. I am grateful to Tony Manela for research on this.

118 **"Interrogators are trained"**: FM 34-52-3-1.

118 **"An individual's value system"**: Ibid., 3-1.

118 **"[The following] factors must be considered"**: Ibid., 3-11.

119 **general principles**: Note, the examples Quinn discusses follow this general approach for exploitation: Quinn's harping on a detainee's adulterous past was a form of shaming; his forcing a Shia and Sunni together in the recreation yard made their hatred of Quinn look innocent compared to their hatred of each other; his rapport building with a female detainee was a way to gain intimacy.

119 **"fear-up harsh" and "pride and ego-down"**: FM 3-14-18. For a chilling first-person account on the use of "fear-up" and "pride and ego-down" and the moral injury of those who use them, see Lagouranis and Mikaelian 2007.

119 **"comfort items"**: FM 3-11-13.

120 **"the greatest potential to violate the law"**: Ibid., 3-16.

120 **To exploit is to take advantage**: For a helpful discussion, see Wood 2004, ch. 16, "Capitalist Exploitation."

121 **consent to cooperate**: For related discussions of consenting to cooperate, see Wood 1995 and 2004.

121 **may choose exploitive work**: I have profited here from discussions with Tea Logar in connection with her Georgetown doctoral dissertation on exploitation.

121 **psychoanalytic insight**: I am grateful here for discussion with Dr. William Kenner, a psychiatrist, psychoanalyst, and forensics expert who has done extensive critical work on the Reid technique used in American law enforcement to secure confessions.

122 **pressed the point about transference**: In remarks at the symposium "Clean or Dirty Hands: The Role of Mental Health Professionals at Guantánamo" (with other copanelists, Josh Colangelo-Bryan and Nancy Sherman), conducted at the winter meeting of the American Psychoanalytic Association, held in New York City in January 2009. For Stuart Twemlow's views, see: www.backoffbully.com.

122 **dependence on the interrogator's picture of reality**: This extreme dependence on the interrogator, no doubt, may also promote circumstances that lead to false confessions.

122 **Stockholm or Patty Hearst syndrome**: So called after a Stockholm bank robbery in 1973 during which four employees were taken hostage for six days and came to identify with their captors. Patty Hearst similarly identified with her captors from the Symbionese Liberation Army.

124 **fails to respect the dignity or worth**: For emphasis on exploitation and failure to respect dignity, see Carse and Little 2009.

124 **famous experiments psychology professor Philip Zimbardo performed**: Zimbardo 1972.

125 **relationships to what we would do in private**: For a very helpful discussion of military obedience and conflicts between what we do in role and privately, see Estlund 2007.

125 **"the Mayor and Montaigne"**: Montaigne, 1993, 1144, Screech edition (replacing "twain" with "separate").

126 **justification for torture**: For a related actual example, read the case of Col. Allen West, a former artillery battalion commander in Iraq charged with beating an Iraqi detainee. See Julian Borger, " 'Mock Killing' by US Colonel," *Guardian*, November 19, 2003, available at: http://www.guardian.co.uk/Iraq/Story/0,2763,1088099,00.html. For a classic article on practical necessity and moral absolutes, see the closing section of Nagel's (1974) "War and Massacre." For the proposal of torture warrants, see Dershowitz 2002. For an interview on this, see: http://edition.cnn.com/2003/LAW/03/03/cnna.Dershowitz/.

126 **"stands in the spaces"**: Bromberg 1998.

127 **Longworth**: "Longworth" is a pseudonym for the counterintelligence liaison officer with whom Arrigo corresponded. I cannot independently corroborate some elements of their correspondence, though much of it touches on contemporary events that have become public knowledge. For our purposes, the correspondence provides a valuable framework for exploring the interrogator's mindset in the context of harsh interrogation. I am grateful to Jean Maria Arrigo for granting permission to review a copy of the correspondence. The original correspondence and additional military documents pertaining to the correspondence are archived in the Intelligence Ethics Collection at the Hoover Institution Archives, Stanford University. I am indebted to Jeff Farrington for his research assistance on this correspondence.

129 **Stoicism as a "therapy"**: For more on Stoicism as a therapy for the soul, see Sherman 2005.

131 **torture does not produce good intelligence**: On the issue of torture not producing good intelligence, see Arrigo 2004. For the contrary opinion, see the memoir of the French general, Paul Aussaresses (2002), who authorized the systematic use of torture as an interrogation technique in the Battle of Algiers.

132 **he *does* control the harming**: For an excellent discussion of complicity, see Kutz 2000, esp. 116–117.

132 **"torture lite"**: From an address by Albie Sachs, "Four Tales of Terrorism," given at the University of Chicago Law School conference on Torture, Law and War, on March 1, 2008. Sachs also lost his right arm in a car bomb planted by agents of South African security forces. See Sachs 2000 for the fuller account. For a compelling account of the history of "stealth" torture and its relationship to democracy and its monitoring of torture, see Rejali 2007.

133 **rarely raised as *moral* burdens**: Some of these concerns are background worries that motivate Jean Maria Arrigo's initiation of the correspondence.

134 **"In my meetings with detainees"**: William Quinn, "Violence Is Easier Than Empathy," *The Hoya*, September 11, 2007, available at: www.thehoya.com/node/13564.

135 **concrete respect**: See Sherman 1998b.

135 **portrait of Longworth**: My remarks in this paragraph and the next are greatly indebted to an insightful discussion of Kutz 2000.

136 **a small group**: The group included U.S. Surgeon General Richard Carmona, Army Surgeon General Kevin Kiley, Joint Staff Surgeon Joseph Kelly, and a number of military and civilian physicians on the staff of Undersecretary of Defense for Health Affairs William Winkenwerder. Also present were

representatives from the American Psychiatric Association, the American Psychological Association, the American Medical Association, and a number of military and medical and ethics writers.

136 **"reverse engineered"**: See Jane Mayer, "The Experiment," *The New Yorker*, July 11 and 18, 2005, 60–71, and "The Black Sites," *The New Yorker*, August 13, 2007, 46–57. Also, M. Gregg Bloche and Jonathan H. Marks, "Doing Unto Others as They Did Unto Us," *New York Times*, Op-Ed, November 14, 2005.

136 **breach of confidential psychiatric records**: On the report of breaches of medical records (including exploitation of a detainee's phobia of dogs and longing for his mother), see Neil Lewis, "Interrogators Cite Doctor's Aid at Guantánamo," *New York Times*, June 24, 2005, A1.

137 **large-scale force-feeding**: See Clive Stafford Smith, "Gitmo's Hunger Strikers," *Nation*, October 17, 2005. See also the transcript for "Guantánamo Force Feeding," *The Kojo Nnamdi Show*, WAMU 88.5, March 13, 2006. I also learned about force-feeding from Marc Falkoff, counsel for Guantánamo detainees at the litigation office of Covington & Burling LLP.

137 **my impressions with those of others**: The account that follows is drawn from a symposium, "Clean or Dirty Hands: The Role of Mental Health Professionals at Guantánamo," in which Josh Colangelo-Bryan, Stuart Twemlow, and I spoke during the winter meetings of the American Psychoanalytic Association January 2009 in New York City.

140 **interrogation and health care**: I draw heavily here on Marks 2009 for analysis of the "mezzo" levels of interrogation and professional health care workers.

140 **various professional organizations**: So, for example, the American Medical Association in 2006 stated that "physicians may participate in developing effective interrogation strategies for general training purposes," but "must neither conduct nor directly participate in an interrogation." The American Psychiatric Association, in an early statement, forbids psychiatrists to "participate or assist in any way, whether directly or indirectly ... in the interrogation of their patients," but allows them to "provide training to military or civilian investigative or law enforcement personnel on recognizing and responding to persons with mental illnesses, on the possible medical and psychological effects of particular techniques and conditions of interrogation." The American Psychological Association released a statement in August 2007 prohibiting "direct or indirect participation" in interrogations involving 19 unethical techniques that it specified. The American Anthropological Association released a statement announcing that it too condemned "the use of anthropological knowledge as an element of physical and psychological torture." The American Psychoanalytic Association released a

statement in January 2007 "condemning the use of torture. As an organization of psychoanalysts who have devoted their lives to helping people undo the effects of trauma in their lives, we strongly protest any governmentally administered and governmentally approved torture of people who are detained.... We also strongly condemn the participation or oversight by any mental health or medical personnel in any and all aspects of torture."

For more on the American Medical Association, see policy *E-2.068, Participation in Interrogation*, on the AMA web site; for more on the American Psychiatric Association, see position statement entitled *Psychiatric Participation in Interrogation of Detainees*, on its web site; for more on the American Psychological Association, see the council resolution from August 2007 on its web site; for more on the American Anthropological Association and the stances of other social science organizations, see Scott Jasachik's article, "Torture and Social Scientists," *Inside Higher Ed*, November 22, 2006. For discussion of the statement of the American Psychoanalytic Association, see Simon Bennett's report in the *American Psychoanalyst*, vol. 41, no. 1, Winter/Spring 2007.

140 **"intervention capital"**: Marks 2009.

141 **subtle identity shift**: Ibid.

141 **International Military Tribunal at Nuremberg**: I take up issues related to Guantánamo and Nuremberg in greater detail and with extensive documentation in Sherman 2007b. A shorter discussion appears in Sherman 2007a.

142 **Lifton interviewed doctors**:   Lifton 1986.

142 **"life unworthy of life"**: Ibid., 45–79.

142 **"The term euthanasia"**: Ibid., 101.

142 **"therapeutic killing"**: Ibid., 14–16.

142 **all added to the legitimization of the process**: Ibid., 65–70.

143 **Stanley Milgram in his famous experiments**: For a revisiting of the Milgram experiments, see Philip Zimbardo, "When Good People Do Evil," *Yale Alumni Magazine*, January/February 2007, 40–47. Zimbardo is the creator of the well-known "Stanford Prison Experiments" on the psychology of incarceration on incarcerators. The Yale magazine article is adapted from Zimbardo 2007.

144 **role of the nonclinicians**: On the importance of critiquing one's institutions, even if only from roles outside them, see Kant's arguments in "What is Enlightenment?" (discussed in ch. 1). I thank Tony Pfaff for comments on this issue.

145 **case of Al-Dossari**: Conversations with Joshua Colangelo-Bryan in the fall of 2006 and winter of 2009.

146 **strapped into restraint chairs**: See Eric Schmitt and Tim Golden, "Force-

Feeding at Guantánamo Is Now Acknowledged," *New York Times*, February 22, 2006. On this, I am also grateful to Kristine Huskey, attorney for several Kuwaitee detainees, for our conversation on March 24, 2006.

146 **diuretics and laxatives**: The force-feeding of laxatives and diuretics while in "the chair" was reported by Brig. Gen. Stephen Xenakis, former commanding general of the Southeast Regional Army Medical Command, during remarks at a conference, "Voices of Guantánamo," at George Washington Law School on March 20, 2006, covered by C-SPAN that evening.

146 **"charged with assuring quality medical care"**: In the words of Dr. William Winkenwerder, former assistant secretary of defense of health affairs, in his letter of invitation to me to travel to Guantánamo Bay.

CHAPTER 6: IN THE FACE OF TORTURE

151 **"Five years down there at least"**: Stockdale 1995, 185.

151 **Epictetus was a slave**: For this biography of Epictetus, see Long 2002, 10–12. Epictetus's *Handbook* was popular in its own times (indeed, the major influence on the emperor-philosopher Marcus Aurelius in his *Meditations*). In recent years, Epictetus has enjoyed a following not only in the military but also in wider circles; for example, see Tom Wolfe's depiction in *A Man in Full* (1998). There are also scores of contemporary self-help books that rely on Epictetus.

151 **common treatment of slaves**: See Pagán 2007/2008. Also duBois 1991. For a colorful case, see Cicero, "In Defense of Cluentius" in Cicero 1927.

152 **"Our opinions are up to us"**: Epictetus 1983, White edition.

152 **"Lameness is an impediment"**: Epictetus 1995, 290, Gill edition.

152 **"Memory is the chief enemy"**: Timerman 1981, 36; italics added.

152 **"professional stoicism"**: Ibid., 37.

153 **rapport building with a jailor or torturer**: In October 2005 I was told by the then-commanding officer of Guantánamo Detention Center, Maj. Gen. Jay W. Hood (who replaced Maj. Gen. Geoffrey D. Miller, who was responsible for "Gitmo-izing" Abu Ghraib with harsh interrogation techniques) that rapport building had now become the preferred method of interrogation at Guantánamo.

153 **"all logical emotions and sensations"**: Timerman 1981, 35.

153 **"penetration from the outside world"**: Ibid., 85.

153 **"The image of my wife's face"**: Ibid., 84.

153 **"blind architect"**: Ibid., 83.

153 **Esfandiari, described a similar approach**: Conversation with Haleh Esfandiari on September 26, 2007, and from Haleh Esfandiari, "Held in My Homeland," *Washington Post*, September 16, 2007, B1.

154 **One West Point colonel**: Conversation with David Luban in April 2005.

154 **victim will break at some point**: See Sussman 2005.

154 **Stockdale**: See Stockdale and Stockdale 1990, e.g., 161ff.

155 **philosophical underpinnings of his survival tool**: See "The Tough Mind of Epictetus" and "Courage under Fire" in Stockdale 1995.

155 **"taking the ropes"**: Stockdale 2001 and interview with Jim Stockdale in October 2001.

155 **Stoicism**: The Greek founders of the Stoic school are Zeno of Citium (335–263 BCE), Cleanthes (331–232 BCE), and Chrysippus (280–207 BCE). Cicero's *Tusculan Disputations* (see Cicero 2002, Graver edition) is a critical analysis of Stoic views on grief and is written after his own turn to Stoic consolations. For further discussion, see Sherman 2005, esp. ch. 6.

156 **"People come eagerly"** : Cicero 2001, 4.52, Annas edition; see 4.53–58 for the accusation that Zeno was just playing with words, "altering the terminology," in excluding certain goods from happiness (using Woolf translation in Annas edition).

156 **"oars of dialectic"**: Cicero, 2002 4.9, 3.25.

157 **"steals upon us"**: Seneca, 1995a, 2.2, Cooper and Procopé edition.

157 **"rehearsal"**: Seneca 1989, 14.3–6, Gummere edition.

157 **"Displays" of imminent and intimate brutality**: The "hook" apparently continues as an instrument of torture (or at least, of its bluster) and was found in a Sadam-era converted "Black Hole" room used by U.S. Special Forces Intelligence interrogation teams in Baghdad. See Eric Schmitt and Carolyn Marshall, "In Secret Unit's 'Black Room,' a Grim Portrait of U.S. Abuse," *New York Times*, March 19, 2006, 11.

158 **"because they overwhelm"**: Herman 1992, 33.

158 **brute sadistic need**: For more on sadistic cruelty and torture, see Seneca 1989, 2.5. For a fuller discussion of types of torture, see Sherman 2006.

158 **non-interrogational torture is harder to endure**: On this epistemic issue, see Shue 1978 and Sussman 2005.

158 **banality of the torturer's techniques**: See Rejali 2007, 380.

158 **"They would start by clanging"**: Interview with Jim Stockdale in October 2001.

159 **decent person's response**: Ancient versions of Stoicism famously hold suicide out as an option when one's will is crippled or where to act requires complic-

ity in evil or utter compromise of one's honor. Some POWs, as well as soldiers in theater or once at home, come to this point. On Stoicism and suicide, see Nussbaum 1996. I am indebted to Ian Hinsdale (in a paper submitted in December 2008) for an excellent discussion.

159 **enlightened emotions**: More broadly, the Greek Stoics allow for three "good" or enlightened emotions (*eupatheiai*) that a sage will feel (plus various subtypes of each): rational caution (*eulabeia*), rational wish (*boulēsis*),and rational delight (*chara*). They correspond to and replace ordinary nonsage emotions of fear (*phobos*), appetite (*epithumia*), and pleasure (*hēdonē*). Tellingly, there is no "good" emotion that maps onto the ordinary emotion of pain or distress (*lupē*) and more specifically, the distress of shame. For more on the classification of ordinary emotions, see Sherman 2005, 81, and for "good" emotions, see 81, 106, 109, 193, and 205. For a key text, see Laertius 7.116, in Long and Sedley 1987, vol. 1, 412, and more generally, 410–423. For an insightful discussion of "good" emotions, see Cooper 2004. Also, Graver 2002 and 2007.

159 **Jean Améry and Primo Levi**: See Améry 1980 on the predicament of the intellectual who does not always have those concrete skills. See Levi 1996 on the threat of moral corruption in the camps.

160 **cases reported to have occurred at Guantánamo**: Remarks by Josh Colangelo-Bryan, an attorney at Dorsey & Whitney LLP who represented detainees at Guantánamo. Colangelo-Bryan spoke at "Voices of Guantánamo," a symposium at George Washington Law School on March 20, 2006, and again at a symposium, "Clean or Dirty Hands: The Role of Mental Health Professionals at Guantánamo," at the winter meetings of the American Psychoanalytic Association in January 2009 in New York City.

160 **"indifferent"**: Epictetus 1995, 4.1.66, 4.1.78–80, 3.22.40–41, Hard translation in Gill edition.

161 **"show concern for nothing"**: Cicero 2001, 4.36. Interestingly, from a metaphysical point of view, the Stoics were physicalists in their conception of what mind actually is; it is *pneuma*, or breath, an animating, fine material.

161 **"When it comes to a happy life"**: Ibid., 3.43.

161 **Stockdale, in his own writings**: See Stockdale 1995.

161 **told me once**: Conversation with Wynona Ward on February 25, 2004. See also Brison 2002.

161 **"depersonalization"**: Conversation with psychiatrist and trauma specialist Rich Chefetz in fall 2006. For treatment of dissociative identity disorders, see Chefetz 2000, 2004; Way 2006; and Shapiro and Maxfield 2002.

161 **personal agency**: The point of much cognitive-behavioral therapy (CBT) in the treatment of trauma is to allow patients to renarrate events more accurately and with greater self-empathy. For an account of CBT in the treatment of rape victims, see Foa and Rothbaum 1998.

162 **remarks of a freed Guantánamo detainee**: At "The Voices of Guantánamo," a symposium at George Washington Law School on March 20, 2006.

162 **bodily or psychological pain**: A conception of torture as only extreme pain is what the notorious Jay Bybee's (then head of the Office of Legal Counsel) "torture memo" suggests: Torture involves the pain "associated with serious physical injury so severe that death, organ failure, or permanent damage resulting in a loss of significant body function will likely result." For this memo and others pertaining to the torture debate, see Greenberg and Dratel 2005. On the infliction of pain as not being the specific moral wrong of torture, see Sussman 1995.

162 **personal and moral agency**: Again, see Sussman 2005 on this important point.

163 **"unimportant matters"**: Timerman, 40–41, 67.

163 **some speak of their ordeals**: From "Voices of Guantánamo," a symposium at George Washington Law School on March 20, 2006.

164 **"The chair"**: On the chair, see the discussion in ch. 5. Also, see Eric Schmitt and Tim Golden, "Force-Feeding at Guantánamo Is Now Acknowledged," *New York Times*, February 22, 2006. I discussed the use of "the chair" with detainee attorney Kristine Huskey on March 24, 2006; Huskey represented Omar Khadr, the young Canadian charged with war crimes under the Military Commissions Act of 2006. For an account of her legal representation of detainees, see Huskey 2007.

164 **forced to urinate and defecate on himself**: As reported by Brig. Gen. Stephen Xenakis, former commanding general of the Southeast Regional Army Medical Command, during remarks at a symposium, "Voices of Guantánamo," at George Washington Law School on March 20, 2006, broadcast by C-SPAN that evening.

165 **way of getting him to experience**: It is also a way to get hunger strikers to stop striking of their own will. Kristine Huskey reported that her client, after hearing screaming in an adjoining cell from a detainee strapped to the chair, said "I won't strike again if it amounts to torture." Conversations with Kristine Huskey on March 24, 2006.

165 **"In my suffering there is nothing"**: Coetzee, 1982, 115.

165 **"the water cure"**: See Paul Kramer, "The Water Cure," *The New Yorker*, February 25, 2008.

165 **"Waterboarding"**: For an account of the recent practice of waterboarding, see Mayer 2008, 171–174.

166 **current evidence suggests**: See Koopman, Classen, and Spiegel 1994.

166 **some have argued**: See, for example, Jessica Wolfendale's (2006) comments on *Stoic Warriors* and torture.

166 **more popular version of the argument**: For discussion of "reverse engineering," see Jane Mayer's "The Experiment," *The New Yorker*, July 11, 2005, 60–71; M. Gregg Bloche and Jonathan H. Marks, "Doing Unto Others as They Did Unto Us," *New York Times*, Op-Ed, November 14, 2005, A21; and Nancy Sherman, "Mind Games at Gitmo," *Los Angeles Times*, Op-Ed, December 12, 2005. For additional citations, see Sherman 2007b.

166 **cornerstone of Socratic teaching**: See Plato, 1997, 280b7–281e1; 281e3–5, Cooper edition.

CHAPTER 7: LOOSENING THE STOIC ARMOR

171 **Maj. Tony DeStefano**: My first interviews with Tony DeStefano were in February and April of 2006 at Walter Reed Army Medical Center. I have corresponded with him and interviewed him many times since.

172 **attack at Camp Doha**: For an account of an attack on Doha by an Ababil-100 (a surface-to-surface missile, similar to the Tony DeStefano report on), see Gordon and Trainor 2006, 178.

172 **resilience**: For research on resilience, and the use of beta-blockers to tamp down traumatic memory formation, see Southwick et al. 1997 and 1999. For work on the role of the amino acid peptide in resilience, see Wilson, Friedman, and Lindy 2004. On a meditation-based resilience model for use in predeployment, I am grateful to Elizabeth Stanley for ongoing discussion. She presented some of her findings in a talk, "Mind Fitness and Mental Armor," at the Center for Peace and Security Studies at Georgetown University on March 3, 2009. For work in the field of positive psychology and non-deficit-based models of mental health and resilience influential in the military, see Seligman 2004 and http://www .defenselink.mil/news/newsarticle.aspx?id=52103. For models of post-traumatic growth, see Tedeschi, Calhoun, and Park 1998.

172 **traumatic responses are imprinted and stored**: See Herman 1992.

172 **"Every contemporary study"**: Van der Kolk 2003, 176, 187.

172 **repeat and relive their traumatic memories**: See Shay 2006.

173 **influential study by Charles Hoge**: According to the study conducted by Charles Hoge et al. (2004), of 222,620 Iraq veterans, 69,012 (31 percent) had at least one outpatient mental health care visit within the first year after deployment, as based on Post-Deployment Health Assessment Forms collected between May 2003 and April 2004.

A subsequent study (Seal et al. 2007) detailing the prevalence of mental health problems among Iraq and Afghanistan veterans reports that of 103,788 of Operation Enduring Freedom or Operation Iraqi Freedom veterans seen at VA health care facilities, 25,396 (25 percent) received a mental health diagnosis, and more than half of these veterans were dually or multiply diagnosed. When the definition was broadened to include psychosocial problems, 32,010 (31 percent) received mental health diagnoses. Mental health diagnoses were detected within days of a first VA clinic visit, and most initial mental health diagnoses (60 percent) were made in non–mental health clinics, mostly primary-care settings. The youngest group of veterans (ages 18–24 years) were at greatest risk for receiving mental health or post-traumatic stress disorder diagnoses, compared with veterans 40 years or older.

173 **Another recent report**: See discussion of the report in Thomas Shanker, "Army Is Worried by Rising Stress of Return Tours," *New York Times*, April 6, 2008, A1.

174 **impact on combat readiness**: In a starkly candid assessment, Gen. Richard A. Cody, the Army vice chief of staff, testified to Congress, "Our readiness is being consumed as fast as we can build it. . . . Lengthy and repeated deployments with insufficient recovery time have placed incredible stress on soldiers and our families, testing the resolve of our all-volunteer force like never before." Ibid.

For an analysis of long-term costs of providing care and disability benefits for veterans of Iraq and Afghanistan, see Linda Bilmes, "Soldiers Returning from Iraq and Afghanistan: The Long-Term Costs of Providing Veterans Medical Care and Disability Benefits," Faculty Research Working Paper Series, John F. Kennedy School of Government, Harvard University, 2007, at: http://ksgnotes1 .harvard.edu/Research/wpaper.nsf/rwp/RWP07-001/$File/rwp_07_001_ bilmes.pdf.

174 **signature injury of the current wars**: See Hoge et al. 2008. See Terry Tanielian and Lisa Jaycox, "Invisible Wounds of War," at: http://www.rand.org/ pubs/monographs/MG720/2008.

174 **"We're still Cartesians here"**: Conversation with senior military officer on April 23, 2008.

174 **meeting of veterans:** November 14, 2007. I am grateful to Henry Kenny for allowing me to attend the meeting.

174 **"PTSD is an anxiety disorder":** See Jeff Schogol, "Pentagon: No Purple Heart for PTSD," *Stars and Stripes*, January 6, 2009, available at: http://www .military.com/features/0,15240,182414,00.html.

175 **"So an enemy bullet could graze":** Conversation with senior military medical officer on January 13, 2009.

175 **"Psychological injuries *are* war injuries":** JSCOPE (Joint Services Conference on Professional Ethics, now, known as "ISME"—International Symposium for Military Ethics) meetings held in Washington, D.C., in January 2006. See also Shay 2006.

175 **"row for a bit":** Cicero, 2002, 4.9, Graver edition.

175 **"No doctor lives here":** Seneca 1989, 68.9: *non medicus, sed aeger hic habitat.* See Wilson 1997.

175 **Epictetus fashions himself:** See Long 2002.

176 **"Is it possible to be altogether faultless?":** Epictetus 1995, 4.12.19, Hard translation in Gill edition.

176 **"zero-defect" mentality:** "Zero-defect" was a term used for a policy in the late 1990s in the wake of various public scandals, such as the sexual harassment scandal called "Tailhook." At the Naval Academy, where I was teaching at the time, the policy was posted around the halls and photocopying rooms. Colin Powell (1995, 46, 323) famously criticized the policy as overly harsh and as knocking out of the military a source of potentially strong leaders who may have made mistakes early in their careers. He is autobiographical: As a junior officer he once lost a sidearm, a fairly serious offense for a junior officer and one that under a zero-defect policy can be career-ending.

176 **he did not suffer from PTSD:** The VA later diagnosed Tony with post-traumatic stress disorder, and with likely mild traumatic brain injury. For reports of pressure to misdiagnose psychological illnesses, including pressure to use diagnoses of preexisting personality disorders in order to save the military money in benefits, see: http://static.salon.com/media/mp3/2009/04/edited_mb_soldier .mp3. Also see the Army's response to an investigation of its mental health care at Fort Carson, including wrongful misdiagnoses: http://www.cbsnews.com/ stories/2007/05/17/health/main2820541.shtml.

177 **before he could be pinned:** Though the period from selection to pinning can, even at the best of times, involve long delays.

178 **mixes with other symptoms:** See van der Kolk 2003, 171.

179 **On another occasion, Walter Clark**: Interview with Walter Clark on April 28, 2006.

179 **are the questions an Army ranger**: Correspondence with Tony Pfaff from April 19 to May 6, 2006.

180 **self-condemnation**: See Williams 1993, 92–93.

180 **deflation from failing to meet goals**: See Deigh 1983.

180 **As one philosopher has put it**: See Velleman 2001.

180 **presentation of self and its limits**: See Goffman 1959 for a discussion that remains seminal. Also, see Darwall 2006 on the notion that guilt, but not shame, is a second personal, reactive attitude, esp. 71–72, 124–125, 163, 166–167.

The discussion of shame in recent philosophical literature is extensive and deserves some comment. Traditionally, some have held that shame is principally about autonomous morality and, in particular, about the loss of self-worth through the collapse of chosen ideals or one's faith in one's ability to carry them out. Others have argued that it concerns more public and social disapproval to which a person is vulnerable. The first view propounded by John Rawls (1971) owes much to Gerhart Piers and Milton Singer's (1953) influential, psychoanalytic account of the distinction between shame and guilt, in which shame is associated with a failure of self to achieve ego ideals, and guilt with a condemnation of self for a transgression against others and a wish for reparation. The second, social view of emotion is the traditional view exposited well by Aristotle: There is public exposure of some sort, or as David Velleman (2001) has put the point recently with a Kantian gloss, we are compromised in our ability to control our public personae.

Despite the initial attractiveness of the Rawlsian view of shame as the deflation inherent in a loss of self-worth, I side with Aristotle that shame is essentially a social emotion not just *induced* by others' disapproval, but *constituted* by a diminished appearance of oneself in their gaze. Moreover, shame does not necessarily signify what a person takes to be a fault in herself or her conception of her excellence, but rather can deprecate a more contingent aspect of her identity. On this, see Deigh 1983; for a related critique of the Rawlsian-influenced view of Bernard Williams in *Shame and Necessity*, see Calhoun 2004a, though to my mind, Calhoun does not adequately analyze the social weight of shame as something other than mechanical.

Sandra Bartky (1990) makes the critical point that a person often cares about how she is viewed by others and can feel shame as a result, even if she ultimately doesn't internalize the critical judgment. That's a point Aristotle seems to accept, as I say below.

180 **"like ourselves"**: Aristotle 1984, Rh. 1384a10, Barnes edition.

181 **"his clipped prick"**: Timerman 1981, 67.

181 **demeaning forms of punishment**: On a critique of shaming as punishment, see Nussbaum 2004, ch.4.

182 **"To this day I still can't talk"**: Interview with Robert Kislow on February 14, 2007.

182 **Article 15 of the Uniform Code of Military Justice**: See the Uniform Code of Military Justice subchapter 3, "Non-Judicial Punishment under Section 815, Article 15," at: http://www.au.af.mil/au/awc/awcgate/ucmj .htm#SUBCHAPTER%20III.%20NON-JUDICIAL%20PUNISHMENT.

183 **in-depth series exposing punitive conditions at Walter Reed**: See Dana Priest and Anne Hull's Pulitzer Prize–winning three-part series on conditions at Walter Reed in the *Washington Post*, February 18, 19, and 20, 2007.

184 **mandatory attendance**: The mandatory attendance, threats of punishment, and bullying went on side by side with state-of-the-art medicine and complementary, alternative medicine, typically offered by outside contractors, for relaxation, massage, yoga, and the like. Many of those alternative practitioners gathered under the umbrella "Camp PTSD" ("Camp" for "Complementary and Alternative Medicine Practitioners), now called "The Trauma Study Group at Walter Reed Army Medical Center." I am grateful to Robin Carnes and Sheila Crye for information about this group over the years.

184 **"They battled an enemy"**: Guy Raz, "Secretary Gates Promises Changes at Walter Reed," NPR, *All Things Considered*, February 23, 2007, available at: http://www.npr.org/templates/story/story.php?storyId=7577560.

185 **unofficial "stoic" patch**: For the art and politics of unofficial "tabs" or patches, see the review of Trevor Paglen's *I Could Tell You But Then You Would Have to Be Destroyed by Me,* in William Broad, "Inside the Black Budget," *New York Times*, April 1, 2008; available at: http://www.nytimes.com/2008/04/01/science/01patc. html?_r=1&oref=slogin; also William Broad, "Top-Secret Research Wears Its Art on Its Sleeve," *Scotsman*, available at: http://news.scotsman.com/latestnews/ Topsecret-research-wears-its-art.3936562.jp.

185 **"Warrior Resilience"**: See http://www.usatoday.com/news/military/2009 -03-24-iraqsuicides_N.htm.

187 **treatment of psychological trauma**: See, for example, the web site of the National Center for the Treatment of PTSD: http://www.ncptsd.va.gov/ncmain/ ncdocs/fact_shts/fs_treatmentforptsd.html?opm=1&rr=rr32&srt=d&echorr =true. I am grateful for conversations with its director, Matthew Friedman, on issues of treatment. For discussion and case study, see Resick and Calhoun 2001. A form of cognitive therapy is eye movement desensitization and reprocessing

(EMDR) (founded by Francine Shapiro), which uses the external stimulus of moving eyes back and forth (or snapping or tapping) in connection with focus on the negative traumatic belief, and emotions paired with a preferred positive belief. See http://www.emdr.com/briefdes.htm.

187 **"you try to challenge their guilt"**: Interview with John Rodolico on March 5, 2007.

189 **most research psychologists and philosophers now agree**: For an excellent critical overview, see Hurley 2006.

190 **"Get rid of judgment"**: Aurelius 1989, 4.7, Farquharson edition. See 4.4.

190 **"Not in being acted upon"**: Ibid., 9:16, reading "being acted upon" for "feeling."

191 **"He who writes these words"**: Seneca 1989, 1.437, Gummere edition.

191 **"Tears fall"**: Ibid., 3. 137.

191 **"a comeliness even in grief"**: Ibid., 143–145.

191 **"We teach Aristotle more than the Stoics"**: Conversations with Roger Herbert on March 18 and 25, 2009.

192 **Aristotelian view**: See Sherman 1989 and 1997.

192 **"Army Strong"**: See " 'Army Strong' to Be New Recruiting Slogan," *Washington Times*, October 9, 2006, available at: http://www.washingtontimes.com/news/2006/oct/09/20061009-104305-9882r/.

193 **"While we still remain among human beings"**: Seneca 1995a, 3.43, Cooper and Procopé edition.

CHAPTER 8: BODY AND BODY PARTS

195 **Dawn Halfaker**: Interview with Dawn Halfaker on December 17, 2007.

197 **"amputee disorder"**: On this, I am grateful to ongoing conversations with Jonathan Shay, who has been zealous in his efforts both to change the stigmatizing *DSM* (*Diagnostic and Statistics Manual*) label and to broaden the criteria of postcombat stress; see Shay 2006 (and for a broader discussion of psychological trauma, see Shay 1994 and 2002). Though combat stress is not a new phenomenon, it was not until 1980 that PTSD became a distinct diagnosis in the *DSM*. A confluence of therapeutic work with Vietnam vets and traumatized rape victims is part of the background story to the diagnosis. For the history, see Herman 1992.

197 **some reports**: *Salon* interview, available at: http://static.salon.com/media/mp3/2009/04/edited_mb_soldier.mp3; also http://www.cbsnews.com/stories/2007/05/17/health/main2820541.shtml.

198 **"If you see a guy"**: Conversation with Will Quinn on April 6, 2009.

198 **At Georgetown one evening**: Juan Luis Alcivar spoke at Georgetown University on March 31, 2009, at an event sponsored by a student social action committee in conjunction with the nonprofit group CAUSE (Comfort for America's Uniformed Services).

198 **received U.S. citizenship**: For an account of his receiving U.S. citizenship and the administering of the oath of allegiance by Homeland Secretary Janet Napolitano see: http://www.cnn.com/2009/US/04/10/soldier .citizen/index.html; also http://www.pbs.org/kcet/tavissmiley/mobile/archive/ shows_20090423.html.

200 **Quinn tells a class**: Will Quinn talked to my class on April 6, 2009, at Georgetown University.

202 **how we occupy our bodies**: I thank Robin Roger for insight here.

202 **"bigorexia"**: See Pope et al. 2000.

202 **wannabe amputees**: For a lucid, critical account, see Elliot 2000. For a different perspective, see Sullivan 2005. For body identity from the points of view of literary, gender, and cultural studies, see Brooks 1993, Bordo 1993, and Wills 1995.

202 **"attentively recessive in a high degree"**: O' Shaughnessy 1995, 175. Consider also Freud's notion of the bodily ego in *The Ego and the Id* (1923) in Freud 1955, vol. 19, 25–27: "The ego is first and foremost a bodily ego; it is not merely a surface entity, but is itself the projection of a surface." By that, he seems to mean that we bear a sense of ourselves derived not only from bodily sensations, from our surfaces, but also, internally, from proprioception (awareness) of our own limbs and body, not dependent on the specific report of the five senses. For a developmental notion of encasement by skin and skin-to-skin contact, see Anzieu 1989, 40: "By Skin Ego, I mean a mental image of which the Ego of the child makes use during the early phases of its development to represent itself as an Ego containing psychical contents, on the basis of its experience of the surface of the body." I am grateful to John Kafka for discussion of this last source.

204 **"carved at the joints"**: See Kinsbourne 1995.

204 **"long term body image"**: See Campbell 1995.

204 **Another wounded warrior**: I am indebted to an interview on April 23, 2007, with Dr. Douglas Price, a VA psychiatrist who has done extensive historical and medical research on phantom limbs. I am also grateful to Peter Cappadona, a leg amputee, for insights on living with limb loss. We spoke on December 7, 2007.

204 **"trapped pain memory"**: See Woodhouse 2005.

205 **"This is the way it is"**: Conversation with Rob Kislow in December 2007.

205 **consciousness of their bodies**: See Butterworth 1995; also Meltzoff and Moore 1995. On psychoanalytic research on developmental notions of embodiment, see Fonagy and Target 2007.

205 **"Things are defined"**: See Aristotle, *Politics*, in Aristotle 1984, 1253a20ff.

206 **"My ankle rolled"**: Huze 2004, quoted with permission from the author through the Susan Schulman Literary Agency.

207 **We grieve for the space**: See Krasner 2004.

208 **a story a friend shared about her mother**: I thank Alisa Carse for sharing this story about her mother with me.

208 **collecting body parts**: For insight on the collection of the dead, see Sledge 2005. In Israel, there is a self-organized group of religious Jews, Zaka (Israel's Disaster Victims Identification organization), now officially sanctioned by the government, that collects body parts for proper burial after bombings. I suspect the nature of the work is in general more familiar to the Israeli public than the work of body collection during war is to Americans. For a related discussion, see "Study of Zaka Volunteers Shows Surprisingly Low Levels of PTSD," *Jerusalem Post,* online edition, January 4, 2005.

208 **"We had to find"**: Interview with Dereck Vines on May 31, 2007.

210 **homicides and suicides**: See the *New York Times* series by Deborah Sontag, "War Torn," including "A Veteran's Descent, a Prosecutor's Choice," January 20, 2008, A1, 20.

210 **"blows they take"**: Aristotle 1984, NE III.9, Barnes edition.

210 **pain that persists**: Here, I am reminded of a book review by Holocaust archivist and psychoanalyst Dori Laub, and his coauthor, Johanna Bodenstab (2007). Laub described soldiers that he had treated in Israel during the Yom Kippur War of 1973. Some decompensated, he reported, out of sheer terror when what they were exposed to in battle resonated with the "extreme violence their parents had been exposed to during the Holocaust.... The traumatic experience of loss and extinction their parents had gone through caught up with them" during the violence of combat.

211 **hedonic utilitarianism**: See, for example, Kahneman and Krueger 2006. For an insightful critique, see Nussbaum 2008.

211 **"Character of the Happy Warrior"**: Wordsworth, "Character of the Happy Warrior" in *English Poetry II: From Collins to Fitzgerald. The Harvard Classics. 1909–14,* available at: http://www.bartleby.com/41/391.html.

211 **"insensibility"**: See Wilfred Owen's poem "Insensibility" in Owen, 1984, 145.

Chapter 9: FROM SOLDIER TO CIVILIAN

215 **Julie Pfaff's**: Interview with Julie Pfaff in June 2006.

216 **familiar account from World War I**: See Le Naour 2006.

216 **some 250,000 soldiers vanished**: Ibid., 2.

216 **"Number 2 Platoon"**: Remarque 1930, renewed 1958, 73.

216 **"secure base"**: Bowlby 1988, 11. Bowlby attributes to Mary D. S. Ainsworth the introduction of the notion of a secure base to attachment theory. For a brief biography, see: http://attachment.edu.ar/bio.html.

218 **wedding photo**: For the photo of Marine Sgt. Ty Ziegel and Renee Kline, see: http://www.ninaberman.com/index3.php?pag=prt&dir=marine. The photo, taken by Nina Berman, won the World Press Photo competition for portraiture in 2007. For an interview with her, see: http://www.salon.com/mwt/feature/2007/03/10/berman_photo/. According to CNN's "Waging War on the VA" (November 17, 2007), Ty and Renee Ziegel separated shortly before their first wedding anniversary.

219 **I visited Jason**: The following account is based on an interview with Pam Estes and Jason Erhart on February 6, 2008.

221 **"Veterans who come to facilities"**: Conversation with Jonathan Shay on February 13, 2007.

223 **Dereck and Clara Vines**: Interview with Derek and Clara Vines and their son, Brandon Douglas, in February 2008.

228 **"in fancy"**: Smith 1976, 47–48; also 53, 58, 140–141, 146, 169. For Hume's account of empathy (or what he calls "sympathy"), see Hume 1968. For an extensive discussion of the notion of empathy and its connection with imagination and how we know other minds, see Sherman 1998a.

229 **knowing others' minds may never come**: For important work on autism and impairment in "mind reading," i.e., "mind blindness," see Baron-Cohen 1999.

229 ***philia***: Aristotle takes up philia or friendship in NE VIII and IX, 1984, Barnes edition. For an extended discussion of his account of friendship, see Sherman 1989, ch 4, and Sherman 1997, ch. 5.

231 **trained to die in a hail of bullets**: Certain military specialties may better prepare soldiers, though even those trained to see bullets, missiles, and mortar may still suffer war's complex, psychological injuries. For a story on the low rate of PTSD among the POWs of the "Hanoi Hilton" era, many of whom were naval aviators, see David Brown, "POW Aftereffects in McCain Unlikely: Research

Shows Past Trauma Probably Won't Affect Candidate's Life Span," *Washington Post*, May 23, 2008, A06.

232 **women make up only about 14 percent**: See: http://www.army.mil/ women/. Also: http://www.army.mil/professionalwriting/volumes/volume6/ october_2008/ 10_08_2.html.

EPILOGUE

237 **Ted Westhusing**: I have assembled my reflections about Ted from several sources, including my own interviews with him in researching my earlier book *Stoic Warriors*, and later, after Ted's death, in conversations with Nick Fotion, Al Gill, Tony Pfaff, Steven Strange, and Jack Zupko. For many of the details of Ted's deployment in Iraq, I have relied heavily on T. C. Miller 2006, ch. 1 and 14. Miller first reported on Westhusing in an article in the *Los Angeles Times*: "The Conflict in Iraq: A Journey That Ended in Suicide," November 27, 2005, A1, A14.

238 **USIS had contracts with the Department of Defense**: T. C. Miller 2006, 278. Some have estimated that 50 percent of the Department of Defense budget is contracted out to private firms. See Minow 2005. For a detailed study of private contractors, see Singer 2003. Both gave presentations on these subjects to a seminar on war that David Luban and I taught at Georgetown University Law Center in 2004–2005.

238 **In March**: T. C. Miller 2006, 279.

238 **But by April**: Ibid.

238 **In May**: Ibid., 280. For more broad-based problems of contractual compliance, see Minow 2005.

239 **Ted was distraught**: T. C. Miller 2006, 281.

239 **"Nothing is easy in Iraq"**: Ibid., 282.

239 **On June 4, 2005**: Ibid., 282–283.

239 **"Cause of Death"**: Censored report the author received from the U.S. Army Criminal Investigation Command. Shortly after the report was released, a senior military officer and friend of Ted's was given permission to read the full document. He told me he had serious doubts at first, but after a critical reading of the report, he was persuaded that Ted committed suicide.

240 **"I cannot support a msn"**: As reported by T. C. Miller (2006), who was allowed to review a copy of the note by a U.S. government source.

241 **"an extremely ancient pastime"**: See Yalichev 1997, 1.

241 **"men for pay"**: Bugh 2006, 265, 265–277.

241 **jurisdiction over civilians is limited**: For a recent test of the permissible limits of military jurisdiction in a contractor abuse case, see Michael Gordon, "U.S. Charges Contractor at Iraq Post in Stabbing," *New York Times*, April 5, 2008, A5.

241 **deepens the sense of betrayal**: This was especially so in the incident involving the marines' jailing of the Zapata security contractors in June 2005. See Josh White and Griff White, "Tension, Confusion between Troops, Contractors in Iraq," *Washington Post*, July 10, 2005, A12. Also: http://www.corpwatch.org/article.php?id=12349.

242 **"The corrupt can come from outside"**: For his developed position on this, see Pfaff 2008.

BIBLIOGRAPHY

Adams, Gordon. 2007. Defense Spending: Embarrassment of Riches. *Bulletin of the Atomic Scientists*, March 5. Available at www.thebulletin.org.

Adams, Marilyn McCord. 1991. Sin as Uncleanness. *Philosophical Perspectives* 5:1–27.

Ajami, Fouad. 1974. *The Global Populists: Third World Nations and World Order Crises*. Research Monograph no. 41. Princeton: Princeton University Center of International Studies.

———. 1978. *Human Right and World Order Politics*. Working paper (World Order Models Project) no. 4. New York: Institute for World Order.

———. 1992. *The Arab Predicament: Arab Political Thought and Practice since 1967*. 2d ed. Cambridge: Cambridge University Press.

———. 1998. *The Dream Palace of the Arabs: A Generation's Odyssey*. New York: Pantheon Books.

———. 2006. *The Foreigner's Gift: The Americans, the Arabs, and the Iraqis in Iraq*. New York: Free Press.

Aldrich, Virgil C. 1939. An Ethics of Shame. *Ethics* 50 (1):57–77.

Améry, Jean. 1980. *At the Mind's Limits*. Bloomington: Indiana University Press.

Anthony, E. James, and Bertram J. Cohler, eds. 1987. *The Invulnerable Child*. New York: Guilford Press.

Anzieu, Didier. 1989. *The Skin Ego*. Translated by C. Turner. New Haven: Yale University Press.

Appadurai, Arjun. 2006. *Fear of Small Numbers: An Essay on the Geography of Anger*. Durham: Duke University Press.

Appiah, Kwame Anthony. 2008. *Experiments in Ethics*. Cambridge: Harvard University Press.

Applbaum, Arthur Isak. 1999. *Ethics for Adversaries: The Morality of Roles in Public and Professional Life*. Princeton: Princeton University Press.

Aristotle. 1984. *The Complete Works of Aristotle: The Revised Oxford Translation*, edited by J. Barnes. Princeton: Princeton University Press.

Army Field Manual 3–14, November 1997, at http://www.globalsecurity. org/wmd/library/policy/army/fm/3–14/index.html, accessed July 15, 2009.

Army Field Manual 3–11, March 2003, at http://www.globalsecurity.org/library/policy/army/fm/3-14/index.html, acessed July 15, 2009.

Arrigo, Jean Maria. 2004. A Utilitarian Argument against Torture Interrogation of Terrorists. *Science and Engineering Ethics* 10 (3).

Aurelius, Marcus. 1989. *The Meditations of Marcus Aurelius Antoninus*, edited by A. S. L. Farquharson. New York: Oxford University Press.

Aussaresses, Paul. 2002. *The Battle of the Casbah: Terrorism and Counter-Terrorism in Algeria 1955–1957*. New York: Enigma Books.

Austin, J. L. 1962. *How to Do Things with Words*. Cambridge: Harvard University Press.

Bacevich, Andrew J. 2005. *The New American Militarism: How Americans Are Seduced by War*. New York: Oxford University Press.

Baier, Annette C. 1993. Moralism and Cruelty: Reflections on Hume and Kant. *Ethics* 103 (3):436-457.

Bar On, Bat-Ami. 1991. Why Terrorism Is Morally Problematic. In *Feminist Ethics*, edited by C. Card. Lawrence: University Press of Kansas.

Barbusse, Henri. 2004. *Under Fire*. Translated by R. Buss. New York: Penguin Books.

Barker, Pat. 1992. *Regeneration*. New York: Penguin.

———. 1993. *The Eye in the Door*. New York: Plume.

———. 1995. *The Ghost Road*. New York: Plume.

Barnett, Roger W. 2003. *Asymmetrical Warfare: Today's Challenge to U.S. Military Power, Issues in Twenty-First-Century Warfare*. Washington, D.C.: Brassey's.

Baron, Marcia. 1988. Remorse and Agent-Regret. In *Midwest Studies in Philosophy*, edited by P. A. French, T. E. Uehling, and H. K. Wettstein. Notre Dame: University of Notre Dame Press.

Baron-Cohen, Simon. 1999. *Mindblindness: An Essay on Autism and Theory of Mind*. Cambridge: MIT Press.

Bar-Tal, Daniel. 2001. Why Does Fear Override Hope in Societies Engulfed by

Intractable Conflict, as It Does in the Israeli Society? *Political Psychology* 22 (3):601–627.

Bartky, Sandra. 1990. *Femininity and Domination: Studies in the Phenomenology of Oppression.* New York: Routledge.

Bazemore, Gordon, and Mara Schiff, eds. 2001. *Restorative Community Justice: Repairing Harm and Transforming Communities.* Cincinnati: Anderson.

Benn, Piers. 1996. Forgiveness and Loyalty. *Philosophy* 71 (277):369–383.

Bermudez, Jose Luis, Anthony Marcel, and Naomi Eilan, eds. 1995. *The Body and the Self.* Cambridge: MIT Press.

Bilton, Michael, and Kevin Sim. 1992. *Four Hours in My Lai.* New York: Penguin.

Black-Michaud, Jacob. 1975. *Cohesive Force: Feud in the Mediterranean and the Middle East.* New York: St. Martin's Press.

Blumenfeld, Laura. 2002. *Revenge.* New York: Washington Square Press.

Boehm, Christopher. 1984. *Blood Revenge: The Anthropology of Feuding in Montenegro and Other Tribal Societies.* Lawrence: University Press of Kansas.

Bordo, Susan. 1993. *Unbearable Weight: Feminism, Western Culture, and the Body.* Berkeley: University of California Press.

Botros, Sophie. 1983. Acceptance and Morality. *Philosophy* 58 (226):433–453.

Bottomley, Gordon, and Denys Harding, eds. 1949. *The Collected Poems of Isaac Rosenberg.* New York: Schocken Books.

Bowden, Mark. 2003. The Dark Art of Interrogation. *Atlantic Monthly* 292 (3):51ff.

Bowlby, John. 1988. *A Secure Base.* New York: Basic Books.

Bradley, F. H. 1927/1876. *Ethical Studies.* 2d ed. Oxford: Oxford University Press. Original edition, 1876.

Brady, James B. March. 1973. Status Responsibility. *Philosophy and Phenomenological Research* 33 (3):408–411.

Bragg, Melvyn. 1999. *A Soldier's Return.* London: Sceptre.

———. 2001. *A Son of War.* London: Sceptre.

———. 2003. *Crossing the Lines.* New York: Arcade.

Braithwaite, John. 2002. *Restorative Justice and Responsive Regulation.* New York: Oxford University Press.

Brennan, Tad. 2005. *The Stoic Life.* New York: Oxford University Press.

Brison, Susan J. 2002. *Aftermath: Violence and the Remaking of the Self.* Princeton: Princeton University Press.

Brock, Dan W. 1983. Desert, Fairness and Persons. *Nous* 17 (1):56–58.

Bromberg, Philip. 1998. *Standing in the Spaces: Essays on Clinical Process, Trauma, and Dissociation.* Hillsdale, N.J.: Analytic Press.

Brooks, Peter. 1993. *Body Work: Objects of Desire in Modern Narrative*. Cambridge: Harvard University Press.

———. Spring 2002. Narrativity of the Law. *Law and Literature* 14 (1):1–10.

Browne, Brynmor. 1992. A Solution to the Problem of Moral Luck. *Philosophical Quarterly* 42 (168):345–356.

Bugh, Glenn. 2006. Hellenistic Military Developments. In *The Cambridge Companion to the Hellenistic World*, edited by G. Bugh. Cambridge: Cambridge University Press.

Burlingham, Dorothy T., and Anna Freud. 1973. *War and Children*. Westport, Conn.: Greenwood Press.

Burns, John Horne. 2004. *The Gallery*. New York: New York Review of Books.

Butterworth, George. 1995. An Ecological Perspective on the Origins of Self. In *The Body and the Self*, edited by J. L. Bermudez, A. Marcel, and N. Eilan. Cambridge: MIT Press.

Calhoun, Cheshire. 1992. Changing One's Heart. *Ethics* 103 (1):76–96.

———. 2004a. An Apology for Moral Shame. *Journal of Political Philosophy* 12 (2):127–46.

———. ed. 2004b. *Setting the Moral Compass: Essays by Women Philosophers*. New York: Oxford University Press.

Campbell, John. 1995. The Body Image and Self-Consciousness. In *The Body and the Self*, edited by J. L. Bermudez, A. Marcel, and N. Eilan. Cambridge: MIT Press.

Campbell, W. Keith. 2001. Is Narcissism Really So Bad? *Psychological Inquiry* 12 (4):214–216.

Card, Claudia. 1972. On Mercy. *Philosophical Review* 81 (2):182–207.

Carse, Alisa L., and Maggie O. Little. 2009. Exploitation and the Enterprise of Medical Research. In *Exploitation in Medical Research*, edited by E. Emanuel and J. Hawkins. Princeton: Princeton University Press.

Caruth, Cathy, ed. 1995. *Trauma: Explorations in Memory*. Baltimore: Johns Hopkins University Press.

Casey, Edward S. 2000. *Remembering: A Phenomenological Study*, 2d ed. Bloomington: Indiana University Press.

Chagnon, Napoleon A. February 1988. Life Histories, Blood Revenge, and Warfare in a Tribal Population. *Science* 239:985–992.

Chandrasekaran, Rajiv. 2006. *Imperial Life in the Emerald City*. New York: Knopf.

Chefetz, Richard A. 2000. Disorder in the Therapist's View of the Self: Working with the Person with Dissociative Identity Disorder. *Psychoanalytic Inquiry* 20 (2):305–329.

———. Fall 2004. The Paradox of "Detachment Disorders": Binding-Disruptions of Dissociative Process. *Psychiatry* 67 (3):246–255.

Childress, James F. 1979. Appeals to Conscience. *Ethics* 89 (4):315–335.

Christopher, Paul. 1999. *The Ethics of War and Peace: An Introduction to Legal and Moral Issues*, 2d ed. Upper Saddle River, N.J. : Prentice Hall.

Cicero. 1927. *The Speeches.* Translated by H. Grose Hodge. Cambridge: Harvard University Press.

———. 1991. *On Duties*, edited by M. T. Griffin and E. M. Atkins. New York: Cambridge University Press.

———. 2001. *On Moral Ends*, edited by J. Annas. New York: Cambridge University Press.

———. 2002. *Cicero on the Emotions: Tusculan Disputations 3 and 4*, edited by M. Graver. Chicago: University of Chicago Press.

Clausewitz, Carl von. 1942. *Principles of War.* Translated by H. W. Gatzke. Harrisburg, Penn.: Military Service Publishing.

Clausewitz, Karl von. 1943. *On War.* Translated by O. J. M. Jolles. New York: Modern Library.

Coetzee, J. M. 1982. *Waiting for the Barbarians.* New York: Penguin.

Conot, Robert. 1983. *Justice at Nuremberg.* New York: Harper and Row.

Conroy, John. 2000. *Unspeakable Acts, Ordinary People: The Dynamics of Torture.* New York: Knopf.

Cooper, David E. 1969. Collective Responsibility: Again. *Philosophy* 44 (168):153–155.

Cooper, John. 2004. The Emotional Life of the Wise. Available at: http://www .princeton.edu/~johncoop/Papers/Stoics-EmotionalLife12.04.pdf.

Cordner, Christopher. 1997. Honour, Community, and Ethical Inwardness. *Philosophy* 72 (281):401–415.

Cornell, Drucilla. 2004. *Defending Ideals: War, Democracy, and Political Struggles.* New York: Routledge.

Crelinsten, Ronald, and Alex Schmid, eds. 1995. *The Politics of Pain.* Boulder, Colo.: Westview Press.

Croft-Cooke, Rupert. 1971. *The Licentious Soldiery.* London: W. H. Allen.

Cua, Anthony S. 2003. The Ethical Significance of Shame: Insights of Aristotle and Xunzi. *Philosophy East and West* 53 (2):147–202.

D'arms, Justin, and Daniel Jacobson. 2000. Sentiment and Value. *Ethics* 110 (4):722-748.

Darwall, Steven. 2006. *The Second-Person Standpoint.* Cambridge: Harvard University Press.

Davies, Roy. 1989. *Service in the Roman Army*. Edinburgh: Edinburgh University Press.

Davis, Nancy. 1985. Rights, Permission, and Compensation. *Philosophy and Public Affairs* 14 (4):374–384.

Davoine, Francoise, and Jean-Max Gaudilliere. 2004. *History beyond Trauma: Whereof One Cannot Speak . . . Thereof One Cannot Stay Silent*. Translated by S. Fairfield. New York: Other Press.

Day Lewis, C. 1943. *Word over All*. London: J. Cape.

Deigh, John. 1983. Shame and Self-Esteem: A Critique. *Ethics* 93 (2):225–245.

———, ed. 1992. *Ethics and Personality: Essays in Moral Psychology*. Chicago: University of Chicago Press.

———. 1996. *The Sources of Moral Agency*. New York: Cambridge University Press.

———. 1999. All Kinds of Guilt. *Law and Philosophy* 18 (4):313–325.

Dennett, Daniel C. 1991. *Consciousness Explained*. Boston: Little, Brown.

Dershowitz, Alan. 2002. *Shouting Fire: Civil Liberties in a Turbulent Time*. New York: AOL Time Warner.

Devji, Faisal. 2005. *Landscapes of the Jihad: Militancy, Morality, Modernity*. Ithaca: Cornell University Press.

Digeser, Peter. 1998. Forgiveness and Politics: Dirty Hands and Imperfect Procedures. *Political Theory* 26 (5):700–724.

Dillon, John M. 1997. *The Great Tradition*. Norfolk, U.K.: Ashgate/Variorum.

Dillon, Robin S. 1997. Self-Respect: Moral, Emotional, Political. *Ethics* 107 (2):226–249.

Djilas, Milovan. 1958. *Land without Justice*. New York: Harcourt Brace.

Dohrenwend, Bruce, et al. August 2006. The Psychological Risks of Vietnam for U.S. Veterans: A Revisit with New Data and Methods. *Science* 313:979–982.

Dolinko, David. 1999. Morris on Paternalism and Punishment. *Law and Philosophy* 18 (4):345–361.

Dower, John D. 1986. *War without Mercy: Race and Power in the Pacific War*. New York: Pantheon.

Downie, R. S. 1965. Forgiveness. *Philosophical Quarterly* 15 (59):128–134.

Driver, Julia. 1997. The Ethics of Intervention. *Philosophy and Phenomenological Research* 25 (99):138-150.

duBois, Page. 1991. *Torture and Truth*. New York: Routledge.

Einstein, Albert, and Sigmund Freud. 1960. The Freud-Einstein Correspondence of 1932 and Psychoanalytic Theories of War. In *Einstein on Peace*, edited by O. Nathan and N. Heinz. New York: Schocken Books.

Eisenberg, Nancy, and Qing Zhou. 2000. Regulation from a Development Perspective. *Psychological Inquiry* 11 (3):166–171.

Elliot, Carl. 2000. A New Way to Be Mad. *Atlantic Monthly* 286 (6):72–84.

Elliot, Ward. 1968. Guilt and Overguilt: Some Reflections on Moral Stimulus and Paralysis. *Ethics* 78 (4):247–254.

Elster, John. 1990. Norms of Revenge. *Ethics* 100 (4):862–885.

Emad, Parvis. 1972. Max Scheler's Phenomenology of Shame. *Philosophy and Phenomenological Research* 32 (3):361–370.

Epictetus. 1983. *The Handbook (The Enchiridion)*. Translated by Nicholas White. Indianapolis: Hackett Publishing.

———. 1995. *The Discourses of Epictetus*, edited by C. Gill. London: Everyman.

Erxleben, Jan, and Jim A. Cates. 1991. Systemic Treatment of Multiple Personality: Response to a Chronic Disorder. *American Journal of Psychotherapy* 45 (2):269–278.

Estlund, David. 2007. On Following Orders in an Unjust War. *Journal of Political Philosophy* 15 (2):213–234.

Etzioni, Amitai, and David E. Carney, eds. 1997. *Repentance: A Comparative Perspective*. Lanham, Md.: Rowman and Littlefield.

Faulks, Sebastian. 1993. *Birdsong*. New York: Vintage.

Feldman, Noah. 2004. *What We Owe Iraq: War and the Ethics of Nation Building*. Princeton: Princeton University Press.

Felman, Shoshana. 1991. Crisis of Witnessing: Albert Camus' Postwar Writings. *Cardozo Studies in Law and Literature* 3 (2):197–242.

Felman, Shoshana, and Dori Laub. 1992. *Testimony: Crises of Witnessing in Literature, Psychoanalysis, and History*. New York: Routledge, Taylor, and Francis.

Ferguson, Tamara J., Hedy Stegge, and Tlse Damhuis. 1991. Children's Understanding of Guilt and Shame. *Child Development* 62 (4):827–839.

Ferracuti, Franco, and Marvin E. Wolfgang. 1969. *The Subculture of Violence: Towards an Integrated Theory in Criminology*. London: Tavistock.

Filkins, Dexter. 2005. The Fall of the Warrior King. *New York Times*, October 23.

Fingarette, Herbert. January 1966. Responsibility. *Mind* 75 (297):58–74.

Fischer, John Martin, and Mark Ravizza, eds. 1991. *Ethics: Problems and Principles*. Orlando: Holt, Rhinehart and Winston.

Foa, Edna B., and Barbara O. Rothbaum. 1998. *Treating the Trauma of Rape: Cognitive-Behavioral Therapy for PTSD*. New York: Guilford Press.

Fonagy, Peter, and Mary Target. 2007. The Rooting of the Mind in the Body: New Links between Attachment Theory and Psychoanalytic Thought. *Journal of American Psychoanalytic Association* 55 (2):493–502.

Fotion, N. 1961. Wickedness. *Philosophical Quarterly* 11 (45):323–327.

Frank, Robert H. 1988. *Passions within Reason: The Strategic Role of the Emotions*. New York: W. W. Norton.

Frankfurt, Harry. 1988. *The Importance of What We Care About*. New York: Cambridge University Press.

French, Peter A. 2001. *The Virtues of Vengeance*. Lawrence: University Press of Kansas.

French, Peter A., Theodore E. Uehling, and Howard K. Wettstein, eds. 1988. *Ethical Theory: Character and Virtue*. Notre Dame: University of Notre Dame Press.

Freud, Anna. 1973. *Infants without Families: Reports on the Hampsted Nurseries, 1939–1945*. New York: International Universities Press.

Freud, Sigmund. 1955. *Standard Edition (SE) of the Complete Psychological Works of Sigmund Freud*. Translated by J. Strachey. London: Hogarth Press.

Friedman, Lawrence. 1985. Towards a Reconceptualization of Guilt. *Contemporary Psychoanalysis* 21:501–547.

Friedman, Matthew. 2004. Acknowledging the Psychiatric Cost of War. *New England Journal of Medicine* 351 (1):75–77.

Frijda, Nico H. May 1988. The Laws of Emotion. *American Psychologist* 43 (5):349–358.

———. 1994. The Lex Talionis: On Vengeance. In *Emotions: Essays on Emotion Theory*, edited by S. H. M. Van Goozen, N. E. Van de Poll, and J. A. Sergeant. Hillsdale, N.J.: Lawrence Erlbaum.

Fussell, Paul. 1975. *The Great War and Modern Memory*. New York: Oxford University Press.

———, ed. 1983. *Siegfried Sassoon's Long Journey: Selections from the Sherston Memoirs*. New York: K. S. Giniger.

———. 1989. *Wartime: Understanding and Behavior in the Second World War*. New York: Oxford University Press.

Gallagher, Shaun. 1995. Body Schema and Intentionality. In *The Body and the Self*, edited by J. L. Bermudez, A. Marcel, and N. Eilan. Cambridge: MIT Press.

Garbarino, James, Nancy Dubrow, Kathleen Kostelny, and Carole Pardo. 1992. *Children in Danger: Coping with the Consequences of Community Violence*. San Francisco: Jossey-Bass.

Garren, David. Winter/Spring 2007. Soldiers, Slaves, and the Liberal State. *Philosophy and Public Policy Quarterly* 27(1/2):8–11.

Gellius, Aulus. 1927. *The Attic Nights of Aulus Gellius* (Loeb Classical Library), edited by E. Capps, T. E. Page, and W. H. D. Rouse. Cambridge: Harvard University Press.

Gibbard, Allan. 1992. Moral Concepts: Substance and Sentiment. *Philosophical Perspectives* 6:199–221.

Gillett, Grant. 1991. Multiple Personality and Irrationality. *Philosophical Psychology* 4 (1):103–118.

Gingell, John. 1974. Forgiveness and Power. *Analysis* 34 (6):180–183.

Ginsberg, Elaine. 1996. *Passing and the Fictions of Identity*. Durham: Duke University Press.

Glatzer, Nahum, ed. 1971. *Philo Judaeus: The Essential Philo*. New York: Schocken.

Glover, Jonathan. 1988. *The Philosophy and Psychology of Personal Identity*. London: Penguin Press.

Glucklich, Ariel. 2001. *Sacred Pain: Hurting the Body for the Sake of the Soul*. New York: Oxford University Press.

Goffman, Erving. 1959. *The Presentation of Self in Everyday Life*. New York: Anchor Books, Doubleday.

———. 1961. *Encounters: Two Studies in the Sociology of Interaction*. Indianapolis: Bobbs-Merrill.

Goldman, Jan, ed. 2006. *Ethics of Spying: A Reader for the Intelligence Professional*. Lanham, Md.: Scarecrow Press.

Goodin, Robert. 1985. *Protecting the Vulnerable: A Reanalysis of Our Social Responsibilities*. Chicago: University of Chicago Press.

Gordon, Michael, and Bernard Trainor. 2006. *Cobra II: The Inside Story of the Invasion and Occupation of Iraq*. New York: Pantheon.

Govier, Trudy, and Wilhelm Verwoerd. 2002. The Promise and Pitfalls of Apology. *Journal of Social Philosophy* 33 (1):67–82.

Graver, Margaret. 1999. Philo of Alexandria and the Origins of the Stoic *Propatheia*. *Phronesis* 44 (4):300–325.

———, ed. 2002. *Cicero on the Emotions: Tusculan Disputations 3 and 4*. Chicago: University of Chicago Press.

———. 2007. *Stoicism and Emotions*. Chicago: University of Chicago Press.

Graves, Robert. 1957. *Good-Bye to All That*. New York: Anchor Books.

Greenberg, Jerald, and Ronald L. Cohen, eds. 1982. *Equity and Justice in Social Behavior*. New York: Academic Press.

Greenberg, Karen, ed. 2006. *The Torture Debate in America*. New York: Cambridge University Press.

Greenberg, Karen, and Joshua Dratel. 2005. *The Torture Papers*. New York: Cambridge University Press.

Greene, Joshua. 2008. The Secret Joke of Kant's Soul. In *Moral Psychology: The Neuroscience of Morality: Emotion, Disease, and Development*, edited by W. Sinnott-Armstrong. Cambridge: MIT Press.

Grossman, Lt. Col. Dave. 1995. *On Killing: The Psychological Cost of Learning to Kill in War and Society*. Boston: Little, Brown.

———. 2004. *On Combat: The Psychology and Physiology of Deadly Conflict in War and Peace*. Illinois: PPCT Research Publications.

Guest, John. 1970. *Broken Images: A Journal*. London: Leo Cooper.

Gunderson, Erik. 2003. *Declamation, Paternity, and Roman Identity: Authority and the Rhetorical Self*. New York: Cambridge University Press.

Halliwell, Stephen. 1986. *Aristotle's Poetics*. Chapel Hill: University of North Carolina Press.

Hardimon, Michael O. 1994. Role Obligations. *Journal of Philosophy* 91 (7):333–363.

Hartman, Geoffrey H. 1994. Is an Aesthetic Ethos Possible? Night Thoughts after Auschwitz. *Cardozo Studies in Law and Literature* 6 (2):135–155.

Hedges, Chris. 2002. *War Is a Force That Gives Us Meaning*. New York: Anchor Books.

Held, Virginia. 1987. Feminism and Moral Theory. In *Women and Moral Theory*, edited by Eva Feder Kittay and D. T. Meyers. Totowa, N.J.: Rowman and Littlefield.

Herman, Judith Lewis. 1992. *Trauma and Recovery*. New York: Basic.

Herr, Michael. 1977. *Dispatches*. New York: Knopf.

Hestevold, H. Scott. December 1985. Justice to Mercy. *Philosophy and Phenomenological Research* 46 (2):281–291.

Hieronymi, Pamela. 2001. Articulating an Uncompromising Forgiveness. *Philosophy and Phenomenological Research* 62 (3):529–555.

Hill, Thomas, Jr. 1983. Moral Purity and the Lesser Evil. *Monist* 66 (2):213–232.

Hinde, Robert A., ed. 1992. *The Institution of War*. New York: St. Martin's Press.

Hinde, Robert A., and Donald A. Parry, eds. 1989. *Education for Peace*. Nottingham: Spokesman.

Hinde, Robert A., and Helen E. Watson, eds. 1995. *War: A Cruel Necessity? The Bases of Institutionalized Violence*. London: Tauris Academic Studies.

Hoge, Charles W., Carl A. Castro, Stephen C. Messer, Dennis McGurk, Dave I. Cotting, and Robert L. Koffman. 2004. Combat Duty in Iraq and Afghanistan, Mental Health Problems, and Barriers to Care. *New England Journal of Medicine* 351 (1):13–22.

Hoge, Charles W., Dennis McGurk, Jeffrey L. Thomas, Anthony L. Cox, Charles C. Engel, and Carl A. Castro. 2008. Mild Traumatic Brain Injury in U.S. Soldiers Returning from Iraq. *New England Journal of Medicine* 385 (5):453–463.

Holmes, Richard. 1989. *Acts of War: The Behavior of Men in Battle*. New York: Free Press.

Homer. 1999. *The Iliad*, edited by R. Fagles. New York: Penguin.

Honneth, Axel. 1992. Integrity and Disrespect: Principles of a Conception of Morality Based on the Theory of Recognition. *Political Theory* 20 (2):187–201.

Howlett, Jana, and Rod Mengham, eds. 1994. *The Violent Muse: Violence and the Artistic Imagination in Europe, 1910–1939*. Manchester: Manchester University Press.

Hubbard, Thomas K., ed. 2003. *Homosexuality in Greece and Rome: A Sourcebook of Basic Documents*. Berkeley: University of California Press.

Hughes, Martin. 1975. Forgiveness. *Analysis* 35 (4):113–117.

Hume, David. 1968/1739. *A Treatise of Human Nature,* edited by L. A. Selby-Bigge. Oxford: Oxford University Press.

Hurley, Elisa. 2006. Beyond Emotional Cognitivism: Feelings, Norms, and Folk-Psychological Kinds. Ph.D. dissertation, Georgetown University.

Huskey, Kristine. 2007. Standards and Procedures for Classifying "Enemy Combatants": Congress, What Have You Done? *Texas International Law Journal* 43 (1):41–54.

Hutton, J. H., ed. 1954. *The Unwritten Law in Albania*. Cambridge: Cambridge University Press.

Huze, Sean. 2004. *The Sand Storm: Stories from the Front* (A play in one act).

Hynes, Samuel. 1997. *The Soldiers' Tale: Bearing Witness to Modern War*. New York: Penguin.

Isenberg, Arnold. 1949. Natural Pride and Natural Shame. *Philosophy and Phenomenological Research* 10 (1):1–24.

Ito, Tiffany A., and John T. Cacioppo. 1998. Representations of the Contours of Positive Human Health. *Psychological Inquiry* 9 (1):43–48.

Jacobson, Richard B. 1992. The Structures of Forgiveness. *Cardozo Studies in Law and Literature* 4 (2):243–253.

James, William. 1902. *The Varieties of Religious Experience*. New York: Modern Library/Random House.

Janoff-Bulman, Ronnie. 1992. *Shattered Assumptions*. New York: Free Press.

Johnson, James Turner. 1999. *Morality and Contemporary Warfare*. New Haven: Yale University Press.

Jones, David H. 1966. Freud's Theory of Moral Conscience. *Philosophy* 41 (155):34–57.

Jünger, Ernst. 1996. *The Storm of Steel*. New York: Fertig.

Kahan, Dan M. 2001. Two Liberal Fallacies in the Hate Crimes Debate. *Law and Philosophy* 20 (2):175–193.

Kahneman, Daniel, and Alan B. Krueger. 2006. Developments in the Measurement of Subjective Well-Being. *Journal of Economic Perspectives* 20:3–24.

Kant, Immanuel. 1949/1797. On a Supposed Right to Lie from Altruistic Motives. In *Critique of Practical Reason and Other Writings in Moral Philosophy*, edited by L. W. Beck. Chicago: University of Chicago Press.

———. 1964/1797. *The Doctrine of Virtue*, edited by M. J. Gregor. Philadelphia: University of Pennsylvania Press.

———. 1970/1784. An Answer to the Question: What Is Enlightenment? In *Kant's Political Writings*, edited by H. Reiss. Cambridge: Cambridge University Press.

Kasachkoff, Tziporah. 1998. Killing in Self-Defense: An Unquestionable or Problematic Defense? *Law and Philosophy* 17 (5/6):509–531.

Keen, Maurice. 1984. *Chivalry*. New Haven: Yale University Press.

Keen, Sam. 1991. *Faces of the Enemy: Reflections of the Hostile Imagination*. San Francisco: Harper.

Kelman, Herbert C., and V. Lee Hamilton. 1989. *Crimes of Obedience: Toward a Social Psychology of Authority and Responsibility*. New Haven: Yale University Press.

Kennedy, David. 2006. *Of War and Law*. Princeton: Princeton University Press.

Kennedy, George. 1972. *The Art of Rhetoric in the Roman World: 300 B.C.–A.D. 300*. Princeton: Princeton University Press.

Kerrigan, John. 1996. *Revenge Tragedy: Aeschylus to Armageddon*. New York: Oxford University Press.

Keynes, Geoffrey, ed. 1970. *The Poetical Works of Rupert Brooke*. London: Faber and Faber.

Kilner, Maj. Peter. March–April 2002. Military Leaders' Obligation to Justify Killing in War. *Military Review*, 82 (2):24–31.

Kinsbourne, Marcel. 1995. Awareness of One's Body: An Attentional Theory of Its Nature, Development, and Brain Basis. In *The Body and The Self*, edited by J. L. Bermudez, A. Marcel and N. Eilan. Cambridge: MIT Press.

Klein, Melanie. 1975. *Envy and Gratitude and Other Works, 1946–1963*. New York: Dell.

———. 1977. *Love, Guilt and Reparation and Other Works, 1921–1945*. New York: Delta.

Klimehuk, Dennis. 2001. Retribution, Restitution and Revenge. *Law and Philosophy* 20 (1):81–101.

Kluft, Richard P. 1988. The Postunification Treatment of Multiple Personality Disorder: First Findings. *American Journal of Psychotherapy* 42 (2):212–228.

Koopman, C., C. Classen, and D. Spiegel. 1994. Predictors of Posttraumatic Stress Symptoms among Survivors of the Oakland/Berkeley, California, Firestorm. *American Journal of Psychiatry* 151:888–894.

Korsgaard, Christine M. 1989. Personal Identity and the Unity of Agency: A Kantian Response to Parfit. *Philosophy and Public Affairs* 18 (2):101–132.

Krasner, James. 2004. Doubtful Arms and Phantom Limbs: Literary Portrayals of Embodied Grief. *Publications of Modern Language Association of America* 119(2):219–232.

Kronman, Anthonoy. 1987. Living in the Law. *University of Chicago Law Review* 54.

Kutz, Christopher. 2000. *Complicity: Ethics and Law for a Collective Age*. New York: Cambridge University Press.

Laertius, Diogenes. 1972. *Lives of Eminent Philosophers* (Loeb Classical Library), edited by R. D. Hicks. Cambridge: Harvard University Press.

Lago, Mary, and P. N. Furbank, eds. 1983. *Selected Letters of E.M. Forster: Volume One, 1879–1920*. Cambridge: Belknap Press of Harvard University Press.

Lagouranis, Tony, and Allen Mikaelian. 2007. *Fear Up Harsh: An Army Interrogator's Dark Journey through Iraq*. New York: NAL Caliber.

Lamb, R. E. 1983. Guilt, Shame, and Morality. *Philosophy and Phenomenological Research* 43:329–346.

Landau, Russ Shafer. 1991. Can Punishment Morally Educate? *Law and Philosophy* 10 (2):189–219.

Lansky, Melvin. 2007. Unbearable Shame, Splitting, and the Forgiveness in the Resolution of Vengefulness. *Journal of American Psychoanalytic Association* 55 (2):571–594.

Laub, Dori, and Johanna Bodenstab. 2007. Psychoanalysis and Trauma. *Journal of American Psychoanalytic Association* 55 (1):335–341.

Le Naour, Jean-Yves. 2006. *The Living Unknown Soldier.* New York: Arrow Books/Random House.

Lear, Jonathan. 2006. *Radical Hope: Ethics in the Face of Cultural Devastation.* Cambridge: Harvard University Press.

LeDoux, Joseph. 1996. *The Emotional Brain.* New York: Touchstone.

Levi, Primo. 1996. *Survival in Auschwitz.* New York: Simon and Schuster.

Levinson, Jerrold. 1995. Still Hopeful: Reply to Karl and Robinson. *Journal of Aesthetics and Criticism* 53 (2):199–201.

Levinson, Sanford, ed. 2004. *Torture: A Collection.* New York: Oxford University Press.

Lewis, David. 1984. Devil's Bargains and the Real World. In *The Security Gamble: Deterrence Dilemmas in the Nuclear Age,* edited by D. MacLean. Totowa, N.J. : Rowman and Allanheld.

Lewis, Meirlys. 1980. On Forgiveness. *Philosophical Quarterly* 30 (120):236–245.

Lewis, Michael. 1989. *Liar's Poker.* New York: W. W. Norton.

Lewis, Norman. 1978. *Naples '44.* New York: Pantheon Books.

Lichtenberg, Judith. 1994. War, Innocence, and the Doctrine of Double Effect. *Philosophical Studies* 74:347–368.

———. 2008. How to Judge Soldiers Whose Cause Is Unjust. In *Just and Unjust Warriors,* edited by D. Rodin and H. Shue. New York: Oxford University Press.

Lifton, Robert Jay. 1973. *Home from the War: Vietnam Veterans: Neither Victims nor Executioners.* New York: Simon and Schuster. Original edition.

———. 1986. *The Nazi Doctors: Medical Killing and the Psychology of Genocide.* New York: Basic Books.

Linderman, Gerald F. 1987. *Embattled Courage: The Experience of Combat in the American Civil War.* New York: Free Press.

———. 1997. *The World within War: America's Combat Experience in World War II.* New York: Free Press.

Lomax, Eric. 1995. *The Railway Man: A POW's Searing Account of War, Brutality and Forgiveness.* New York: W. W. Norton.

Long, A. A. 2002. *Epictetus: A Stoic and Socratic Guide to Life.* Oxford: Oxford University Press.

Long, A. A., and D. N. Sedley. 1987. *The Hellenistic Philosophers.* Vols. 1 and 2. Cambridge: Cambridge University Press.

Lord, Catherine. 1969. Tragedy without Character: Poetics VI. 1450ᵃ 24. *Journal of Aesthetics and Criticism* 28 (1):55–62.

Luban, David. 1988. *Lawyers and Justice*. Princeton: Princeton University Press.

——. 2004. Preventive War. *Philosophy and Public Affairs* 32 (3):207–248.

——. 2005. Liberalism, Torture and the Ticking Time Bomb. *Virginia Law Review* 91 (6):1425–1461.

——. 2008. *Legal Ethics and Human Dignity*. New York: Cambridge University Press.

Luckhardt, C. G. 1975. Remorse, Regret and the Socratic Paradox. *Analysis* 35 (5):159–166.

Luria, Zella, Miriam Goldwasser, and Adena Goldwasser. June 1963. Response to Transgression in Stories by Israeli Children. *Child Development* 34 (2):271–280.

Luthar, Suniya S., Dante Cicchetti, and Bronwyn Becker. May 2000. Research on Resilience: Response to Commentaries. *Child Development* 71 (3):573–575.

——. 2000. The Construct of Resilience: A Critical Evaluation and Guidelines for Future Work. *Child Development* 71 (3):543–562.

Lyons, Daniel. 1966. "Entitled to Complain." *Analysis* 26 (4):119–122.

Maass, Peter. 2002. A Bulletproof Mind. *New York Times*, November 10.

MacLean, Douglas, ed. 1984. *The Security Gamble: Deterrence Dilemmas in the Nuclear Age*. Totowa, N. J. : Rowman and Allanheld.

Mahler, Margaret, F. Pine, and A. Bergman. 1975. *The Psychological Birth of the Human Infant*. New York: Basic Books.

Manchester, William. 1980. *Goodbye, Darkness: A Memoir of the Pacific War*. Boston: Little, Brown.

Manning, Frederic. 1986. *Her Privates, We*. London: Hogarth Press.

Mansfield, Sue. 1991. *The Rites of War: An Analysis of Institutionalized Warfare*. London: Bellew.

Margalit, Edna Ullmann. 1990. Revision of Norms. *Ethics* 100 (4):756–767.

Marks, Jonathan. 2009. Looking Back, Thinking Ahead: The Complicity of Health Professionals in Detainee Abuse. In *Interrogations, Force Feedings and the Role of Health Professionals*, edited by R. Goodman and M. J. Roseman. Cambridge: Harvard University Press.

Marongiu, Pietro, and Graeme Newman. 1987. *Vengeance: The Fight against Injustice*. Totowa, N.J. : Rowman and Littlefield.

Marshall, S. L. A. 1978. *Men against Fire: The Problem of Battle Command in Future War*. Gloucester, Mass.: Peter Smith.

Martin Ramirez, Jesus, Robert A. Hinde, and Jo Groebel, eds. 1987. *Essays on*

Violence, International Colloquium on the Brain and Aggression (6th: 1986: Seville, Spain). Sevilla: Publicaciones de la Universidad de Sevilla.

Marvin, Carolyn. 1999. *Blood Sacrifice and the Nation: Totem Rituals and the American Flag.* New York: Cambridge University Press.

Matthews, Steve. March 1998. Personal Identity, Multiple Personality Disorder, and Moral Personhood. *Philosophical Psychology* 11 (1):67–88.

May, Larry. 2005. *Crimes against Humanity.* New York: Cambridge University Press.

———, ed. 2008. *War: Essays in Political Philosophy.* New York: Cambridge University Press.

May, Larry, Eric Rovie, and Steve Viner, eds. 2006. *The Morality of War.* Upper Saddle River, N.J.: Pearson/Prentice Hall

May, Larry, and Robert Strikwerda, eds. 1992. *Rethinkig Masculinity: Philosophical Explorations in Light of Feminism.* Lanham, MD: Rowman and Littlefield.

Mayer, Jane. 2008. *The Dark Side: The Inside Story of How the War on Terror Turned into a War on American Ideals.* New York: Doubleday.

McKelvey, Tara, ed. 2007. *One of the Guys: Women as Agressors and Torturers.* Emeryville, Calif.: Seal Press.

McMahan, Jeff. July 2004. The Ethics of Killing in War. *Ethics* 114:693–733.

———. 2006a. Liability and Collective Identity: A Response to Walzer. *Philosophia* 34:13–17.

———. 2006b. Killing in War: A Reply to Walzer. *Philosophia* 34:47–51.

———. 2008. The Morality of War and the Law of War. In *Just and Unjust Warriors*, edited by D. Rodin and H. Shue. New York: Oxford University Press.

McMaster, H. R. 1997. *Dereliction of Duty.* New York: HarperCollins.

McNally, Richard, et al. August 2006. Psychiatric Casualties of War. *Science* 313:923–924.

McPherson, James M. 1997. *For Cause and Comrades: Why Men Fought in the Civil War.* New York: Oxford University Press.

Meltzoff, Andrew, and M. Keith Moore. 1995. Infants' Understanding of People and Things: From Body Imitation to Folk Psychology. In *The Body and the Self,* edited by J. L. Bermudez, A. Marcel, and N. Eilan. Cambridge: MIT Press.

Mikhail, John. 2007. Universal Moral Grammar: Theory, Evidence and the Future. *TRENDS in Cognitive Sciences* 30 (10).

Miles, Steven. 2006. *Oath Betrayed: Torture, Medical Complicity, and the War on Terror.* New York: Random House.

Milgram, Stanley. 1969. *Obedience to Authority.* New York: Harper and Row.

Mill, J. S. 1978. *On Liberty*, edited by E. Rapaport. Indianapolis: Hackett Publishing.

Miller, Arthur. 1944. *Situation Normal*. New York: Reynal and Hitchcock, Lester Cowan Productions.

Miller, Rowland S. 2001. On the Primacy of Embarrassment in Social Life. *Psychological Inquiry* 12 (1):30–33.

Miller, T. Christian. 2006. *Blood Money: Wasted Billions, Lost Lives, and Corporate Greed in Iraq*. New York: Little, Brown.

Miller, William Ian. 1990. *Bloodtaking and Peacemaking: Feud, Law, and Society in Saga Iceland*. Chicago: University of Chicago Press.

———. 2006. *An Eye for an Eye*. Cambridge: Cambridge University Press.

Minow, Martha. 2005. Outsourcing Power: Private Police, Prisons, and War. Cecil A. Wright Lecture. University of Toronto Faculty of Law.

Modell, Arnold. 1971. The Origin of Certain Forms of Pre-Oedipal Guilt and the Implications for a Psychoanalytic Theory of Affects. *International Journal of Psychoanalysis* 52:337–346.

Montagu, Ewen. 1954. *The Man Who Never Was*. Philadelphia: J.B. Lippincott.

Montague, Phillip. 1984. Rights and Duties of Compensation. *Philosophy and Public Affairs* 13 (1):79–88.

Montaigne, Michel de. 1993. *Michel de Montaigne: The Complete Essays*, edited by M. A. Screech. New York: Penguin.

Moore, Michael S. 1987. The Moral Worth of Retribution. In *Responsibility, Character, and the Emotions: New Essays in Moral Psychology*, edited by F. Schoeman. Cambridge: Cambridge University Press.

Moran, Richard. 1993. Impersonality, Character, and Moral Expressivism. *Journal of Philosophy* 90 (11):578–595.

Morris, Herbert. 1971. Guilt and Suffering. *Philosophy East and West* 21 (4):419–434.

———. 1976. *On Guilt and Innocence*. Berkeley: University of California Press.

———. 1981. The Status of Rights. *Ethics* 92 (1):40–51.

———. 1987. Nonmoral Guilt. In *Responsibility, Character, and the Emotions*, edited by F. Schoeman. New York: Cambridge University Press.

———. 1988. The Decline of Guilt. *Ethics* 99:62–76.

———. 1999. Some Further Reflections on Guilt and Punishment. *Law and Philosophy* 18 (4):363–378.

Morstein-Marx, Robert. 2004. *Mass Oratory and Political Power in the Late Roman Republic*. New York: Cambridge University Press.

Morton, Jerry. 2004. *Reluctant Lieutenant: From Basic to OCS in the Sixties*. College Station: Texas A&M University Press.

Moss, Donald, ed. 2003. *Hating in the First Person Plural*. New York: Other Press.

Moyers, Bill. 2006. *Message to West Point*. CommonDreams.org [cited November 30 2006].

Muller, John P., and Jane G. Tillman, eds. 2006. *The Embodied Subject: Minding the Body in Psychoanalysis*. Lanham, Md.: Aronson/Rowman and Littlefield.

Murphy, Audie. 1949. *To Hell and Back*. New York: Henry Holt.

Murphy, Jeffrie. 1999. Shame Creeps through Guilt and Feels Like Retribution. *Law and Philosophy* 18 (4):327–344.

———. 2003. *Getting Even: Forgiveness and Its Limits*. New York: Oxford University Press.

———. 2006a. Well Excuse Me!–Remorse, Apology, and Criminal Sentencing. *Arizona State Law Journal* 38 (2):371–386.

———. 2006b. Legal Moralism and Retribution Revisited. *Criminal Law and Philosophy* 1 (1):5–20.

Murphy, Liam. 2000. *Moral Demands in Nonideal Theory*. Oxford: Oxford University Press.

Nagel, Thomas. 1974. War and Massacre. In *War and Responsibility*, edited by M. Cohen, T. Nagel, and T. Scanlon. Princeton: Princeton University Press.

———. 1979. *Mortal Questions*. New York: Cambridge University Press.

Nathanson, Donald L., ed. 1987. *The Many Faces of Shame*. New York: Guilford Press.

Neblett, William. 1974. Forgiveness and Ideals. *Mind* 83 (330):269–275.

———. October 1974. The Ethics of Guilt. *Journal of Philosophy* 71 (18):652–663.

Newark, Tim. 2007. *Camouflage*. New York: Thames and Hudson and Imperial War Museum.

Nichols, David, ed. 1986. *Ernie's War: The Best of Ernie Pyle's World War II Dispatches*. New York: Random House.

Nietzsche, Friedrich. 1994. *On the Genealogy of Morality*, edited by Keith Ansell-Pearson. Translated by C. Diethe. Cambridge: Cambridge University Press.

North, Joanna. 1987. Wrongdoing and Forgiveness. *Philosophy* 62 (242):499–508.

Novitz, David. 1998. Forgiveness and Self-Respect. *Philosophy and Phenomenological Research* 58 (2):299–315.

Nozick, Robert. 1975. *Anarchy, State, and Utopia*. Oxford: Blackwell.

Nunner-Winkler, Gertrud, and Beate Sodian. 1988. Children's Understanding of Moral Emotions. *Child Development* 59 (5):1323–1338.

Nussbaum, Martha C. 1986. *The Fragility of Goodness: Luck and Ethics in Greek Tragedy and Philosophy*. New York: Cambridge University Press.

———. 1996. Comments on Englert's "Stoics and Epicureans on the Nature of Suicide." In *Proceedings of the Boston Area Colloquium in Ancient Philosophy*, edited by John J.Cleary and William Wians. Lanham, Md.: University Press of America.

———. 2004. *Hiding from Humanity: Disgust, Shame, and the Law*. Princeton: Princeton University Press.

———. 2006. *Frontiers of Justice: Disability, Nationality, Species Membership*. Cambridge: Harvard University Press.

———. 2008. Who Is the Happy Warrior? Philosophy Poses Questions to Psychology. *Journal of Legal Studies* 37 (2):81–113.

Oakley, Justin, and Dean Cocking. 2001. *Virtue Ethics and Professional Roles*. Cambridge: Cambridge University Press.

Orwell, George. 1952. *Homage to Catalonia*. New York: Harcourt Brace.

———. 1993. *A Collection of Essays*. San Diego: Harcourt Brace.

O'Shaughnessy, Brian. 1995. Proprioception and the Body Image. In *The Body and the Self*, edited by J. L. Bermudez, A. Marcel, and N. Eilan. Cambridge: MIT Press.

O'Shaughnessy, R. J. 1967. Forgiveness. *Philosophy* 42 (162):336–352.

O'Toole, Patricia. 2005. *When Trumpets Call: Theodore Roosevelt after the White House*. New York: Simon and Schuster.

Owen, Wilfred. 1984. *The Complete Poems and Fragments*, edited by Jon Stallworthy. Vol. 1. New York: W. W. Norton.

Pagán, Victoria Emma. 2007/2008. Teaching Torture in Seneca *Controversiae* 2.5. *Classical Journal* 103 (1):165–182

Perry, David G., Louise C. Perry, Kay Bussey, David English, and Gail Arnold. 1980. Processes of Attribution and Children's Self Punishment following Misbehavior. *Child Development* 51 (2):545–551.

Peters, R. S. 1962. Moral Education and the Psychology of Character. *Philosophy* 37 (139):37–56.

Pfaff, Tony. 2005. Military Ethics in Complex Contingencies. In *The Future of the Army Profession*, edited by L. Matthews and D. Snider. Boston: McGraw-Hill.

———. 2008. Development and Reform of Iraqi Police Forces. *Strategic Studies Institute of the U.S. Army War College*, available at: http://www.strategicstudies institute.army.mil/pubs/people.cfm?q=45.

Pfaff, Tony, and Jeffrey R. Tiel. 2004. The Ethics of Espionage. *Journal of Military Ethics* 3 (1):1–15.

Pfeiffer, Ernst, ed. 1972. *Sigmund Freud and Lou Andreas-Salome Letters*. New York: Harcourt Brace Jovanovich.

Phillips, D. Z., and H. S. Price. 1967. Remorse without Repudiation. *Analysis* 28 (1):18–20.

Piers, Gerhart, and Milton Singer. 1953. *Shame and Guilt*. Springfield, Ill.: Charles C Thomas.

Plato. 1980. *Plato: Symposium*, edited by K. Dover. Cambridge: Cambridge University Press.

———. 1989. *Symposium*. Translated by A. Nehamas and P. Woodruff. Indianapolis: Hackett Publishing.

———. 1997. *Euthydemus*. In *Plato: Complete Works*, edited by John M. Cooper. Indianapolis: Hackett Publishing.

Plessner, Helmuth. 1970. *Laughing and Crying: A Study of the Limits of Human Behavior*. Translated by J. S. Churchill and M. Grene. Evanston: Northwestern University Press.

Plutarch. 1906. *Pelopidas*, translated by John Dryden. In *Plutarch's Lives*, vol. 2, edited by A. H. Clough. Boston: Little, Brown.

Pope, Harrison, Katherine Phillips, and Roberto Olivardia. 2000. *The Adonis Complex*. New York: Touchstone.

Powell, Colin, with Joseph Persico. 1995. *My American Journey*. New York: Random House.

Proctor, Robert. 1988. *Racial Hygiene: Medicine under the Nazis*. Cambridge: Harvard University Press.

Purshouse, Luke. 2001. Embarrassment: A Philosophical Analysis. *Philosophy* 76 (298):515–540.

Pyle, Ernie. 1941. *Ernie Pyle in England*. New York: Robert M. McBride.

Quinlan, Michael. 1993. Controversy: Ethics in the Public Sphere. *Governance* 6 (4):538–544.

Radden, Jennifer. 1996. *Divided Minds and Successive Selves: Ethical Issues in Disorders of Identity and Personality*. Cambridge: MIT Press.

Rashdall, Hastings. 1900. The Ethics of Forgiveness. *International Journal of Ethics* 10 (2):193–206.

Rawls, John. 1971. *A Theory of Justice.* Cambridge: Belknap Press of Harvard University Press.

Read, Herbert. 1966. *Collected Poems.* New York: Horizon Press.

Rejali, Darius. 2007. *Torture and Democracy.* Princeton: Princeton University Press.

Remarque, Erich Maria. 1931. *The Road Back.* Translated by A. W. Wheen. Boston: Little, Brown.

Resick, Patricia A., and Karen Calhoun. 2001. Posttraumatic Stress Disorder. In *Clinical Handbook of Psychological Disorders: A Step by Step Treatment Manual,* edited by D. Barlow. New York: Guilford Press.

Richards, Norvin. 1988. Forgiveness. *Ethics* 99 (1):77–97.

Richardson, Henry S. 1999. Institutionally Divided Moral Responsibility. *Social Philosophy and Policy* 16:218–249.

———. 2008. Incidental Findings and Anciliary-Care Obligations. *Journal of Law, Medicine, and Ethics* 36 (2):256–270.

Ricks, Thomas E. 1997. *Making the Corps.* New York: Touchstone.

Robinson, JoAnne L. May 2000. Are There Implications for Prevention Research from Studies of Resilience? *Child Development* 71 (3):570–572.

Robinson, Wade L., and Michael S. Pritchard, eds. 1983. *Profits and Professions: Essays in Business and Professional Ethics.* Clifton, N.J. : Humana Press.

Rodin, David. 2002. *War and Self-Defense.* Oxford: Clarendon Press.

Roosa, Mark W. 2000. Some Thoughts about Resilience versus Positive Development, Main Effects versus Interactions, and the Value of Resilience. *Child Development* 71 (3):567–569.

Rosenblatt, Roger. 1983. *Children of War.* Garden City, N.Y. : Anchor Press/ Doubleday.

Ross, Colin A., and Pam Gahan. 1988a. Cognitive Analysis of Multiple Personality Disorder. *American Journal of Psychotherapy* 42 (2):229–239.

———.1988b. Techniques in the Treatment of Multiple Personality Disorder. *American Journal of Psychotherapy* 42 (1):40–52.

Rosthal, Robert. 1967. Moral Weakness and Remorse. *Mind* 76 (304):576–579.

Rotberg, Robert, and Dennis Thompson, eds. 2000. *Truth v. Justice: The Morality of Truth Commissions.* Princeton: Princeton University Press.

Rowse, A. L., ed. 1978. *The Annotated Shakespeare: The Histories, Sonnets and Other Poems.* New York: Clarkson N. Potter.

Sachs, Albie. 2000. *The Soft Vengeance of a Freedom Fighter.* Berkeley: University of California Press.

Sample, Ruth. 2003. *Exploitation: What It Is and Why It's Wrong*. Lanham, Md.: Rowman and Littlefield.

Sanborn, Herbert C. January 1927. The Function of Clothing and of Bodily Adornment. *American Journal of Psychology* 38 (1):1–20.

Sassoon, Siegfried. 1968. *Selected Poems*. London: Faber and Faber.

Satel, Sally. 2004. Post-Traumatic Stress Disorder and Iraq Veterans. Testimony to House Committee on Veterans Affairs (Washington, D.C.), March 11. Available at: http://www.aei.org/speech/ 20106.

———. 2007. The Trouble with Traumatology: Is It Advocacy or Is It Science? *Weekly Standard*, February 19.

Scary, Elaine. 1985. *The Body in Pain*. New York: Oxford University Press.

Scheffler, Sam. 1992. *Human Morality*. New York: Oxford University Press.

Scheler, Max. 1972. *On the Eternal in Man*. Translated by B. Noble. Hamden, Conn.: Archon Books.

Schlenker, Barry R., and Bruce W. Darby. September 1981. The Use of Apologies in Social Predicaments. *Social Psychology Quarterly* 44 (3):271–278.

Schoeman, Ferdinand, ed. 1987. *Responsibility, Character, and the Emotions: New Essays in Moral Psychology*. Cambridge: Cambridge University Press.

Schueler, G. F. 1983. Akrasia Revisited. *Mind* 92 (368):580–584.

Schulfhofer, Stephen J. 1992. Taking Sexual Autonomy Seriously: Rape Law and Beyond. *Law and Philosophy* 11 (1/2):35–94.

Scott, J. W. 1911. Idealism and the Conception of Forgiveness. *International Journal of Ethics* 21 (2):189–198.

Seal, Karen H., Daniel Bertenthal, Christian R. Miner, Saunak Sen, and Charles Marmar. 2007. Bringing the War Back Home: Mental Health Disorders among 103 788 US Veterans Returning from Iraq and Afghanistan Seen at Department of Veterans Affairs Facilities. *Archives of Internal Medicine* 167:476–482.

Seligman, Martin. 2004. *Authentic Happiness*. New York: Simon and Schuster.

Seneca. 1989. *Epistulae Morales* (Loeb Classical Library), edited by R. Gummere. Cambridge: Harvard University Press.

———. 1995a. *On Anger*. In *Moral and Political Essays*, edited by J. M. Cooper and J. F. Procopé. New York: Cambridge University Press.

———. 1995b. *On Mercy*. In *Moral and Political Essays*, edited by J. M. Cooper and J. F. Procopé. New York: Cambridge University Press.

Seneca, the Elder. 1974. *Declamations*. Vol. 1 and 2 (Vol. 1: *Controversiae*, Books 1–6. Vol. 2: *Controversiae*, Books 7–10. *Suasoriae*). Translated by M. Winterbottom. Cambridge: Harvard University Press.

Shalev, A. Y., T. Peri, L. Canetti, and S. Schreiber. 1996. Predictors of PTSD in

Injured Trauma Survivors: A Prospective Study. *American Journal of Psychiatry* 153:219–225.

Shapira, Avraham, ed. 1970. *The Seventh Day: Soldiers' Talk about the Six-Day War.* New York: Scribner.

Shapiro, Francine, and Louise Maxfield. 2002. Eye Movement Desensitization and Reprocessing [EMDR]: Information Processing in the Treatment of Trauma. *Journal of Clinical Psychology* 58/ In Session: Psychotherapy in Practice (8):933–946.

Shapiro, Ian, ed. 1994. *The Rule of Law: NOMOS XXXVI.* New York: New York University Press.

Shapiro, Tamar. 2003. Compliance, Complicity, and the Nature of Nonideal Conditions. *Journal of Philosophy* 100 (7):329–355.

Sharpe, R. A. 1992. Moral Tales. *Philosophy* 67 (260):155–168.

Shay, Jonathan. 1994. *Achilles in Vietnam: Combat Trauma and the Undoing of Character.* New York: Touchstone.

———. 2002. *Odysseus in America: Combat Trauma and the Trials of Homecoming.* New York: Scribner.

———. 2006. The Pen and the Dollar Bill: Two Philosophical Stage Props. Washington, D. C., presented at the meeting of the PTSD Subcommittee, Institute of Medicine.

Sherman, Nancy. 1989. *The Fabric of Character.* New York: Oxford University Press.

———. 1992. Virtue and Hamartia. In *Essays on Aristotle's Poetics*, edited by A. O. Rorty. Princeton: Princeton University Press.

———. 1997. *Making a Necessity of Virtue.* Cambridge: Cambridge University Press.

———. 1998a. Empathy and Imagination In *Philosophy of Emotions*, edited by Peter A. French and Howard Wettstein, 82–119. Vol. 22 of *Midwest Studies in Philosophy* series. Notre Dame: University of Notre Dame Press.

———. 1998b. Concrete Kantian Respect. *Social Philosophy and Policy* 15:119–148.

———. 2005. *Stoic Warriors: The Ancient Philosophy behind the Military Mind.* New York: Oxford University Press.

———. 2006. Torturers and the Tortured. Symposium: Torture and the Stoic Warrior. *South African Journal of Philosophy* 25 (1):77–88.

———. Winter 2007a. From Nuremberg to Guantánamo: Medical Ethics Then and Now. *Dissent* 54 (1):9–13.

———. 2007b. From Nuremberg to Guantánamo: Medical Ethics Then and Now. *Washington University Global Studies Law Review* 6 (3):609–619.

————. 2009a. The Fate of a Warrior Culture. *Philosophical Studies* 144 (1):71–80.

————. 2009b. Review of N. Szajnberg, *Reluctant Warriors: Israelis Suspended between Rome and Jerusalem* (2006). *Journal of the American Psychoanalytic Association* 57:251–256.

Shklar, Judith N. May 1993. Obligation, Loyalty, Exile. *Political Theory* 21 (2):181–197.

Shue, Henry. 1978. Torture. *Philosophy and Public Affairs* 7 (2):124–43.

Siegel, Daniel J. 1999. *The Developing Mind: How Relationships and the Brain Interact to Shape Who We Are*. New York: Guilford Press.

Simmons, A. John. January 1996. External Justifications and Institutional Roles. *Journal of Philosophy* 93 (1):28–36.

Sims, Jennifer E., and Burton Gerber, eds. 2005. *Transforming U.S. Intelligence*. Washington, D.C.: Georgetown University Press.

Singer, P. W. 2003. *Corporate Warriors: The Rise of the Privatized Military Industry*. Ithaca: Cornell University Press.

Sledge, E. B. 1981. *With the Old Breed: At Peleliu and Okinawa*. Novato, Calif.: Presidio Press.

Sledge, Michael. 2005. *Soldier Dead*. New York: Columbia University Press.

Smith, Adam. 1976 (1759). *The Theory of Moral Sentiments*. Indianapolis: Liberty Classics.

Smith, James M. 1965. Punishment: A Conceptual Map and a Normative Claim. *Ethics* 75 (4):285–290.

Smith, T. V. 1961. Wordsworth and the Sense of Guilt. *Ethics* 71 (4):233–245.

Smith, Theodate L. 1915. Note on the Psychology of Shame. *American Journal of Psychology* 26 (2):229–235.

Solomon, Marion, and Daniel J. Siegel, eds. 2003. *Healing Trauma: Attachment, Mind, Body, and Brain*. New York: W. W. Norton.

Solomon, Robert. 2004. *In Defense of Sentimentality*. New York: Oxford University Press.

Solomon, Robert, and Mark Murphy, eds. 2000. *What Is Justice? Classic and Contemporary Readings*, 2d ed. New York: Oxford University Press.

Sophocles. 1967. *The Women of Trachis*. Translated by D. Green and R. Lattimore. New York: Washington Square Press.

Sorabji, Richard. 2000. *Emotion and Peace of Mind: From Stoic Agitation to Christian Temptation*. Oxford: Oxford University Press.

Southwick, Steven, J. D. Bremner, A. Rasmusson, and C. A. Morgan. 1999. Role of Norepinephrine in the Pathophysiology and Treatment of Posttraumatic Stress Disorder. *Biological Psychiatry* 46 (9):1112–1204.

Southwick, Steven, C. A. Morgan, A. Douglas Bremner, Christian Grillon, et al. 1997. Noradrenergic Alterations in Posttraumatic Stress Disorder. *Annals of the New York Academy of Sciences* 821:125–141.

Speziale-Bagliacca, Roberto. 2004. *Guilt: Revenge, Remorse and Responsibility after Freud.* New York: Brunner-Routledge.

Spiller, Roger J. 1988. S.L.A. Marshall and the Ratio of Fire. *RUSI Journal* 133:63–71.

Starbuck, Edwin Diller. 1897. A Study of Conversion. *American Journal of Psychology* 8 (2):268–308.

Stareke, C. N. 1892. The Conscience. *International Journal of Ethics* 2 (3):342–372.

Staub, Ervin. 2003. Notes on Cultures of Violence, Cultures of Caring and Peace, and the Fulfillment of Basic Human Needs. *Political Psychology* 24 (1):1–21.

Stern, Daniel. 1985. *The Interpersonal World of the Infant: A View from Psychoanalysis and Developmental Psychology.* New York: Basic Books.

Stockdale, James. 1995. *Thoughts of a Philosophical Fighter Pilot.* Stanford, Calif.: Hoover Institution Press.

———. 2001. Stockdale on Stoicism II: Master of My Fate. An Occasional Paper. No. 2. U.S. Naval Academy, Annapolis, Md.

Stockdale, James, and Sybil Stockdale. 1990. *In Love and War.* Annapolis, Md.: Naval Institute.

Suedfeld, Peter. 1997. Reactions to Societal Trauma: Distress and/or Eustress. *Political Psychology* 18 (4):849–861.

Sullivan, Nikki. 2005. Integrity, Mayhem, and the Question of Self-Demand Amputation. *Continuum: Journal of Media and Culture Studies* 19 (3):325–333.

Sussman, David. 2005. What's Wrong with Torture? *Philosophy and Public Affairs* 33 (1):1–33.

Swanton, Christine. 2003. *Virtue Ethics: A Pluralistic View.* New York: Oxford University Press.

Tangney, June Price, and Kurt W. Fischer, eds. 1995. *Self-Conscious Emotions: The Psychology of Shame, Guilt, Embarrassment, and Pride.* New York: Guilford Press.

Taylor, Gabriele. 1985. *Pride, Shame, and Guilt: Emotions of Self-Assessment.* Oxford: Oxford University Press.

Taylor, Telford. 1992. *The Anatomy of the Nuremberg Trials.* New York: Knopf.

Tedeschi, Richard, Lawrence Calhoun, and Crystal Park, eds. 1998. *Posttraumatic Growth: Positive Changes in the Aftermath of Crisis.* Mahwah, N.J.: Lawrence Erlbaum Associates.

Teichman, Jenny. 1973. Punishment and Remorse. *Philosophy* 48 (186):335–346.

———. 1986. *Pacifism and the Just War: A Study in Applied Philosophy*. Oxford: Basil Blackwell.

Telfer, Elizabeth. 1968. Self-Respect. *Philosophical Quarterly* 18 (71):114–121.

Thalberg, Irving. 1963. Remorse. *Mind* 72 (288):545–555.

———. April 1968. Rosthal's Notion of Remorse and Irrevocability. *Mind* 77 (306):288–289.

Thomson, Judith Jarvis. 1986. *Rights, Restitution, and Risk*. Cambridge: Harvard University Press.

Tietz, Jeff. 2006. The Killing Factory. *Rolling Stone*, April 20, 54–76.

Timerman, Jacobo. 1981. *Prisoner without a Name, Cell without a Number*. New York: Knopf.

Trouern-Trend, Jonathan. 2006. *Birding Babylon: A Soldier's Journal from Iraq*. San Francisco: Sierra Club Books.

Trudeau, G. B. 2005. *The Long Road Home: One Step at a Time, A Doonesbury Book*. Kansas City, Mo.: Andrews McMeel.

Tudor, Steven. 2001. Accepting One's Punishment as Meaningful Suffering. *Law and Philosophy* 20 (6):581–604.

Tuttle, William M. 1993. *"Daddy's Gone to War": The Second World War in the Lives of America's Children*. New York: Oxford University Press.

Twambley, P. 1976. Mercy and Forgiveness. *Analysis* 36 (2):84–90.

Twining, W. L., and P. E. Twining. 1973. Bentham on Torture. *Northern Ireland Legal Quarterly* 24 (3):305–356.

Upadhyaya, K. N. 1969. The Bhagavad Gita on War and Peace. *Philosophy East and West* 19 (2):159–169.

The U.S. Army Intelligence Interrogation Manual FM 34-52. 1992. Available at: http://www.globalsecurity.org/intell/library/policy/army/fm/fm34-52/toc.htm. The U.S. Army Intelligence Interrogation Manual FM 2-22-1, 2002. Available at: www.army.mil/institution/armypublicaffairs/pdf/fm2-22-1.pdf.

U.S. Army/U.S. Marine Corps. *The U.S. Army/Marine Corps Counterinsurgency Field Manual*. 2007. Chicago: University of Chicago Press.

Van der Kolk, Bessel A. 2003. Postraumatic Stress Disorder and the Nature of Trauma. In *Healing Trauma: Attachment, Mind, Body, and Brain*, edited by Marion Solomon and Daniel J. Siegel, 168–195. New York: W. W. Norton.

Van Goozen, Stephanie H. M., Nanne E. Van de Poll, and Joseph A. Sergeant, eds. 1994. *Emotions: Essays on Emotion Theory*. Hillsdale, N. J. : Lawrence Erlbaum Associates.

Van Wees, Hans, ed. 2000. *War and Violence in Ancient Greece*. London: Duckworth.

Vandergriff, Donald. 2002. *The Path to Victory: America's Army and the Revolution in Human Affairs*. Novato, Calif.: Presidio Press.

Velleman, David. 1999. A Rational Superego. *Philosophical Review* 108:529–558.

———. 2001. The Genesis of Shame. *Philosophy and Public Affairs* 30 (1):27–52.

———. 2006. *Self to Self*. New York: Cambridge University Press.

Vermetten, Eric, et al. 2007. PTSD and Vietnam Veterans: Letters (and replies) on McNally's "Psychiatric Casualties of War." *Science* 315:184–187.

Vidal, Gore. 2003. *Williwaw: A Novel*. Chicago: University of Chicago Press.

Vitoria, Francisco de. 1991. On the Law of Wars. In *Political Writings/Francisco de Vitoria*, edited by A. Pagden and J. Lawrance. New York: Cambridge University Press.

Volkan, Vamik. 2006. *Killing in the Name of Identity*. Charlottesville, Va.: Pitchstone.

Vonnegut, Kurt. 1969. *Slaughterhouse-Five or the Children's Crusade*. New York: Delacorte Press.

Walker, Margaret Urban. 1991. Moral Luck and the Virtues of Impure Agency. *Metaphilosophy* 22:14–27.

———. 1998. *Moral Understandings: A Feminist Study in Ethics*. New York: Routledge.

Walker, Nigel. 1995. The Quiddity of Mercy. *Philosophy* 70 (271):27–37.

Walsh, W. H. 1970. Pride, Shame, and Responsibility. *Philosophical Quarterly* 20 (78):1–13.

Walzer, Michael. 1977. *Just and Unjust Wars: A Moral Argument with Historical Illustrations*. New York: Penguin.

———. 2006. Response to McMahan's Paper. *Philosophia* 34:43–45.

Watson, G. R. 1969. *The Roman Soldier*. Ithaca: Cornell University Press.

Watson, Gary. 1987. Responsibility and the Limits of Evil: Variations on a Strawsonian Theme. In *Responsibility, Character, and the Emotions: New Essays in Moral Psychology*, edited by F. Schoeman. Cambridge: Cambridge University Press.

Way, Karen. 2006. How Metaphors Shape the Concept and Treatment of Dissociation. *Psychiatric Clinics of North America* 29:27–43.

Wertheimer, Alan. 1996. *Exploitation*. Princeton: Princeton University Press.

Wertsch, Mary Edwards. 1991. *Military Brats: Legacies of Childhood inside the Fortress*. St. Louis: Brightwell.

Weschler, Lawrence. 1998. *A Miracle, a Universe: Settling Accounts with Torturers*. Chicago: University of Chicago Press.

Westhusing, Ted. 2003a. Taking Terrorism and ROE Seriously. *Journal of Military Ethics* 2 (1):1–19.

———. 2003b. The Competitive and Cooperative Aretai [Virtues]. Dissertation, Emory University of Atlanta.

Whitely, C. H. 1979. Love, Hate and Emotion. *Philosophy* 54 (208):235.

Wiener, Tom, ed. 2004. *Voices of War: Library of Congress Veterans History Project*. Washington, D.C.: National Geographic.

Williams, Bernard. 1981. *Moral Luck*. New York: Cambridge University Press.

———. 1993. *Shame and Necessity*. Berkeley: University of California Press.

———. 2006. *The Sense of the Past*. Princeton: Princeton University Press.

Williams, Craig. 1999. *Roman Homosexuality: Ideologies of Masculinity in Classical Antiquity*. New York: Oxford University Press.

Williams, Kayla. 2005. *Love My Rifle More Than You: Young and Female in the U.S. Army*. New York: W. W. Norton.

Williams, Oscar. 1945. *The War Poets, an Anthology of the War Poetry of the 20th Century*. New York: John Day.

Williams, Richard Hays. March 1942. Scheler's Contributions to the Sociology of Affective Action with Special Attention to the Problem of Shame. *Philosophy and Phenomenological Research* 2 (3):348–358.

Williamson, Ronald. 1989. *Jews in the Hellenistic World: Philo*. Cambridge: Cambridge University Press.

Wills, David. 1995. *Prosthesis*. Stanford: Stanford University Press.

Wilson, John. 1988. Why Forgiveness Requires Repentance. *Philosophy* 63 (246):534–535.

Wilson, John P., Matthew J. Friedman, and Jacob Lindy, eds. 2004. *Treating Psychological Trauma and PTSD*. Madison, Conn.: Guilford Press.

Wilson, Marcus. 1997. The Subjugation of Gried in Seneca's "Epistles." In *The Passions of Roman Thought and Literature*, edited by Susanna Morton Braund and Christopher Gill. Cambridge: Cambridge University Press.

Wolfe, John D. 2006. *A Different Species of Time*. At: www.wolfestudio.com/ Reprinted from *War, Literature & the Arts* [cited November 22, 2006].

Wolfe, Tom. 1999. *A Man in Full*. New York: Bantam.

Wolfendale, Jessica. 2006. The Moral Psychology of Military Torture. Symposium: Torture and the Stoic Warrior. *South African Journal of Philosophy* 25 (1):62–77

Wollheim, Richard. 1984. *The Thread of Life*. Cambridge: Harvard University Press.

Wood, Allen. 1995. Exploitation. *Social Philosophy and Policy* 12 (2):136–158.

———. 2004. *Karl Marx*. New York: Routledge.

Wood, Trish. 2006. *What Was Asked of Us*. New York: Little, Brown.

Woodhouse, Annie. 2005. Phantom Limb Sensation. *Clinical and Experimental Pharmacology and Physiology* 32:132–134.

Woodward, Bob. 2008. *The War Within: A Secret White House History 2006–2008*. New York: Simon and Schuster.

Wright, Quincy. 1965. *A Study of War*, 2d ed., with a Commentary on War since 1942. Chicago: University of Chicago Press.

Yalichev, Serge. 1997. *Mercenaries of the Ancient World*. London: Constable.

Young, Iris Marion. 2005. *On Female Body Experience*. New York: Oxford University Press.

Zehr, Howard. 1969. *Transcending: Reflections of Crime Victims: Portraits and Interviews*. Intercourse, Penn.: Good Books.

Zimbardo, Philip. 1972. Pathology of Imprisonment. *Society* 9 (6):4–8.

———. 2007. *The Lucifer Effect: Understanding How Good People Turn Evil*. New York: Random House.

Zoch, L. N. 1986. Remorse and Regret: A Reply to Phillips and Price. *Analysis* 46 (1):54–57.

CREDITS

p. 10   U.S. Navy photo by Photographer's Mate Second Class Charles E. Alvarado

p. 38   U.S. Marine photo by Lt. Cpl. Brian A. Tuthill

p. 64   Mehdi Fedouach/AFP/Getty Images

p. 88   U.S. Marine photo by Cpl. Brian Reimers

p. 112   Exclusive iStockphoto Photographer

p. 148   Gina Smith/Shutterstock

p. 170   U.S. Marine photo by Cpl. Daniel J. Redding

p. 194   U.S. Army photo by David Melancon

p. 214   U.S. Army photo by Sgt. Robert J. Strain

INDEX

Page numbers beginning with 249 refer to endnotes.

A-1 aircraft, 59
Abu Ghraib, Iraq, 36, 150, 154
    interrogation at, 5, 113–14, 133
    torture in, 116, 120, 131, 133
academe, 117, 142
accidents, 86, 90, 94–95, 98
    see also fratricide
accountability:
    of command, 36–37, 42
    in *Henry V,* 42
    personal, 37, 40–41, 63, 143
    professional, 135
    of soldiers, 2, 40, 42–45, 48, 63, 91,
        109–10
Achilles, 70, 74, 78, 82–83, 103, 199
acquiescence, 146, 161, 163–65
    consent vs., 146
Afghanistan, 13, 65, 257
    Bagram, 150, 163–64
    culture of, 77
    military detention centers in, 140
    Paktika Province, 80
Afghanistan war, 6, 32, 46, 47, 171, 238

casualties in, 198, 205
initial U.S. invasion in, 150
insurgency/counterinsurgency in, 66
as a just mission, 53–54
National Guard in, 13
officers in, 42
older veterans of, 50
racial slurs in, 34
rules of engagement in, 76
sectarian violence in, 66
Africa, northern, 61
Agamemnon, 74
agathos, 74
aidoia, 181
aidōs, 181
Air Force, U.S., 127, 200
Alcivar, Juan Luis, 198, 204
alcohol abuse, 60, 128, 218
Al Qaeda, 54, 114
Al Shuayba, Kuwait, 171
Amazon warriors, 199
American Medical Association, 267
American Psychiatric Association, 267

American Psychoanalytic Association, 267–68
American Psychological Association, 267
American Red Cross, 225
Améry, Jean, 159
Amos, James, 76
amphibious tractors (amtraks), 101, 108
amputees:
  bodily awareness of, 203–4
  emotional struggles of, 210
  grief at limb loss of, 204, 210
  phantom limb pain of, 201, 204, 205, 210
Andover, 61
Andrews, Dana, 217
anger, 65–67, 84–85, 91, 235, 257
  revenge compared with, 66, 84
  warnings against, 85
  of warriors, 67–71, 78
anguish, 177, 200
Annapolis, *see* Naval Academy, U.S.
anorexia, 202
anthropologists, 71–73
Antilochus, 83
Aquinas, Thomas, 2, 115
Argentina, Argentinians, 152, 181
Aristotle:
  on anger, 65, 80, 85
  on courage and fear, 62, 210
  on emotions, 31, 189
  Ethics of, 229
  on happiness, 211–12
  mimēsis of, 28
  on objects and function, 205–6
  on pity, 29
  Poetics of, 28, 98
  on resilience, 30
  on revenge, 70, 78
  on shame, 180–81
  teachings of, used in military training, 191–93
  Vitoria influenced by, 43
armed forces, *see* military

armies, volunteer, 44
Army, U.S., 11, 12, 18, 46, 49, 80, 200
  Baghdad headquarters of, 95
  branches of, 32
  Charlie Company, 6th Infantry, First Armored Division of, 94–95
  82nd Airborne Division of, 67, 80
  404th Reserve Unit of, 53
  Green Berets of, 185–87
  infantry of, 67, 90, 110
  101st Airborne Division of, 40
  rangers of, 11, 23, 67
  recruiting motto of, 192
  Special Forces of, 125
  3/17th Air Cavalry ("A" Troop) of, 49
  World War II draftees in, 13
Army Combined Arms Center, U.S., 76
Army reserves, *see* military reserves
Army surgeon general's Mental Health Advisory Team, 174
Arrian, 151
Arrigo, Jean Maria, 127
atrocities, 49, 52
Augustine, Saint, 2
Aulus Gellius, 156
Austin, John Langshaw, 32
authority, 43, 143
  attention to, 92–93
  fear of, 47
  political, 41
  questioning of, 24
  submission to, 92–93
aviators, 109–10

Ba'athists, 107, 134
Bachelor Officer Quarters (BOQs), 21
BACK US, 155, 163
Baghdad, Iraq, 23, 84
  Camp Dublin, 239
  Green Zone, 239
  Sunni Triangle, 107
  U.S. Army headquarters in, 95
Bagram, Afghanistan, 150, 163–64

Baker, James, 58, 227
Balad, Iraq, 220, 224–25
Bancroft Hall, 12
basic training, 12, 16, 50, 219, 234
    and sense of family, 56
battle-readiness, need for, 13
Battlestar Galactica, 203
behavioral scientists:
    Behavioral Science Consultation
        Teams (BSCTs), 143
    and interrogation teams, 140, 144
Bentham, Jeremy, 211
bereavement, 72
Best Years of Our Lives, The, 217–18
betrayal, 41, 46, 55–57, 63, 84, 100–106
    defined, 55
    of detainees, 123
    guilt for, 91, 235
    by leaders, 55, 57, 60–61
    moral, 133
    of POWs, 159
    of self, 163
"bigorexia," 202
Bin Laden, Osama, 54, 65
Black-Michaud, Jacob, 73
black sites, 131
blame:
    for conduct, 52
    praise vs., 47
    of self, 104
body:
    awareness of, 203
    bodily ego and, 160, 279
    Cicero on, 161
    disembodied parts of, 205–8
    dysmorphic disorders of, 202
    Epictetus on, 160–61
    Freud on, 160, 279
    identity and, 202
    image, 202
    in pain, 160–62
    and "wannabe" amputees, 202
Boggs, Tim, 30–31

bootcamp, *see* basic training
BOQs (Bachelor Officer Quarters), 21
Bosnia, Bosnians, 53
    war in, 47, 53, 65, 223
Boston College, 58
Bowlby, John, 216–17
Bradley Fighting Vehicle, 90–91, 95–96,
    180
Bragg, Fort, *see* Fort Bragg
Brenner, Marvin, 77, 209–10
British Airways, 15
British military, 13, 81
Bromberg, Philip, 126
Brooke Army Medical Center, 220
brotherhood, 103
Brummell, George, 51
bureaucracy, 2, 26, 63, 226
Burns, John Horne, 61
Bush, George W., 34, 253
Bybee, Jay, 272

camaraderie, 40, 41, 48, 55, 128–29
Camp Doha (Iraq), 172
Camp Dublin (Baghdad), 239
Camp Liberty (West Baghdad), 185
Camp Pendleton, 89
Camp X-Ray, 116
Canada, Canadians, 90
career military, 40, 41, 74, 79
Carter, Phil, 40
casualties, 29, 46
catharsis, 28, 73
causes:
    accountability of soldiers for, 44–45
    challenging of, 49
    conduct and, 42, 48
    dying for, 58
    of enemy, 71
    examination of, 22, 43, 55
    in *Henry V,* 41–42
    just, 42, 61–62
    loyalty to, 39
    and morale, 40

causes (*continued*)
  popular, 61
  soldiers' ignorance of, 42
  soldiers' inner debate of, 22, 47
  unjust or unworthy, 41, 42, 60
cell phones, cell phone technology, 13
  as detonators, 76
censorship, 200
Central Intelligence Agency (CIA), 140
Cervantes, Victor, 81
Chagnon, Napoleon, 72
chain of command, 45, 74, 75
  among POWs, 152, 163
  among private defense contractors,
    241
character, 33
  moral, 2, 76
"Character of the Happy Warrior"
    (Wordsworth), 211
Charles, Prince of Wales, 21
Charlie Company, 6th Infantry, First
    Armored Division, 94–95
Chicago, University of, Law School of,
    132
Chicago Tribune, 108
child abuse, 161
children, injury or death of, 107–10
choice, *see* decisions, decision making
Chriseis, 74
Cicero, 68, 155, 185
  on Stoicism, 161, 175
citizens, moral concerns of, 118
citizen-soldiers, 44–45, 48, 72, 241
civil affairs, 13
  order, 108
  soldiers in, 13
civilians, 13–14
  as new soldiers, 26, 37
  values of, 2, 14, 90, 243
  in war zones, 13, 76, 239
Civil War, 32
clandestine sites, 131, 133
Clark, Walter, 66, 179, 203–4

Clausewitz, Carl von, 72
Cleland, Max, 50, 197, 253
CNN, 224
coercion:
  of detainees, 121
  in interrogation, 130, 144
  as part of military function, 45
  of soldiers, 35, 47, 53
  in torture, 159, 162
Coetzee, J. M., 165
Colangelo-Bryan, Josh, 137–39
collateral damage, 1, 107–10
combat, 20
combatants, 13, 60, 134
  nonuniformed, 117
  as police, 108
  unjust, 44
combat readiness, 174
command, 37, 41
  practice of torture under, 116
  responsibility of, 105
command structure, *see* chain of
    command
compartmentalization:
  emotional, 25–26, 62
  of mission from war, 48
  moral, 22, 25–26, 125–26
  psychological, 62, 126
  of roles, 20–21, 25
  as a soldiering skill, 63
complicity, 254
  denial of, 133
  of health professionals, 140
  legal, 51
  soldiers' internal struggle over, 63
  and taint, 52
  in torture, 131, 133, 135, 140–41, 147
  of torture victims, 162
  victims' shame of, 161
  in *Waltz with Bashir,* 126
concealment, 115
conduct, 43, 50, 52, 70
  cause vs., 42, 48

moral, 85, 262
conflicts, inner, 25–26, 63
conscience, 2, 41, 43, 45, 74
    Freud on, 93
    and guilt, 91, 92
    and internal peace, 50
    Kant on, 92
    reflection and, 44
    see also superego
conscientious objection, 44, 234–35
    cowardice vs., 47
    Harvard classes on, 234
consent:
    absence of, 121
    acquiescence vs., 146
Constitution, U.S., 32
Constitutional Court of South Africa, 132
conversion experience, 14–19
    of Alysha Haran, 14–16
    defined, 17
    of former civilians, 26, 37
Coriolanus (Shakespeare), 179
Corsica, 73
cosmopolitans, 85
counterinsurgency, 34, 66, 75, 108
    field manual for, 76
counterintelligence, 127, 133
counterterrorism, 117, 127–28, 134
courage, 208, 212
court martial, 24, 40
cowardice, 48, 73
    conscientious objection vs., 47
Craiglockhart hospital, 40
Crawford, Susan, 116
crimes against humanity, 141
crimes of obedience, 125
criminologists, 144
Cunard Line, 46

death, dying:
    for causes, 58
    natural, 72

understanding of, 89
debate, 44
deception, 115
    of detainees, 117
    public, 59
decisions, decision making, 26, 28
    coerced, 53
Defense Centers of Excellence for Psychological Health and Traumatic Brain Injury, 174
Defense Department, U.S. (DOD):
    civilian health affairs officials in, 136, 137, 146
    in contract with USIS, 238
    interrogation influenced by, 140
    military health officials in, 146
    on PTSD and Purple Heart, 175
dehumanization:
    of the enemy, 26, 34–35, 123–24
    racial slurs and, 34–35
    of self, 26
Deianeira, 98–99
democracies, 44
Department of Veterans Affairs (VA), 173, 226
Department of Veterans Affairs Hospitals, 90, 183, 220, 226, 229, 233, 274
depression, 50, 128, 183, 218
desensitization, 30
DeStefano, Noi, 172–73, 192, 229–35
DeStefano, Poi, 230–35
DeStefano, Tony, 6, 171–73, 229–35
    Al-Samoud missile attack on, 6, 172, 230
    as mentor, 181, 185
    postwar mental and emotional suffering of, 178, 180, 190, 197, 210
    as victim of diagnostic abuse, 197
    at Walter Reed, 6, 176–77
    Walter Reed nicknamed by, 183
    "war after the war" coined by, 192, 210
    and *Washington Post,* 183–84

DeStefano, Tony-Michelle, 230–35
detainees:
    at Abu Ghraib, 114
    admiration for, 133–34
    capture of, 118
    deception of, 117
    dehumanization of, 146–47
    empathic identification with, 115–16,
        133–34
    exploitation of, 1, 117–20
    family members of, 138
    force-feeding of, 116, 137, 145–47,
        164–65
    in Guantánamo Detention Center,
        137, 163
    health care for, 117
    health officials and abuse of, 140
    hunger strikes of, 116, 136–37,
        145–47, 164–65
    as intelligence sources, 118
    mental state of, 119, 139, 145–47
    moral vulnerability of, 156
    physical state of, 119
    respect for, 133–34
    "softened," 136
    suicide and, 139
detention:
    conditions of, 145, 156, 162
    as enslavement, 121
    in wartime, 116
diagnostic abuse, 197
Diogenes the Cynic, 85
discipline, 41, 45
Discourses (Epictetus), 151
disillusionment, 59–60
dissociation, 126, 161, 164, 166
Dix, Fort, 53
Doha, Camp (Iraq), 172
Dominican Republic, 198
Domitian, 151
Dorsey & Whitney, 137
Dossari, Jumah Al-, 137–39, 145
doubt, 43, 44, 47, 48, 53, 63

Douglas, Brandon, 223–29
draft, draftees, 13–14, 35, 40, 48, 52
    in Vietnam era, 198
dreams, 60
dual identities, 13–14
Dublin, Camp (Baghdad), 239
Dugway Proving Ground, 68
Durkin, Bob, 107
duty, 22, 25, 32, 37, 41, 43, 48, 74, 82, 91
    dereliction of, 75
    moral relativism disguised as, 125

Edinburgh, 16, 40
Edmonson, John, 145
Ego and the Id, The (Freud), 279
Egypt, 171
82nd Airborne Division, 67, 80
Eisenhower, USS, 13
Ellis, Albert, 188
Elsten, Irv, 107
email, 12–13, 224, 233
embedding, 3
emergency-preparedness kits, 224
Emory University, 6, 67, 237
emotions, 71–72
    appropriateness of, 31, 106
    cognitive mediation of, 189
    detachment from, 30
    in killing, 33
    maladaptive, 188
    of soldiers, 29
    Stoics on, 84, 106, 154–56, 163, 251,
        271
    toughening and, 30
    of war, 28
    see also specific emotions
empathy, 23, 97, 105
    defined, 228
    for enemy, 90
    feigned, 119
    of interrogator for detainee, 115–16,
        133–34
    sympathy compared with, 228

Enchiridion (*Handbook*) (Epictetus), 151, 188

enemy:
  benefit of discrimination for, 35
  causes of, 71
  dehumanization of, 26, 34–35, 75, 130, 134
  demonization of, 70, 130
  derogatory terms for, 71, 130
  empathy for, 90
  exploitation of, 120
  external vs. internal, 1
  invisible, 77
  killing by, 85
  killing of, 37, 71–72
  as prisoner of war (EPW), 119
  respect for, 71, 85
  revenge against, 65
  similarity with, 35
enhanced interrogation techniques, 116
  see also torture
Enlightenment, Age of, 23, 85
  German, 23, 92
  philosophers in, 23, 85, 92
enlistment, 16
  reasons for, 18–19, 32, 39, 41
Epictetus, 150, 185
  biography of, 151–52
  on detachment, 29–30, 165–66
  Discourses of, 151
  Handbook of, 151, 188
  Long on, 155
  on moral education, 175–76
  on respect vs. anger, 85
  on tragedy and hardship, 29–30, 165–66
  on the will, 177–78
Erhart, Jason, 219–23, 228
Esfandiari, Haleh, 153–54, 163, 227
Estes, Kerry, 222
Estes, Mike, 218
Estes, Pam, 218–23, 228
ethics, 240

civilian vs. military, 33
codes of, 21
debates of, 28
education programs in, 74
military, 23, 124
professional, 26
euphemisms:
  for killing, 142
  for torture, 130–31, 147
executive power, 43
exploitation, 117–27
  of detainees, 117–18, 123
  of enemy, 120
  in everyday life, 120
  labor, 117
  nonharsh, 120
  and sadism, 122
  sexual, 117
explosives, 107
  see also improvised explosive devices

F-18 fighter aircraft, 109
Fallujah, Iraq, 76
families:
  of detainees, 138
  of soldiers, 215–16
  of wounded, 221
Fascism, 35
fear, 28–31, 62, 78, 211
"fear-up" tactic, 114
  at Abu Ghraib, 114
  at Guantánamo, 114
  "harsh," 119–20
  used by CIA, 114
fedayeen, 107
Federal Bureau of Investigation (FBI), 139
  harsh interrogations opposed by, 140
fidelity, 39–41, 57, 104
  see also loyalty
1st Division, Marines, 89
Firth of Clyde, 46
507th Maintenance Company, Marines, 100

flashbacks, 173, 210, 215, 218, 226, 231
FM 2-22-3 (Army intelligence manual), 264
FM 34–52 (Army intelligence manual), 118–19
force-feeding, 116, 137, 145–47, 164–65
forensics experts, 144
Fort Bragg, 136, 186–87
    Army Special Operations at, 186
    SERE program at, 157, 186
    STRAC soldiers at, 187
Fort Dix, 53
Fort Huachuca, 113
Fort Leavenworth, 76
Fort Lewis, 51
Fort Polk, 234
Fotion, Nick, 237–38
404th Army Reserve Unit, 53
France, 78–79
Frankfurt, Harry, 63
fratricide, 84, 94, 99, 260
Freedom of Information Act, 139
Freud, Sigmund, 20, 63, 73, 91
    on conscience, 93
    on ego, 177, 279
    on guilt, 92–94
    on the irrational, 3
    on morality, 94
    on superego, 91, 94, 177
    on trauma, 172

Galleria Umberto Primo, 61
Gallery, The (Burns), 61–63
    Hal in, 62–63
Gates, Robert, 184
Gaza, 46
gender, 89, 123
Geneva Accords, 117, 150
Geneva Convention Relative to the
    Treatment of Prisoners of War, 120
genocide, 65
Georgetown University:

author as teacher at, 5, 196
Collegiate Gothic campus of, 26
faculty of, 154
Gaston Hall of, 31–32
graduates of, 37
history of, 32
newspaper of, 134
ROTC at, 26–27, 31–32, 41
students at, 18, 23, 48, 113, 125, 196
Georgia, 50
Germany, 26, 86, 208
    Nazi, 50
Gifford Lectures, 16
Gill, Al, 6, 26–33, 41–42
global communication, 12–13
Goffman, Erving, 19, 22
Good-Bye to All That (Graves), 35
Gourock, Scotland, 46
Graves, Robert, 35, 40
    Good-Bye to All That, 35
Great Santini, 178
Greece, ancient, 83, 199, 240–41
    Amazon warriors, 199
Greenbelt, Md, 224
Green Berets, 185–87
Green Zone (Baghdad), 239
grief, 82–85, 177
    Stoics on, 155–56
Grossman, Dave, 11
Guantánamo Detention Center, 116–17, 136–41, 145–47, 150, 154
    Camp 5 of, 145
    detainees in, 137, 162
    torture at, 116, 142–43
guilt, 2, 89–110, 260
    for accidents, 1, 107, 130, 189
    for collateral damage, 107–10
    emotion of, 90, 106
    Freud on, 92–94
    irrational, 106
    Kant on, 92–94
    Klein on, 97
    legal, 96

of luck, 1, 100–106, 107, 204, 234
pathological, 91
rational, 106
researchers on, 51
shame compared with, 180
and soldiers' mental anguish, 177
survivor, 3, 100, 103–4, 235
and Ted Westhusing, 243
of torture victims, 159
for triumph, 90
for wrongdoing, 107–10
Gulf of Tonkin Resolution, 59
Gulf War, first (1990–1991), 5, 12, 48,
105, 238, 241–42
Basra road, 5

Hadamar, 142
Haditha massacre, 66, 75–78, 242
Hal, 62–63
Halfaker, Dawn, 6, 195–97, 200, 203–5,
209–11
hamartia, 28
Hamas, 66
Hamilton, Lee H., 58, 227
Hamlet, 73
Handbook (Epictetus), 151, 188
Hanoi, Vietnam, 51
Hanoi Hilton, 59, 149–52, 163
happiness, 155, 211
upon returning from war, 211
Haran, Alysha, 6, 14–16, 18–19, 31
Harvard University:
conscientious objector classes at, 234
graduates of, 61
McLean Hospital of, 187
Rawls at, 35
William James at, 16
Harvey, Francis, 184
hatred, 70, 79–80
Healey, Daniel, 104–6
health professionals:
combatant vs. noncombatant status of,
141

in detainee abuse, 140
in Guantánamo, 139
in interrogation, 136
military, 116–17, 141
Hector, 70, 78, 83
hedonic utilitarianism, 211
Henry V (Shakespeare), 41–42, 57
Heracles, 29, 98–100, 199
Herbert, Roger, 191
Herman, Judith, 158
Herr, Michael, 51
high-tech age, 13
war in, 13
Hitler, Adolf, 61
Hoge, Charles, 173
Holocaust, 103, 159
Homer, 74
Iliad, 70
homicides, 210
honor, 2, 242
cultures of, 72
group, 242
and kinship obligation, 72
and revenge, 72
sexual, 75
traditional codes of, 74, 76–77, 82
in tribal cultures, 72–75, 242
of warriors, 73–75
Hood, Jay W., 137
hospitals:
Department of Veterans Affairs (VA),
90, 183, 220, 226, 229
military, 220, 225
see also specific hospitals
hostility, 43
Hoya Battalion, 31–32, 33, 42
Huachuca, Fort, 113
Hude, Henri, 79
humanity, humanization, 26, 77, 134,
193
of enemy, 134–35
of soldier, 2, 23, 25–26, 29, 37
human rights, 130, 134–35

human rights workers, 137
Hume, David, 228
humiliation:
    nudity, 116
    sexual, 114, 116
hunger strikes, 116, 136–37, 145–47,
    164–65
hushuwo, 72, 75, 82
Huze, Sean, 206
Hydra, 29
hyperarousal, 172, 178, 209
hypocrisy, 52

identity, group, 72, 74, 77
Iliad (Homer), 70, 74, 83
    see also specific characters
improvised explosive devices (IEDs), 76,
    77, 127, 186, 198–99, 219
information, access to, 44
In Love and War (Stockdale and Stock-
    dale), 150
instant messaging, 23
insularism, 25–26
insurgents, insurgency, 66, 67
    in ambush on Dereck Vines's convoy,
        224
    in Baquba, Iraq, 195
    killed by private military contractors,
        239
    motivation of, 33, 86
integrity, 74
intelligence:
    ethics of, 127
    FM 34–52 (Army intelligence
        manual) and, 118–19
    gathering of, 115, 123, 147
international law, 45, 47, 135, 141
International Military Tribunal at
    Nuremberg, 141
Internet, 13
    Abu Ghraib images on, 120
interrogation, interrogators, 1, 18,
    113–47, 127–41, 198

    at Abu Ghraib, 5, 113–14, 133
    behavioral scientists' role in, 140, 143
    coercive, 131, 140
    control over detainees, 119
    descriptions of, 138–39
    empathic identification with detainee
        by, 115–16
    establishing rapport with detainees by,
        1, 119
    exploitation training of, 118–19
    "fear-up" tactics of, 114, 119–20
    feigned empathy used in, 119
    FM 34–52 (Army intelligence
        manual) and, 118–19
    freelance, 131
    Level 1 "harsh coercive interrogation"
        in, 131–32
    manipulation of detainees in, 119
    moral ambiguity of, 117
    "pride and ego-down" tactic in, 119,
        124
    profile of, 127–28
    sadism and, 122, 124
    torture used in, 158
    transference in, 147
Iran, 153
    Evin prison in, 153, 227
Iraq, 58
    Baghdad in, 33, 84, 95, 107, 239
    Balad in, 220, 224–25
    Baquba in, 195
    Camp Doha in, 172
    Camp Dublin in, 239
    Camp Liberty in, 185
    Kirkuk in, 224
    military detention centers in, 140
    Mosul in, 224
    Sunni Triangle in, 195
Iraqi military police, 48
Iraqi Ministry of Interior, 23
Iraqi police, 40, 195–96, 238, 239, 242
    Emergency Response Unit of, 238
Iraqis, 23, 71

racial slurs for, 34
Iraq Study Group, 58
Iraq War, 42, 46–48, 53, 71, 105–6, 195,
      198, 215, 223, 238–43
   American military casualties in, 174
   battle descriptions in, 195–96, 224
   collateral damage in, 107–10
   departure of soldiers for, 1, 32, 89, 171
   effect on older veterans of, 50
   Haditha massacre in, 75–77
   National Guard in, 13, 66
   officers in, 12, 23, 90, 230–31
   as Operation Iraqi Freedom, 150, 171
   as Operation Iraqi Freedom II, 107
   private defense contractors in, 240–41
   reservists in, 13, 30
   run-up to, 45
isolation, 114, 116, 123, 152
   psychological death by, 121

James, William, 16–17, 19
Janet, Pierre, 172
Japanese, 77
Jarrett, Thomas, 84, 185–89
Johnson, Lyndon B., 59
Joint Service Commendation Medal, 171
journalists, 51, 137, 209
judgment, 89, 180
   self, 92
Jumanji (1995), 138
Jünger, Ernst, 86
Just and Unjust Wars (Walzer), 42–43,
      252
justification, 91
just-war theory, 42, 45, 48, 107, 115

Kant, Immanuel:
   on conscience, 92–93
   on enlightenment, 23–24
   on guilt, 92–94
   on moral insularism, 25–26
   on questioning authority, 24–25
   on respect for others, 85, 124

Karpinski, Janet, 36
kathexis, 20
Kennedy, John F., 58
Kerry, John, 52
Kiley, Kevin C., 184
killing, 26
   becoming accustomed to, 11–12, 92
   of children, 107–10
   of civilians, 1, 36, 37, 71–72, 75,
         107–8, 239
   from a distance, 109–10
   emotional response to, 33
   by enemy, 37, 71–72
   euphemisms for, 142
   of fellow humans, 37, 89
   glory of, 78
   for identity, 73
   indiscriminate, 89
   of innocents, 86, 91, 108
   just, 90, 91, 115
   lawful vs. murder, 11, 37, 252
   with malice, 89, 108
   medicalized, 142
   mock vs. real, 33
   for necessity, 79
   for pleasure, 79
   revenge, 76–77
   as right of combatants, 43
   tribal, 76–77
Kilo Company, Marines, 75–77
kinship wars, 72–73
Kirkuk, Iraq, 224
Kislow, Robert, 6, 80–81
   flashback incident of, 183, 210
   limb injury of, 181, 205
   psychological trauma of, 181–84,
         192
   and revenge, 85
   at Walter Reed, 181–84, 232–33
Klein, Melanie, 97
Koestner, Katie, 74
Kohn, Pierre-Richard, 79–80
Koran, 66

Korea, 67, 238
  prisoners of war from, 113
Kosovo, 67, 238, 257
Kutz, Christopher, 254
Kuwait, 6, 48, 101, 171, 230
Kuwait City, 101

Laird, Melvin, 150
Landstuhl Regional Medical Center
  (Germany), 171, 220, 225
law, international, 45
lawyers, lawyering, 20, 21, 40, 137, 161
leadership, 46
  betrayal by, 55, 57, 60–61
  just, 93
  legislative, 93
  military, 67
  untrustworthy, 60
Lear, 73
Leavenworth, Fort, 76
Lebanon war (1982), 126
letter-writing, 4, 13
Levi, Primo, 159
Lewis, Fort, 51
Lewis, Norman, 81
Liberty, Camp (West Baghdad), 185
Lifton, Robert Jay, 142
limb injuries, 197–98, 205, 228
Lives of Others, The (2006), 116
Long, A. A., 155
Longworth, Ray:
  Arrigo's correspondence with, 127,
    266
  on black sites, 131
  and individual vs. collective responsi-
    bility, 143, 147
  profile of interrogators, 127–28
  on psychological vs. moral stress of
    interrogators, 127–28
  and questions of complicity, 135–36
  on rapport with detainees, 133–34
  on rapport with subordinate interroga-
    tors, 128–29

  on relationship with Level 1 harsh
    interrogators, 131–33
  Stoic doctrine and, 130–31
  William Quinn compared with, 135
Loy, Myrna, 217
loyalty, 39, 74
  see also fidelity
Lubavitch Hasidism, 19
Lynch, Jessica, 100

Macbeth (Shakespeare), 14
McCain, John, 150
machismo, 73, 77, 78, 84, 141
McMahan, Jeff, 44–45, 47, 48
McQueeny, Hank, 46, 58–60
Mangin, Anthelme, 216
March, Fredric, 217
Marcus Aurelius, 85, 154, 185, 190
  Meditations of, 154, 188, 190
Marine Corps, U.S.
  burden of war on, 200
  and collateral damage, 107–9
  1st Division of, 89
  507 Maintenance Company of, 100
  at Haditha, 75–77
  Kilo Company of, 75–77
  motto of, 39, 56
  officers in, 12, 71, 100, 104–5
  role of, 75
  young Marines in, 105
Marks, Jonathan, 140
Marshall, S. L. A., 249
Maryland, University of, 223
masks, 19, 21
  of the workplace, 22
massacres, 66, 75–78
  see also specific massacres
Mattis, James, 77–78
Mayek, Joseph, 94–95, 180
media, 44
Medical Holding Companies, 184
Meditations (Marcus Aurelius), 154
memories, 55

Menninger Clinic, 122
metamorphosis, 19, 21
Metropolitan Museum of Art, 199
Meyer, Nancy, 56
Milgram, Stanley, 143
military:
    civilian relations with, 115
    clergy in, 141
    identity in, 13–14
    and sense of family, 56
    spouses of, 17–18
    stoic culture of, 173–80
    see also specific branches
military detention centers, 140
    see also specific detention centers
military reserves, 5, 13–14, 40, 180
    Army, 30, 40, 53
    Navy, 16
Military Tribunal I, 141
Mill, John Stuart, 211
Miller, Arthur, 39
mimēsis, 28
mines, 77
Modell, Arnold, 104
Monchy-au-Bois, France, 86
Montaigne, Michel de, 20–23, 37, 124
Mooney, Michael, 100–102, 104–6
morality, 36, 40, 47, 68, 252, 262
    compromise in, 129
    Freud on, 94
    idealism in, 240
    insulation and, 20, 141–42, 147
    internal dialogue and, 22
    leadership and, 29
    luck in, 46, 53, 82, 134
    permissibility in, 110
    relativism in, 125
    see also ethics
Mosul, Iraq, 224
murder, 75
    just killing vs., 11, 37
Musonius Rufus, 151
My Lai massacre, 66, 78, 254, 257

Naples, Italy, 61
Naples '44 (Lewis), 81
National Guard, U.S.:
    in Afghanistan and Iraq, 5, 13–14
    NCOs in, 66, 203
    officers in, 180
    on responsibility, 40
National Security Agency (NSA), 140
Naval Academy, U.S.:
    author as teacher at, 4–5, 12–13, 21,
        149, 159, 261
    faculty of, 25, 70–71
    Marine and Navy officers interviews
        at, 100–105
    moral teaching standards at, 74
Naval reserves, U.S., *see* military reserves
Navy, U.S., 200
    clergy, 89, 107
    creed, 74
    hospitals, 137
    John F. Kennedy in, 58
    midshipmen in, 14–15
    officers in, 14–15, 25, 100
    rank in, 21–22
    retired officers of, 58
    Seals, 71, 191–92
    WAVE (Women Accepted for Volun-
        teer Emergency Service), 15
Nazaria, 100–101
    Ambush Alley, 100
Nazi Doctors, The (Lifton), 142
Nazis, 26, 50, 61, 141–43
    at Nuremberg, 141–42
Nero, 151
Nessus, 98
New York City, 62, 199
New York University, 186
Nicopolis, Greece, 151
Nietzsche, Friedrich, 91, 96–97
9/11, terrorist attacks of, 15, 42, 66,
    150
Nixon, Richard, 150
noncombatants, 13, 108

noncommissioned officers (NCOs), 57,
    65, 66, 174
Normandy, invasion of, 46, 90
North Vietnam, see Vietnam, North
North Vietnamese Army (NVA), 35
Nuremberg, see International Military
    Tribunal at Nuremberg
nurses, nursing corps, 51

oaths of office, 31–32, 37
obedience, 42, 45, 58
    crimes of, 125
Ohio University, 30
Okinawa, Japan, 77, 209
On Anger (Seneca), 66
On Combat (Grossman), 11
One Day in the Life of Ivan Denisovich
    (Solzhenitsyn), 159
101st Airborne Division, Army, 40
On Killing (Grossman), 11
Operation Enduring Freedom (Afghani-
    stan), 150
Operation Iraqi Freedom, 150, 171
Operation Iraqi Freedom II, 107
Opinion, La, 152
Oran, Algeria, 62
orders:
    disobeying of, 24, 25, 41
    illegal or immoral, 24, 41
    protesting unlawful, immoral or
        unwise, 24, 45
    questioning of, 24
    see also obedience
Orwell, George, 35
Owen, Wilfred, 211–12
Oxford English Dictionary, 55

pacifism, 22, 40
Paktika Province, Afghanistan, 80
panic attacks, 183, 231
patriotism, 3, 41, 52, 54, 66
Patriot missiles, 172, 230
Patroclus, 82–83, 103

Patty Hearst syndrome, 122–23
PBS (Public Broadcasting Service), 108
peace, peacetime, 19, 90
    intelligence gathering in, 115
Peloponnesian War, 241
Pendleton, Camp, 89
Pentagon, 25, 59, 144, 174
Petraeus, David, 76, 238–39
Pfaff, Julie, 23, 215
Pfaff, Tony, 22–23, 48, 215, 241–42
Phaedrus, 40
philia, 229
Philo Judaeus, 156
philosophers, 47, 121, 180
    ancient Greek, 63
    ancient Roman, 63
    contemporary, 63, 99
    expulsion of, from ancient Rome, 151
    see also specific philosophers
photojournalism, 197
physical abuse, 132
physicians, 136
Piaget, Jean, 229
pity, 28–31, 36
Plato, 144
    Republic of, 67
    Symposium of, 40
    technē of, 144
Poetics (Aristotle), 28, 98
police, 75, 108
    combatants acting as, 108
    in interrogation, 140
Polk, Fort, 234
Pope, Harrison, 202
post-traumatic stress disorder (PTSD),
    30–31
    flashbacks in, 173, 210, 215, 218, 226,
        231
    "The Iron Monkey" and, 233
    and multiple military deployments,
        174–76
    on returning from war, 174, 183, 197,
        229–31

support groups for, 226
symptoms of, 30–31, 178, 183, 231
praise, 47
Priam, 83
"pride and ego-down" tactic, 119, 124
Prior, John, 90, 94–100, 106, 180
prisoners of war (POWs), 59, 141, 155
    exploitation of, 120
    Korean, 113
    moral vulnerability of, 156
    U.S., 149–50, 154, 158–59
    see also detainees
private defense contractors, 6, 201, 209,
    241
    USIS, 238–39
propaganda, 54
prostheses, 200, 204
psychiatrists, 136, 222, 267
    breach of confidentiality by, 116–17,
        136
    in Guantánamo, 139
psychoanalysts, 3, 122, 136, 267–68
    on guilt, 107–8
    Washington Psychoanalytic Institute
        and, 3
psychological health, 22, 27
    breakdown of, 46, 76
    convalescence and, 40, 84
    of detainees, 123
    military treatment centers for, 174
    trauma and, 30
psychology, psychologists, 167, 267
    clinical, 2, 30, 187
    cognitive, 188–89
    developmental, 229
    in Guantánamo, 139–40, 143
    involved in Jason Erhart's TBI treat-
        ment, 222
    military, 11
    research on intelligence work by,
        127–28
    on traumatic experiences, 172
    on well-being, 211

PT-109, 58
PT boats, 59
PTSD, *see* post-traumatic stress disorder
Public Broadcasting Service (PBS),
    108
public criticism, 52
public deception, 59
public opinion, 43
Purple Heart, 198
    PTSD and, 174–75

Qahtani, Mohammed al-, 116
Quan Loi, 49
Queen Elizabeth I, 46, 208
Quinby, Ripley, IV, 33–37, 251
Quinn, William, 5, 18, 113–15, 117–18,
    120–27, 133–35, 149, 198, 200,
    264
    and female detainee, 122–24

Rabinowitz, Boudin, and Standard,
    48–49
racial slurs, 34–35, 71
rage, *see* anger
Rambo, 71
rank:
    and promotion, 37
    significance of, 21–22
rape, 161
rationalism, 23, 155
rationalization, 49, 53
Rawls, John, 35–36, 276
Raytheon, 230
Reagan National Airport, 101
religion, 133
Remarque, Erich Maria, 216–17
remorse, 51, 99, 115
Republic (Plato), 67
Reserve Officer Training Corps
    (ROTC), 16, 21, 41, 117, 198
    Army, 26, 31, 125
    Hoya Battalion, 31–32, 42
    Naval, 21

resilience training, 136, 166, 185
  reverse engineering of, 136
  Warrior Resilience and Thriving, 185
respect:
  for civilians, 71
  for culture, 71
  for the enemy, 71, 85, 135
  for religion, 71
responsibility:
  of command, 37
  of leaders, 42, 43
  public, 43
  of soldiers, 28, 40–41, 46, 109–10
  see also accountability
returning from war, 3, 31, 39, 40, 50, 89,
      192, 209, 227
  aggression in, 209
  alcohol abuse in, 218
  anxiety and, 174–75
  depression and, 174, 218
  with emotional problems, 173, 226
  flashbacks in, 173, 210, 215, 218, 226,
      231
  happiness in, 211
  homicides and, 210
  hyperarousal in, 209
  idealized image of, 199, 225
  impact on families in, 215–17, 219–23
  with injuries, 192
  personality change in, 215
  recovery in, 211, 212
  risky behavior in, 209
  stress in, 174
  suicides in, 210
  "war after the war" in, 192, 210, 216
revenge, 2, 3, 63–86
  anger compared with, 66
  anticipation of, 70
  cycles of, 72–74
  emotions of, 78–82
  injury and, 70
  vigilantism, vendettas, 71
revenge cultures, 71–73, 77, 82

Rhinelander, Philip, 151
Richmond Polytrauma Rehabilitation
      Center, 220
rituals of the workplace, 22
Rivers, W. H. R., 102
Road Back, The (Remarque), 216
roadside bombs, 13, 174
Rodolico, John, 187
Roger, Ralph, 90
Roger, Robin, 90
roles:
  civilian, 115
  emotions and, 31
  of interrogators, 116
  lawyers' adversarial, 20
  occupational, 20, 24, 26
  shift of, 124
  social, 19–20
  in uniform, 115
Roman Empire, 151
Roosevelt, Theodore, 16–17
ROTC, *see* Reserve Officer Training
      Corps
rules of engagement, 36–37, 70, 76, 109
Rupp, John, 12, 109–10
Russell, Bertrand, 40
Russell, Harold, 217

Sabra massacre, 126
Sachs, Albie, 132
sadism, 122, 124
Saigon, Vietnam, 51
Saint-Cyr (French military academy),
      78–79
San Antonio, Tex., 220
Sander, August, 197
San Diego, Calif., 150, 201
San Diego, University of, 12, 14, 21–22,
      149
Sand Storm, The (Huze), 206
Sarajevo, 79
Sarra, Rob, 108–9
Sassoon, Siegfried, 40, 102–4

Saudi Arabia, 116
sectarian violence, 66
self-defense, 34, 61, 85
Seneca, 185
  on compassion, 191, 193
  on feigned anger as motivation, 68
  on grief, 207
  on moral development, 175
  On Anger of, 66
  on preemotions, 156–57
  on rage, 78
  on respect for others, 85
  on revenge, 65, 91
  on self-control, 63, 69–70
  on Stoicism as therapy, 129
  on torture, 158
sensory deprivation, 114, 116
September 11, 2001, terrorist attacks of,
    15, 42, 66, 150
Serbians, 53
SERE (Survival, Evasion, Resistance,
    Escape), 157, 166
sexual humiliation, 114, 116
sexual motif of war, 78–79
Shakespeare, William, 6, 14, 26–27
  Coriolanus of, 179
  Henry V of, 41–42, 57
shame, 2, 276
  engendered through love, 40
  guilt compared with, 180
  and postwar mental illness, 176–77,
    180–85
  of rape and abuse victims, 161
  and shaming, 180–85, 234
  from shifting civilian and military
    roles, 115
  of Ted Westhusing, 243
  of torture victims, 158–59
  for wartime acts, 1, 51, 235
Shatillah massacre, 126
Shay, Jonathan, 175, 221
Sherman, Seymour, 7, 46
Shia, 114

shift:
  of realities, 125–26
  of roles, 124
"Sick Leave" (Sassoon), 102
Singleton, Jerry, 21–22
sleep disorders, 128, 178
Smith, Adam, 228
Socrates, 2, 151, 166–67
soldiers, soldiering:
  accountability or responsibility of, 40,
    42–45, 48, 63, 91, 109–10
  conflict with personal morals of,
    25–26, 63
  duties of, 22, 32, 37, 41, 43, 48, 91
  enlisted, 34
  humanity of, 2, 23, 25, 29, 37
  as identity, 4
  ignorance of cause of, 42
  as a job, 80, 81
  in peacetime, 19
  personal transformation of, 3, 20, 29,
    45, 71
  preparation for war by, 89
  as psychological phenomenon, 20, 72
  public face of, 19
  public investment in, 41, 47
  ready-to-kill vs. reluctant-to-kill, 11
  returning from war, *see* returning from
    war
  as sociological phenomenon, 20
  training of, 12
  U.S. citizenship for service granted to,
    198
  in wartime, 20
  wounded, 42
solidarity, 29, 66, 104
solitary confinement, *see* isolation
Solomon Islands, 58
Solzhenitsyn, Aleksandr, 159
Sophocles, 98–100
Sorabji, Richard, 155
South Africa, 165
Spanish Civil War, 35

Spanish Inquisition, 165
Spinoza, Baruch, 97
Stalin, Joseph, 105
Stanford Prison Experiment, 124
Stanford University, 23, 124, 151
Steck, Bob, 5, 46, 48–53, 58, 78
steroids, 202
Stockdale, James, 6, 12, 59, 149–53,
        154–55, 158–59, 163, 185, 190
   on Stoics and pain, 161
Stockdale, Sybil, 150, 152
Stockholm syndrome, 122–23
Stoics, Stoicism:
   on anger, 68, 85–86
   compassionate, 189–93
   on detachment, 29–30
   on emotions, 84, 106, 154–56, 163,
        251, 271
   goals of, 129–30
   Greek, 155, 175, 193
   on mental illness, 175–79
   and military culture, 173–80, 185–93
   on pain, 160–62
   on preemotions, 156–57
   on reason, 80, 106
   on resisting temptation, 166
   on revenge, 65, 80
   Roman, 154, 193, 207
   sages of, 175, 189
   as therapy, 129–30
   of torture victims, 149–54
   on virtue, 166
   and warrior ethos, 29–30
Stoic Warriors (Sherman), 49, 149, 178
stomach tubes, 137, 145–46
Storm of Steel, The (Jünger), 86
stress, 30, 179
   from multiple military deployments,
        174
   physical symptoms of, 129
   in a war zone, 180
stressors, 20
   traumatic, 157

stress positions, 114, 116
suicide bombers, 107, 108, 126, 133–34
suicides, suicide attempts, 6, 239–40
   by detainees, 139
   by soldiers returning from war, 210,
        231, 233
   of Ted Westhusing, 237–43
Sunni, 114
Sunni Triangle, Baghdad, 107
superego, 91
survivor guilt, *see* guilt, survivor
Swift Boat controversy, 52
Symposium (Plato), 40

taint, 51–52, 60, 63
   and complicity, 52
Taylor, Telford, 141
technē, 144
Tehran, Iran, 153
telephone, 12
Terrazas, Miguel, 75–76
terrorists, terrorism, 33, 67, 128, 130,
        134–35
   of detainees, 116
   Islamic, 134
text messaging, 12
Theseus, 199
Thompson, Hugh, 254
Thoughts of a Philosophical Fighter Pilot
        (Stockdale), 149
3/17th Air Cavalry ("A" Troop), 49
thumos, 67, 85–86
Ticonderoga, USS, 58–59, 151
timē, 21, 74
Timerman, Jacobo, 152–53, 154, 163,
        181
Tombs restaurant, 27, 41
torture, 126, 130–32
   in Abu Ghraib, 116, 120, 131, 133
   American victims of, 149–63
   in ancient Rome, 151
   under command structure, 116
   day/night confusion in, 132

denial of relief for bodily functions in, 164
descriptions of, 116, 138–39, 146, 157–59, 163–66, 272
electric shock, 132
euphemisms for, 131–32, 147
exposure to extreme cold in, 116
force-feeding in, 116, 137, 145–47, 164–65
at Guantánamo, 116
and health professionals, 144, 167
hooding in, 132
ineffectiveness of, 118, 131
isolation in, 114, 116, 121, 123, 139, 152
loud music in, 116
military dogs in, 115
morality of, 134, 144
nudity in, 116
proof of, 132
public debate on, 116, 133
as punishment, 158
resilience training for, 157, 166
resistance of, 162–63
sadism and gratuitous use of, 158
and self-betrayal, 163
sensory deprivation in, 114, 116, 132
sexual humiliation in, 114, 116
sleep deprivation in, 132
soldiers' approval of use of, 257
as spectacle, 158
stoicism of victims of, 149–54
stress positions in, 114, 116, 132
systematic or state-sanctioned, 117, 132–33, 135, 147, 151
terror in, 116
"torture lite" in, 132
by U.S. allies, 131–32
in Vietnam, 131
waterboarding in, 114, 116, 165
tours of duty, length of, 45
transference, 115, 143
in detainees, 147

erotic, 123
in interrogators, 147
regressive, 121–22
trauma, 73
from accidents, 95
from battle, 55, 172, 188, 225
from captivity, 121, 123
from injury, 219
medical science of, 167
from observing torture, 157–58
traumatic memories, 172–73, 192
of war, 203
as war injury, 175
Trauma and Recovery (Herman), 158
traumatic brain injury (TBI), 174, 198, 219–25
Alzheimer drugs as treatment for, 220
family's role in recovery from, 221
and PTSD symptoms, 222
traumatic syndromes, 115, 192
tribal communities, 72–74
honor in, 73
militias of, 242
Troy, 78, 83
Twemlow, Stuart, 122, 124
24, 118, 263–64

Uniform Code of Military Justice, 182
uniforms:
combatant's lack of, 13, 77, 117
concealment of, 140
descriptions of, 14, 41–42, 49
effacing individual identity, 2, 12, 71
improper, 50
infatuation with, 217
meaning of, 19–26, 60–61, 117
as moral insulation, 110
moral responsibility of, 24–25
Navy, 14
in peacetime, 19
and personal transformation, 234–35
pride in, 54, 58
removal of, 20

uniforms (*continued*)
  representation of solidarity in, 2
  roles requiring wearing of, 115
Union Army, 32
United Nations, 45, 53
urban warfare, 108
Utah, 68

Van Allsburg, Chris, 138
van der Kolk, Bessel A., 172
Varieties of Religious Experience, The
  (James), 16–17
vehicle checkpoints, 107
veterans, 206
  of Afghanistan war, 50, 80, 274
  anti-war, 49
  of combat, 50
  family health insurance needed for,
    232
  homelessness among, 233
  of Iraq war, 50, 274
  of Korean War, 222
  of Vietnam War, 50, 78, 149–50, 154,
    158–59, 174, 197, 222, 233
  of World War I, 102, 197
  of World War II, 46, 50, 77, 90, 209,
    222, 233–34
  wounded, 51, 80
Vietnam, 51–52
Vietnam, North, 59, 150, 152
Vietnam Memorial, 233
Vietnam Veterans Against the War, 50,
  52
Vietnam War:
  dehumanizing of the enemy in, 34–35
  lessons from, 51
  officers in, 149, 215
  opponents of, 48–49
  POWs of, 149, 152–53
  public reaction to, 51–52
  soldiers in, 49–50, 234
  USS *Ticonderoga* in, 58–60

  veterans of, 50, 78, 149–50, 154,
    158–59, 174, 197, 222, 233
Vietnam War Memorial, 51
Vines, Clara, 223–29
Vines, Dereck, 5, 40, 46, 53–58, 60, 65,
  208, 223–29
Virgin Airlines, 15
Vitoria, Francisco de, 43–44, 55

Wahlmann, Adolf, 142
Waiting for the Barbarians (Coetzee), 165
Walter Reed Army Institute of Research,
  173
Walter Reed Army Medical Center, 229
  bureaucracy at, 226
  Clara Vines at, 227–28
  communications systems of, 171
  Deployment Health Clinical Center
    of, 176
  diagnostic abuse in, 176–77
  hospital conditions scandal at, 183–84
  Iraq veterans in, 66, 179
  isolation of, 6, 203
  Malone House of, 176
  psychiatric patients in, 6, 50, 56–57,
    80–81, 173–74, 225, 229
  veterans counseling patients in, 50–51,
    181
  as "Wally World," 183
  Warrior Transition Brigade and, 185,
    198
  wounded in, 80–81, 197, 205, 225
Waltz with Bashir (2008), 126
Walzer, Michael, 42–43, 252
war correspondents, *see* journalists
war crimes, 89, 141
  see also atrocities
Ward, Wynona, 161
war on terror, 142
wars, wartime, 20, 90
  causes of, 37, 39–50, 60
  Chagnon on, 72

Clausewitz on, 72
corruption in, 61
detention in, 117
in Europe, 1
intelligence gathering in, 115
internalization of, 62
just, 42, 45, 62
modern, 72
morality of, 37, 252
in the Pacific, 1
preemption of, 45
pretexts for, 46
prevention of, 45
prosecution of, 61
sexual motif in, 78–79
trauma of, 203
unjust, 42, 43, 44, 53, 140, 240, 251
unpopular, 44, 76
urban, 108
violence of, 62
Washington, D.C., 14, 31, 49, 50, 58, 65, 171
National Mall in, 234
Washington and Lee University, 48
Washington Post, 116
on Walter Reed Army Medical Center scandal, 183–84
Washington Psychoanalytic Institute, 3
waterboarding, 114, 116, 165
WAVES (Women Accepted for Volunteer Emergency Service), 15
weapons of mass destruction, 54
Webb, James, 261
Webber, Tom, 89, 108
Weightman, George, 184
Westhusing, Michelle, 239
Westhusing, Ted:
as Army ranger, 6, 67
at Emory University, 6, 67, 237
in graduate studies at Emory University, 67

as philosopher, 6, 67
suicide of, 237–43
on use of anger as motivation, 68–69, 257
at West Point, 6, 67, 238
West Point, U.S. Military Academy at:
graduates of, 6, 195
mandatory medical training at, 196
teachings of, 200
Ted Westhusing at, 6, 67, 238
"What is Enlightenment?" (Kant), 23–24
William and Mary, College of, 74
Williams, Robin, 138
wiretapping, 116
wisdom, 43
Wolfe, John, 27–29, 35, 85
Women Accepted for Volunteer Emergency Service (WAVES), 15
"Women Can't Fight" (Webb), 261
Women of Trachis, The (Sophocles), 98–100
Woodrow Wilson International Center for Scholars, 5, 50, 53, 153, 227, 233
Middle East Program at, 227
newsletter of, 227
Wordsworth, William, 211–12
World War I, 35, 40, 86, 115, 216
veterans of, 102, 198
World War II:
cause of, 39
dehumanization of the enemy in, 34
draftees in, 234–35
Gestapo in, 208
Jewish victims of, 208
letters home vs. contemporary communications in, 13
low kill ratios in, 12
Nazi doctors in, 142
Norman Lewis memoir of, 81

ued)
ion of, 61–62
rience in, 35–36
_of, 46, 50, 77, 90, 209, 222,_
_33–34_
ded, 42, 50, 51, 201
descriptions of, 208–9
see also casualties
wounds, visible vs. invisible, 4
Wyler, William, 217

X-Ray, Camp 116

Yale University, 5, 48, 143
Yanomamö, 72–73, 78, 82

Zimbardo, Philip, 124